CONFRONTING THE PERPETRATORS

CONFRONTING THE PERPETRATORS

A HISTORY OF THE
CLAIMS CONFERENCE

Marilyn Henry

Foreword by
SIR MARTIN GILBERT

VALLENTINE MITCHELL
LONDON • PORTLAND, OR

First published in 2007 in Great Britain by
VALLENTINE MITCHELL
Suite 314, Premier House,
112–114 Station Road,
Edgware, Middlesex, HA8 7BJ

and in the United States of America by
VALLENTINE MITCHELL
c/o ISBS, 920 NE 58th Avenue, Suite 300
Portland, Oregon, 97213-3786

Website: www.vmbooks.com

British Library Cataloguing in Publication Data
A catalogue record for this book has been applied for

ISBN 0 85303 628 4 (cloth)
ISBN 978 0 85303 6289
ISBN 0 85303 629 2 (paper)
ISBN 978 0 85303 6296

Library of Congress Cataloging-in-Publication Data
A catalog record for this book has been applied for

Enfield, Middx.
Printed in Great Britain by MPG Books Ltd., Bodmin, Cornwall.

In memory of
Ruth Cohen
and
Rabbi Israel Miller

פתחו לי שערי צדק, אבא בם אודה יה.
זה השער ליי, צדיקים יבאו בו.

Open for me the Gates of Righteousness;
I will enter them and thank God.

This is the Gate of the Lord;
only the righteous shall enter through it.

Contents

Preface

At the end of the twentieth century, the world seemed to rediscover Holocaust survivors. Ceremonies commemorating the fiftieth anniversary of Second World War-era events offered occasions for reflection about the war, its heroes and its victims. In the US, broad interest in the Holocaust was sparked by two cultural phenomena: the 1993 opening of the US Holocaust Memorial Museum and the film *Schindler's List*. The collapse of communism, the opening of archives in Eastern Europe and the approach of the millennium – and with it a desire to 'clean the slate' – also sparked a series of confrontations with the past.

Among those confrontations was an extraordinary focus on the material losses and injuries suffered by Nazi victims. Class-action lawsuits filed in American courts against European governments and enterprises, improvised commissions, national historical reviews and international conferences attempted, at the end of the century, to deal with the material, historical, legal and moral issues stemming from the Holocaust.

These initiatives built on groundwork laid in 1951, when Israel and an *ad hoc* consortium of voluntary Jewish organizations received an invitation to negotiate with West Germany for 'moral and material amends' for Nazi-era damages. The consortium became the Conference on Jewish Material Claims Against Germany (known as the Claims Conference).

This book is a history of the Claims Conference, the vehicle representing Jewish victims of Nazi persecution for material claims against Germany and Austria. Despite its unprecedented accomplishments, the Claims

Conference has remained largely unrecognized by the public during most of its existence. It is generally known that Germany paid 'reparations' and that Holocaust survivors received 'compensation.' However, it is not well known that the Claims Conference was responsible for the agreements that culminated in Germany's payments of some DM 100 billion to individual Nazi victims. This was not 'humanitarian' compensation. Instead, these were payments based on landmark legal and moral principles developed and demanded by the Conference and accepted by West Germany that established precedents for redress for victims of human rights abuses.

The publication of this work was commissioned in 2000 by Rabbi Israel Miller and Saul Kagan, the long-time leaders of the Claims Conference. We had become acquainted when I reported for the *Jerusalem Post* on Holocaust-related issues, from 1995 through 2000. Miller and Kagan provided full access to the Claims Conference records and archives at its headquarters in New York, as well as in Jerusalem and Frankfurt; were readily available to answer any and all questions; and arranged the funds to cover the research expenses for this book. Miller, Kagan and Gideon Taylor, Kagan's successor, reviewed the manuscript for factual errors and glaring omissions. They offered suggestions, as well; some were accepted and some were not. I profoundly regret that Rabbi Miller did not live to see the publication of this book.

This is not the first book about or supported by the Claims Conference. In *German Reparations: A History of the Negotiations* (Jerusalem: Hebrew University, 1980), Nana Sagi provided a detailed account of the original negotiations between Israel, the Claims Conference and West Germany. Those negotiations culminated in the Luxembourg Agreements, which form the basis for West Germany's bulk payment to Israel for refugee absorption, as well as its commitments to the Claims Conference.

The second book, by Ronald W. Zweig, focuses specifically on the Claims Conference. In *German Reparations and the Jewish World: A History of the Claims Conference* (2nd edn, London: Frank Cass, 2001), Zweig reviews the Conference's history from its founding through 1965. He focuses on its organization and the allocations of German funds for relief programs for individuals and reconstruction of Jewish communities that were destroyed by the Nazis.

An important book on the Conference's early agreements with German companies for payments for slave labour is Benjamin B. Ferencz's *Less Than Slaves: Jewish Forced Labour and the Quest for Compensation* (Cambridge, MA: Harvard University Press, 1979; reissued by Indiana University Press, 2002). Ferencz, a former Nuremberg prosecutor who tried the *Einsatzgruppen*, was the founding director in 1947 of the Jewish Restitution Successor Organization, a long-time Claims Conference negotiator and its counsel. He also spent decades pursuing the establishment of the International Criminal Court, and was instrumental in ensuring that the 1998 Rome Statute mandated the court to establish principles for reparations to victims – a legacy of the Luxembourg Agreements.

Another work deserves special mention. Ernst Katzenstein, a German-born Jewish lawyer who fled to Palestine after Hitler's rise to power, returned to West Germany as the Claims Conference's representative and laboured for decades as a draftsman, legal monitor and relentless lobbyist for German legislation to expand compensation for Nazi victims. In his final years, he began to prepare a history of the Conference's efforts to develop and improve German compensation legislation. His strength failing, he abandoned the project in 1983. However, over the years, he had maintained extensive and exhaustive correspondence and memos – in English, German and occasionally Latin. These collectively are known as the 'Katzenstein bible' and, although it has not been published, this bible is an extraordinary source-book of the history of the Conference's struggles and successes in securing compensation, as well as the limits of the German indemnification laws.

This book, while it draws on the work of the others, is far broader. Its prism is the Claims Conference as a vehicle for compensation, restitution and aid for Jewish victims of Nazi persecution. The book includes previously undisclosed material from the period after 1965, with special attention to the Conference's work since 1990. The Conference's efforts ensured that in the rush toward German reunification, the rights of Nazi victims would be protected. Its activities in unified Germany have produced substantial compensation and property restitution for tens of thousands of Nazi victims, and generated the largest-ever unrestricted source of funds to finance social welfare services for Holocaust survivors around the world.

A NOTE ON SOURCES

The Claims Conference records from 1951 to 1979 are housed in Jerusalem at the Central Archives for the History of the Jewish People (CAHJP). Materials from the last two decades are scattered among Claims Conference offices and are not systematically organized. The records include correspondence, memoranda, minutes and unedited transcripts of meetings, as well as copies of documents obtained from the US National Archives and Records Administration (NARA). Unless otherwise noted, the materials cited in this book were located in the files of the Conference headquarters in New York. When the materials have titles, these are used. This book relies heavily on meeting transcripts, which are indicated in the notes by the name and date of the meeting.

A number of historians generously have reviewed this manuscript, in whole or in part, and provided valuable comments and criticism. I thank Jens Hoppe and Peter Heuss (Frankfurt), Laurie Cohen (Vienna), Constantin Goschler (Humboldt University, Berlin), Yitzchak Mais (Jerusalem), Anita Shapira (Tel Aviv University) and Ivan Marcus (Yale University).

This book also has benefited from a decade of my reporting on the efforts to recover Nazi-looted properties. In my reporting and in my research I have been helped by scores of people in the US, Israel and Europe. I especially would like to acknowledge Hadassah Assouline, Andrew Baker, John Becker, J.D. Bindenagel, Gisela Blau, David Brinn, Arie Bucheister, Ariel Colonomos, Kurt Donnelly, Keri Douglas, Jeanettea Dunbar, Nilene Evans, Allyn Ilan Fisher, Ricki Garti, Rivka and Alex Glickman, Ann Goldstein, Judah Gribetz, Lawrence Grossman, Ruth Ellen Gruber, Raynelle Hall, Meryl Hyman Harris, Shelley Helfand, Ben Helfgott, Cyma Horowitz, Zvi Imbar, Alec Israel, Sara Kadosh, Stanislaw Krajewski, Antony Lerman, Steve Linde, Sybil Milton, Mikhail Mitsel, Jan Munk, Matt Nesvisky, Sam Norich, Thomas Preiswerk, David Raab, Shari Reig, Fran Rivera, Jüergen Roth, Carl Schrag, Israel Sela, Christopher Simpson, Brigitte Sion, Lonnie Stegink, Eric Thomason, Barbara Tzoukermann, Nancy Gruskin Warner and Eliot Zimelman. I am deeply indebted to Jeff Barak, the editor who enthusiastically encouraged my extensive travels in Europe for the *Jerusalem Post*; to Sherry Hyman, for her wisdom and compassion; and to Esther Hecht, an extraordinary editor and friend. None of this would have been possible without the love and support of Shammai Engelmayer.

I am, of course, responsible for errors.

Marilyn Henry
New York, 2006

Abbreviations

AJC	American Jewish Committee
ASVG	*Allgemeines Sozial Versicherungsgesetz* (General Social Insurance Law)
BARoV	*Bundesamt zur Regelung offener Vermögensfragen* (German Federal Office for the Settlement of Open Property Issues)
BDI	*Bundesverband der Deutschen Industrie* (Federal Association of German Industries)
BEG	*Bundesentschädigungsgesetze* (German federal indemnification laws)
CAHJP	Central Archives for the History of the Jewish People
CDU	Christian Democratic Union
CJCA	Committee for Jewish Claims on Austria
CSU	Christian Social Union
DM	Deutschmark
DP	displaced person
FRG	Federal Republic of Germany
FSU	former Soviet Union
GDR	German Democratic Republic
ICHEIC	International Commission for Holocaust Era Insurance Claims
IKG	*Israelitische Kultusgemeinde* (Austrian Jewish Community)
JDC	American Jewish Joint Distribution Committee (also known as 'the Joint')
JRSO	Jewish Restitution Successor Organization
JTA	Jewish Telegraphic Agency

JUVA	*Judenvermögensabgabe* (confiscatory property taxes specifically aimed at Jews)
MK	Member of the Knesset (Israel)
NARA	US National Archives and Records Administration
OFG	*Opferfürsorgegesetz* (Victims' Assistance Law, Austria)
SPD	Social Democratic Party
TCG	Tripartite Gold Commission
URO	United Restitution Organization
WJC	World Jewish Congress
WJRO	World Jewish Restitution Organization

Foreword

The story of the Conference on Jewish Material Claims Against Germany – known as the Claims Conference – is the story of a massive undertaking: the attempt at finding the means to compensate survivors of the Holocaust for at least some of their suffering and loss during the war years. In a scholarly and gripping account, Marilyn Henry takes the reader behind the scenes both of international diplomacy and the practical, day-to-day work of an organisation that, while sometimes criticised for obscurantism and lack of transparency, has served the Jewish people well.

Ronald W. Zweig, in his book *German Reparations and the Jewish World: A History of the Claims Conference*, first published by Westview Press in 1987 and subsequently by Frank Cass, tells the story of the first 10 years of the Claims Conference. Marilyn Henry builds on this pioneering work to provide a comprehensive study of conscience and philanthropy in action.

The basis of the work of the Claims Conference was the series of agreements signed in Luxembourg in 1952, under which the then West German Government, headed by Konrad Adenauer, agreed to pay money both to Israel and to the Claims Conference, and at the same time agreed to enact legislation to provide compensation and restitution to individual victims of Nazi persecution, wherever they might be living.

The process of reparation was continuous. In 1980 the Claims Conference set up a special Hardship Fund for Jewish immigrants from the Soviet Union. Originally intended to benefit 80,000 people, it was eventually to make payments to four times that number. In the late 1990s a further fund, the Central and Eastern European Fund, was set up to help those survivors in former Communist countries who had never been eligible for German compensation. Most recently, the question of wartime slave labour compensation has been high on the Claims Conference agenda, leading to payments to Jewish victims in 40 countries. Marilyn Henry does not shy away from the controversies, disappointments and even litigation that these important initiatives generated; her account is scrupulously documented, clear and fair.

Not only individual survivors, but also educational institutions and projects related to Jewish history and culture have been the beneficiaries of the generosity of the Claims Conference. These include such major enterprises as Yad Vashem, the Holocaust memorial and archive in Jerusalem, and a wide range of social services and educational institutions throughout Israel; as well as individual efforts such as Vladka Meed's annual teachers seminars in Poland and Israel, and Esther Goldberg's Holocaust Memoir Digest, an ongoing series for teachers and students, published by Vallentine Mitchell.

One of the strengths of Marilyn Henry's work is that she enables the reader to see just how many individuals and institutions were involved, first in putting the whole concept together and then in enabling it to work efficiently. These are, in many cases, the unsung heroes of post-war Jewish history: the civil servants of the Jewish people, led in this enterprise by Nahum Goldmann, the president of the Claims Conference from its inception until his death in 1982.

Goldmann's work, and that of myriad other officials who worked with him in their long and complex negotiations with the German government, is given full credit in these pages. So too, are the Claims Conference's capital projects, which in the first decade alone included, in still war-torn Europe, support for the establishment of 150 schools, 107 community and youth centres, 56 homes for the aged and 41 children's homes and kindergartens. In the words of Charles Jordan, then director of the European operations of the American Jewish Joint Distribution Committee (the 'Joint'), the effect of these initiatives by the Claims Conference 'in the development of Jewish life, the prestige of the Jewish community and the inspiration to other communities in Europe, are immense'. They provided, he wrote, 'a spirit of hope that attracts people back to the community'.

That legacy has continued until today. A new initiative that continues to this day began in 1992, with the fall of the Iron Curtain. That year, the Claims Conference initiated the creation of the World Jewish Restitution Organization, a consortium of seven international Jewish organizations, as well as survivors' organizations in Israel and the United States, to seek the recovery of Jewish property in Central and Eastern Europe that had been confiscated or nationalised during both the Nazi and Communist eras.

Marilyn Henry shows how much has been accomplished, by so many, and with so much effort, in the 50 years since the Luxembourg Agreements. Today, more than 90,000 Jewish victims of Nazism continue to receive monthly pensions direct from Germany, totalling more than 450 million Euros each year. A further 70,000 receive monthly payments totalling almost 300 million Euros each year through three funds administered by the Claims Conference. The Conference's international allocations programme has, in Marilyn Henry words, 'altered the cultural and physical landscape of Jewish communities in western Europe', as well as the 'scope and nature' of social welfare and medical services to the elderly in both Israel and the former Soviet Union.

Marilyn Henry shows how these achievements came into being, the struggles and problems in their paths, and the intensity of Jewish self-help and rebirth in the former charnel houses of Europe, in Israel, and in the wider Jewish Diaspora.

Sir Martin Gilbert
August 2006

Chapter 1

Confronting the Perpetrators: Jewish Material Claims for Nazi Atrocities

Isolated from the outside world by a moat and a phalanx of security agents, delegations from Israel, Jewish organizations and West Germany convened in a castle in Wassenaar, near The Hague, on 21 March 1952. This was the first formal meeting between representatives of the Jewish people and Germany since the Holocaust. It was the most implausible of encounters: negotiations for the Jewish 'material claims' against West Germany for the damages and destruction wrought on the Jewish world by a dozen years of Nazi persecution.[1]

These unprecedented talks were based on two momentous ideas: That West Germany should pay reparations to a Jewish state – Israel – for acts committed before the birth of that state, and that West Germany should reach an agreement with an *ad hoc* organization of Jewish agencies on compensation for injuries and losses sustained by Jewish victims of Nazi persecution. Neither Israel nor a voluntary Jewish organization had standing to press claims against Germany. Yet they were the voices of the Jewish people undertaking this audacious, historic mission to recover funds to rebuild Jewish life and to establish the principle of accountability for wrongs committed against victims of persecution. 'If you look back to the destruction of the Temple, the Crusades, the expulsion of the Jews from Spain in 1492, or, in more recent times, the pogroms in Russia in the 1890s, these catastrophes inflicted on the Jewish people over 3,000 years of its history resulted in mass exiles. They were major human disasters, followed by exile and resettlement,' said Saul Kagan. 'Only in the late 1930s and early 1940s did the organized Jewish world begin to think seriously about facing the perpetrators.'[2]

When the Germans and the Jews convened, seven years after the devastation of European Jewry, the mood in the castle 'was one of devastating tension,' recalled Kagan, who was part of the Jewish delegation in The Hague and whose career spanned a half-century of efforts to secure compensation for Nazi victims. 'At the opening session, not a greeting was exchanged between the Jews and the Germans; every word spoken was icily correct, but no more. Every Jew at the conference was keenly aware of an invisible presence haunting that room, the presence of six million dead.'[3]

The surviving victims were represented by a consortium of Jewish organizations from the west – the Conference on Jewish Material Claims Against Germany, known as the Claims Conference. Since Wassenaar, and for more than five decades, the Claims Conference secured funds for hundreds of thousands of Jewish Nazi victims and for the restoration of Jewish communities in western Europe; and pursued measures for the restitution of Jewish properties in Germany, primarily for tens of thousands of individual Jewish victims and their heirs.

The Wassenaar discussions, as traumatic as they were, culminated in agreements signed in Luxembourg in 1952 under which Germany agreed to pay some DM 3 billion to Israel and another DM 450 million to the Claims Conference for projects for the rehabilitation of Holocaust survivors outside of Israel. More important, West Germany pledged to enact legislation to provide compensation and restitution to individual victims of Nazi persecution. These individual payments amounted to more than DM 100 billion by century's end.[4]

By the close of the twentieth century, the idea of 'reparations' to individual victims of atrocities and human rights abuses, while not common, was no longer novel. In 1988, the US Congress authorized the Justice Department to pay $20,000 each to surviving Japanese-Americans who, because of their race, were interned or relocated in the US during the Second World War.[5] The Korean 'comfort women' had made claims against Japan, and American descendants of nineteenth-century slaves raised reparations claims against the US and private companies.[6]

However, in 1952, such individual claims on such a massive scale were historic. Post-war law was not equipped to deal with the extraordinary status or demands of the surviving victims of the Nazis. International law had developed the concept of war reparations, but reparations were matters between governments – the victors and the vanquished. There was no expectation of individual compensation for persecution and no role for individual victims in the proceedings.[7] Instead, national governments advocated for their citizens' interests in bilateral diplomatic negotiations. However, a significant proportion of surviving Nazi victims were displaced and stateless. Jewish victims lacked a government to whom to appeal to represent their interests, and the nature of their claims differed from traditional reparations. They were not presenting general war-damage claims. Instead, they sought indemnification for material damages and losses resulting from persecution, arguing that the perpetrators should not enjoy the spoils of their slaughter of the Jews.[8] The Nazis' first declaration of war was against the Jewish people, and 'its aim was not conquest and enslavement, but the complete physical extermination of the Jews, the utter destruction of their spiritual and religious heritage, and the confiscation of all their material possessions,' Chaim Weizmann, then president of the quasi-governmental Jewish Agency for Palestine, told the Allies in 1945. 'In executing their declaration of war, Germany and her associates murdered some six million Jews, destroyed all Jewish communal institutions wherever their authority extended, stole all the Jewish treasures of art and learning, and seized all Jewish property, public and private, on which they could lay their hands.'[9]

As the Jewish claims were historic, the Luxembourg Agreements were unprecedented. Restitution was made not to victors, but to the individual victims via agreements between West Germany and Israel and the Claims Conference, 'descendant' entities of the perpetrators and the victims.[10] The 1952 negotiations were held among nascent entities: West Germany, which had become a state only three years earlier; Israel, which had been established four years earlier; and the Conference, an *ad hoc* non-governmental organization based in New York and representing 'Jewry.'[11] The Jews had moral, not legal, claims. 'All we had was justice and morality on our side and, in this world, justice and morality do not count for very much,' said Moses Leavitt, the executive secretary of the American Jewish Joint Distribution Committee, and the chairman of the Claims Conference delegation that faced the German negotiators in The Hague. 'They once said to us, "There was no basis in international law for these negotiations." We then asked, "What was the basis in international law for the murder and spoliation of six million people?" That ended the discussion.'[12]

The Luxembourg Agreements were unique in international relations. It was extraordinary that the government of a sovereign state would enter an agreement with a voluntary organization to pay compensation to individuals dispersed around the world for damages the state's predecessor had inflicted. 'In no previous case in history had a state paid indemnification directly to individuals, most of them not even its own citizens,' wrote Nehemiah Robinson, a Lithuanian-born émigré who was the architect of the legal basis of Jewish claims. 'Countries paid indemnification when they were defeated in war; the fact is as old as human history itself. But that a government should pay for crimes committed, not only to its own citizens, which was unusual enough, but to hundreds of thousands of non-citizens, or to another state, the State of Israel, which was not even in existence at the time the crimes were committed and had no legal claim to anything, was truly a revolutionary idea.'[13]

The Claims Conference itself was unique. Jewish organizations had set aside their profound – and often bitter – political, ideological and religious differences to focus on one central task: aid to Nazi victims. From its origins as an improvised collective, the Claims Conference evolved into an internationally recognized agency representing the interests of individual Jewish Nazi victims in negotiations with the Federal Republic of Germany (FRG), a mission it persistently pursued for more than a half-century.

Between 1945 and 1949, Germany was divided in four Occupation zones under the control of the Allies – the United States, Britain, France and the Soviet Union. Nazi victims had received limited compensation under fragmentary general claims laws that had been enacted in some of the individual German states – the *Länder* – under the post-war western Occupation authorities, primarily the US. 'These laws varied from state to state and represented no more than a modest beginning in their scope and execution,' said Nahum Goldmann, who served as the Claims Conference's president from its founding until his death in 1982.[14] In the newly sovereign West Germany, the prospect of compensation for Nazi victims was first raised in 1949 by the political opposition, in a vigorous response to the first speech by Konrad Adenauer as the first chancellor of the Federal Republic. In his 20 September 1949 address to the Bundestag, Adenauer made only limited reference to the Jews. He condemned anti-Semitism, saying, 'After all that happened in the National Socialist period, we view it as unworthy and unbelievable there are still people in Germany who would persecute or despise the Jews because they are Jews.' Instead, he focused on his domestic problems, including the integration of millions of ethnic Germans, the *Volksdeutsche*, who had been expelled from Central and Eastern Europe after the Second World War, and on German prisoners of war in the Soviet Union.

The leader of the opposition Social Democratic Party (SPD), Kurt Schumacher, criticized Adenauer because the chancellor had uttered 'not one word' about the victims of fascism or the anti-Nazi resistance.[15] One could not be against Nazism 'without thinking about its victims,' Schumacher said the day after the chancellor's speech. 'What was said yesterday in [Adenauer's] statement about the Jews and the frightful tragedy of the Jews in the Third Reich was too feeble and too weak. Resigned comments and a tone of regret in this matter don't help at all. It is not only the duty of international socialists to place the fate of the German and European Jews in the forefront of attention and to offer help where it is needed. It is also the duty of every German patriot to do so. By the extermination of six million Jewish human beings, Hitler barbarism disgraced the German people. We will have to bear the consequences of this disgrace for the unforeseeable future.'[16]

The chancellor's first gesture toward the Jews came in November 1949, when he offered goods valued at DM 10 million to Israel 'as a first direct token that the injustice done to the Jews all over the world has to be made good.' It was offensive. 'Dr Adenauer's offer of 10 million marks, or about 2 marks per murdered Jew, was regarded by the Jewish people as an insult,' said the World Jewish Congress's A. L. Easterman of London.[17] An invitation for negotiations between Germany and the Jews came two years later in Adenauer's dramatic declaration in the Bundestag on 27 September 1951 – the eve of Rosh Hashanah, the Jewish new year. 'The federal government, and with it the vast majority of the German people, is conscious of the immeasurable suffering that was brought to bear upon the Jews in Germany and in the occupied territories during the period of National Socialism. The great majority of the German people abhorred the crimes committed against the Jews and had no part in them,' he said. 'During the time of National Socialism, there were many Germans who, risking their own lives for religious reasons, obeying the commands of their conscience, and feeling ashamed that the good name of Germany should be trodden upon, were prepared to help their Jewish compatriots. But unspeakable crimes were perpetrated in the name of the German people, which impose upon them the obligation to make moral and material amends, both as regards the individual damage that Jews have suffered and as regards Jewish property for which there are no longer individual claimants... The Federal Government is prepared, jointly with representatives of Jewry and the State of Israel, which has admitted so many homeless Jewish refugees, to bring about a solution of the material reparation problem, in order to facilitate the way to a spiritual purging of unheard-of suffering.'[18]

A constellation of factors led to the invitation. Adenauer, a devout Catholic, had received support from his Jewish friends when he was ousted in 1933 as mayor of Cologne. Alongside his moral convictions, there also was the matter of West Germany's self-interest. The invitation could have practical benefits for West German foreign policy. In a March 1951 diplomatic note, the State of Israel had sought aid from the four Occupation powers in gaining compensation from Germany.

'When the victorious Allies at the end of the war allocated the reparations due from Germany, the Jewish people had as yet no *locus standi* in the community of sovereign nations,' Israel said in its note to the United States, Great Britain, France and the Soviet Union. 'As a result, the claims, though morally perhaps stronger than those of any other people that had suffered at the hands of the Nazis, went by default. The time has come to rectify this omission.' Israel at the time was virtually a bankrupt state struggling with its defense, development and the influx of refugees. 'The State of Israel regards itself as entitled to claim reparations from Germany by way of indemnity to the Jewish people,' it said. Israel asked for $1.5 billion, which it calculated as the cost of resettling some 500,000 refugees from or survivors of the Nazi-conquered territories. However, Israel cautioned, 'No indemnity, however large, can make good the loss of human life and cultural values or atone for the suffering and agonies of the men, women and children put to death by every inhuman device.'[19]

The Soviet Union ignored the Israeli note, while the western Allies suggested that Israel deal directly with the German government in Bonn.[20] The Cold War was under way, and US High Commissioner John J. McCloy believed that West Germany might be accepted by the Americans as a trustworthy ally if it met Jewish claims. He told Adenauer that the FRG's reconciliation with the Jews was 'significant' for Germany's international position.[21]

Adenauer's invitation to negotiations came more than a decade after Jewish organizations around the world began formulating the basis for claims against Germany – long before the extent of the devastation of the Holocaust was known. In 1940, the American Jewish Committee appointed a 'Committee on Peace Studies,' which considered the question: 'Will it be possible for those who have been deprived of their business or professional calling to be restored to the position they occupied before the advent of the Hitler régime?'[22] That was followed by conferences in Baltimore (1941) and Atlantic City (1944) convened by the World Jewish Congress. Preparatory work on the legal basis of claims and the scope of Jewish material losses had been done by Jacob and Nehemiah Robinson of the World Jewish Congress's Institute of Jewish Affairs. In Mandatory Palestine, Dr Siegfried Moses, of the Association of Central European Immigrants in Palestine, in 1943 had prepared a broad outline of the philosophical and practical issues in seeking compensation for the Jewish people as a nation. Weizmann, of the Jewish Agency, called for compensation from Germany, and for heirless Jewish property to be turned over to the Jewish Agency, saying the agency was the official representative of the Jews and bore the cost of resettling Jewish refugees in Palestine.[23]

Within the Jewish world, however, the prospect of direct negotiations with West Germany posed a profound quandary. Every instinct militated against negotiations, while reason demanded them. Both Israel and Jewish agencies were in dire need of funds to aid and resettle Nazi victims, which made some sort of payment from Germany vital. In addition, if no claims were pressed, the German people would have enriched themselves through the success of the Nazi extermination programme. The damages the Jews had sustained for loss of life, deprivation of liberty, injuries to health, and pain and suffering were incalculable; the Jewish material losses at Nazi hands had been 'authoritatively estimated' at some $30 billion.[24] It grated, said Abba Eban, then the Israeli ambassador to the US, that 'there has been no tangible effort to expiate this sin, even if it were capable of expiation. Israel is startled to observe the easy acceptance in many quarters of the doctrine that the German people, with this hideous responsibility still lying on its shoulders, can fittingly be associated as an equal partner in the defense of human freedoms and moral values.'[25]

Weeks after Adenauer's invitation, a conference of some two dozen Jewish organizations assembled at the Waldorf-Astoria hotel in New York. It had been convened by Goldmann, the pre-eminent Jewish statesman of his era, at the behest of Israeli officials. 'I did so because I realized that Israel would not be able to negotiate with Germany alone and that a body as representative as possible of all Jews, whose authority both the Jewish public and the German Federal Republic could respect, would be required,' said Goldmann, who simultaneously represented Jewish interests in the diaspora and in Israel as the head of both the World Jewish Congress and the Jewish Agency for Palestine.[26]

The Waldorf participants represented international and national Jewish organizations in the west, primarily from the United States, Britain and France.[27] These nations were the Occupation authorities in West Germany, and the Jewish organizations were expected to influence their respective governments to support the Israeli claim of $1.5 billion against Germany. The conference's original mission, though, had been changed both by Adenauer's declaration and the Allies' reluctance to directly intervene. 'This hope – which has existed for some time among many of us, and which everybody would have been delighted if it had materialized – that there would be other powers, the western Powers, the Occupying Powers, the United Nations, God knows who – who would do this work for us, and they would either influence or impose or get the Germans to make these arrangements and we will just be on the receiving end – I never believed in the seriousness of such a policy and it is clear that it cannot be done. We know that no other power will step in and take over this job,' Goldmann said as he opened the two-day Waldorf meeting on 25 October 1951. 'So if we want seriously to get something out of this destruction of the Nazi decade of the Holocaust, we must be ready to talk by ourselves or take a position [that] we don't expect anything.'[28]

Eban told the conference that Israel's claim was symbolic and did not take into account the actual losses of property destroyed or plundered by the Germans. 'In the name of Jewish security and Jewish honor, Israel now solemnly invites Jews everywhere to rally unreservedly to the support of this claim, for if it were to be historically established that six million Jews could be consigned to the slaughterhouse and that this event could be passed over by history in silence, having no effect upon Germany's relations with the international community, what conclusion would be drawn as to the value of Jewish life, as to the price of Jewish honor, as to the stability of Jewish security in any part of the world?' the Israeli ambassador asked.

However, to Eban's consternation, the conference would not limit its focus to Israel's claim. Israel was not universally recognized as the representative of the Jewish people, nor did its claim focus on individuals' losses and rights. 'The claim, of course, is preponderantly that of Israel, but it is not only an Israel claim,' said Jacob Blaustein, a prominent industrialist who led the American Jewish Committee. He insisted that 'we must press equally for the claims of all Jewry.'

The scope and nature of those claims were unclear. The Israeli claim had not arisen in a vacuum. International Jewish organizations had been pressing for compensation measures and generating claims under indemnification and restitution laws in the western Occupation zones since 1947. At issue was how to distinguish a general Jewish claim from that of the State of Israel, and how to reconcile those claims with existing laws. "Whether we have energetically pursued all aspects of the problem or pursued some with dubious hope of success, we have nonetheless pushed a program that asks for the return of all plundered Jewish property, either to individuals or to successor organizations, as may befit the case," Jerome Jacobson, counsel of the Joint Distribution Committee, wrote shortly before the Waldorf meeting.[29] Benjamin Ferencz, the founding director of the Jewish Restitution Successor Organization, estimated that some $25 million had been collected under the Occupation-era laws,[30] and he thought that the Waldorf participants were naïve in discussing claims. 'As I listened here this morning to all these speeches about $1.5 billion, and about a few billions here and another few billions there … I thought: "If anybody thinks that Adenauer is waiting like Santa Claus with a big bag of packages to give to the Jews who come marching by at Christmas time, forget about it."

That is not the way it works,' he told the assembly. 'It is going to take a lot of hard work before you get anything.'

Eban warned that an amorphous Jewish claim could obscure and undercut the Israeli claim, which was based on the premise that Israel had provided refuge and rehabilitation for victims who were weakened and impoverished by the Nazis. He urged the conference 'to ponder very seriously whether the specific nature of the Israel claim – its formal character as a claim which now lies before all the governments concerned, its clear-cut and well-defined properties, the obvious feasibility of its implementation – whether these attributes of the Israel claim do not argue for it at this at stage at least primacy, if not monopoly, of Jewish attention and support'.

The Waldorf participants were not swayed by the Israeli ambassador. They gave 'wholehearted support' to Israel's claims, but they also demanded 'satisfaction of all other Jewish claims against Germany, including claims for restitution and indemnification by individuals, successor organizations and others, and for rehabilitation of the Jewish victims of Nazi persecution,' and called for immediate steps to improve existing restitution and indemnification legislation. They organized themselves as the Conference on Jewish Material Claims Against Germany,[31] agreeing that they could, as a group, negotiate with West Germany, but only if the discussions were limited to material claims. 'Every elementary principle of justice and human decency requires that the German people shall, at the least, restore the plundered Jewish property, indemnify the victims of persecution, their heirs and successors, and pay for the rehabilitation of the survivors,' the Conference said at the meeting's end.[32] Adenauer's declaration would be judged by the speed and extent of its implementation, the Conference said. It did not deal with Germany's relations with Jewry. History alone can settle the question of relations, said Goldmann, adding, 'To seek to get back what is ours from the Germans does not mean we are forgiving our debtors.'[33]

Eban hailed the Waldorf conference. 'We neither honor our dead nor do justice to their survivors if we continue to maintain an attitude of oblivion, of acquiescence, forgetfulness, or inaction in all the questions affecting the surviving remnant of the Jewish people,' he said. 'The Jews in Israel, through their accredited representatives, and Jews throughout the world, through their recognized organizations, have today reached a united definition of German obligations and of Jewish rights.'

In Israel, however, Adenauer's invitation prompted wrenching debates, demonstrations and riots. Negotiations with the Germans were vehemently criticized as 'sacrilege' and payments called 'blood money'. Menachem Begin of the Heruth Party led the movement against German reparations to Israel, arguing that Jewish honour would not be sold. Prime Minister David Ben-Gurion called in the police when Begin's supporters stoned the Knesset. After a stormy two-day session, the Knesset voted 61–50 on 9 January 1952 to accept Adenauer's invitation.[34] To those who argued that talks with Germany were immoral, Goldmann countered: 'The opposite is true. We would have committed a moral injustice, a sin of omission, had we refused to negotiate, however delicate and difficult it all seemed in its initial stages. Even if these negotiations had not involved material benefits to Israel and the Jewish victims of Nazism, our generation still would have been morally bound to make every possible effort to obtain recognition of the moral principle that a nation which has committed crimes against our people must make amends. The fact that a powerful and sovereign state has done so establishes a historic precedent of importance to all people.'[35]

When the negotiations began in Wassenaar, Moses Leavitt of the Joint Distribution Committee said the Conference had accepted Adenauer's invitation because of a sense of duty toward and responsibility for survivors. 'We are ready to negotiate on certain claims of a material nature,' he said. 'But we want to make clear from the beginning that there can be no negotiation on moral claims.' The material claims were for payments to individual victims for damages resulting from Nazi persecution. The Conference sought uniform compensation and restitution legislation for the surviving victims, by extending Occupation-era measures to the whole of the FRG, and expanding the laws to add new categories of claimants. It also sought to transfer unclaimed and heirless property to organizations caring for survivors. 'The millions who have perished are, together with their survivors, the ones whose rights are at stake here,' the Jewish delegation said. 'Though they are absent, their assets must not be abandoned. Germany should not retain any benefit from the thoroughness of the Nazi extermination program.'[36]

The negotiations were strained. 'We sat there for six months wrestling with the Germans in 1952 trying to create the basis both for compensation and for the principle of justice which had to underlie all of these efforts,' Kagan recalled.[37] The magnitude could be gauged from the number of claims that already had been filed under limited *Länder* compensation measures. Some 125,000 claims had been filed in the US Occupation Zone alone.[38]

The Wassenaar talks culminated in the Luxembourg Agreements, which were signed on 10 September 1952. The mood was somber. 'That the Hitler-created heritage of hate cannot be quickly dispelled was evident in the stiff and self-conscious atmosphere as Chancellor Konrad Adenauer, Foreign Minister Moshe Sharett of Israel and Dr Nahum

Goldmann, chairman of the presidium of 24 world Jewish organizations, penned their signatures to the series of accords,' the *New York Times* reported in a front-page account. 'Scarcely a word was spoken as the German and Jewish representatives faced each other across a long table in Luxembourg's City Hall in their first officially amicable ceremony in almost two decades. There was no public handshaking.'[39]

Under the Luxembourg Agreements, West Germany agreed to pay Israel DM 3 billion in goods and services, over the course of a dozen years.[40] These payments (*Shilumim*) had a dramatic effect on the economic development of the impoverished state,[41] which was understood immediately. 'The Hague agreement was received very well in Israel. Even the opposition parties (with the exception of Heruth) appreciate the economic importance of reparations,' said Giora Josephthal of the Jewish Agency. However, he was not entirely sanguine. 'In spite of that we may have to face some acts of terrorism when the first [German] goods reach Israel.'[42]

The German agreements with the Conference were in two 'protocols,' which covered individual and collective claims.[43] Under Protocol I, West Germany was obliged to enact federal legislation to provide compensation and restitution to individual victims of Nazi persecution. Under Protocol II, which dealt with the Conference's collective claim, West Germany agreed to provide DM 450 million to the Conference for 'the relief, rehabilitation and resettlement of Jewish victims of National Socialist persecution, according to the urgency of their needs as determined by the Conference on Jewish Material Claims Against Germany ... living outside of Israel.'[44]

Protocol II had been especially difficult to achieve. West Germany resisted payments to the Claims Conference, saying that the material settlement should be with Israel, and that the Conference negotiations should be restricted to improving legislation affecting restitution and indemnification claims of individuals. That attitude rankled the Conference members. Adenauer had invited 'jointly' representatives of Jewry and of Israel to enter negotiations; it was pointless to meet if West Germany would not consider collective claims. West Germany contended that the Conference's claim duplicated the Israeli claim, and the FRG feared that the Conference's claim was a 'trick' to obtain more money for Israel, according to Goldmann.[45]

'Naturally both the Israel delegation and we maintained that we have two separate and different claims,' Leavitt said. 'Fundamentally, however, we must admit that the two claims were based on the same set of circumstances. Although we said our claim was for heirless and unclaimed property and Israel said its claim was for the resettlement of penniless immigrants, Germany was being asked to pay for the looting and spoliation of millions of Jews, for the physical damage which she did.'[46] However, by that time, Jewish organizations had spent more than $1 billion for the relief and rehabilitation of hundreds of thousands of Nazi victims, and more funds were required. 'There was cast upon the Jews of the world the monumental task of caring for this vast mass of innocent victims. Broken bodies had to be made whole, tortured minds restored, children had to be reared and educated. All had to be housed, fed and clothed, and provided with the means to achieve new livelihoods. They had to be established in lands, notably Israel, where they could live in peace and security,' the Conference delegation said. 'These enormous undertakings, engaged in by Jews everywhere, involved expenditures on a scale unparalleled in the whole history of social endeavor by private groups and institutions, while Germany benefited and continues to benefit from the great mass of Jewish property looted, confiscated and extorted by the Nazi régime.'[47]

The agreement for DM 450 million under Protocol II left the Conference with some 20 per cent of its original claim for $500 million. In The Hague, Conference negotiators conceded on the collective claim to gain improvements in compensation for individual victims through German legislation under Protocol I. The delegation had been instructed that 'the satisfaction of individual claims should have priority over the aggregate claim. In other words, if the satisfaction of the most pressing individual claims will appear impossible at the same time as the assignment of an aggregate amount, concessions should be made on the latter.'[48]

The two protocols defined the Conference's dual responsibilities: pursuing compensation for individuals through German legislation, and using the collective claim to rehabilitate Jewish victims and communities. Protocol I detailed West Germany's commitment to the principle of compensation and its pledge to enact indemnification and restitution laws. On behalf of individual victims, the Conference focused on the development and passage of additional German legislation, on the implementation of existing legislation, and on assisting needy victims with their legal claims. Between 1953 and 1965, after negotiations with the Conference, the West German government enacted three federal indemnification laws (*Bundesentschädigungsgesetze,* or BEG) – built on the inherited Occupation laws – that established the legal framework for compensation for 'victims of National Socialist persecution'[49] in the west for a range of damages caused by Nazi persecution, including deprivation of liberty, loss of property, and damage to health.

At the time, the long-term financial and political significance of

Protocol I was unknown and wildly underestimated. 'The global payments and the legislative program will cost Germany up to $2 billion, and there was considerable resistance within the [German] government – not to the principle of meeting Jewry's and Israel's claims, but to the amounts involved in these claims,' Goldmann told the Conference shortly after the signing of the Luxembourg Agreements.[50] This was the pattern that would prevail for more than a half-century, in which the Conference would approach negotiations to discuss principles, and its German counterparts would focus on the costs. Five years after the agreements, indemnification costs had jumped to four times the original estimates. The laws were expanded through Claims Conference negotiations, Parliamentary amendments and German court rulings into a complicated matrix of one-time payments and on-going compensation based on the type and duration of persecution the victim suffered, and on the victim's location before, during and after the Second World War – all of which vastly increased the volume of payments. Despite the breadth of the German federal legislation, the disparities in compensation were wide, and created privileged, underprivileged and neglected classes of victims.[51]

The Protocol II funds presented an opportunity and a challenge. While the funds would help rehabilitate Holocaust survivors and reconstruct Jewish communities, the needs were overwhelming. 'The directors of the Claims Conference entered their task with history at their elbow and a deep sense of responsibility for utilizing the Conference's funds to make a permanent contribution toward the rebuilding of Jewish life and lives,' Kagan said. However, requests for funds 'were coming across our desks at the rate of many millions of dollars a week,' far in excess of the amounts available.[52] Over a dozen years, it allocated the DM 450 million, primarily for relief and social welfare programmes in the western European communities that had been decimated by the Nazis. A significant amount also was used to assist institutions in countries of resettlement, such as in Latin America and Australia, and for indirect aid to tens of thousands of survivors in Eastern Europe, which was known by the vague name 'relief in transit'.

There also were massive programmes for the construction of essential communal facilities in western Europe – including schools, synagogues, community centres and clinics. 'The reconstruction of the Jewish communities brought with it a revival of the Jewish spirit in country after country,' the Conference said. 'In a growing roster of communities, a will for accomplishment and a closer identification with Jewish life, Jewish values and the Jewish spiritual heritage has developed.'[53] When the Conference met on 30 May 1965, in Geneva, to vote on the last of its Protocol II allocations, it was generally expected that the organization would close. 'Having lived out its ordained lifespan, the Conference on Jewish Material Claims Against Germany has entered the corridor of history,' Kagan said.[54]

However, the Conference had residual responsibilities. The third and final West German indemnification law, the *Schlussgesetz*, was not passed until 1965 – two full decades after the end of the Second World War. Despite improvements in the law, large numbers of victims remained without compensation, and legal challenges to the earlier laws had not yet been resolved by the courts.[55] At the end of its first decade, the Conference decided it would continue its role as the watchdog of German indemnification legislation until it could transfer this task to another organization that was properly equipped to handle it. No such organization representing survivors' interests world-wide emerged.

Since Wassenaar, and for more than fifty years, the Conference engaged in continual negotiations to expand compensation measures for Jewish victims of Nazi persecution. 'Because the Nazi onslaught on the Jews was so global in scope and so extensive in execution, the existing program – despite its wide scope and large costs – provided most of the survivors of the Nazi Holocaust with too little material redress of the damage done; many have been totally excluded,' Nehemiah Robinson wrote on the tenth anniversary of the German indemnification legislation.[56] Among those who were excluded were the Jewish victims living in Eastern Europe. In the geopolitics of the day, West Germany was unwilling to provide compensation to victims in countries with which it did not have diplomatic relations.[57] That sentiment endured until after German reunification.

After 1965, the Conference maintained only a skeletal staff. A representative in West Germany, who also worked for the United Restitution Organization, continually pressed the German federal and state authorities on the implementation of the German compensation legislation. At stake was the protection of the rights of hundreds of thousands of Nazi victims. At the end of 1965, nearly 244,000 pensions were paid under the FRG's indemnification programme; that number would reach its peak of some 278,000 at the end of 1972.[58] The Conference also had several small, on-going responsibilities, such as providing funds for refugee rabbis and for former European communal leaders. In addition, in 1963 it had created a fund for *Hassidei Umot Haolam*, Righteous Gentiles who had been recognized by Yad Vashem, Israel's Holocaust Martyrs' and Heroes' Remembrance Authority, for saving Jews during the Nazi era. These tasks were handled by the New York office, whose operations took place in a corner of the Memorial Foundation for Jewish Culture. The Conference had founded the Memorial Foundation with its last $10 million from Protocol II.

Conference board meetings were limited to a few hours tacked on to the end of those of the Memorial Foundation, which shared many of the same board members. 'We functioned as an appendage to the Memorial Foundation because we didn't have the money to reimburse expenses of delegates attending our meetings,' said Jack J. Spitzer, the former president of B'nai B'rith and a long-time Conference official.[59] Smaller Conference meetings occasionally were held over breakfast in Blaustein's home.

From 1953, the Conference also pursued claims against the Republic of Austria, with only modest success in the early years. It was caught in a paradox. West Germany refused to pay compensation to Austrian victims, arguing that Austria itself was a successor state to the Nazi régime and thus was obliged to pay for damages.[60] Austria refused, relying on the first paragraph of the Allies' 1943 Moscow Declaration, in which Austria was labelled the 'first victim' of the Nazis. 'As a result of their government's basic attitude, the Austrian Jews have come out worst in the matter of compensation,' Goldmann said. 'Our completely inadequate achievements in the negotiations with Austria are another impressive illustration of how much was achieved in the long years of negotiations with Germany.'[61] It was not until 1991 that Austria broke the taboo of its 'first victim' status. 'We must not forget that there were not a few Austrians who, in the name of this [Nazi] régime, brought great suffering to others, who took part in the persecutions and crimes,' said Austrian Chancellor Franz Vranitzky. 'We own up to all facts of our history and to the deeds of all parts of our people. As we take credit for the good, we must apologize for the evil.'[62] However, from the end of the Second World War until 1995, Austria offered only limited compensation, and it was provided as a 'humanitarian' gesture for poor and elderly Nazi victims, not as an obligation of the state. In 1995, in conjunction with the 50th anniversary of the Second Republic, the Austrian Parliament created the 'National Fund' to make symbolic payments to an estimated 30,000 surviving Austrian-born victims. 'The fund will recognize that we are responsible for the fact Austrians also took part in the crimes of National Socialism,' said the chairman of the Social Democrats, Peter Kostelka.[63] An agreement to resolve remaining the Second World War-era Jewish property claims against Austria and Austrian enterprises was not reached until January 2001.

Austria was not alone in refusing to see itself as a Nazi successor state. The same was true for East Germany, which was occupied by the Soviet Union immediately after the Second World War and remained a Soviet satellite for the next four decades. In 1973, West Germany and the German Democratic Republic (GDR) became members of the United Nations, and East Germany and the US began talks to establish diplomatic relations. The Conference immediately initiated efforts to induce the GDR to acknowledge responsibility for Nazi-era compensation and restitution. East Germany, however, clung to the idea of its 'virgin birth', insisting that it was an anti-fascist state and not a successor to the Nazi régime. Further, it said, its 'reparations debt' had been paid by the Soviet Union's post-war seizure of its assets. The Conference pursued claims against the GDR for some 17 years. But it was not until April 1990, after the fall of the Berlin Wall and its first free elections, that East Germany acknowledged its Nazi-era obligations. In a declaration, the GDR's Parliament, the *Volkskammer*, admitted 'joint responsibility on behalf of the people for the humiliation, expulsion and murder of Jewish women, men and children,' and said the country was prepared to provide 'just compensation' for material losses. 'We feel sadness and shame as we acknowledge this burden of German history,' it said.[64]

West Germany had considered its obligations to Jewish victims to have been met by the passage of three indemnification laws between 1953 and 1965. However, the victims' need for additional compensation remained urgent. Détente between the east and west in the 1970s suddenly permitted thousands of Jews, including Nazi victims, to leave Eastern Europe. These victims had been unable to get payments from West Germany in their home nations. By the time they arrived in the west, where they would have been eligible for the FRG's compensation programmes, the filing deadlines for the programs had long expired. West Germany adamantly refused to reopen the filing period, despite passionate protests by the Conference that these victims should not be penalized for having been trapped behind the Iron Curtain. 'The days of 1965, when victims who were excluded from the law were allowed to have access to it, are over,' lamented Ernst Katzenstein, the Conference director in West Germany. 'The world has changed; so have its problems – the political scenery, the atmosphere, the general conditions, the financial situation.'[65]

However, the Conference persisted in seeking compensation. Bonn was wary. Compensation for Jewish victims competed with other demands – including those of non-Jewish persecutees in East Bloc nations with which West Germany had begun to normalize relations. The director-general of the West German Finance Ministry, Ernst Feaux de la Croix, once estimated that indemnification for bodily injury and material damage in all the western and eastern territories formerly occupied by the Nazis would amount to $200 billion.[66] For political reasons, West Germany would not endorse measures that solely benefited Jews; at the same time, the government rejected any plan that would expose it to massive claims from other groups of victims, or to charges that the measures were inequitable. 'The Germans are sensitive, once they enact a measure, that they don't find themselves under attack for not providing equal or analogous compensation to non-Jewish Nazi victims,' Kagan said.[67]

This concern also had played a role in the Wassenaar negotiations. Originally, the Germans 'were not prepared to pay one penny' to Jews from Eastern Europe, Leavitt recalled. That position excluded the single largest group of Jewish survivors. However, the FRG feared that providing compensation for Jewish victims would set a precedent for the non-Jews who had been persecuted in the east. This was resolved when the Conference and West Germany crafted eligibility criteria that were narrowed with distinctions based on the harshness of treatment the victims had endured: Bonn would accept indemnification claims of those victims from the east who had been confined in concentration camps or ghettos. The criteria included the majority of Jews, because they had been incarcerated, but excluded most other groups of victims – without specifying them.[68]

It was again victims from the east at the heart of an agreement with West Germany in 1980. After seven years of negotiations, the Conference entered its second phase when it reached an agreement with the FRG to establish the 'Hardship Fund'.[69] Unlike the indemnification program, in which compensation was a legal right for those who met the eligibility criteria, all German measures after 1965 were predicated on the principle of 'hardship' and could be viewed as 'humanitarian' gestures. 'The Germans' point of view was that the BEG was closed and that these extra measures were for unusual hardships which have arisen for people who could not take advantage of the BEG,' Kagan said. 'This is not an accident; this is part of their philosophy and approach to this whole issue.'[70]

The Hardship Fund, which began with an initial West German commitment of DM 400 million, was for Jewish victims who had 'suffered in their health because of National Socialist violence, and therefore [are] in a hardship situation, who for formal reasons did not obtain compensation,' including those who, for legitimate reasons, failed to file timely claims.[71] However, the German authorities refused to operate the new fund, which was primarily for victims emigrating from the Soviet Union. Instead, the German government conditioned the fund on the Conference's agreement to administer it. This thrust the Conference into a new role that profoundly changed its fundamental nature and its relationship to survivors. It was no longer solely an advocacy organization pressing German authorities for the rights of Nazi victims. Instead, it acquired a second mission as an operating agency that approved or rejected individual victims' claims.

Under the arrangement, the German government established the guidelines and criteria for the Hardship Fund, which permitted one-time payments of DM 5,000 to Jewish Nazi victims who qualified. The fund was originally expected to benefit 80,000 victims – such a sizeable number that the Conference members thought they could not jeopardize the fund by rejecting the German conditions. But the individual payments were small, the inequities apparent, and the terms were profoundly disturbing. The intended recipients were doubly persecuted and deserved more than a small payment, complained Conference counsel Benjamin B. Ferencz. 'They were persecuted by the Nazis, they were behind the Iron Curtain and only recently managed to come out after all the filing deadlines had expired, and all they will get is a one-time grant of 5,000 marks,' he said.[72] When the emigration of Jews from the Soviet Union exploded in the late 1980s, the Conference insisted that West Germany expand the programme. The German authorities agreed, and by the end of 2001, the Conference had made more than 263,000 Hardship Fund payments to Jewish victims.[73]

The extraordinary global changes brought by the collapse of communism and the reunification of Germany opened the Conference's third phase. Although the Conference initially struggled to gain attention for its demands amid the general euphoria over the fall of the Berlin Wall, it had two dramatic successes that profoundly changed the scope of restitution and compensation for Nazi victims.

Unified Germany rushed to incorporate the former East Germany into the framework and institutions of the West, passing hundreds of German federal laws between 1990 and 1992. Among those were measures intended to reprivatize the GDR's nationalized, state-supported economy. The Conference fought to ensure that the restitution legislation would not be limited to property that had been nationalized by the previous communist régime, but also would cover Nazi-era Jewish properties in the former GDR that had been confiscated, transferred or sold under duress between 1933 and 1945.[74]

The original pre-war Jewish owners and their heirs gained the right to claim their properties in the former East Germany, and the Conference was designated as the successor organization for all heirless and unclaimed individual Jewish property and for the property of dissolved Jewish communities and organizations.[75] While the overwhelming majority of former Jewish properties were restored to the original owners and heirs, by the end of 2000, the Conference had been awarded the rights to more than 8,200 properties. In the decade since the fall of the Berlin Wall, it acquired some $1 billion from compensation or sales of these Nazi-era Jewish properties.[76]

From 1995 through 2000, the Claims Conference distributed more than $400 million from the funds generated by these sales. In one year, 2000, it allocated $81.86 million to projects in 26 countries. The bulk of the proceeds were allocated to institutions and agencies that provided medical and social welfare services to Nazi victims, primarily in Israel and the former Soviet Union. About 20 per cent was for research, documentation and education about the Shoah.[77]

In addition to the recovery of properties, the Conference secured a commitment that, as an adjunct to the '2+4' agreement on reunification, Germany would provide compensation to Nazi victims who had received minimal or no compensation in the past.[78] In 1992, after 16 months of negotiations, it reached an agreement with Germany on the terms of compensation. 'It requires a lot of time and a lot of effort and a lot of worry, sweat and blood and tears, to move even friendly people, and not all of them are particularly friendly,' said Rabbi Israel Miller, who succeeded Goldmann and served as Conference president until his death in 2002. 'When it comes to money, it's very difficult to get statesmen to be friendly.'[79] Under the 'Article II' fund – named after the provision associated with the 2+4 agreement – Germany financed monthly payments for these survivors living in the west. Five years later, a similar agreement was reached that, for the first time, provided on-going compensation to Jewish victims living in Central and Eastern Europe; they were known as the 'double victims' of both Nazism and communism.[80] As with the Hardship Fund, the Conference was obliged to administer the two post-unification pension programmes, which in 2001 made payments to more than 70,000 victims.[81]

From its earliest days, the Claims Conference's mission has been profoundly influenced by external political events, which provided opportunities to pursue compensation and also imposed constraints. In 1952, its negotiations in Wassenaar on behalf of victims were conducted at the same time that West Germany, at the London Debt Conference, was dealing with its war-era liabilities to nations. This appeared to pit the victims' claims against those of Bonn's creditors.[82] However, the FRG's favourable treatment of Nazi victims' claims was taken into account when the Allies granted West Germany's sovereignty. Over its first four decades, the Cold War militated against the Conference's ability to directly aid victims behind the Iron Curtain. Conversely, the fall of the Berlin Wall enabled it to reach these victims and insist that unified Germany make good on the GDR's debts to Nazi victims.

The collapse of communism and the restructuring of the political and economic institutions of Central and Eastern Europe also created opportunities to resolve other Nazi-era claims. In 1992, the Conference initiated the creation of the World Jewish Restitution Organization, a consortium of seven international Jewish organizations, as well as Israeli and American survivors' organizations, which undertook to recover Jewish properties in Central and Eastern Europe that had been confiscated or nationalized during the Nazi and communist eras.

In the mid-1990s, the Conference's role was expanded again by a series of class-action lawsuits, filed in US federal courts, against Swiss banks, European insurers and German industries for the recovery of Nazi-era assets. The Conference had a long-standing interest in recovering funds from German industry for compensation for Nazi-era slave labourers, and had reached limited compensation agreements in the 1950s and 1960s with a handful of West German firms. The Conference had not initiated the legal actions in the late 1990s, but, as an agency organized to represent survivors' interests, and experienced with individual claims and the distribution of funds, the Conference was actively involved in the negotiations to resolve the lawsuits and was assigned a prominent role in the settlements. It also was a founding member, in October 1998, of the International Commission on Holocaust Era Insurance Claims, which was organized to resolve claims for Nazi-era insurance policies and annuities issued by European insurers.

By century's end, the estimated number of surviving Jewish victims was substantially higher than ever imagined – between 832,000 and 935,000, or some six per cent of the Jewish population worldwide.[83] 'At the time of its establishment in 1951, we could not have envisioned that fifty years after the Shoah there would continue to be so urgent a need for the services of the Conference on Jewish Material Claims Against Germany,' Miller said. 'The Claims Conference's overriding priority throughout its existence has been, and remains, securing compensation and restitution to satisfy individual claims.'[84]

The Germans refer to the payments as *Wiedergutmachung* ('making good again'). It is a highly inappropriate word within the Jewish community. 'We do not use the word *Wiedergutmachung* because the losses suffered by the Jewish people can never be made whole through material compensation,' Miller said. 'However, indemnities obtained by the Claims Conference from German successor governments have brought recognition of suffering, and needed relief and assistance, to the victims who did not perish.'[85]

The history of the Claims Conference is recounted in the chapters that follow. When it was founded in 1951, it had two major objectives: to obtain funds for the relief, rehabilitation and resettlement of Jewish victims, and to aid in rebuilding Jewish communities and institutions devastated by Nazi persecution; and to secure compensation for individual victims for injuries inflicted by Nazi persecution and restitution for properties confiscated by the Nazis.[86] A half-century later, it had added two objectives: To administer individual compensation programmes for Nazi victims; and to recover unclaimed Jewish property and allocate the proceeds to institutions that provide social services to needy Nazi victims and that engage in Holocaust research, education and documentation.[87]

The Conference's achievements in negotiations led to German legislative programmes and other funds for Nazi victims that have made one-time or on-going payments to more than 500,000 Jewish victims in 67 countries. The formidable amounts of compensation originating from the West German indemnification laws – the achievement of Protocol I – dwarf all other forms of compensation to victims. At the end of the twentieth century, nearly five decades after the passage of the first German federal indemnification law, more than 94,000 Nazi victims continued to receive monthly pensions directly from Germany – totalling some DM 955 million a year.[88] Another 70,000 Jewish victims receive monthly payments via Conference-administered programmes that are financed by Germany. In 2001 alone, the Conference distributed DM 571 million to individual survivors through these programmes.[89] The Conference's institutional allocations programmes, from its first and fourth decades, altered the cultural and physical landscape of Jewish communities in Western Europe, as well as the scope and nature of social welfare and medical services to the elderly in Israel and the former Soviet Union.

With little more than moral arguments and dogged determination, the Conference undertook the difficult, painful and tragic task of trying to heal some of the wounds and to cope with some of the consequences of the Shoah. 'Our generation of Jews witnessed the greatest disaster in all Jewish history, but also the greatest achievement in contemporary Jewish history – the creation of the State of Israel. The rebuilding of Jewish life from the horror perpetrated by the Nazis confronted us with unparalleled and unprecedented problems. The negotiations with Germany were among the most formidable of these problems,' said Goldmann. 'We met the challenge with dignity, solemnity and a high sense of responsibility. Above all else, we should be proud of our spetacular contribution toward the triumph of justice and morality.'[90]

NOTES

1   For a detailed account of negotiations, see Nana Sagi, *German Reparations: A History of the Negotiations*, Jerusalem: Hebrew University, 1980.
2   Aufbau, 22 August 2002. Kagan's career is inextricably linked with the history of the Claims Conference; he ordered its first piece of stationery and served as executive director until his retirement in 1998. He subsequently served the Conference as a consultant.
3   Saul Kagan, 'The Claims Conference and the Communities,' *Exchange,* Vol. 22, 1965.
4   That sum is expected to reach some DM 124 billion by the year 2030. German Foreign

Minister Klaus Kinkel, speech to national assembly of the American Jewish Committee, 8 May 1996, Washington.

5   On signing US Public Law 100-383, Restitution for the Wartime Internment of Japanese-American Civilians, on 10 August 1988, President Ronald Reagan said: 'The legislation that I am about to sign provides for a restitution payment to each of the 60,000 surviving Japanese-Americans of the 120,000 who were relocated or detained. Yet no payment can make up for those lost years. So what is most important in this bill has less to do with property than with honor. For here we admit a wrong; here we reaffirm our commitment as a nation to equal justice under the law.'

6   *New York Times*, 4 June 2001.

7   When the Allies met in Paris in 1945 to discuss reparations and refugee relief, they did not deal with the question of restitution and indemnification for individuals, but focused on funds, from unclaimed and heirless Jewish properties, that could be used for the resettlement of refugees. The Allies reasoned that it would be difficult to determine the validity of individual claims, and that the number of claims was likely to be overwhelming.

8   Although there was no practical effect, the West German budget designation of its indemnification payments vexed Ernst Katzenstein, the Conference director in West Germany. The Finance Ministry labeled the payments *Kriegsfolgenlast,* meaning an expenditure for a 'consequence of war.' The persecution of the Jews began when Hitler came to power in 1933; the Second World War began six years later, Katzenstein said. 'Indemnification went back to criminal acts perpetrated by the German government of the Third Reich against the Jews. Compensation for war damage went back to sufferings and losses sustained in the course and as consequence of the war that the Third Reich had waged,' he wrote in a memo to Kagan dated 14 January 1980. 'Expenditures for indemnification and for consequences of the war therefore were on [a] completely different footing; their joint listing as *Kriegsfolgenlast* was a perversion of historical facts.'

9   Weizmann letter to the Allied Powers, 20 September 1945, State of Israel, Ministry for Foreign Affairs, *Documents Relating to the Agreement Between the Government of Israel and the Government of the Federal Republic of Germany.* The Jewish Agency for Palestine later became the Jewish Agency for Israel.

10 The concept of 'descendants' is from Elazar Barkan, 'Between Restitution and International Morality,' *Fordham International Law Journal*, Vol. 25, 2001.

11 The Claims Conference was not incorporated until 21 November 1952.

12 Minutes, Claims Conference Policy Committee meeting, 24 September 1952, CAHJP 16723.

13 Robinson, 'Ten Years of German Indemnification,' New York: Conference on Jewish Material Claims Against Germany, 1964.

14 Nahum Goldmann, *The Autobiography of Nahum Goldmann: Sixty Years of Jewish Life,* New York: Holt, Rinehart and Winston, 1969, p. 252.

15 Schumacher (1895–1952) was a non-Jewish Nazi victim. Between 1933 and 1944, he was incarcerated by the Nazis on political grounds and survived a number of camps, including Dachau and Flossenburg. In a 1947 speech in San Francisco, he called for Germany to pay compensation to the Jews for material losses and injuries.

16 Jeffrey Herf, *Divided Memory: The Nazi Past in the Two Germanys*, Cambridge, MA: Harvard University Press, 1999. Adenauer was more in tune with German public sentiment than was Schumacher. A December 1951 survey conducted by US Occupation authorities revealed that 68 per cent of the German public supported compensation for Jews. However, that was far behind support for German war widows and orphans (favoured by 96 per cent); for people who suffered damage by bombing (93 per cent); and for 'refugees and expellees,' ethnic Germans who had been expelled, primarily from the Sudetenland, after 1945 (90 per cent). See also Constantin Goschler, 'German Compensation to Jewish Nazi Victims after 1945,' in Jeffrey Diefendorf (ed.), *Lessons and Legacies VI: New Currents in Holocaust Research*, Evanston, IL: Northwestern University Press, 2004.

17 Adenauer's offer came in an interview with Karl Marx, the editor of the German Jewish newspaper *Allgemeine Wochenzeitung der Juden in Deutschland*; it was reported in the *New York Times*, 25 November 1949. Easterman's 'Note of conversation with Lord Henderson, Under-Secretary of State for Foreign Affairs, (accompanied by Mr. Wilson), at the Foreign Office, London, on Thursday, January 11, 1951.'

18 *New York Times*, 28 September 1951. Adenauer's specific reference to Israel's admission of refugees bolstered the basis for the Israeli claim, even though the state was not established

until three years after the end of the Nazi era. The speech, however, was an affront to large segments of the Jewish community because of the way in which Adenauer referred to the atrocities. It was not simply that the chancellor used a passive tone to acknowledge the crime, but that he did not specify the criminals. Isaac Lewin of the Agudath Israel World Organization, representing Orthodox Jewry, was deeply offended at Adenauer's defense of his countrymen. 'The Jewish people would commit moral suicide if the offer of Mr. Adenauer would not be immediately rejected,' Lewin said at the founding meeting of the Claims Conference. 'What will we tell our children ... That we sold this memory for some dinars to Germans who dare to whitewash "the majority of the German people" in stating that – in contradiction to all facts – "they had no part in the crimes committed against the Jews"?'

19 *Documents Relating to the Agreement Between the Government of Israel and the Government of the Federal Republic of Germany.*

20 While the Western Allies propelled the Israeli government toward Bonn, they did not divorce themselves from the resolution of these claims. Although the Allies relinquished their prerogatives in West Germany, the 1952 and 1954 Contractual and Transition Agreements between the Allies and the FRG enshrined West Germany's commitment to preserve compensation and restitution for Nazi victims.

21 Adenauer was aware of this. After the 1953 Bundestag vote to ratify the West German agreements with Israel and the Claims Conference, the chancellor said, 'The reputation of the German people, which has suffered so much through crimes committed by the Nazis against the Jews, will gain much ground in the free world as a result of the agreement.' (See Sagi, p. 187; *New York Times*, 19 March 1953.) After the signing of the Luxembourg Agreements, Goldmann said: 'It is true that the German government's conduct in this case was dictated by political considerations, but these were mainly to restore her moral prestige, and this, in turn, was born out of a moral desire to demonstrate to the world that the Germany of today is not the Nazi Germany of yesterday.' West Germany's moral commitment was confirmed by Adenauer's successor, Ludwig Erhard. In a speech on 18 October 1963, two days after he was elected chancellor, Erhard said: 'We have repeatedly demonstrated that we are responsible for the crimes perpetrated by the Nazi leaders in the name of the German people during the course of those 12 years. We will atone for these crimes as far as it may lie in the power of human beings. We therefore view the indemnification programme as a binding obligation.' (See Claims Conference, *Annual Report 1965*.) On McCloy, see Thomas Alan Schwartz, *America's Germany: John J. McCloy and the Federal Republic of Germany*, Cambridge, MA: Harvard University Press, 1991.

22 Nicholas Balabkins, *West German Reparations to Israel*, New Brunswick, NJ: Rutgers University Press, 1971.

23 This description is by no means exhaustive. In addition to the public efforts of Jewish organizations, there also were sustained, behind-the-scenes activities, by organizations and individuals, designed to press West Germany to confront its obligations to the Jewish people. These actors also included Salomon Adler Rudel, a German-Jewish official of the Jewish Agency; Noah Barou, of the British section of the World Jewish Congress; A.L. Easterman, of the WJC's Political Section; and Josef Rosensaft, a survivor who was the leader of the Jewish displaced persons in the British Occupation Zone. See Sagi, pp. 16–27, and Menachem Z. Rosensaft and Joana D. Rosensaft, 'The Early History of German-Jewish Reparations,' *Fordham International Law Journal*, Vol. 25, 2001. For Weizmann letter, see *Documents Relating to the Agreement Between the Government of Israel and the Government of the Federal Republic of Germany.*

24 Claims Conference, *Annual Report 1965*.

25 Jewish Telegraphic Agency, 26 October 1951.

26 Goldmann, *Autobiography*, p. 255. In his memoirs, Goldmann wrote: 'Israeli Foreign Minister Moshe Sharett (Shertok) approached me with the suggestion that, as chairman of the Jewish Agency, I should invite the leading Jewish organizations of the United States, the British Commonwealth and France to a conference to support Israel's demands and create a body to execute them.'

27 These were primarily the members of the Jewish Restitution Successor Organization, which was formed in 1947 to recover unclaimed Jewish properties in the US Occupation Zone of Germany. Holocaust survivors were not directly represented. See Chapter 10.

28 The following account, unless otherwise noted, is taken from the official transcript of the meeting at Waldorf-Astoria hotel, New York, 25–26 October 1951, CAHJP 16600.

29   Jacobson memo to Moses Beckelman, 11 October 1951, JDC Archives, New York, 45/64
     Collection, File No. 4480.
30   Ferencz report to Administration Committee of the Joint Distribution Committee, 30 October
     1951. JDC Archives, New York, 45/64 Collection, File No. 4262.
31   The membership of the Claims Conference remained essentially the same as the founding
     membership of: Agudath Israel World Organization; *Alliance Israélite Universelle*; American
     Jewish Committee; American Jewish Congress; American Jewish Joint Distribution
     Committee; Anglo-Jewish Association; B'nai B'rith International; Board of Deputies of British
     Jews; Canadian Jewish Congress; Central British Fund for World Jewish Relief; *Conseil
     Representatif des Institutions Juives de France*; Council of Jews from Germany; *Delegacion de
     Asociaciones Israelitas Argentinas*; Executive Council of Australian Jewry; Jewish Agency for
     Israel; Jewish Labour Committee; South African Jewish Board of Deputies; World Jewish
     Congress; World Union for Progressive Judaism; and *Zentralrat der Juden in Deutschland*.
     Another founding member, the Synagogue Council of America, is defunct. The Jewish War
     Veterans of the US signed the October 1951 statement in support of the claims, but declined
     to join the Conference.
32   Jewish Telegraphic Agency, 29 October 1951.
33   Jewish Telegraphic Agency, 26 October 1951. For a detailed account of the Conference's
     origins and history until 1965, see Ronald W. Zweig, *German Reparations and the Jewish
     World: A History of the Claims Conference*, 2nd edn, London: Frank Cass, 2001.
34   'By accident, I was in the neighborhood of the Knesset building at that time, in 1952, when
     the discussion took place in the Knesset. I saw with my own eyes, and I will never forget, the
     attack,' recalled Moshe Sanbar, the president of the Israeli survivors' organization and a
     member of the Claims Conference Executive Committee. 'It was a real attack on behalf of
     supporters of Begin … With stones they attacked the Knesset. Unfortunately I was in the
     middle. I didn't know who would kill me – the people with the stones or the people who were
     protecting the Knesset. It was a terrible experience, especially to see the Jewish people attack
     the Parliament of the Jewish people. Outside they were shouting against the agreement and,
     inside the Knesset at the same time, Ben-Gurion delivered a speech on its importance of the
     future of the State of Israel.' For more on the Israeli government debate, see Sagi, pp. 81–2.
35   Jewish Telegraphic Agency, 25 September 1952. It should be noted that Jewish organizations
     already had established de facto agreements with West German entities for the restitution of
     properties. However, these agreements had been established under the auspices of Occupation
     authorities. The Jewish Restitution Successor Organization operated in the American
     Occupation Zone to recover heirless and unclaimed Jewish properties in Bavaria, Bremen,
     Hesse and Wüerttemberg-Baden. In the British zone, the Jewish Trust Corporation was
     responsible for Hamburg, Lower Saxony, North Rhine-Westphalia and Schleswig-Holstein.
     The Branche Francaise de la Jewish Trust Corporation operated in the French zone. Israeli
     interests were represented in the Jewish Restitution Successor Organization by the Jewish
     Agency, and Israel was a primary beneficiary of the organization's proceeds, which were used
     for the rehabilitation and resettlement of immigrants.
36   Claims Conference Delegation Statement, *Documents Relating to the Agreement Between the
     Government of Israel and the Government of the Federal Republic of Germany*.
37   Claims Conference Planning Committee meeting, 23 November 1999, New York.
38   Claims Conference background paper, 'Negotiations Between the Conference On Jewish
     Material Claims Against Germany and the Federal Republic of Western Germany,' 29
     September 1955, CAHJP 15010.
39   *New York Times*, 11 September 1952.
40   The agreement was structured to be paid over time, and in goods and services, because West
     Germany was cash-strapped, and there were doubts about its ability to pay. In addition to the
     claims of Nazi victims and the costs of absorbing the *Volksdeutsche*, Bonn also was
     negotiating with its creditors to settle its pre-war commercial debts.
41   The impact of the West German payments on the economic development of the State of Israel
     cannot be overstated. The country was in the midst of a radical austerity programme,
     struggling to finance its defense, build its infrastructure and industry, provide basic social
     services and absorb refugees from Europe, North Africa and the Middle East. Pinhas Lavon,
     then a minister without portfolio in the Israeli government, said that the funds promised by
     the Luxembourg Agreements exceeded the capital Israel had received since its founding in
     1948 from all foreign sources, including investments, gifts, loans, grants, the sale of Israel

Confronting the Perpetrators

25

Bonds in the US, and the transfer of funds by immigrants (*New York Times*, 11 September 1952). Some 1,400 initiatives in Israel – transport, power, port, agriculture and communications – received equipment and machinery with funds generated by the Luxembourg Agreements. 'When you use a telephone, it's German. When you go in a railway, it's German. When you use electricity, the machines come from Germany,' Goldmann told the Conference in 1960. 'You cannot make a step in Israeli life without feeling the effect, the impact, of the Luxembourg Agreements.' Although the goods provided were essential, Goldmann recalled in his autobiography that a German negotiator once had suggested that Germany could send its surplus butter to Israel. Goldmann rejected the butter as an amenity. With an austerity crisis in Israel, butter was beyond the means of the Israelis, who would have to subsist on margarine until local conditions improved, he said.

42 Josephthal letter to Leavitt, 7 October 1952, JDC Archives, New York, 45/64 Collection, File No. 4262.

43 Because a voluntary organization could not sign a treaty with a sovereign state, the agreements were called 'protocols.'

44 This was known as the so-called 'purpose clause.' The payment to the Conference came via Israel, which agreed to supply the monetary value of the Conference's share of the goods and services that served as payment from West Germany. At the time, no one was certain of West Germany's capacity to pay, although it did meet its financial obligations to Israel and the Conference.

45 Goldmann interview, 24 November 1971, American Jewish Committee (William E. Wiener) Oral History Library, New York Public Library, Dorot Jewish Division.

46 Minutes, Claims Conference Policy Committee meeting, 24 September 1952, CAHJP 16723. Sagi, p. 144.

47 Claims Conference Delegation Statement.

48 Claims Conference Executive Committee, 13 March 1952, instructions to delegation.

49 Victims were identified as those persecuted for their political convictions, race, religion or ideology during the National Socialist régime. Although the number of Jewish claimants is unknown, they are estimated to be at least 80 per cent, based on the residence of the recipients. As of 2000, only 20 per cent of those receiving compensation lived in Germany. About 40 per cent were in Israel, and the remaining 40 per cent were primarily in the United States.

50 Claims Conference Policy Committee meeting, 24 September 1952.

51 The German laws gave preference to former German nationals. Although the German compensation legislation was federal, the costs were shared by the federal government and the *Länder*, which were responsible for implementing the programmes. The effect was that the measures were plagued by legal and administrative problems, including conflicting interpretations of the laws at the state levels, and various agencies' inexperience and resistance to the programmes. 'In no other area of law are the administration and courts so narrow-minded, sometimes heartless, so petty, or do they act in such a hairsplitting and quibbling fashion,' Dr Adolph Arndt, a Social Democratic deputy, complained in 1954. 'Thus, a task whose generous fulfillment should move an entire people has fallen to the ink-blotters and pen-pushers.' See Chapter 2 on German indemnification legislation.

52 Kagan, *Exchange*. See Chapter 9 on Claims Conference allocations.

53 Claims Conference, *Twenty Years Later: Activities of the Conference on Jewish Material Claims Against Germany, 1952–1972*.

54 Kagan, *Exchange*.

55 The United Restitution Organization, a legal-aid society originally organized to aid claimants in the Allied Occupation zones, assisted more than 200,000 individuals with some 300,000 indemnification and restitution claims between 1949 and 1972; the awards exceeded $800 million. The organization was financed, in part, with Conference funds, as well as modest fees from victims. *Twenty Years Later*.

56 Katzenstein quoting Robinson, Claims Conference Board meeting, 4 July 1972, Geneva.

57 This did not apply to Israel, with which West Germany did not establish relations until 1965.

58 Annual statistical report from German Ministry of Finance, December 1999. Some 80 per cent of the beneficiaries were Jewish. The total number of pensions does not correlate directly to the number of beneficiaries because victims could file multiple claims, one for each category of damage or injury.

59 Claims Conference Board meeting, 17–18 July 2001, Washington.

60 The wildly eager reception that Nazi troops received from the Austrians during the 1938 *Anschluss* was widely noted at the time. In his memoirs *Von Moskau nach Berlin 1936–1939*,

French Ambassador Robert Coulondre observed: 'The only injuries the German soldiers received on entering Vienna was from the stems of the flowers that were enthusiastically thrown at them as they marched by.' See Chapter 8.

61 Goldmann, *Autobiography*, p. 282.
62 *New York Times*, 19 July 1991.
63 Reuters, 1 June 1995.
64 Translation by GDR Embassy, Washington, 12 April 1990. See Chapter 4.
65 Claims Conference Board meeting, 3 July 1980, Amsterdam.
66 Katzenstein letter to Goldmann, 1 April 1970.
67 Kagan interview, 12 January 2001.
68 Although obtaining compensation for Jewish victims from the east was one of the Conference's most significant achievements because of the number of individuals who would be covered, it came at a cost. 'This category represented the most difficult problem. In a sense it is something unique for a successor government to give indemnification to people who were victims of a war but who had received far-worse treatment than had been given to the non-Jewish population of the occupied country,' Leavitt said. 'But there were many non-Jews who also received similar treatment to that of the Jews and whose property was confiscated. Because of that we had our greatest difficulty. We had to make concessions on eligibility on the one hand, but on the other hand, we got additional benefits in return.' Minutes, Claims Conference Policy Committee meeting, 24 September 1952, CAHJP 16723.
69 In 1981, a DM 100 million fund for non-Jewish persecutees was established; it also made one-time payments of DM 5,000.
70 Kagan interview, 12 January 2001.
71 Guidelines, Hardship Fund, *West German Federal Gazette*, 14 October 1980.
72 Claims Conference Board meeting, Geneva, 8–9 July 1981.
73 Claims Conference, *Annual Report 2001*. See Chapter 3.
74 There also were measures under which Germany provided compensation in cases in which the property could not be returned. See Chapter 6.
75 In addition to the Jewish claims, there also were claims by US citizens for some 2,000 properties in the GDR.
76 Claims Conference, *Annual Report 2002*.
77 See Chapter 9 for a discussion of Claims Conference allocations.
78 The 1990 treaty on the Final Settlement with Respect to Germany ('2+4') was signed in Moscow by the '2' – referring to the two Germanies – and the '4' – the post-war Occupation authorities: the US, Britain, France and Soviet Union. In conjunction with reunification, Germany pledged to continue the Federal Republic's pre-unification policy on restitution and to establish an additional fund for Jewish victims of Nazi persecution. The Conference was able to insert its demands into the German reunification pact by appealing to the US government.
79 Claims Conference Board meeting, 6 July 1990, Jerusalem.
80 The Article II pensions for victims in the West are DM 500 a month; however, pensions in the east were limited to DM 250 per month, on grounds that the cost of living in Central and Eastern Europe is lower than in the West.
81 Claims Conference, *Annual Report 2001*. See Chapter 5.
82 From the outset, Adenauer linked compensation to Nazi victims to West Germany's ability to pay. In his 1951 declaration, he specifically referred to the 'limitations of the German financial capacity due to the bitter necessity to provide for the countless war victims and to care for [German] refugees and exiles.'
83 Ukeles Associates, 'An Estimate of the Current Distribution of Victims of Nazi Persecution,' in *A Plan for Allocating Successor Organization Resources*, report of the Claims Conference Planning Committee (28 June 2000). Ukeles Associates uses a wide definition of a Nazi victim: any Jew who lived in a country when it was under a Nazi régime, Nazi occupation or Nazi collabourators, or who fled to a country or region not under Nazi rule or occupation to escape the Nazis.
84 Rabbi Israel Miller, 'The Conference on Jewish Material Claims Against Germany,' *Cardozo Law Review*, Vol. 20, No. 2, December 1998.
85 Ibid.
86 *Twenty Years Later*.
87 Claims Conference, *Annual Report 2000*.

88   Annual statistical report from German Ministry of Finance, December 1999. The actual numbers of claimants from the period was not known, because individuals submitted multiple claims for different categories of losses and injuries.
89   Claims Conference, *Annual Report 2001.*
90   Claims Conference Policy Committee, 24 September 1952.

Chapter 2

Establishing the Legal Right to Compensation: West German Indemnification and Restitution Legislation

The telegram was short and sweet. 'Ratified, gratified. Felix,' the Israeli negotiator Felix Shinnar said in a message to the Claims Conference in New York on 18 March 1953, when the German Parliament ratified the Luxembourg Agreements.[1]

Chancellor Konrad Adenauer had accepted the moral duty of West Germany to remedy Nazi injuries and, in Luxembourg on 10 September 1952, signed a treaty with the State of Israel and two 'protocols' with the Conference that spelled out West Germany's obligations to the Jewish world. Protocol I of the Luxembourg Agreements called for the enactment of West German legislation that would make direct payments to Nazi victims for indemnification and restitution claims arising from Nazi persecution. The Luxembourg Agreements were accords under international law that were intertwined with German domestic law. It was the 18 March vote in the Bundestag that established the legal right of individual victims to material redress for Nazi persecution.

The Bundestag's approval of the Luxembourg Agreements was more complicated and, in some respects, was more problematic than the original agreement, Goldmann said.[2] The US supported the agreements, while Arab states had tried to pressure West Germany not to reach a settlement with Israel. 'The Arabs coupled threats and inducements in their effort to dissuade Germany from entering into these agreements,' he said.[3]

On the domestic front, Adenauer did not command the full support of his own faction, the Christian Democratic Union (CDU)/Christian Social Union (CSU).[4] The vote came shortly before midnight on 18 March, after three hours of debate, and only two days before the end of the Parliamentary term. The tally was 238 in favour, 35 against, and 86 abstaining. The opposition Social Democratic Party (SPD) was unanimously in favour of ratification. Among the abstentions were 39 members of the CDU/CSU faction. Forty-four deputies did not attend the session.[5]

In the Luxembourg Agreements, the Federal Republic of Germany (FRG) 'resolved to supplement and amend the existing compensation legislation,' referring to the various indemnification and restitution measures that had come into force in the postwar Allied Occupation zones before the 1949 creation of the West German state. Protocol I was a list of specific commitments the Federal Republic was obliged to address in legislation to remedy some of the injuries that Nazi persecution had inflicted on its victims.[6] It was intended to benefit those who were persecuted for their political convictions, race, religion, or ideology during the National Socialist régime and who were stateless or were political refugees. There also were geographical limits: Protocol I referred to those who lived within the boundaries of the German Reich as of 31 December 1937.

Over the course of a dozen years, beginning in 1953, with the Conference pressing the government to craft meaningful legislation, the West German Parliament passed three laws on indemnification for Nazi victims that were landmarks establishing their legal right to redress. Collectively, the federal indemnification laws were known as the *Bundesentschädigungsgesetze* (BEG).[7] The BEG, as expanded through Conference negotiations, Parliamentary amendments and German court rulings, evolved into a bewildering matrix of compensation to groups of victims for a variety of damages. Indemnification was for those who suffered loss of life, damage to limb or health, liberty, property, possessions, or vocational or economic pursuits.

Once the individual met the German eligibility requirements concerning persecution and territoriality, he could file multiple claims, one for each type of damage suffered. Compensation was made in the form of a one-time payment or an annuity (also known as a pension), depending on the nature of the damages. 'The lifelong annuity is the most precious stone in the whole indemnification building, a continuing governmental obligation which is viewed with disapproval and dislike by many Germans who would prefer to have it abrogated,' said Ernst Katzenstein, who served as the Conference's representative in Germany for some three decades.[8]

Compensation to individuals under the legislation quickly dwarfed West Germany's global payments to Israel and to the Conference under the Luxembourg Agreements. 'When the Luxembourg Agreements were signed in 1952, the belief was widespread that reparations [paid in] goods and services, in the value of $716 million [DM 3 billion], would represent the great bulk of the payments moving from Germany to Israel,' Goldmann said on the tenth anniversary of the legislation. Payments to individual Nazi victims 'were expected to serve as a source of supplementary income, a "something extra for good measure". But in this instance, events have left expectations far behind, and the "something extra for good measure" is now looming up larger, financially speaking, than the reparations deliveries themselves.'[9] Hundreds of thousands of victims had received lump-sum payments of varying amounts from West Germany. At its peak, in December 1972, the German indemnification programme paid 278,000 pensions a year.[10] An estimated 85 per cent of the beneficiaries were Jews.

As sweeping as they were, the compensation laws did not apply equally to all Nazi victims. Indemnification was based not only on the nature and duration of persecution suffered by victims of 'National Socialist persecution,' but largely was governed by 'territoriality,' which included the survivor's citizenship, legal status and residence before and after the Second World War.

This was the historic anomaly: Victims of the same circumstances received different redress. 'The country of origin made no difference during the Holocaust,' said Benjamin Meed, the head of the American Gathering of Jewish Holocaust Survivors. 'It should make no difference in reparations.'[11] But it did. The German law was structured around the government's view that the Federal Republic's primary obligation was to its former citizens, and they were compensated for a broader range of losses and damages than other Nazi victims. Those who were displaced persons or who had refugee status before 1965, but who were not German citizens, got compensation, but it was limited to personal suffering or injury.[12] In the prime years of the BEG, the majority of all annuities were paid to victims who suffered damage to health. However, the average pension for damage to health was lower than one for damage to profession.[13]

Former German citizens were entitled to monthly pensions for loss of economic opportunity if their professional careers had been disrupted or damaged by Nazi persecution. A lawyer from Berlin who had been barred from practice and compelled to flee Germany could claim such a pension. 'The assumption is that, were it not for Hitler, this person would have attained the level of a judge in the German civil service. Therefore, his pension would be calculated on the basis of the pension of a judge,' said Kagan. A lawyer from Warsaw who survived deportation to Auschwitz and was displaced after the war was entitled to less. He would get a one-time payment for deprivation of liberty and, if he could establish that as a result of persecution his earning capacity was impaired by at least 25 per cent, he would be entitled to a pension for damage to health, but not for the fact that Nazi persecution had disrupted his career.[14] A French lawyer who was deported to a German concentration camp and who was repatriated to France had no right to file a claim under the German compensation law, because he was never stateless and was never a refugee. However, a German-born victim of the same fate who lived in France after the war was entitled to file indemnification claims.

The exclusion of the Western Europeans in the indemnification legislation was based on the concept of *territorialitatsprinzip*, which required a personal or local link between the victim and the area of the Federal Republic. Bonn also had argued that these Nazi victims were to be compensated for damages from the reparations the FRG already paid to Western European governments. The Conference and European Jewish communities contended, however, that claims arising from persecution were clearly distinct from and required a separate remedy than general war-damage claims. For instance, the war-damage legislation in Britain dealt with claims for property damage unrelated to damages, losses or harms that individuals suffered as victims of Nazi persecution. Further, large numbers of Jewish persecutees had been excluded from war-damage compensation in Western Europe because they were alien residents; lacking citizenship, they were ineligible to recover war-damage claims from host governments.[15]

Under prodding from the Conference and European governments, between 1959 and 1964 entered into bilateral 'global agreements' with 11 Western European states. Under these agreements, West Germany paid almost DM 900 million, which was intended for payments to Nazi victims in those countries who were not eligible under the BEG.[16] Unlike the BEG, which is a compensation programme for individuals, the bilateral lump-sum payments were agreements between governments. The Western European governments had discretion to determine how to allocate the funds to local victims of Nazi persecution.[17] There were vast differences among the programmes that developed under the domestic measures of each country. For instance, France, which supplemented the German funds, permitted payments to resistance fighters, while the German compensation legislation excluded payments to combatants. The Netherlands also supplemented the German funds. In 1973, it enacted a programme of benefits for people who were victims of persecution between 1940 and 1945; the aim was to maintain or restore, within limits, the standard of living the victims would have enjoyed had the persecution not occurred. By contrast, in Greece, compensation was earmarked for victims who were Greek citizens when the German funds became available, in 1960, which excluded Greek survivors who emigrated. Britain designated its payment for British subjects, such as resistance workers, who were incarcerated or otherwise ill-treated by the Nazis during the war.[18]

The gaping hole in German compensation concerned Eastern Europe, reflecting the geopolitical conflicts of its time – the division between East and West. Bonn did not have diplomatic relations with Eastern European states when it entered the bilateral agreements with Western Europe. In the 1950s, benefits for Nazi victims from the East were predicated on emigration; the German law excluded all the victims from Eastern Europe who did not emigrate to a non-communist country by the end of 1965.[19] 'The Germans were not ready under any circumstances to include people who remained behind the Iron Curtain,' Kagan said.[20]

In December 1970, Chancellor Willy Brandt heralded the West German policy of *Ostpolitik* with a dramatic trip to Warsaw during which he knelt in front of the monument to Jewish Nazi victims. By the time Brandt established diplomatic relations with Eastern Europe, however, the FRG was unwilling to establish significant new indemnification commitments. Although Bonn entered limited bilateral agreements with Yugoslavia, Poland, Hungary and Czechoslovakia, these were not for compensation for persecution.[21] It was only decades later, after reunification, that Germany reached bilateral agreements with Poland, Russia, Ukraine, Belarus and the Czech Republic to compensate all victims of Nazi persecution.[22]

The majority of Holocaust survivors are in Israel, where the compensation they receive varies widely. Some 40 per cent of the BEG pensions are paid to Nazi victims in Israel. The German-born Nazi victims received monthly pensions from West Germany for economic losses, while formerly stateless and refugee victims got one-time payments for deprivation of liberty. However, for a significant benefit – annuities for damage to health – Nazi victims in Israel were treated differently than their counterparts elsewhere. At the time of Luxembourg Agreements, the Germans insisted that the Israeli government provide compensation to Nazi victims who were in Israel by 1953. 'Their point was that they were giving Israel funds for the resettlement of Jewish victims and they did not want to pay twice,' Leavitt said.[23] The Israeli Knesset in 1957 enacted a disability law for Holocaust survivors – the Disabled Victims of Nazi Persecution Law – which covered Nazi victims in Israel who would have been eligible for BEG payments for damage to health had Germany not specified otherwise. At least twenty thousand Nazi victims received the Israeli annuities, which were substantially less than the German payments.[24]

The West German compensation agreement did not begin on a *tabula rasa*. Under the Allied Occupation régimes, compensation laws were enacted in some West German states, the *Länder*, which had paid DM 738 million to Nazi victims before the BEG became law.[25] Where the *Länder* laws existed, however, none was considered satisfactory. They differed considerably in eligibility and residency requirements, and provided no benefits to persecutees other than to current or former residents of the particular German state and of DP camps in the US Occupation Zone.[26]

The most comprehensive and uniform laws were those in the US Occupation Zone, which had been promulgated in August 1949.[27] Protocol I committed West Germany to enact indemnification legislation that would cover all of West Germany and would be 'no less favourable' than the General Claims Law in the American Zone.[28] Bonn originally anticipated amending and extending the General Claims Law, rather than writing new legislation.[29] This turned out to be 'impossible' because, when the American law was enacted, there had been little actual experience with indemnification, Robinson said. 'The [American Zone] law was therefore chiefly a set of principles, which had to be complemented by various local implementing regulations,' he said. 'It was necessary to prepare a new law which would leave as little as possible to administrative procedure.'[30]

In addition to establishing the framework for compensation in Protocol I, the Conference also secured a mechanism to protect payments against erosion: Victims' annuities were to be adjusted in line with improvements in payments to comparable categories of pensions paid to German officials.[31] One of 'the brilliant things that we were able to achieve in The Hague was to hitch the cost of living adjustments of annuities to Nazi victims to the cost of living adjustments of pensions to German civil servants,' Kagan said. 'Our constituents are not voters in Germany, and therefore the political clout we can have in terms of increases and adjustments would be limited. The lobby of the German civil servants is strong, powerful, voting, and is there.'[32] It was an expensive provision and, on at least one occasion, a Finance Ministry official asked whether the Conference would be amenable to severing the link between the Nazi victims' annuities and that of German civil servants. 'I just looked at him and laughed,' Katzenstein said.[33]

The first national indemnification law, the Supplementary Federal Law for the Compensation of the Victims of National Socialist Persecution (*Bundesergänzungsgesetz zur Entschädigung für Opfer des Nationalsozialismus*), was enacted in July 1953 and became effective on 1 October. 'Getting the law passed was a race against time,' Robinson told the board. The Bundestag was due to adjourn for the summer recess, and the Conference scurried to get the measure through the Parliament, 'a task which was made much more difficult because of everybody's preoccupation with the forthcoming elections,' he said.[34] The Conference also encountered resistance from the Finance Ministry, which found the prospect of the programme expensive and which had not yet set a formula to share costs with the *Länder*. The extent of the expense was unknown, and no ceiling for individual indemnification was specified in Protocol I. Both sides underestimated the value. The Finance Ministry had estimated the cost at DM 5 billion. 'While our experts feel that the sum would be appreciably lower, it is still a substantial sum,' Goldmann said.[35]

The legislation was an important first step in federal compensation for Nazi victims, but it was seriously deficient and did not fully meet the terms of Protocol I. 'The law was dotted with flaws and shortcomings that called for early remedy, and it reflected the haste with which the German Parliament had come to grips with it, on the eve of its dissolution for elections,' the Conference reported.[36] The Conference was not alone in finding the law inadequate; the measure did not satisfy the conditions expected by the Allies in the Contractual Agreement that restored German sovereignty. But there was a limit to the Allies' willingness to intervene and influence the German legislation. US Secretary of State John Foster Dulles said the problems raised by the Conference would receive 'my full and sympathetic consideration.' However, he said: 'I also believe that any new all-German government must be completely free to determine which of the international obligations ... it may wish to conclude. Otherwise it would not be genuinely free.'[37]

The German law attracted enormous attention. 'Hardly any other law has ever aroused so much interest both in the Jewish and the non-Jewish world as did the BEG. On the one hand, there were the thousands of former victims of Nazi persecution who became eligible for compensation and who evinced an active interest in the law. Jewish organizations in every nook and corner of the globe also took great interest in the law because large numbers of residents of their area were or might be affected,' Robinson said. 'On the other hand, the law produced a flood of criticism and of proposals for amendments.' Some were 'reasonable,' he said, while 'others would make the law applicable to practically every case of Nazi persecution wherever it took place – a justified but hardly feasible proposal.'[38]

The law defined as eligible those who sustained injuries due to persecution 'by National Socialist oppressive measures' because of 'political opposition to National Socialism, or because of race, religion or ideology'. To qualify for compensation, victims must have been incarcerated in concentration camps and ghettos, subjected to 'compulsory labour,' or to have lived under conditions similar to incarceration or 'underground' under conditions 'unworthy of human beings'. The West German government saw its obligations under domestic law as being limited to former German citizens or residents, and the law had a territorial boundary, dealing primarily with the Federal Republic and West Berlin. Former residents of the Soviet Occupation Zone were ineligible for indemnification payments because Bonn viewed East Germany as a puppet state of the Soviet Union. A claimant must have 'had his domicile or place of permanent sojourn within the Federal Republic on 31 December 1952,' or meet the definition of a repatriate, expellee, refugee or stateless person.[39] The deadline for applications was 1 October 1953, the effective date of the law.[40]

'The ink on the Official Gazette in which the law was promulgated had not yet become dry when the Conference began to work for amendment of the law,' Robinson reported.[41] The Conference quickly assembled experts to draft revisions of the legislation, and submitted to the German government wide-ranging recommendations for basic improvements in the law.[42] Some were included in the new law the Bundestag passed on 29 June 1956. 'In the process of amendment, the 1953 law was rewritten almost totally, so that it may now be regarded as a new law, rather than a modified version of the previous one,' Robinson said.[43]

The second law, the Revised Federal Indemnification Law (*Bundesgesetz zur Entschädigung für Opfer der Nationalsozialistischen Verfolgung*), extended coverage to the whole of Germany within the borders of 31 December 1937, and victims who emigrated from German areas outside the Federal Republic – primarily East Germany and former German territories belonging to Poland – became eligible. This was a political statement, signifying that the Federal Republic considered itself the only legitimate successor to the National Socialist state. Goldmann convinced Adenauer that, if East Germany was an artificial state, the Federal Republic was obliged to be responsible for compensation for all victims in Germany. As Goldmann recounted telling Adenauer: '"You claim that you represent the whole of Germany and you do not recognize the GDR. In that case, be consistent and pay its share!" After months of negotiations he accepted, and now a Jew from Leipzig receives the same pension as a Jew from Frankfurt.'[44]

Refugees and stateless persons also gained benefits under the revised law, and there were improvements in compensation for damages to life, health, property and career; deprivation of liberty; and payment of discriminatory taxes and special fines.[45] The law extended the filing deadline to 1 April 1958.

The Revised BEG also codified several important principles, although they were plagued by problems of application and interpretation. A vital principle established the probability of the causal link between persecution and the damage to the Nazi victim's health. But claimants still faced the burden of proving to German doctors and judges that their injuries resulted from persecution. In the early years of the programme, there were horror stories about examinations by unsympathetic 'Nazi doctors'. 'If you had to prove that you were physically disabled as a result of persecution in order to qualify for a lousy small pension, they wanted to know, "Was your father also crippled? Did he have heart trouble? How about your neighbor?"' Conference negotiator Benjamin Ferencz recalled. 'And they had to put him through an examination, and he thought he was back being examined by Mengele. It was horrible.'[46]

The 1956 law also stated that West Germany was responsible for payments for Nazi-era incarceration and other damages caused by foreign governments. This was the notion of *Veranlassung*, or instigation or inducement, by Nazi Germany that drove its satellite states to persecute the Jews. Under the 1956 BEG, claimants could receive compensation from West Germany for deprivation of liberty by a foreign government 'when the deprivation of, or restriction on, liberty was the result of an "inducement" of the foreign government by the Nazi Government'.

Such instigation was evident to the Conference. 'True, the Romanians were anti-Semites and many Hungarians, too,' Goldmann said. 'But the deportation to Bessarabia and the concentration camps were imposed and demanded by the German government.'[47] However, what was apparent to the Conference was a contentious topic for the Germans. Compensation to tens of thousands of victims who were oppressed outside of Germany was dependent on proving that the Nazis had instigated persecution over a wide swathe of Europe. 'Volumes of documents, prepared mainly by the United Restitution Organization, had to be assembled for each country and sometimes for individual camps to demonstrate the pressure exercised by the Third Reich upon these [satellite] governments to persecute the Jews, the conditions of life in internment, and the period involved,' said Robinson.[48]

West Germany also provided compensation to its own 'war victims' – primarily ethnic Germans who moved from the German region that became Poland after the war, or who had been expelled from territories in the East, especially the Sudetenland, which were known as the 'expulsion areas.'[49] Some 10 million of the so-called German 'expellees' had been absorbed in the FRG, and in March 1953, when the Luxembourg Agreements were ratified, the expellees accounted for nearly 20 per cent of West Germany's population. Relief to the German expellees was provided under the Equalization of Burdens law

(*Lastenausgleich*). During The Hague negotiations, 'the Germans were afraid of the pressure they would be under if they would do for Jews what they could not do for these ... expellees,' Leavitt said.[50]

However, the Conference wanted to ensure that Jewish victims would not receive less than the expellees. This was achieved when Protocol I established the right to compensation for individual Jewish victims who lived in territories from which the Germans had been expelled.[51] This provision overcame the geographic limitations of the BEG, which favoured victims from Germany over those from other countries. But it also entailed convoluted logic. Unlike Germans who found themselves in hostile territory after the Second World War, Jews fled or were driven from the 'expulsion areas' as a result of Nazi persecution. But, because West Germany did not want to open the door to war claims from non-Jews, it adopted a 'legal fiction' that if Jews had not left the expulsion areas, they would have been expelled along with the ethnic Germans, and therefore were entitled to benefits under the *Lastenausgleich*.[52]

The Revised BEG applied to 'expellees' who had been part of the 'German folk' on 31 December 1937. In effect, to be treated under the law as 'German folk', Jews had to demonstrate they were 'quasi-Germans,' which entailed an affinity with German culture.[53] German-language tests were the tool used to gauge this affinity. Although Yiddish was the mother tongue of much of European Jewry, there had been significant pockets in the expulsion areas in which, during the period between the two world wars, Jewish youth had been educated in elite German-language gymnasia and in which the principal language in the family was German. 'Obviously we couldn't suddenly come to the Germans and say, "Yiddish is German,"' Kagan said. But the Conference successfully argued that the Jews from certain areas, educated in German-language schools, had the requisite linguistic affinity. Thus victims who passed language examinations could qualify for pensions because they belonged to the German linguistic and cultural circle.[54] However, this also had its discriminatory features: a Jew from Prague who spoke German became eligible, but a Jew who spoke Czech did not. And, although successfully claiming membership in the 'German cultural group' expanded eligibility for compensation, it was traumatic for victims. 'Never again saw my wife, my three sons, mother, and siblings. Everyone dead in Auschwitz,' one Nazi victim wrote in the test booklet. 'I ask myself how I manage to sit here and say I am part of the German cultural sphere.'[55]

After 1956, the Conference continued to aggressively pursue the West German government and the Bundestag to improve the scope and amount of payments. It pressed the German authorities to enact dozens of amendments to the laws, both to repair wrongs that had emerged over the course of the years, and to provide redress to groups of Nazi victims to whom compensation was denied. Among those excluded were a mass of migrants from Eastern Europe. The BEG was limited to Nazi victims in the West and, specifically, those who arrived in the West by 1 October 1953.

The so-called 'residency tests' had been a profound irritant since they first had been imposed by the *Länder* for the indemnification measures in the Allied Occupation zones. A. L. Easterman of the World Jewish Congress had complained to the British Foreign Office, as an occupying power overseeing *Länder* laws, that the dates were arbitrary and excluded many Nazi victims from compensation. 'To limit and even to abrogate the just rights of these victims by fixing a terminal date of residence in Germany is unreasonable and unjust. No such limitation was fixed by the Nazi Government in pursuing and executing the measures of persecution,' Easterman wrote.[56]

This was the principle the Conference used to advocate for the rights of an estimated 125,000 to 150,000 victims who had been unable to flee to the West from Eastern Europe before the BEG deadline. They became known as the 'post-1953' victims, a reference to the deadline that rendered made them ineligible for compensation under the existing law. For years, the Conference insisted that the German authorities treat these refugees on an equal footing with those who had left before October 1953. 'Some of these Nazi victims who, through no fault of their own were only able to come out into the free world after the Hungarian Revolution, are barred from filing claims under the indemnification law (BEG), which limits eligibility to those who were out by October 1953,' the Conference said. 'Having been exposed to both Nazi and communist privations, these persecutees find themselves excluded from the benefits which the law provides for those who were fortunate to escape entrapment behind the Iron Curtain.'[57]

However, a dozen years after the Luxembourg Agreements, Goldmann did not expect to prevail. 'It is a source of deep regret that in the final stage of negotiations for the amendment of the laws for indemnification and restitution, many of our proposals face stormy weather.' The Conference's position is 'beset with exceptional difficulties, not merely by virtue of the laws and their substance, but in light of the political climate,' he said. 'In every political negotiation, the state of the political weather counts for a great deal. In the political scales, psychology can outweigh ideology. We like to believe that a strong case can be won if convincing arguments in sufficient numbers can be mustered in support. But the most rational and convincing arguments may be doomed to defeat if the political climate grows unfavourable. Today, the psychological winds in Germany are not blowing in our direction. The political climate in 1964 is far less favourable that it was in 1952.'[58]

West Germany had been convinced to pay compensation not only as part of its 'atonement' for Nazi crimes, but as the price of its re-admission to 'family of nations'. 'The reputation of the German people, which has suffered so much through crimes committed by the Nazis against the Jews, will gain much ground in the free world as a result' of the Luxembourg Agreements, Adenauer said after the Bundestag ratified the pacts.[59] However, that incentive had been deflated. 'In the matter of political rehabilitation, I am afraid that the German government no longer feels the need for it, as it did in 1952. If anything, it may be said to be over-rehabilitated, for it is now courted on every side for its political, diplomatic, economic and financial support,' Goldmann said.[60]

German officials were tiring of Conference demands and were losing their tempers with its negotiators. At one meeting, when West German officials mentioned the country's budget woes, Robinson apparently referred to the sums Germans spent on whiskey, implying that West Germany could ease the financial strain by limiting liquor consumption. The head of the Finance Ministry's indemnification office, Hermann Zorn, jumped up as if to assault Robinson, 'culminating in the furious reproach that the Jews did not appreciate under what trying financial circumstances the Germans did in terms of indemnification, and wildly protesting against the unheard-of attempt now to subject the German people to a Jewish prescription of what they were allowed to drink and what not, and how much,' Katzenstein recalled.[61]

Despite the hurdles, the Conference's demands led to the second revision of the BEG (*Bundesentschädigungsschlussgesetz*, or BEG *Schlussgesetz*) of 18 September 1965. This was the 'final' indemnification law.[62] It contained some important improvements, including a special fund of DM 1.2 billion for the claims of Nazi victims who had left Eastern Europe between 1 October 1953 and 31 December 1965.[63] However, the fund was restricted and did not provide annuities.[64]

Under earlier laws, victims claiming damage to health had been handicapped by the rigid requirement to prove that permanent injury, with a constant reduction of earning capacity of at least 25 per cent, was the direct consequence of Nazi persecution. 'We have argued for years that it is not only unjust, but also immoral, to impose the burden of proof on the claimant, because basically the difficulties are the result of the lapse of time between the persecution (or damaging event) and the medical examination, the lapse of time varying between 13 to 30 years,' Robinson said.[65] The Final BEG relieved some of the victims' burden by granting the legal presumption that those who were incarcerated in concentration camps for a year or more had sustained damage to health.[66] However, the German authorities refused to extend that presumption to other inmates. 'The German claim that they could not apply the presumption to inmates of ghettos, forced labour camps, etc., because only for concentration camps lists of inmates exist (not all lists, incidentally). This is just an excuse to save money,' Robinson said. The exclusion of ghettos and labour camps seemed especially egregious. 'It is well known that the conditions in ghettos and forced labour camps were, at times, even worse than in concentration camps; the incidence of diseases and deaths greater,' Robinson said.[67]

This was tragic, for instance, for the survivors of the ghetto of Lodz, Poland. That ghetto was closed less than a year before the end of the war, and the surviving victims' confinement in concentration camps lasted less than a year. Thus, they were not entitled to the presumption regarding damage to health. The German authorities were not swayed by survivors' accounts. 'We brought from the [United] States three former inmates of the Lodz Ghetto who testified to the horrible conditions there before a German governmental committee. Deadly silence reigned in the committee room when testimony was given. One witness, overwhelmed by memories, broke down, had stated how newly born Jewish babies were thrown out of the window of the operating room upon a lorry in the courtyard and were driven away,' Katzenstein said. 'All this was not relevant. What mattered was that the concentration camps had been under the supervision of the SS *Wirtschaftsverwaltungshauptamt, Amtsgruppe D* [Main Economic Administrative Office of the SS, Group D], and the ghetto had not. Hence, the former ghetto inmates must render full proof that their illnesses were due to the incarceration, difficult and often impossible after the lapse of so many years and because of the meticulous requirements of German physicians.'[68]

The Final Law also created a two-tier system of Holocaust compensation in Israel. West Germany in 1952 had insisted that, for Nazi victims who were in Israel by 1953, the Israeli government provide compensation that would be analogous to German payments for damage to health. However, the Final BEG allowed claims for damage to health to be filed by some victims living in Israel, even though, in principle, they were ineligible. This is because, when classified as members of the German 'linguistic and cultural group', they were considered persecutees who could claim compensation from Germany, despite the fact that they lived in Israel.

The name of the 1965 law expressed its intent: To the German government, the 1965 indemnification law was *schluss*, final. The Conference's victories were bittersweet. It had succeeded in obtaining substantial benefits for hundreds of thousands of survivors. But the laws were marked by deficiencies and inequities, as well as laggardly implementation and restricted interpretation.

More than 4.3 million indemnification claims were submitted for a variety of persecution-related damages; 2.014 million were approved.[69] In addition, some two million claims had been rejected or retracted, an untold number had not been filed, and there were hundreds of thousands of victims for whom the statutes made no provision. 'And how many with great sufferings and in misery had been shown out of agencies and courts with negligible one-time compensation payments only?' Katzenstein asked.[70] Among the glaring exclusions was the failure to provide compensation for the slave labour of concentration camp inmates, or for Nazi victims who endured less than one year in a 'recognized' concentration camp, or those living in Eastern Europe. The last possible date for filing a claim was 31 December 1969.

With the Final Law came a new – and costly – condition for refugees and stateless persons who had been part of the 'German cultural and linguistic group' and who filed claims for damage to health.[71] The Final Law imposed a cut-off date: claimants must have left the expulsion areas before 1 October 1953. But there was no such deadline in the earlier law, the 1956 BEG. The effect was to create two categories of expellees, each with a distinct legal status. The first group was the *Altberechtigte*. These were German citizens or members of the 'German nation,' within the meaning of the Federal Expellees Law, who were vested with certain legal rights under the 1956 law. They were exempt from the deadline and were eligible for compensation even if they left the expulsion areas after 1 October 1953. By contrast, there were the *Neuberechtigte* – or the 'newly eligible' – were neither German citizens nor members of the 'German nation' but who were members of the German 'cultural or linguistic group.' They were eligible for compensation under the final BEG, which had a deadline of 1 October 1953. The Federal Constitutional Court ruled in 1971 that the 1953 deadline was unconstitutional, but it failed to simultaneously reopen the filing period for substantiating claims. The result was that thousands of Nazi victims who had left the expulsion areas after 1 October 1953 were denied the opportunity to substantiate their claims. Their predicament was untenable, the Conference complained, saying, 'The absurdity of the judgment of the Federal Supreme Court is evident.'[71] The legal position of this group remained complicated and controversial, subject to conflicting court judgments and to restrictive and obstructive interpretations.[73]

Deadlines were a problem across the board. Many victims had sustained medical and psychiatric injuries that became evident only long after the claims deadlines expired. Deadlines were a severe handicap for victims in the communist states. The BEG was not available behind the Iron Curtain, and many victims did not receive permission to emigrate until the end of the 1950s, if not later. Originally, these victims did not meet the BEG residency requirements. By the time they emigrated to the West, they had missed the filing deadlines for compensation.

There were other instances in which victims lost the opportunity for compensation because, while their eligibility was under legal review, deadlines had lapsed and were not reopened to accommodate them once the courts had ruled in their favour. For instance, Jews who fled from the Nazi advance in Western Poland in September 1939 and crossed the German-Soviet 'demarcation line' had no legal standing for BEG compensation for the damage to health that they suffered, for instance, in Siberia – until a 1961 ruling by the Federal Supreme Court for Indemnification, the *Bundesgerichtshof* (BGH). By that time, the filing period was closed. 'It was the legal situation prevailing during the filing time which disqualified them from filing,' Katzenstein said. 'When, in 1961, the BGH reversed the legal situation and vested the group with a legal status, all deadlines had expired.'[74]

The indemnification programme itself had come with a deadline. In Protocol I, Adenauer agreed that the FRG would 'endeavor to carry out the whole compensation programme as soon as possible but not later than within 10 years'.[75] However, a year before the BEG was due to reach its statutory end, Goldmann said: 'When the law was enacted, it was expected that 10 years following the signing of the agreements at Luxembourg would be long enough to witness the completion of the programme. These expectations have unhappily fallen short of fulfillment.' In December 1961, nearly 900,000 claims were still pending.[76]

There were numerous causes for the miscalculation of timing. The pivotal factor was the extent of the Nazis' destruction of Jewish life, health and property, which led to millions of claims and a thorough underestimate of the costs. The laws intended to provide redress were complex – and became ever more mired in masses of detail. The original law in the American Zone contained 53 paragraphs that covered basic damages of loss of life, health, liberty, property, vocational and economic pursuits. The 1953 German law had 'well over 100 different articles, each of which is divided into several paragraphs, and even a regulation in the comparatively simple area of claims of widows and orphans is over 25 pages long,' Ferencz said.[77]

There were disparities within the laws that, coupled with the slow pace of judicial rulings, hampered the programmes. In addition, the process was impeded by what the Conference called the 'formalistic and bureaucratic' approach of the restitution agencies. German authorities had the tendency to protect the national Treasury, irrespective of West Germany's rapid post-war transformation into a prosperous industrial state and of the small per centage allocated for Nazi victims, especially contrasted with amounts paid to Nazi-era functionaries – the so-called '131-ers'.[78] For instance, in 1958, the German Institute for Economic Research calculated that 'the total costs of *Wiedergutmachung* were 4 per cent of all expenditures occasioned by the war,' Goldmann said. '... Expenditures for the so-called "131-ers" come to 8 per cent, or double that amount.'[79]

Compensation to Nazi victims was not immune from federal budget cuts. Within 90 days of the enactment of the 1965 BEG law, the government introduced a 'budget protection' measure that cut or deferred for several years funds for highway and canal construction, road repairs and housing projects – and also delayed some indemnification payments. The Conference protested vigorously; the amount for Nazi victims – about DM 200 million – was so small that it could 'scarcely help secure the German government's budget'. And, Katzenstein argued, the deferral of compensation 'constitutes a flagrant breach of a solemn promise; it shakes all confidence in the German Government's statements'. The budget 'forces a moratorium upon persecutees who have been waiting for five, for ten or more years, or upon whom, for the first time for 20 years, have been bestowed at last some (restricted) rights under the Final Indemnification Law', he said. 'It is little consolation that they are not to be deprived of part of their claims; that such part – probably 30 or 40 per cent – is "only" to be deferred to future years. Many of the persecutees are old; they may not have months to wait, not to speak of years.'[80]

The compensation programmes were created by federal legislation, which shared with the states the costs of the payments. The operations of the programmes, however, were the responsibility of the *Länder*. Elabourate indemnification agencies were created in the eleven West German states, and thousands of employees were recruited to process claims.[81] Under the terms of an agreement among the *Länder*, claims were distributed among the states according to the nature of the claim or the claimant's country of residence at the time he filed the claim.

The law established the basic rules for compensation, which, in turn, depended on regulations enacted by the federal government. There were substantial delays: The first regulation, which concerned claims for loss of life, was published on 17 September 1954, a year after the law was passed. The second regulation, regarding damage to health, was published on 24 December 1954, while the third regulation, regarding professional damage, was published on 6 April 1955 – ten years after the end of the war.[82]

The implementation of the compensation programmes was hampered by the law's scope, intricacy and interpretation; the lack of precedents; problems with funding; and agencies' inexperience. The myriad problems were logistical and ideological. The 'legal-historical background' of the FRG fostered some of the shortcomings. West Germany was a decentralized state; there was no centralized coordination of the indemnification and restitution programmes. Many of the states detested and resisted the responsibility for the programmes, which were created by federal law but which the federal government had no authority to enforce. 'The whole complex of the financial equalization – the vertical one between Federal and *Länder* Governments and the horizontal one between the economically weak and economically strong *Länder* – was and is the subject of heated discussion within Germany and the fertile soil for considerable resentment against the Federal Government on the part of the *Länder*,' Goldmann said. Although this was a domestic German problem, it had serious consequences for Nazi victims, who, Goldmann said, 'should not bear the burden for conflicts in internal German financial policies'.[83]

'It was quite unavoidable that the implementation of such a law on separate bases would create difficulties of a legal and practical nature,' according to Robinson. 'There is hardly any major provision of the law which, in one way or another, did not become controversial.' Within the first decade of the indemnification laws, the German Supreme Court rendered almost 2,000 decisions, courts of secondary jurisdiction issued more than 37,000 decisions, and courts of original jurisdiction issued more than 256,000 rulings on the measures.[84]

Local officials, with latitude in the administration of the programmes, also took their cues from Fritz Schäffer, who served as the first federal finance minister, and went on to become justice minister. Schäffer had a running battle with the Conference from Day One and 'made every effort to delay ratification' of the Luxembourg Agreements, Goldmann said.[85] He was among the members of Adenauer's CDU/CSU faction who abstained from the March 1953 Bundestag vote that ratified the German-Jewish compensation agreements. Schäffer opposed financing the BEG with funds from the Federal Treasury; US State Department officials intervened to try to soften his resistance and to ensure the passage of the BEG legislation in 1953.[86] He then opposed the rapid revision of the original legislation. 'There have been several difficulties in the way of achieving a speedy and satisfactory amendment, though practically everyone agrees that changes are required,' Robinson said. 'First, the opposition by the Federal Minister of Finance, Schäffer, to any increase in the financial burden; this precludes any substantive changes because there are practically no amendments which have no financial repercussions.'[87]

After the law was amended, Schäffer complained in an interview with the German-Jewish newspaper *Aufbau* about the cost of the indemnification programme and its effect on the German national budget and on the currency – without referring to the cost of pensions paid to Nazi-era government officials.[88] The Deutsche mark had become the proud national symbol of post-war West Germany, and Schäffer warned, in an 'avalanche of estimates' to the German public, that the indemnification costs had jumped to four times the original estimates, and were a menace to the security of the currency. His speeches frequently blamed the large 'increase' in the compensation costs on the stateless victims and refugees, referring to those who were non-Germans who lived abroad. His speeches, which triggered some anti-Semitic reaction, were followed by stiffened requirements in the local adjudication of claims, with fewer favourable decisions.[89] However, while the Conference routinely called the Finance Ministry's estimates exaggerated, in fact, the indemnification programme grew dramatically, in large part because the Conference's success in widening the criteria had expanded the volume of payments.

'Where the delivery of goods and materials under the terms of the reparations agreements is flowing [to Israel] at a smooth and even pace, the gravest and most determined attack ever launched on the programme of indemnification is currently confronting us,' Goldmann warned the Conference in 1958. At a CSU party meeting in Bavaria, 'Dr Schäffer proclaimed that the indemnification programmes to Nazi victims had swollen to proportions so vast and far-ranging as to threaten the very security of the Deutsche mark and to open the way for its devaluation. Conjuring up fantastic estimates in support of his economic fantasies, Dr Schäffer set the sum that the demands of the indemnification programme would call for, by the year 1961, at DM 28 billion, matched against the modest DM 8 [billion] to 9 billion envisaged originally ... The Schäffer speech gained widespread coverage up and down the German press, and the so-called peril to the Deutsche mark posed by the problem of *Wiedergutmachung* stirred up excitement in every quarter,' Goldmann said. '*Wiedergutmachung*, we ought not forget, does not enjoy the widest appeal in many German circles.'[90]

Despite Adenauer's commitment to compensation, in the *Länder*, which bore half the costs of the programme, 'ministers proceeded to toss oil on the flames of the controversy in an apparent drive to lighten the *Länder* share of the indemnification burden,' Kagan reported. 'The assaults on *Wiedergutmachung* have failed to taper off since the closing days of January 1958, and the pressures generated by them represent the first formidable threat to the indemnification programme that it has been called upon to meet.'[91]

The problems with Schäffer were not confined to the costs of the indemnification programme. He also challenged how the Claims Conference spent the funds it had received under Protocol II. 'It looks like the Finance Ministry people are out to give us a rough time,' Kagan warned in 1957. 'One of the principal attacks, according to advance information, will be made upon our cultural programme because "the needs of individual victims of Nazi persecution were still so urgent and not sufficiently remedied". In addition, of course, they will protest against our unwillingness to deal with individual hardship cases,' he said.[92]

The *Länder* bureaucracies and the judiciary could not be compelled to be generous. 'The indemnification law is being implemented too bureaucratically, generally speaking, and the tragic background that led to indemnification and restitution, and sometimes the very spirit of it, is frequently forgotten,' a Conference 'study mission' reported after a monthlong tour of German indemnification agencies.[93] The bottlenecks were grave. There were reports of catastrophic delays in which claims based on decades-old persecution and with longstanding favourable judgments standing went unpaid. 'In not a few cases, the claim derives from events that occurred 22 years ago; in other cases, 20 years ago,' Professor Franz Boehm, who had co-chaired the German delegation in The Hague in 1952, said during a 1955 Bundestag debate on the indemnification legislation. During the same debate, Dr. Adolph Arndt, of the SPD, recounted 'typical' court verdicts in indemnification cases that were 'incomprehensible.' He cited the 1954 rejection of a Jewish shop-owner's claim by a Mannheim court, which ruled that the anti-Jewish boycott measures of 1 April 1933, were not directed at the shop-owner personally but were a collective measure 'countering the anti-German propaganda prevalent in those days.' Arndt also cited the case of a non-Jewish wife who followed her Jewish spouse to live underground during the Nazi period. Her claim for indemnification was rejected by a Berlin court on the ground that she had the option of deserting her husband; therefore, her suffering was the result of a voluntary act, not Nazi persecution.[94]

Frustrated at the tardy pace, the Conference in 1955 simultaneously sought to abolish the 'maze of technicalities which are strangling the law' and to craft new legislation to address the law's inadequacies. 'Most important of all, however, the spirit which animated the enactment of the law must somehow be communicated down to every official until the compensation which was promised to the claimants becomes not merely a hope but a reality,' the board said in a resolution.[95]

In a letter to Adenauer, Goldmann commended the 'admirable' manner in which West Germany was meeting its obligations to Israel, but complained that commitments to individual Nazi victims were not being 'satisfactorily fulfilled.' When the law was passed in 1953, 'it was generally recognized as an inadequate piece of legislation,' he wrote. 'The major deficiencies in the law have been recognized by all important political parties, and the persecutees were led to expect early improvements.'[96] While Adenauer expressed regret at the delays – 'which almost of necessity resulted from the difficulties of the legislative material and the administrative burden on the appropriate authorities' – he said there had been achievements in individual compensation. The chancellor also said that a committee of federal agencies, the *Länder* compensation authorities and parties in the Bundestag was preparing 'as speedily as possible' an amendment to the indemnification law. 'In the preparation of the law, the suggestions and wishes of the victims shall be considered as far as at all possible,' Adenauer wrote.[97]

The law was amended the next year. But delays persisted. 'New laws are useless unless they are implemented in keeping with their original conception,' Goldmann said. As a practical matter, the Conference sought simplified and standardized procedures for the treatment of claims throughout the FRG. 'We wish to avoid what happened on various occasions when on the same set of facts, in Bavaria, for example, [authorities] may make one decision, in West Berlin another,' Goldmann said.[98]

The Conference also called on German authorities to advance funds to supplement the budgets of the German states when the volume of claims was greater than anticipated.[99] It wanted to avoid disruptions such as those in Berlin, where indemnification payments were suspended for several months in 1956 when the earmarked funds were exhausted.[100] Rhineland-Pfalz, which had only limited sums available monthly, dealt with claims in what amounted to a de facto quota system.[101] Although it was one of the weakest *Länder* economically, Rhineland-Pfalz had jurisdiction over the claims of stateless persons and political refugees residing outside of Europe, which were some of the most difficult.

But not all backlogs could be attributed to a shortage of funds. In fact, of the DM 2.6 billion set aside for the indemnification programme in the federal and state budgets in 1959, DM 1 billion was not spent, because not enough claims had been approved to use the funds. 'When you consider that the average value of an indemnification claim is below DM 10,000, this means that ... more than 100,000 claims were not settled, although the necessary funds were at hand,' Goldmann said.[102]

At the insistence of the Conference, Adenauer on 26 June 1959 convened the first of two extraordinary meetings of the finance minister, the minister-presidents of the eleven *Länder* and the Conference, to discuss the delays. Some of the *Länder* were irked at the idea that Adenauer would call 'prime ministers together to meet with a private organization in which the people are not even German citizens,' Goldmann recalled. 'Germans stick very much to protocol. It's a bureaucratic nation. But he [Adenauer] insisted on it with his usual stubbornness, and nearly all of them came.'[103] At the meeting at the Palais Schaumburg, Goldmann warned that the indemnification law was 'a *ruhmesblatt* [source of pride] of the new Germany. It should be implemented in the same spirit that prompted its enactment.'

'The Federal Indemnification Law is an extraordinary document, which makes one conscious once again of a dark past, forces the smallest portion of unimaginable suffering into a sober legal language, and translates it into so-called indemnification claims. It is by no means an ordinary statute, which can be implemented amid comfortable lounging behind the desk or on the bench, without an eye on the clock,' he said. 'With foresight, the legislator subjected the programme to a time limit. For the sooner this dark past is overcome, the less fuss is made about its final settlement, the less old wounds are torn open through piercing questions and tormenting demands for evidence, the less bureaucratic routine and judicial hairsplitting are put into motion, the more manifest the effort to bring about a *restitutio in integrum* of the mortally wounded sense of justice, the better for all concerned. Time is measured here not only by the yardstick of the date of expiration; and the amount of the payments measured not only with the slide-rule. The dissimilar treatment of similar claims, whether caused by the differences in locale or time, awakens in the persecutees the almost unbearable feeling of helpless delivery into the hands of an arbitrary executive power.'

After outlining the structural and financial problems with the indemnification programme, Goldmann warned: 'Nothing would be more regrettable than that a law – whose enactment and unanimous passage by the Bundestag and Bundesrat has done so much to raise Germany's prestige in the world, whose explicit goal, confirmed on the federal and state level on various occasions, is to bring about the most extensive and speediest *Wiedergutmachung* possible – should, through its manner of implementation, occasion bitter complaints and disappointments among those persecuted and entitled. Many of these persecutees, who had survived the collapse of the Third Reich, are no longer alive; most of the survivors have been waiting for more than twenty years for their indemnification.'[104]

Adenauer vowed: 'You may be certain that all levels of government are imbued with the strong and serious determination to carry out the *Wiedergutmachung* as quickly and as favourably as possible.'[105] After the meetings, new funds were made available, indemnification offices were opened, and staffs were enlarged. But that was not sufficient. 'We reached a very paradoxical situation, that much more money was allocated by the *Länder* and the Federal Republic for this item,' Goldmann said. 'In the first years, we had to fight to get the allocation of money with Schäffer, who always wanted to hold back. Now we have the allocations of money; there is no problem. But we haven't the machinery to use the money.'[106]

From the outset, the Conference sought not only special legislation for Nazi victims, but also endeavoured to ensure that they would not be excluded from the benefits provided by standard German social welfare programmes.[107] When Nazi actions struck victims in their early years, the persecution interrupted, disrupted or prematurely ended their education and professional or vocational training. Under the indemnification law, certain groups of survivors could receive a one-time payment of DM 10,000 for that injury. In addition, the Conference was able to secure the rights of Jewish victims of Nazi persecution to participate in conventional German social insurance programmes, such as pensions for invalids and for old-age social insurance. Because they were expelled or deported, Nazi victims had been prevented from making the customary contributions that citizens made to the German system to earn pensions that were paid in their old age. The Conference was able to ensure that the German government gave victims 'credits' for the years of persecution, and the right to make retroactive contributions, when necessary, to meet the minimum eligibility requirements for these pensions.[108] This was subsequently broadened for victims in Lodz, Poznan and other areas in Poland that had been incorporated into Nazi Germany.[109]

The Conference also devoted enormous effort to preserving benefits from deterioration. The protection of annuities was a complicated effort involving not only attention to fluctuating currency exchange rates and vigilance over German federal budget appropriations, but regular and prolonged lobbying of the indemnification authorities in each of the eleven German states. Significant benefits were at stake; in the early 1980s, for instance, a five per cent adjustment in indemnification meant additional benefits to victims of some DM 100 million per year.[110]

Katzenstein had grudgingly accepted that the 1965 law was final. However, he insisted that West Germany had failed to honour the terms of Protocol I and its indemnification laws. 'The BEG is a piece of codified law,' he said. 'What is not in the statute is not in the world. But what is in the statute has to be provided.'[111] Specifically, Katzenstein charged that the FRG had failed to meet its obligations to match victims' compensation to that of German civil servants, as specified in

Protocol I. German civil servants received a '13th payment' each year, which had originated as a Christmas bonus. As of January 1977, after pressure from the trade unions, it had evolved from a holiday gratuity to an annual 13th salary payment. Nazi victims did not receive the payment, which infuriated Katzenstein. He was relentless in pursuing it, arguing that once the payment had become standard for German civil servants, it was a right of Nazi victims under Protocol I.

The amount was considerable. For instance, in 1979, some 230,000 Nazi victims were receiving pensions; if they received the thirteenth payment, collectively they would have received an additional DM 100 million that year. Katzenstein consistently argued that the rights under the BEG were immune to what he called 'budgetary distress'. When it came to compensation for Nazi victims, Katzenstein thought German financial problems were irrelevant. 'I have seen too many cases of severest persecution and lifelong damage without compensation to be impressed by fiscal considerations,' he said. The German Parliament, 'the father and creator of the BEG, has to provide whatever is necessary to meet the obligations it has stipulated.'[112]

Germany's failure to provide the additional annual payment 'confronts us with a serious situation – constitutional, political, legal and moral; it is in line with the declining climate and atmosphere in the field of indemnification,' said Katzenstein.[113] He was angry that Bonn had disregarded the demand for the payment and frustrated with the Conference, as well. 'Presentations year after year of the same demands, continuously submitted throughout more than a decade and just as persistently annually rejected, restating the same arguments of evasiveness or inconsistency again, year after year, rebutted but never followed up by action from our side, must come to an end,' he said. 'It has been going on for much too long already.'[114] Nearly three decades after the Luxembourg Agreements, Katzenstein wanted the Conference to make some kind of move that would compel West Germany to pay additional benefits. However, by that time, the Conference had just concluded a bruising seven-year battle for a hardship fund for Nazi victims who emigrated to the West after 1965, and it was clear that West Germany would not undertake any additional commitments.[115] The issue was finally resolved in 1988, when the *Bundesgerichtshof* ruled that Nazi victims and their surviving relatives were not entitled to the extra month's pension paid to German civil servants.[116]

In addition to individual compensation, Protocol I committed West Germany to extend the Allies' restitution laws, which dealt with purely material losses. As with the case of indemnification, the German restitution legislation expanded on principles that had been developed by the Allied forces in the Occupation zones. These measures were intended to restore identifiable assets – in kind or in compensation – that had been 'Aryanized'. The seminal measure was US Military Government Law Number 59 of 10 November 1947, whose restitution provisions called for compensation for assets that had been confiscated by the Nazis.[117] The Allies also empowered successor organizations to recover Jewish property that had been made heirless by Nazi persecution.[118]

The Allied laws also anticipated the subsequent passage of German legislation on property restitution. The effect, however, was to confuse Nazi victims, because it was not clear when claims would be handled under Allied or German laws. There were instances in which victims were advised by the Allied authorities, the United Restitution Office and their own lawyers that it might be a waste of time to file claims under Allied laws, and instead were told to wait for German legislation.[119] It was not until 1957, five years after the Luxembourg Agreements, that West Germany enacted the Federal Restitution Law, known as the BRüG.[120] That law compensated Nazi victims for household furnishings, personal valuables, bank accounts, securities and other movable properties that had been confiscated by Nazi authorities and that could be specifically identified but could no longer be restored.[121] And in conjunction with the Equalization of Burdens law, there were payments for claims for individual properties in the 'expulsions areas', because the loss of the property was a 'consequence of the war'.[122]

Like the indemnification legislation, the BRüG was fraught with serious flaws and onerous burdens that stymied claimants. As with the BEG, the restitution law used territorial limits, so that not all victims were eligible to file property claims. Unlike indemnification, which was open-ended, there originally was a ceiling of DM 1.5 billion on BRüG payments.

That created what Robinson called a 'thorny problem'. The ceiling was a feature of Protocol I, whose terms could be negotiated between the FRG and the Conference. But the ceiling also was specified in the Contractual Agreement, and represented one aspect of the settlement with the Allies that restored German sovereignty. Under those terms, West Germany was obliged to satisfy restitution claims against the Nazi régime, but its liability was capped at DM 1.5 billion.[123] That amount bore no direct relationship to loss.

As interpreted by the Allies – particularly the Americans – the ceiling referred to West Germany's obligation to pay first the claims of Nazi victims who filed their claims in time under the existing restitution laws in the American and British zones and in Berlin. Those claims would have to be paid in full before claimants who missed the filing deadlines could obtain compensation, according to Robinson. The effect was that, by 1964, approved individual claims with a value of up to DM 20,000 had been paid in full, but victims with claims above that amount received only 50 per cent of their value, because the payments ceiling had been reached by 1962.[124]

In addition to the financial inadequacies, there were more serious flaws in the BRüG. It was extremely confusing. Just as it had been unclear earlier whether restitution claims should be filed under Allied or German laws, claimants were confused about whether claims should be filed under the German indemnification or restitution laws. Further, there was considerable uncertainty regarding the definition of identifiable property, and many claimants did not know they were entitled to file claims for property that was no longer available.[125]

The law, which bore a tight claims deadline of 1 April 1959, imposed onerous requirements of proof. Claimants or heirs were expected to prove that goods confiscated outside Nazi Germany were shipped subsequently to Germany, or property owners were required to prove that plundered goods were in port or in transit, via France, Belgium and Holland. Many victims apparently abandoned claims because it was impossible to trace or document the shipment of confiscated assets. After protests from the Conference, Germany eased some of the criteria. In 1958, it waived the requirement for 'proof of shipment' for movable goods seized in France. Between 1959 and 1961, it also shelved the proof requirement for goods confiscated in Belgium, Holland and occupied territories in Eastern Europe. However, the waivers were more theoretical than real because they were not accompanied by an extension of the 1959 deadline.[126]

The Conference began negotiating with Bonn in 1960 to expand the restitution law. An amended law went into force on 8 October 1964. It enlarged the volume of compensation payments and expanded the scope of eligibility. Under the amendments, the FRG also created a 'hardship fund' for new restitution claimants. These included claimants whose moveable properties were confiscated from what became East Berlin, and recent migrants from Central and Eastern Europe.[127] The 1964 amendments added DM 800 million – twice the sum Germany originally offered – for the new fund, and raised compensation from 50 per cent to 100 per cent.[128]

In the negotiations in Wassenaar, West Germany agreed to keep the Conference informed about the preparation of indemnification and restitution legislation; to invite the Conference to comment on draft measures; and to consult it on the implementation of Protocol I. That set into motion the Conference's 'legislative' program. Despite Protocol I's anticipation that West Germany would carry out the compensation programme within ten years, instead, for more than a half-century the

Conference negotiated with Germany to enhance benefits for Nazi victims, monitored the implementation of the indemnification and restitution measures, and protected the rights of Jewish persecutees.

From the earliest pursuit of indemnification, Jewish advocates have insisted that 'the determining factor in the payment of compensation should be the fact and the extent of the damage inflicted' and that other eligibility criteria deprive them of justice.[129] Nonetheless, the German indemnification laws excluded categories of victims who endured the same horrific persecution, but who qualified – or did not – for indemnification based on their countries of origin and on their legal status and residency after the Holocaust. Victims' anger at the German criteria often was vented at the Conference. However, despite the detractors, the Conference's success with indemnification has been remarkable. By the end of the century, as the result of agreements with the Conference, Germany had paid more than DM 100 billion in compensation to individual Nazi victims. While international agreements initially limited West Germany's obligations under the BRüG to DM 1.5 billion, the FRG ultimately paid DM 3.9 billion.[130] At the end of 2000, under the original indemnification legislative programmes of the 1950s, some 89,000 Nazi victims – the overwhelming majority of them Jewish – continued to receive BEG pensions from Germany; the average monthly payment was DM 1,003.[131]

'We cannot convey that the BEG is heavenly. It is important. It has meant for literally hundreds of thousands of survivors – particularly those who could not build a new, significant economic existence for themselves – an additional income. One hundred billion Deutsche marks, so far paid under implementation of the BEG, is not an insignificant amount, especially in terms of what it meant for individuals,' said Kagan. 'It certainly is meaningful. Is it adequate? Nothing is adequate in relation to the totality of what people suffered.'[132]

NOTES

1   Telegram, CAHJP 16808. Because the Luxembourg Agreements were negotiated in The Hague, they often are referred to as The Hague Agreements.
2   Claims Conference Board meeting, 11 May 1953, CAHJP 14145
3   Claims Conference Policy Committee, 24 September 1952.
4   The CSU is active in Bavaria, and serves as the CDU's 'partner'; in the Bundestag, these two parties are one faction and are known colloquially as 'the unions.'
5   There was vigorous Arab pressure and protests against West Germany's agreements with Israel and the Conference. 'Arab propagandists descended upon Germany with the avowed purpose of preventing ratification by Parliament. Their intemperate campaign reached a climax with the threat to boycott German goods,' if the agreements were ratified, Goldmann told the Claims Conference Board at its 4 July 1972 meeting in Geneva. According to the *New York Times* (19 March 1953), 30 minutes after the announcement of the Bundestag's ratification,

the West German foreign office announced it would continue economic negotiations with Egypt and that German engineers were in Cairo to discuss significant irrigation projects.

6   See Appendix for Protocols I and II.

7   The abbreviation of the programme was based on its initials – B.E.G. It was not pronounced 'beg.'

8   Katzenstein report to Claims Conference Board, 3 July 1979.

9   Summary, Claims Conference Board meeting, 2–3 March 1963, CAHJP 14164

10 Katzenstein report to Claims Conference Board, 3 July 1979. The total number of victims who received annuities under the German indemnification measures could not be determined. The official German government statistics indicate the number of pensions paid each year, but do not indicate the aggregate number of individuals who received pensions over the course of the BEG programme.

11 *Jerusalem Post*, 26 January 1996.

12 Benefits also were treated differently. For instance, a victim's income was taken into account when calculating pensions for damage to health, but it was not taken into account for payments for harm to career.

13 Claims Conference, *Report for the period October 1, 1975 to September 30, 1978*.

14 Kagan interview, 4 January 2001.

15 Memo by Julien Samuel, Fonds Sociale Juif Unifié (Paris), 3 December 1956. JDC Archives New York, 45/64 Collection, File 4388.

16 The nations and amounts paid were: Belgium (DM 80 million), Denmark (DM 16 million), France (DM 400 million), Great Britain (DM 11 million), Greece (DM 115 million), Holland (DM 125 million), Italy (DM 40 million), Luxembourg (DM 18 million), Norway (DM 60 million), Switzerland (DM 10 million), and Sweden (DM 1 million). 'Focus On ... German Restitution for National Socialist Crimes,' New York: German Information Center, January 1997.

17 Austria also had a bilateral agreement with West Germany under which it received some DM 100 million. However, unlike the German agreements with the 11 Western European countries, in which the use of the funds was discretionary, the German-Austrian pact specified how Austria would use the funds. Nazi victims from Austria were not entitled to 'Holocaust' compensation from the FRG. Bonn had refused to accept obligations for Austria, arguing that the birthplace of Hitler also was guilty of Nazi crimes. Austria, in rejecting a legal duty to pay compensation, relied on the Moscow Declaration of 1943, in which the Allies regarded Austria as the 'first victim,' not as a collabourator, of the Nazi régime. See Chapter 8.

18 Katzenstein, report to Claims Conference Board, 1981. The Netherlands programme was quite broad; it was intended for Dutch citizens at home or abroad and their next of kin, as well as for specific groups of aliens who were persecuted on account of their race, religion or 'worldview' during the occupation of the Netherlands and the former Dutch East Indies. Claims Conference Board meeting, 27 July 1984, Jerusalem; Kagan interview, 25 February 2001; *Jewish Chronicle* (London), 12 June 1964.

19 Nazi victims who remained in Central and Eastern Europe did not qualify for compensation until 1998, after the Conference and Germany reached an agreement for a special fund for survivors in the East. See Chapter 5.

20 Kagan interview, 4 January 2001.

21 In its financial agreements with Poland and Yugoslavia, Germany arranged for long-term credits; the FRG also made payments to the Polish social security agency in 1975.

22 The agreements with Poland and the former Soviet republics were concluded between 1991 and 1993. Germany concluded a separate agreement with the Czech Republic in 1997.

23 Minutes, Claims Conference Policy Committee meeting, 24 September 1952, CAHJP 16723

24 Kagan letter to Ferencz, Katzenstein, et. al., 7 October 1987. For decades, the disparity in payments rankled the survivors in Israel. In 1995, hundreds of survivors crowded into the Israeli Supreme Court in support of a petition filed by Avraham Hirschenson, a member of the Knesset, who argued that there was discrimination against survivors who arrived in Israel in the early years. Survivors in Israel received less than half the level of compensation (*Los Angeles Times*, 8 May 1995). The differences subsequently were narrowed, to some extent, when the Israeli government agreed to provide additional compensation or tax breaks to survivors in the country.

25 Claims Conference, *Annual Report 1964*.

26 Robinson, *Ten Years of German Indemnification*. Victims were eligible if they were resident

in the American Zone on 1 January 1947, in the British Zone on 1 January 1948, and in Hamburg as late as 1 January 1949. As the Allies prepared to reinstate German sovereignty and withdraw Occupation authority, Jewish organizations sought to have the existing claims legislation strengthened and to win Allied assurances that the laws would be preserved. However, the Allies maintained that indemnification was a prerogative of the Germans and was not a reserved power.

27   The laws varied, in part, because the Allied Occupation zones were governed by different legal systems, financial concerns and sentiments about Jewish claims. In the British Zone, compensation was provided primarily for the loss of liberty; in the French Zone, extensive bills had been drafted but had not become law. In the US Occupation Zone, authorities worried about imposing a financial requirement on German states that would have to be subsidized by American taxpayers, while the British feared that funds could assist illegal Jewish immigration to Mandatory Palestine. See Ronald W. Zweig, 'Restitution and the Problem of Jewish Displaced Persons in Anglo-American Relations, 1944–1948,' *American Jewish History*, Vol. LXXVIII, No. 1, 1988, pp. 54–78.

28   The General Claims Law in the US Zone, in effect, not only set the minimum standard for indemnification, but could be treated as the 'ceiling,' as well, in which the Germans would argue that if the government was bound to provide no less than the General Claims Law, neither was it obliged to provide more.

29   This expectation was evident in the language of Protocol I, in which the FRG agreed to enact a 'Federal Supplementing and Coordinating Law.'

30   Claims Conference Board meeting, 11 May 1953, CAHJP 14145

31   Protocol I, Item 7.

32   Claims Conference Board meeting, Jerusalem, 6 July 1990.

33   Katzenstein letter to Ferencz, 6 June 1983.

34   Robinson, 'Implementation of The Hague Protocol I,' report to Claims Conference Board, 20 March 1954, CAHJP 14146

35   Claims Conference Board meeting, 11 May 1953, CAHJP 14145

36   Claims Conference, *Annual Report 1965*.

37   Dulles letter to Goldmann, 1 February 1954.

38   Robinson, 'Implementation of The Hague Protocol I.'

39   Each definition had specific geographical parameters and dates that were related to different Nazi-era conditions. A 'repatriate' was a former German prisoner of war or a German who had been interned outside of the Federal Republic or Berlin. An 'expellee' was a member of the 'German folk' (the German cultural or linguistic group) who resided outside the borders of the German Reich as of 31 December 1937, or in the German territories that in 1953 were under Polish or Russian administration, and who had fled or been expelled from those territories. A 'refugee' was defined as someone who emigrated or who was deported from an area that was German on 31 December 1937, while 'stateless persons' referred primarily to Holocaust survivors who were in displaced persons camps after the Second World War. These definitions referred to the victims' status up until 1 October 1953.

40   Many claimants who would have received compensation under the previous *Länder* indemnification laws in the American Zone found their payments withheld after the enactment of the BEG. 'There is no doubt that the promulgation of the BEG resulted in a partial paralysis of the implementation of the old legislation,' Robinson reported to the Claims Conference Board in 1954.

41   Robinson, 'Implementation of The Hague Protocol I.'

42   *Activities of the Claims Conference 1952–1957*.

43   Report by Institute of Jewish Affairs, 13 June 1956.

44   Nahum Goldmann, *The Jewish Paradox*, New York: Fred Jordan Books/Grosset & Dunlap, 1978, p. 136.

45   Among the improvements: The payment for 'damage to property and assets' was increased to DM 75,000, and the compensation for 'damage to professional and economic advancement' was raised to DM 40,000, from DM 25,000. 'Damage to life' referred to the death of the survivors' breadwinner, for whom a pension was paid. 'Damage to health' meant that the victim was 'not insignificantly' harmed in body or health and that there was probably a 'causal connection' between the harm and persecution. Compensation included medical care, pensions, re-training and, if the victim died from the effects of persecution, support of his survivors. Additional compensation was granted if the victim's earning capacity was reduced

by at least 25 per cent (instead of the previous threshold of 30 per cent) because of injuries resulting from persecution. 'Deprivation of liberty' was expanded to include being compelled to wear the Star of David. Finally, the law addressed the rights of heirs to inherit compensation, an issue that was important because claimants died before the BEG was implemented

46 Claims Conference Board meeting, 10 September 1997, New York.

47 Claims Conference Board meeting, 30–31 January 1960, Amsterdam, CAHJP 13630

48 Robinson, *Ten Years of German Indemnification*. The URO was a legal aid organization that assisted Holocaust survivors with indemnification and restitution claims against West Germany. The Conference estimated that its financial support of the URO enabled 115,000 people to secure indemnification and restitution payments.

49 The Equalization of Burdens law (*Lastenausgleich*) provided compensation for damages and losses caused by war and expulsion.

50 Minutes, Claims Conference Policy Committee meeting, 24 September 1952, CAHJP 16723. The expellees were not a unified political force; they had different socioeconomic backgrounds and political orientations. However, they received substantial benefits because, as a significant per centage of the population, Adenauer's government was intent on integrating them peacefully into West German society.

51 Protocol I (Item 12) refers to benefits for people who were persecuted because of their political convictions, race, faith or ideology, and who settled in the Federal Republic or emigrated abroad from expulsion areas within the meaning of that term in the 'Equalization of Burdens' law. This provision applied only if they settled in the Federal Republic or emigrated abroad before the general expulsions took place.

52 Minutes, Claims Conference Policy Committee meeting, 24 September 1952, CAHJP 16723

53 The concept of the 'German folk' was vague. Claimants originally were required to prove they were expelled by reason of German citizenship or 'membership in the German nation' – a condition that would have excluded Jewish victims. The German Federal Constitutional Court ruled on 23 March 1971 that this requirement was unconstitutional. In a ruling affecting some 35,000 victims' claims, the court declared that those who were expelled would qualify if they were members of the German 'cultural and linguistic group,' rather than the German 'nation.' Claims Conference *Report for the period October 1, 1975 to September 30, 1978*.

54 Kagan interview, 25 February 2001.

55 Christian Pross, *Paying for the Past: The Struggle Over Reparations for Surviving Victims of the Nazi Terror*, Baltimore: The Johns Hopkins University Press, 1998.

56 Easterman letter to Lord Henderson, British Under Secretary of State for Foreign Affairs, 25 July 1950.

57 Claims Conference, *Annual Report 1964*. Claims Conference memorandum, 'Regarding German Federal Republic indemnification and restitution programmes for victims of Nazi persecution – Crisis has developed during this final stage,' attachment to 2 June 1964 letter from Blaustein to Secretary of State Dean Rusk.

58 Goldmann to Claims Conference Board, 7 March 1964, Brussels.

59 *New York Times*, 19 March 1953.

60 Goldmann to Claims Conference Board, 7 March 1964, Brussels.

61 Katzenstein letter to Ferencz, 6 June 1983.

62 Goldmann explained the delay in the *Schlussgesetz* to the Conference board in March 1963, saying that, some two years earlier, the Conference had submitted a plan for a draft law to expand indemnification. However, 'our *mazal* [luck] has been bad,' he said. The government delayed consideration of the plan because of the 1961 elections. Then, Finance Minister Franz Etzel, who was familiar with the indemnification programmes, fell ill and resigned. He was succeeded by Heinz Starke, who asked for a delay to become acquainted with the issue. 'The fates frowned again and l'affaire Spiegel took the spotlight,' Goldmann said. After a Cabinet shake-up, Starke was succeeded in February 1963 by Rolf Dahlgruen. The draft law then became bogged down in negotiations between the government and the *Länder* over the division of the costs.

63 Of special concern were Hungarian survivors. After the enactment of the Revised BEG, tens of thousands of refugees fled to the West after the 1956 Hungarian uprising. Among them were Jewish victims of Nazi persecution who were ineligible for compensation from West Germany because of the prior deadline.

64 Claims Conference, *Twenty Years Later*. The DM 1.2 billion was twice the sum that the FRG

originally offered to pay. In addition, the Bundestag supplemented the BEG in 1976 with DM 400 million, for payments to Jewish victims whose health was seriously impaired by the Nazi persecution but who had not been able to obtain compensation previously because they had missed the filing deadline or had not met residency requirements.

65 Robinson, memo, 'Status of the bill to amend the Federal Compensation Law (BEG),' May 1963.
66 Claims Conference, *Twenty Years Later.*
67 Robinson, memo, 'Status of the bill to amend the Federal Compensation Law (BEG)', May 1963.
68 Katzenstein report, 3 July 3 1979.
69 Claimants were both Jewish and non-Jewish. German Foreign Ministry, 'State payments made by the Federal Republic of Germany in the area of indemnification,' January 2000.
70 Katzenstein letter to Ferencz, 6 June 1983.
71 These were claims under Section 150 of the law.
72 Claims Conference *Report for the period October 1, 1975 to September 30, 1978.*
73 Katzenstein report to Claims Conference Board, 1982.
74 Katzenstein memo to Kagan, 'The DM 400 Million hardship fund and the Polish/Russian flight cases of old Pre-65 applicants,' 27 February 1985.
75 Protocol I, Item 15.
76 Claims Conference Board meeting, 24 March 1962, Copenhagen.
77 Claims Conference Board meeting, 5–6 February 1955, Paris.
78 Protocol 1 (Item 15) had predicated compensation to Nazi victims on West Germany's capacity to pay. The original compensation for deprivation of liberty (*Schaden an Freiheit*) was a one-time payment of DM 150 per month of internment – or DM 5 a day. (That amount was set before the enactment of the BEG; it was based on compensation that had been initiated under measures enacted when the German states were under the Allied Occupation authorities.) In June 1987, when West Germany was no longer an impoverished country, the Conference presented the Bundestag's Committee on Internal Affairs (*Innenausschuss*) with a demand that the compensation for deprivation of liberty be doubled. According to the Conference, as of 30 June 1965 – the last date for which the data was certain – some 474,000 awards for *Schaden an Freiheit* were made to individuals living outside of Germany. The Conference's demand was ignored.
79 Section 131 of Grundgesetz entitled former German civil servants, including former Nazi functionaries, to recover their posts. Goldmann speech, meeting with Adenauer and *Länder* officials, 26 June 1959, CAHJP 14007
80 Katzenstein memo, 19 November 1965. In addition to cutting expenditures, the budget also imposed higher taxes on some luxury items, such as brandy. Katzenstein resented the manner in which the German government identified which groups would be affected by the budget measure. 'Of all persons affected by the [budget], consumers of champagne and spirits are listed just after victims of Nazi persecution – those whose life, health, liberty, etc., were willfully impaired by state-organized crime on an unprecedented scale,' he wrote. CAHJP 14340
81 Claims Conference, *Annual Report 1965.*
82 Robinson, *Ten Years of German Indemnification.*
83 Claims Conference memo, 26 June 1959, CAHJP 14007
84 Many of the court decisions dealt only with the circumstances of individual cases, while others were matters of principle and had broad application. Robinson, *Ten Years of German Indemnification.*
85 Claims Conference Board meeting, 11 May 1953, CAHJP 14145. Schäffer's objections to compensation were not limited to Jewish victims; he also aggressively attempted to guard the German treasury against measures to aid the *Volksdeutsche* who came to West Germany after they were expelled from Eastern Europe. See Moeller, Robert G., *War Stories: The Search for a Usable Past in the Federal Republic of Germany*, Berkeley: University of California Press, 1999.
86 Sagi, pp. 187, 190.
87 Robinson, 'Implementation of The Hague Protocol I.'
88 Kagan letter, 22 July 1957.
89 Kagan memo to Claims Conference Board, 1 October 1958, CAHJP 14157
90 Claims Conference Board meeting, 25–26 January 1958, Rome, CAHJP 13626.

91 Kagan memo to Claims Conference Board, 26 March 1958, CAHJP 14156. After Schäffer gave a speech in Plattling, Bavaria, representatives of the United Restitution Organization, which provides legal aid to survivors, found a significant increase in rejections of compensation applications.

92 Kagan letter to Mark Uveeler, 26 August 1957. Under Section 171 of the Federal Indemnification Law, discretionary hardship payments could be made by the government to individual persecutees 'for whom funds for special purposes' are not otherwise provided. Although the *Länder*, which administered the law, had made some hardship payments to Jewish applicants, in April 1957, they halted the funding. The authorities said that hardship payments to Jewish refugees were the responsibility of the Conference, and that Germany's DM 450 million payment to the Conference, under Protocol II, represented a fund for 'special purposes.' However, in The Hague negotiations, the Conference rejected the German idea that the Protocol II funds should be used for grants to individuals. See Chapter 9 on the Claims Conference's institutional allocations.

93 Conference Study Mission, 'Summary of report on trip to German indemnification offices,' 7 October–7 November 1957, CAHJP 14154. In November 1954, the Senate for indemnification cases of the Federal Supreme Court (*Wiedergutmachungssenat des Bundesgerichtshofes*) admonished, to no apparent avail, that 'the aim and purpose of the restitution and indemnification legislation is to provide compensation for the injustice caused as soon and as comprehensively as possible,' and said that 'an interpretation of the law corresponding to this goal should have precedence over every other interpretation that would render *Wiedergutmachung* difficult, or destroy it.' See Goldmann speech, meeting with Adenauer and *Länder* officials, 26 June 1959, CAHJP 14007.

94 Summary of 23 February 1955, Bundestag debate was prepared by the Conference and distributed as a memo to Claims Conference Board, 1 April 1955, CAHJP 14148

95 Claims Conference Board meeting, 5–6 February 1955, Paris, CAHJP 14282

96 Goldmann letter to Adenauer, 6 February 1955, CAHJP 14282

97 Adenauer letter to Goldmann, 9 February 1955, CAHJP 14282

98 Claims Conference Board meeting, 19 January 1957, New York. Goldmann subsequently recounted to the board that a German official had told him that government jobs in the field of indemnification were the most unpopular in the German civil service. 'If we are generous, the [Finance] Minister will blame us, and if we are ungenerous the Jews will blame us,' the official told Goldmann.

99 *Activities of the Claims Conference 1952–1957.*

100 Claims Conference Board meeting, 19 January 1957, New York.

101 Conference Study Mission, 'Summary of report on trip to German indemnification offices,' 7 October–7 November 1957, CAHJP 14154

102 Claims Conference memo, meeting of minister-presidents of *Länder*, 26 June 1959, CAHJP 14007

103 Claims Conference Board meeting, 30–31 January 1960, Amsterdam, CAHJP 13630

104 Claims Conference memo, meeting of minister-presidents of *Länder*, 26 June 1959, CAHJP 14007

105 Claims Conference Executive Committee, 30 June 1959.

106 Claims Conference Board meeting, 30–31 January 1960, Amsterdam, CAHJP 13630

107 There also were other measures that complemented the indemnification law and that applied to specific groups. This included a system of pensions, which had been set up under the Luxembourg Agreements, for former officials of dissolved Jewish communities and organizations. The Conference established a committee of experts to screen applicants and make pension recommendations to the German authorities. In addition, on the basis of Cabinet decisions, payments were provided to some victims of Nazi medical experiments.

108 Social insurance benefits are governed according to the bilateral agreements and the conditions and social insurance requirements that prevail in different countries. In addition to negotiations with the German authorities, the Conference was involved in talks dealing with West Germany's bilateral agreements with the United States and Israel to establish the right of reciprocity under the social insurance systems, so that residents and citizens of another country could obtain social insurance payments from Germany.

109 Claims Conference Board meeting, 6 July 1990, Jerusalem.

110 Katzenstein report to Claims Conference Board, 1983.

111 Katzenstein letter to Kagan, 7 June 1981.

112 Ibid. Katzenstein also dismissed Chancellor Helmut Schmidt's 17 May 1974 declaration that the federal government considered indemnification legislation closed. The declaration, he said, 'has nothing to do with, and does not affect, the governmental obligation to see the indemnification programme through as envisaged in Hague Protocol I and enacted in the German indemnification laws until 14 September 1965.'

113 Katzenstein letter to Kagan, 22 February 1980.

114 Katzenstein letter to Kagan, 7 June 1981.

115 See Chapter 3 on the Claims Conference Hardship Fund.

116 Jewish Telegraphic Agency, 5 June 1988.

117 Restitution traditionally refers to the restoration of a material asset to the individual, institution or community from which it was seized. In this instance, however, restitution also refers to compensation for assets, as distinguished from the German indemnification programmemes, which entailed compensation for personal damages, such as deprivation of liberty.

118 See Chapter 6 on the Claims Conference as Successor Organization.

119 Charles I. Kapralik, *Reclaiming the Nazi Loot: The History of the Work of the Jewish Trust Corporation for Germany*, London: The Corporation 1962–1971.

120 Its full name is *Bundesgesetz zur Regelung der rüückerstattungsrechtlichen Geldverbindlichkeiten des Deutschen Reichs und gleichgestellter Rechtsträäger*, or in short form, *Bundesrüückerstattungsgesetz*.

121 Claims Conference, *Twenty Years Later*.

122 The number of claims for Jewish victims cannot be ascertained because the data on these property claims does not distinguish between Jews and ethnic Germans. At the time of the payments, it was not anticipated that Germany would be reunified and that claimants who had properties in East Germany would, decades later, have the opportunity to recover them. Under the post-unification property law, which applied to properties in the former East Germany, claimants who received a monetary settlement under Protocol I for properties were obliged to return the post-war *Lastenausgleich* payment to the government when they recovered property.

123 Ferencz report to Claims Conference Board, 5–6 February 1955, Paris. The Western Allies initially had agreed to limit the total amount to be paid under this law to DM 1.5 billion, in consideration, in part, for other financial burdens West Germany was expected to assume, such as its military contribution to the NATO. See Constantin Goschler, 'German Compensation to Jewish Nazi Victims after 1945,' Jeffrey Diefendorf (ed.), *Lessons and Legacies VI: New Currents in Holocaust Research*, Evanston, IL, Northwestern University Press, 2004.

124 Claims Conference, *Twenty Years Later*.

125 Robinson report to Claims Conference Board, 20 March 1954.

126 Claims Conference, *Twenty Years Later*.

127 The BRüG hardship fund is distinct from the 1980 Claims Conference Hardship Fund. But the BRüG fund established an important principle in compensation: that a 'hardship fund' was an acceptable alternative to extending filing deadlines for statutory compensation programmes. This was the case in the 1980 fund, which was an alternative, and extremely limited, substitute compensation programme for Nazi victims who had been unable to file timely claims for the BEG.

128 The BRüG regulations set payments for household goods at DM 8,000 per claimant, and at DM 2,000 for gold and jewelry. The losses and liability reflected different historical circumstances. For instance, French Jews lost household contents when German authorities in Occupied France were instructed to empty Jewish flats to provide furniture for Germans whose property had been lost when the Allies bombed Germany.

129 Easterman letter to Lord Henderson.

130 German Foreign Ministry, 'State payments made by the Federal Republic of Germany in the area of indemnification.'

131 Annual statistical report from German Ministry of Finance, 2002.

132 Kagan interview, 4 January 2001.

Chapter 3

From Legal Right to Humanitarian Aid: The Claims Conference Hardship Fund

Twenty years after the Shoah, turmoil again struck the Jews in Central and Eastern Europe. After 1965, Jews began to emigrate from Romania. They were ejected from Poland in anti-Semitic purges and were leaving Czechoslovakia after the crackdown following the Prague Spring in 1968. In the 1970s, with the early thaw of détente, Jews began to bolt from the Soviet Union. Among them were tens of thousands of survivors of Auschwitz, Babi Yar and other Nazi atrocities.

Under its indemnification legislation – the *Bundesentschädigungsgesetze* (BEG) – the Federal Republic of Germany paid compensation to individual Nazi victims. However, it was limited to former German citizens, refugees and stateless persons in the West. Survivors living in the Soviet bloc were not eligible. But once these Nazi victims migrated to the West, they could qualify as refugees. 'That opened the whole issue of compensation for Holocaust survivors from an area that was more brutally exposed to Nazi persecution than any other part of Europe,' said Kagan.[1] However, when these victims arrived in the West, they were still excluded from the German compensation programs because the deadline of the 1965 Final BEG had passed.[2]

The Conference appealed repeatedly to Bonn to reopen the filing period, arguing that the BEG should be available for this 'post-1965' group. It contended that compensation for this group was simply an extension of the principle the German authorities had already accepted. It also argued that the Eastern European survivors' failure to file timely claims was not due to their negligence, and that these Nazi victims should not be forsaken because they had faced the extraordinary obstacle of having been trapped behind the Iron Curtain. 'We asked for the reopening of the filing deadline – not for everyone, only for the group that was excluded by force majeure, and we lost,' Kagan said. The West German government and all major political parties were adamant in their refusal. 'They were not ready to reopen the indemnification law. That was made absolutely clear to us, by the government and the opposition.'[3]

The emigration from the East exposed the extreme disparities in the German benefits for different groups of survivors. The Conference had succeeded in ensuring that the German indemnification law provided pensions for Jews who fled from Germany, but not in gaining compensation for Jews from the Soviet bloc who had endured brutal incarceration and imminent death. 'A German Jew who left Frankfurt in 1934, and had to abandon his property and his practice and his profession and his business and his education, suffered a great deal,' said Kagan. 'But I would say that someone who survived Babi Yar suffered more'.[4]

The Conference did not relent in seeking compensation. The idea of a 'hardship fund' began to emerge in 1969 as a limited substitute for indemnification legislation for the so-called 'post-1965' group when a Finance Ministry official, Ernst Feaux de la Croix, suggested that West Germany enter an agreement for a 'global' payment to the Claims Conference for the post-1965 refugees. It would be feasible, he said, only if it were financed from existing indemnification programmes and if the German government were not obliged to administer the fund.[5]

This was a political, as well as a financial, matter. After Chancellor Willy Brandt's 1970 visit to Warsaw and the initiation of his *Ostpolitik* policy, for instance, Yugoslavia approached the German government with an indemnification claim for DM 2 billion, and West Germany feared other compensation claims from the East.[6] The Conference argued that the claims of the post-1965 refugees were distinct from the reparations claims of Eastern European governments, and that 'the cost of aiding the Jewish victims is but a tiny fraction of those envisioned for the others,' Goldmann said.[7] Bonn, in effect, was seeking a mechanism that would permit payments to one group of Nazi victims but not open the floodgates to claims from other victims in Eastern Europe.

Over the years, the Conference's demands were buffeted by the changing German diplomatic and financial conditions. Originally, the Conference demanded DM 1 billion for the 'post-1965' group.[8] When Helmut Schmidt became chancellor in 1974, he told the Bundestag that the federal government considered indemnification legislation closed. But he was willing to make a final payment, of DM 600 million, for Nazi victims, of which 90 per cent would be for Jews. However, the German government refused to administer or distribute the fund; and, the chancellor said, the Conference and the Israeli government would have to formally renounce any further legislative demands.[9]

Although the sum was lower than the Conference considered necessary, Goldmann had urged the Conference to accept it. The amount was 'twice as much as the Claims Conference received as a result of The Hague Agreements over a period of 12 years,' Goldmann said. And, in light of the deteriorating budgetary conditions in Germany, he said, 'I see no realistic possibilities to obtain a larger amount.'[10] But that plan came to naught.

It was not until July 1980 that the Conference reached an agreement with West Germany for the Hardship Fund, or *Härteausgleich*. By then, the amount had shrunk. The FRG would provide up to DM 400 million for the 'amelioration of hardships in individual cases'. Of the DM 400 million, five per cent was set aside for the Conference to distribute to institutional programmes that provided services to survivors. In addition to the DM 400 million, funds were allocated for the *Zentralrat der Juden in Deutschland* (Central Council of Jews in Germany).

The differences between the two forms of compensation were substantial. The Hardship Fund, unlike the original German indemnification law, did not establish the legal right to compensation. Instead, it was a humanitarian gesture to needy Nazi victims without any German recognition of a legal obligation. Unlike the German indemnification programmes, under which scores of thousands of survivors received lifelong monthly payments known as 'pensions', the Hardship Fund provided one-time payments of DM 5,000. Cost-of-living adjustments protected victims' pensions against erosion, and pension funding was open-ended; the government paid compensation to those who had met the eligibility criteria and had filed their claims before the deadline. The Hardship Fund originally was capped. The West German government agreed to commit up to DM 400 million, which was based on the Conference's estimate that some 80,000 Jews would qualify for a one-time payment.[11]

The fund was a bitter compromise for the Conference. It was burdened with restrictions and conditions. The Conference accepted the terms on the eve of German elections, in part due to the Conference negotiators' fear that any delay would jeopardize the fund, and that negotiations would have to begin anew after elections – when they might fail. By that time, Bonn had resisted new commitments when, facing financial pressures, it was cutting popular domestic programmes, including subsidized housing. The FRG already had paid more than DM 60 billion under the indemnification legislation,[12] and the government was under pressure to widen its compensation programme by making payments to non-Jewish Nazi victims who had been excluded from the BEG.

In the meantime, a Bundestag resolution had drawn attention to another group of potential domestic German claimants: war victims. This group included Nazi-era functionaries and members of the elite SS guard as well as ethnic Germans who had been expelled after the Second World War from regions outside Germany. On 14 December 1979, the Bundestag passed a resolution calling for a commitment of DM 440 million to the Conference and *Zentralrat* for the Hardship Fund as a 'final indemnification gesture.'[13] It also passed a resolution asking for a 'report' on the hardship situation of the German war victims. Schmidt was said to want 'to avoid coupling of the fate of victims and their oppressors'.[14] But although that resolution did not request funds to alleviate the hardship of Germans, it implied a linkage between the two.[15] These political and financial factors convinced the Conference that this was the last moment to make a deal. 'Germany is in a much worse position today than before,' Goldmann later reported to the board. 'If we wouldn't have gotten this [last year], we wouldn't have gotten it. Today it would be impossible to get.'[16]

The Hardship Fund had been a decade in the making. Negotiations for the original German indemnification programme took two years, from Adenauer's declaration in September 1951, until West Germany enacted its initial compensation legislation, which became effective in October 1953. By contrast, the Hardship Fund took seven years to arrange. 'In all the 30 years of negotiations, this lousy [DM] 440 million is the most difficult one,' Goldmann complained soon after the agreement was reached. 'If I were to have the slightest inkling that it would take so long, I would never have suggested it.'[17]

Not only had the Hardship Fund changed the nature of compensation from a legal right to a humanitarian gesture, it also confronted the Conference with a condition that changed its fundamental nature, structure and relationship to victims. West Germany refused to shoulder any new administrative compensation task. When it agreed to operate the fund, the Conference was transformed from primarily an advocacy and monitoring organization into an operating agency that handled tens of thousands of individual claims.

In its first decade, dating back to Protocol II of the Luxembourg Agreements, the Conference allocated DM 450 million to Jewish communities and to communal, commemorative and cultural programmes.[18] With the exception of specialized, modest programmes that aided surviving leaders of the former Nazi-occupied Jewish communities, *Hassidei Umot Haolam* (the 'righteous Gentiles'), and limited programmes, financed by a handful of German companies, to provide compensation for slave labour, the Conference did not deal with individual Holocaust-related claims.[19] Yet, years before the fund was established, the Conference had pronounced itself ready to assume the task. 'The administration of even a limited hardship fund is entangled with difficulties. But if the choice reads: accept responsibility or renounce the fund, the outcome is a foregone conclusion,' it said. 'The Conference cannot in good conscience reject the administration of an aid program for the benefit of Nazi victims.'[20]

By accepting the terms of the Hardship Fund, the Conference would examine applications, determine the victims' eligibility, reject or approve claims, and distribute German funds to individuals. Having achieved the fund, however, the Conference's veteran negotiators were distressed by its limits. 'I could not bear that on the stationery of the Conference on Jewish Material Claims Against Germany, we would have to tell thousands of survivors, the answer is no,' Kagan said.[21]

Kaztenstein complained that the fund was 'alms for the poorest and the most miserable ones'. He also argued that the Conference 'is not to receive orders from the German Government nor is it the agent of the German Finance Ministry; it is now being expected to administer, more like a social worker, a fund for sick and invalid Nazi victims in distress'.[22]

'Never before has the Claims Conference taken on a function that is essentially German as hardly any other one, namely to mete out payments related to damage caused by Nazi persecution,' he wrote. To administer harsh German rules 'is a painful assignment for a Jewish organization called into being to protect the interests of Jewish persecutees all over the world. And, as expected and feared, it is just these thousands of unsuccessful and disappointed Jewish indemnification claimants, now in special need, who pin their last hope to the moderate grants the conference has no alternative but to deny.'[23]

A German-born Jewish lawyer who fled the Nazis, Katzenstein was painfully and personally aware of the profound disparity in benefits for the 'post-1965' group. 'All I had suffered when the Nazis came to power was the ousting from the German Bar on May 1, 1933, whereupon I emigrated to Palestine. That was all the persecution I personally suffered, and for this I draw a BEG annuity for damage to profession, which now amounts to DM 2,200 – per month,' Katzenstein wrote after a 1983 visit with some Eastern European survivors living in Israel. They had been in concentration camps, or were driven underground, or had lived under the shadow of the threat of violent death. Each one, he wrote, 'was totally excluded from any BEG benefits, needy and in poor health as result of the persecution suffered, and all he could hope for was a one-time *ex gratia* payment of DM 5,000.'[24]

The fund was not discretionary. The Conference and the West German government negotiated the criteria for the programme. But this was negotiation in name only; the terms were restricted in eligibility, which the Conference had little leverage to improve. 'They established priorities and criteria and requirements of proof of evidence to which we are bound,' said Kagan.[25] Goldmann originally had refused to accept any guidelines for the Hardship Fund. The notion was insulting. 'My argument was that 30 years ago I signed an exchange of letters on behalf of the Claims Conference with Adenauer. He gave us [DM] 450 million ... He never had guidelines,' Goldmann told the board. 'Why did I accept some of the guidelines? Because it was the same thing we would have done anyhow.' More important, he said: 'I didn't want to end with a conflict with the finance minister, even if the chancellor would have overruled him. He is the master of when to give the money ... He can veto every law which involves expenses.'[26]

However, over time the Conference succeeded in liberalizing the criteria, their interpretation and practical applications. The initial German guidelines called for the applicants to have suffered considerable damage to health due to persecution, to be in special need, and to have survived at least 24 months in a concentration camp. 'It took me two years to bring it down from two to one year in a concentration camp,' Kagan said. The Conference also was able to negotiate new terms under which if an applicant had endured a year in a concentration camp, he automatically was presumed to have sustained damage to his health.[27]

There were substantial gaps in benefits in the original indemnification programme, and a paramount issue for the Conference was whether the new fund would have the same limits or if it would cover acts of Nazi persecution that had not been recognized under the BEG. The Conference also wanted to ensure that Nazi victims did not get trapped in the 'Catch-22' that had harmed the rights of some survivors to BEG benefits. There were instances in which survivors were retroactively made eligible for the BEG, but then were denied those benefits because they had missed the deadline.[28] As the Hardship Fund's initial administrative deadline of 31 December 1982 approached, the Conference advised Nazi victims to file claims, even if they were from groups or regions that were not covered by the eligibility criteria for the fund. 'We will be flooded with a lot of registrations which we may have to reject at a later time, but I consider it unavoidable and preferable to have to deny consideration of requests [later] due to the failure of an individual to register with our fund,' Kagan said.[29]

One significant gap in the criteria concerned the so-called 'flight cases.' For those who were incarcerated, the German indemnification law provided compensation for deprivation of liberty and for damage to health that stemmed from persecution. There was no compensation for the flight cases, the 'fugitives' who fled from Soviet-held territory into the interior of the Soviet Union in advance of the approaching Nazi troops, and escaped persecution in the territories that the Nazis later occupied, such as Kiev. The *Einsatzgruppen* mass-slaughtered 33,171 Jews there in September 1941. 'God forbid, if we stayed here, we would be in Babi Yar,' said Bronislava Rozenblum, who, during the Second World War was a municipal health department employee who rescued orphans from Kiev. As far as the Conference was concerned, these fugitives were victims of Nazi persecution. 'They were running for their lives. They were running from the certainty of being murdered,' Kagan said.[30] Although the flight cases originally were excluded from the Hardship Fund, the Conference ultimately was able to establish the principle that they should be eligible for compensation.

Almost a decade after the fall of the Iron Curtain, the German government voided its traditional criteria of territoriality. In 1998, Germany and the Conference reached an agreement for on-going compensation for Jewish Nazi victims who had been incarcerated or were in hiding during the Second World War and who were still residing in Eastern Europe. From the moment territoriality was no longer a factor, Karl Brozik, who succeeded Katzenstein as the Conference's representative in Germany, began to press for an extension of the Hardship Fund to fugitives in the East who were not eligible for on-going payments. 'Those who suffered persecution and now live in Warsaw, Kiev or Riga have received nothing,' he said. These victims had lost their families and property 'and when they eventually returned home they were treated like unwelcome guests or suffered further persecution under nationalists and Stalinists. In addition to all these strokes of fate was the fact that nobody was prepared to help this group of victims, not even with a one-time compensation payment,' Brozik said. 'After the war they continued to be dogged by fate and they were not given the chance to be integrated into society – in their case, Soviet society – that those living in the West had.' If the Hardship Fund was available for flight cases in the West, Brozik contended, by that same principle, the fund should be available in the East. The original residency requirement was irrelevant after the collapse of communism. 'This is a complete anachronism and must be rectified,' he said.[31]

However, as of 2002, the German government had not agreed to provide hardship payments for the flight cases in the East. 'For a long time I have been bothered by the unfairness of the compensation system where residence determines who is eligible for payment. The injustice began when the compensation law was passed and excluded all victims living on the other side of the Iron Curtain for political reasons,' Brozik said. 'The injustice still reigns today.'[32]

One of the original conditions of the Hardship Fund called for the moneys to channeled through a German entity, a stipulation that later exposed the fund to a multi-million-mark financial scandal.

While Goldmann was negotiating with West German officials for the Hardship Fund, the chairman of the *Zentralrat*, Werner Nachmann, also was negotiating with government officials. In addition to seeking compensation for Nazi victims, Nachmann insisted 'that the *Zentralrat* must assume a leading role in any arrangements concerning the creation of the proposed fund, and that a sum of money be made available directly to the *Zentralrat* over and above the funds intended for payments to individual claimants.' When the then Finance Minister Hans Matthoefer at the end of 1979 proposed the commitment of DM 440 million, of which DM 40 million would be earmarked for the *Zentralrat*, he also proposed that the funds be channeled via the *Zentralrat* as an 'entity under German public law.'[33] Goldmann agreed because Foreign Minister Hans-Dietrich Genscher 'would prefer payment of the DM 400 [million] to the German Jews rather than to the Claims Conference in order not to antagonize the Arabs.'[34]

Under the initial terms of the Hardship Fund, the West German government transmitted the funds to the *Zentralrat*, which held them in trust for the Conference. The Conference, in turn, advised the *Zentralrat* of the number and amount of the approved claims, and distributed one-time payments of DM 5,000 to victims who met the criteria.[35] That system worked. At the time of Nachmann's death in January 1988, the Conference had received from the *Zentralrat* some DM 387 million of the DM 400 million that had been committed by the German government.[36]

Nachmann, whose family had fled from Germany to France in 1938, was a Karlsruhe businessman who led the *Zentralrat* since 1965. He was an esteemed public and communal figure. When he died of a heart attack at the age of 62, the German political elite turned out for his funeral and, in a nation-wide televised broadcast, praised his achievements.[37] Four months after Nachmann's death, his one-time adversary and successor at the *Zentralrat*, Heinz Galinski, announced that German government funds entrusted to the *Zentralrat* for hardship payments had been mishandled, and that millions of marks in interest income were missing. 'We have all been deceived, lied to, and cheated,' said Galinski.[38]

The total amount of interest misappropriated by Nachmann amounted to DM 29.7 million, according to a joint communiqué by

Federal Interior Minister Dr Wolfgang Schäuble and Galinski on the investigation of the 'Nachmann Affair'. The communiqué, issued on 14 December 1989, stated that the misappropriated funds had been shifted into Nachmann's tottering enterprises. The prosecutor was unable to determine that Nachmann had accomplices, and the efforts to trace the funds were unsuccessful. No charges or suspicion of financial wrongdoing were leveled against the Conference, which argued that the work of the Hardship Fund must proceed without interruption. The Nachmann Affair was 'not the Claims Conference scandal; it is not even the Claims Conference problem,' said Ferencz. 'Everything the Claims Conference requested, it received. Everything it received, it has fully accounted for.'[39]

The Conference also noted that the German government had selected the *Zentralrat* as the conduit for funds, and that the Finance Ministry had failed to demand reports on its status. The *Zentralrat* agreed to withdraw as the intermediary, and the Finance Ministry agreed that funds would be sent directly to the Conference.[40] 'The embezzlement is based on the one side on Nachmann's criminal actions and on the other on a lack of oversight,' said the final report released by Schäuble and Galinski.[41] It concluded by saying that 'the work of the Claims Conference to assist the surviving victims of Nazi persecution should continue.'[42]

Goldmann had directed Kagan to create the Hardship Fund operations, using the machinery and procedures the Conference had developed earlier to distribute slave labour payments from German companies.[43] Kagan established regional offices in Tel Aviv, New York and Frankfurt. But administrative problems plagued the Hardship Fund because it had dramatically exceeded all expectations. The fund was established in anticipation of making payments to 80,000 Holocaust survivors – an estimate based on the prevailing political conditions at the time governing emigration from the Soviet Union. Within three years, however, 120,000 people had applied, close to 70,000 from Israel, alone.[44] From the outset, there were serious lags, of several years, between the time survivors applied to the fund and when they received the payments. The German government covered the administrative expenses of the fund, but these were inadequate to accelerate the claims processing. The Conference also feared that the DM 400 million allocated by the FRG would run out and that the Conference would be unable to cover all the eligible claimants. By 1989, the money that had been allocated by West Germany for the Hardship Fund was exhausted, and the Conference had to negotiate with Bonn to replenish the funds.[45] Then the collapse of communism led to the unprecedented emigration of

Jews – including victims of Nazi persecution – from the former Soviet Union, and the number of applicants soared. The Conference demanded assurances from the FRG that there would be no deadline on the Hardship Fund; it had to be open-ended to ensure that the payment would be available to Nazi victims whenever they emigrated from Eastern Europe. 'People will continue to come out. Among them are many Holocaust survivors,' Kagan said. 'Someone should not be shut out [of the Hardship Fund] in the beginning of 1993 because the gate was locked in 1992.'[46]

Because the fund was conceived to be a hardship fund, the immediate priority was payment to older claimants, who were defined, in agreement with the German authorities, as women who were 60 and older, and men 65 and older, as well as claimants who were incapacitated, regardless of age. Because the Conference had succeeded in gaining a number of presumptions in favour of these groups, the documentary requirements were relatively simple, and the claims processing moved fairly quickly.[47] However, determining the eligibility of others did not proceed as quickly. Applicants had to establish the amount of time during which they were deprived of liberty. Younger claimants had to prove that, because of persecution, they had suffered a significant loss of earnings capacity. There also were special problems for victims who were children during the Nazi occupation, because they often were ignorant of and unable to document the circumstances of persecution.

And then there was the problem of geography. It was relatively simple to determine the eligibility of the victims who fled from Poland and Czechoslovakia, because these nations had been occupied by the Nazis. However, as a practical matter, the Hardship Fund was concerned primarily with Jews from the Soviet Union. The Conference had to determine who was a victim of Nazi persecution. 'Flight cases' could qualify depending on where they had been during the Nazi era, when they had been there, and the route over which they fled.

Under their non-aggression pact of August 1939, Germany and the Soviet Union divided Poland, which was marked with a demarcation line. The eastern part of the dismembered state came under Soviet sovereignty within a month. Germany invaded western Poland on 1 September 1939, leading to a wave of flight. Between 300,000 and 350,000 Jewish refugees crossed the demarcation line, fleeing east from the Germans. The next wave of Jewish refugees followed Hitler's attack on Russia on 21 June 1941. It was estimated that 180,000 Jews fled East, deeper into the Soviet Union, from Russian-occupied eastern Poland.[48]

In 1974, the *Bundesgerichtshof* ruled that crossing the demarcation line was a condition of eligibility for indemnification. Compensation was for refugees and stateless people; to be a 'refugee', one had to cross an international border. That meant that, in theory, the first wave of refugees could qualify for payments, but not the second. Katzenstein, in arguing for hardship payments for the 'Russian' flight cases, contended that the 1939 demarcation line was unnatural, and that it was equally unnatural to make a legal distinction between two categories of persecutees with the same or similar refugee fate: those who crossed the official border and those who did not.[49]

In reviewing applications for the Hardship Fund, the Conference did not use the official 1939 line, but rather looked at the path of the Nazi troops. According to a 1940 census, there were 3 million Jews in the former Soviet Union at the time. There were more than 1.5 million more Jews in Eastern Poland, southeastern Romania and the Baltic states who came under Soviet control. 'On that fateful day in June 1941, we estimate that somewhere over three and a half million Jews were suddenly exposed to the Nazi onslaught,' Kagan said. 'We all know what a thorough murderous job the *Einsatzgruppen* had done but, nonetheless, in such a mass, people survived, and among the people who are coming out today, in the older generation, there are a substantial number of Holocaust survivors.'[50]

To qualify for the Hardship Fund, the individual had to have been in the parts of the Soviet Union that were occupied by Germany after 21 June 1941. That included the Baltic states, Ukraine, Belarus, Moldova and Western Russia up to the gates of Leningrad (St Petersburg) and Moscow. A Jew who, for instance, was in Moscow, east of Leningrad, or in Samarkand was not a victim of Nazi persecution under the guidelines, and was excluded. 'We are not a policing agency, but we have to exert due diligence,' Kagan said.[51]

In addition to the Conference's Hardship Fund, West Germany had established smaller hardship funds for non-Jewish Nazi victims. Those funds, which were modeled on the Conference fund of one-time payments, had an important additional provision under which certain categories of victims who had experienced unusual hardship – such as extended periods of imprisonment in camps and forced labour – could receive supplemental recurring payments. Brozik in 1987 began lobbying the Bundestag, arguing that the same principle had to be applied to the Jewish victims. Brozik sought DM 150 million for modest on-going 'emergency' payments for an estimated 20,000 of the neediest victims. In 1989, the Finance Ministry was prepared to accede to it, and the Bundestag earmarked funds for the supplemental payments. However, while the Conference was negotiating for the programme's implementation, the two Germanies had begun reunification talks; the compensation plan was held in abeyance.[52]

The Conference negotiations with Germany after reunification led to additional compensation programmes that changed the focus of the Hardship Fund. Between 1980 and 1993, the one-time hardship payments were the only new source of German compensation for Holocaust survivors in the West, regardless of the Nazi persecution they had endured. The volume of applications for the fund in those years reflected the high numbers of Jews who emigrated from the former Soviet Union who would not have been eligible for the original German federal indemnification programme, such as the flight cases. However, among the applicants, there also were people who had survived concentration camps and ghettos and who would have qualified for the BEG had they been able to apply before the deadline.

After reunification, the Conference secured funding for pensions – the 'recurring hardship payments' that Brozik had sought – for Nazi victims who had survived concentration camps and ghettos,[53] while the Hardship Fund was reserved for Nazi victims who had not been confined in camps or ghettos or who had been living in hiding.

The Conference made more than 263,000 Hardship Fund payments to Jewish victims by the end of 2001.[54] 'Who would have imagined that the Germans would have raised this from DM 400 million to more than DM 1 billion,' said Haim Huller, the director of the Conference's office in Israel, where almost 60 per cent of the recipients live.[55] In 2000, the Hardship Fund still received more than 15,000 applications a year.[56] There was an enduring connection between *aliya* [immigration to Israel] and the number of applicants to the fund. Many of the immigrants from the former Soviet Union were from regions that had been occupied by the Nazis, over the age of 55, and could qualify for the fund. 'For people landing in Israel without a penny, to get the equivalent of 10,000 shekels, which is was about what DM 5,000 was, as modest as it can be by our standards, it meant something,' Kagan said.[57]

NOTES

1   Kagan interview, 22 December 2000.
2   See Chapter 2 on West German indemnification legislation.
3   Kagan interview, 12 January 2001.
4   Saul Kagan, 'Morality and Pragmatism: A Participant's Response,' Symposium on Shilumim in the 1950s, 15 March 1991, Deutsches Haus of Columbia University, New York.
5   Katzenstein letter to Kagan, 15 December 1969. The idea of shifting funds from one indemnification programme to finance another fund was soon abandoned.
6   Katzenstein letter to Goldmann, 1 April 1970.
7   Claims Conference Board meeting, 4 July 1972. Geneva. Walter Scheel, the foreign secretary of the Free Democratic Party (Liberals), told Goldmann in 1973 that the Eastern European governments, with the exception of Romania, would present the FRG with demands of 'astronomic figures' of more than DM 100 billion.

8   Katzenstein memo to Kagan, 10 September 1981.
9   Goldmann memo to Claims Conference board, 22 October 1974.
10 Ibid.
11 The 80,000 estimate was comprised 60,000 Russians and 20,000 Romanians, according to a memo from Katzenstein to Kagan, 10 September 1981. The German government subsequently agreed to replenish the fund as the number of eligible claimants increased.
12 Claims Conference Board meeting, 6 July 1982, Paris.
13 Goldmann memo to Claims Conference Board, 27 October 1980.
14 *New York Times*, 28 December 1979.
15 Katzenstein memo to Kagan, 14 January 1980. Katzenstein also reported that a Finance Ministry official said that the Nazi victims whose interests were safeguarded by the Conference were not German voters – unlike the war victims.
16 Claims Conference Board meeting, 8–9 July 1981, Geneva. Despite that pledge, however, this was not the last payment. New compensation programmes were established after German reunification.
17 Claims Conference Board meeting, 7 July 1980, Amsterdam.
18 See Chapter 9 on Claims Conference institutional allocations.
19 Even as the Conference made strenuous moral arguments that the 'post-1965' Eastern European victims were entitled to compensation, there were internal debates about the uses of a possible fund. Goldmann did not favour direct aid to individuals. 'In general, I regard it as much more important to use the greatest share possible for cultural purposes, rather than giving a thousand dollars more or less to individuals,' he said in a letter to Kagan, dated 22 February 1979. 'This would be significant both from the Jewish and the German point of view, as a permanent memorial for what they have done. I have not yet decided whether, in the agreement with the Germans, we should specify the proportion which it goes individuals and that to be allocated for cultural activities.'
20 Claims Conference, *Twenty Years Later*.
21 Kagan interview, 26 December 2000.
22 Katzenstein letter to Kagan, 26 July 1980.
23 Katzenstein draft report to 1981 Claims Conference Board meeting.
24 Katzenstein letter to Kagan, 10 March 1983.
25 Claims Conference Board meeting, 1 July 1986, Herzliya, Israel. On 14 October 1980, the German guidelines for the Hardship Fund were published in the official government gazette. The restraints on the Conference were noted by a US federal court in Illinois in a 1997 case in which a survivor who had been denied compensation subsequently brought action against Germany and the Conference. The Conference's role in administering the Hardship Fund is limited to 'reviewing whether applicants for such payments meet the clearly-defined qualifications set forth by Germany. The Claims Conference does not have, and has never had, any decision-making or discretionary authority with respect to benefits for claimants,' according to the ruling in *Sampson* v. *Federal Republic of Germany and the Conference of Jewish Material Claims Against Germany*, 975 F. Supp. 1108 (N.D. Ill. 1997).
26 Claims Conference Board meeting, 3 July 1980, Amsterdam. The Conference, in its earliest days, had adversarial experiences with the West German Finance Ministry under the leadership of Fritz Schäffer. See Chapter 2 on German indemnification legislation.
27 Kagan interview, 4 January 2001.
28 Katzenstein memo to Kagan, 'The DM 400 million Hardship Fund and the Polish/Russian flight cases of old pre-65 applicants,' 27 February 1985.
29 Kagan letter to Katzenstein, 26 August 1982. That position subsequently exposed the Claims Conference to considerable wrath from victims. Some survivors, who did not originally qualify, were not rejected outright. Instead, their applications were suspended in limbo. The Conference reasoned that it would continue to demand expansion of the eligibility criteria, and it did not want to be compelled to reject newly eligible claimants in the future on grounds that they previously had been rejected.
30 *Jerusalem Post*, 26 September 1997.
31 Brozik letter to Miller, 14 December 1998. See Chapter 5 on German post-reunification compensation programmes.
32 Brozik correspondence with author, 22 May 2002.
33 Kagan memo to Claims Conference Hardship Fund Review Committee, 14 May 1990.
34 Katzenstein letter to Kagan, 21 January 1980.

35 In a letter to Nachmann dated 17 September 1980, Matthoefer said the *Zentralrat* could release funds for hardship payments only to the extent that they were required for approved claims.

36 Kagan memo to Claims Conference Hardship Fund Review Committee, 14 May 1990. The 1980 German guidelines called for the *Zentralrat* to account annually to the German government for the use of the funds. Kagan, as the administrator of the Hardship Fund, each year sent Nachmann multiple copies of 'The Claims Conference Hardship Fund Statement of Cash Receipts and Disbursements and Other Financial Information.'

37 Claims Conference Board meeting, 14 July 1988, Tarrytown, NY.

38 *Los Angeles Times*, 17 May 1988.

39 Claims Conference Board meeting, 14 July 1988, Tarrytown, NY.

40 Kagan memo to Claims Conference Hardship Fund Review Committee, 14 May 1990.

41 *Los Angeles Times*, 14 December 1989.

42 Kagan memo to Claims Conference Hardship Fund Review Committee, 14 May 1990.

43 Goldmann memo to Claims Conference Board, 27 October 1980. All offices had uniform procedures; the Conference resisted an Israeli recommendation calling for different procedures to govern the Tel Aviv operation. 'We would end up with three defective funds, which could only be a source of confusion, if not chaos,' Kagan said in a letter to Katzenstein on 6 December 1982.

44 Claims Conference Board meeting, 27 July 1984, Jerusalem.

45 Claims Conference Board meeting, 28–29 May 1992, Madrid.

46 Claims Conference Board meeting, 6 July 1990, Jerusalem.

47 Claims Conference Board meeting, 6 July 1982, Paris.

48 Katzenstein memo to Kagan, 'The DM 400 million Hardship Fund and the Polish/Russian flight cases of old pre-65 applicants', 27 February 1985.

49 Ibid.

50 Claims Conference Board meeting, 28–29 May 1992, Madrid.

51 Claims Conference Board meeting, 8–9 July 1981, Geneva.

52 Brozik interview, 29 April 2002.

53 These payments are via the Article II and the Central and Eastern Europe Funds. See Chapter 5.

54 Claims Conference, *Annual Report 2001*.

55 Interview, 30 April 2002.

56 Claims Conference Board meeting, 17–18 July 2001, Washington. Because the Hardship Fund was primarily for immigrants from the former Soviet Union and because so many had received one-time payments, it developed a flawed reputation among immigrants as something of an entitlement. Many routinely applied for the fund shortly after they arrived in Israel. A lawsuit was filed in March 2002 in the District Court of Tel Aviv against the Claims Conference on behalf of 1,900 people who were rejected by the fund. Many were under the age at which certain presumptions about disability would have applied. Huller recalled that when he suggested that immigrants defer their applications, he was told: 'You want us to wait five years till we die.' Unable to prove persecution-related disability, younger applicants were rejected. Once rejected, they could not reapply to the Hardship Fund at the later age when they would have received a presumption of disability. At the end of 2002, the suit was pending.

57 Kagan interview, 4 January 2001.

Chapter 4

From East Berlin to Bonn: Recovering Jewish Assets from the German Democratic Republic

From the moment East Germany was admitted to the United Nations in 1973, until the moment it dissolved in 1990, the Claims Conference sought compensation for Nazi-era losses from the German Democratic Republic (GDR). It failed. In retrospect, that failure was a blessing, said Miller, because the Conference had set its sights too low. 'Fortunately, they said no,' he said. 'We would have settled for $100 million.'[1]

But, for 17 years, from its first meeting in 1974 with the GDR's Antifascist Committee, to lunches in New York and Washington with the East German foreign minister, to a tête-à-tête with Communist Party leader Erich Honecker in East Berlin, the Conference doggedly pushed the GDR to accept moral responsibility and make restitution for its share of the damages caused by the Nazi régime. The GDR refused to discuss any measures to restore property or to compensate individuals outside of East Germany. But it appeared willing to consider a global payment to the Claims Conference – which the GDR linked to trade with the US.

Meeting with American and GDR officials, the Conference discussed the prospect of trading East German goods on the American market – just enough to raise the cash to cover Nazi-era claims. At the same time, it warned East Germany that compensation to Jewish victims of Nazi persecution was a moral issue that should not be viewed as a business transaction.

Following *perestroika*, Honecker had sought recognition for his régime and was seeking an invitation to the White House. Jewish claims were among the issues that might help his cause.[2] East Germany maintained that it was ready on 'humanitarian grounds' to aid Jewish victims of the Nazi régime. However, it steadfastly denied any obligation to meet Jewish claims. It insisted it had no moral obligations because its leadership had fought against and had been persecuted by the Nazis. Nor did the GDR recognize any legal obligations; East Berlin said those had been discharged under the Potsdam Agreement by paying reparations to Poland and the Soviet Union. The East German leadership saw its state as the product of a 'virgin birth', said Kagan. 'They said they are a de novo state; they have no responsibility for the past and, besides which, all the Nazis were in the West.'[3]

The breakthrough came in the spring of 1990. Only months after Honecker was ousted, then-Prime Minister Hans Modrow recognized 'the responsibility of the entire German people for the past.'[4] Two months later, the first freely elected representatives of the East German Parliament, the Volkskammer, held their first session and issued a dramatic declaration.

'We, the first freely elected Parliamentarians of the GDR, acknowledge the responsibility of the Germans in the GDR for their history and their future and unanimously declare before the international public: It was Germans who during the time of National Socialism inflicted immeasurable suffering on the people of the world. Nationalism and racist madness led to genocide, particularly among Jews from all European countries, among the peoples of the Soviet Union, the Polish people and the Sinti and Roma. This guilt must never be forgotten, and we want to perceive it as the source of our responsibility for the future. The first freely elected Parliament of the GDR accepts, on behalf of the citizens of this country, its share of the responsibility for the humiliation, expulsion and murder of Jewish women, men and children,' the Volkskammer said on 12 April 1990, in a declaration read by Speaker Sabine Bergmann Pohl during a televised session of Parliament.

'We feel sadness and shame as we acknowledge this burden of German history. We ask the Jews all over the world for their forgiveness. We ask the people of Israel to forgive us for the hypocrisy and hostility shown in official East German policy toward the State of Israel and to forgive the persecution and degradation of Jewish compatriots in our country also after 1945,' the statement said. 'We declare that we will do everything we can to help heal the mental and physical wounds of the survivors and to bring about just compensation for material losses.'[5] The vast majority of the 400 deputies in the Volkskammer voted to support the statement, and then the entire House stood in silence. The declaration was welcomed by the Claims Conference. 'Its language could probably not have been written better by ourselves,' Kagan said.[6]

However savory after so many years, the sentiment was short-lived. The newly democratic East Germany quickly began to crumble, its absorption into West Germany advanced at a break-neck speed, and the Conference scrambled to ensure that the rights of Nazi victims would not be swept aside in the rush toward German reunification.

Within four weeks of the Volkskammer declaration, Kagan and Brozik were in East Berlin, attempting to start negotiations with the fledgling democratic government under the new prime minister, Lothar de Maiziere. On 29 June 1990, the first negotiations, lasting two days, were held on a similar, but reduced, scale as those that had been held in The Hague nearly 40 years earlier with West Germany. In the initial meeting, Kagan and Brozik told the East German representatives what legislative measures the Conference expected the state to enact to assume its share of the obligations for compensation and restitution for Jewish victims. 'No one was qualified to tell us what was going on, but they were very friendly,' Brozik said.[7] The two sides agreed to meet again within five weeks.

'We attempted for five weeks to set a date. But it became clear that the GDR, the new GDR, was administratively disintegrating,' according to Kagan. 'Furthermore, we were dealing with a Social Democratic foreign minister and a CDU prime minister who had their own political problems to fight out.'[8]

The unification of Germany – originally scheduled for December 1990 – was accelerated to the fall. Brozik simultaneously lobbied the two German governments and Parliamentary bodies in East and West Germany. 'I lived in Bonn more than Berlin,' he said.[9] Meanwhile, Miller sent letters to the leaders of the FRG and the GDR, calling on them to ensure that the reunification treaty would safeguard the minimum rights of the Jewish victims. He specifically sought to have two provisions included in the treaty. The first would extend the FRG's principles on property restitution throughout united Germany. The second would assure 'adequate compensation' for Holocaust survivors who had received little or no compensation, as well as for those who needed institutional support.[10]

Miller and Kagan also pressed the State Department to ensure that a unified Germany would retain and extend West Germany's commitment to restitution and indemnification for Nazi victims. The failure of Germany at the moment of reunification to adequately deal with its historic responsibility would be 'morally reprehensible', and would violate the declarations and obligations proclaimed by the two Germanies, Miller warned the State Department. He reminded the US of the commitments it had undertaken 50 years earlier, in which sovereignty to the new West German state was conditioned on a pledge to honour certain obligations to Nazi victims – which had been initiated by the Allies. 'It is inconceivable to me that the Allied governments would now say that the same obligations need not apply to the whole of a reunited Germany. Surely if confiscated Jewish property in Frankfurt-on-Main must be restituted, the same should apply to property located in Frankfurt-on-Oder,' Miller said. 'Surely, if the West German state was not allowed to be enriched by the stolen property of murdered Jews, neither can the East Germans retain any benefit from heirless Jewish property. Surely, if for 40 years the Eastern part of Germany failed to pay compensation, a united Germany cannot now ignore this continuing obligation to Nazi victims.' He called on the Allies to make clear to East and West Germany that these provisions remained valid legal obligations that must be reconfirmed before sovereignty could be restored to the reunified German state. 'We urge you to take all necessary steps to avert what would otherwise be a historical calamity unworthy of past efforts to heal some of the wounds inflicted by the Third Reich. The three Allied powers should refuse to sign any treaty for reunited Germany until this gross inequity has been corrected.'[11]

However, there was no firm legal commitment enshrined in the Treaty on the Final Settlement with Respect to Germany, which was signed in Moscow on September 12. It was known as the '2+4' agreement – referring to the two Germanies and the four Allied powers: the US, Britain, France and the Soviet Union.[12] 'Despite our efforts and those of others, the unification agreement fails to make any written reference to the Holocaust and the obligations of a united Germany toward the victims of Nazi persecution,' Miller advised the Conference the day after the treaty was signed.[13] This was an unpardonable omission, the Conference charged. It had an unfinished agenda with East Germany – and by extension, with unified Germany. Tens of thousands of Jewish Nazi victims had not received compensation, or had obtained only one-time payments from West Germany. East Germany, which for 40 years had failed to aid Nazi victims outside its territory, had not assumed its share of responsibility to help eliminate the shortcomings and inequities in the indemnification measures.[14]

At the 2+4 signing ceremony in Moscow, German Foreign Minister Hans-Dietrich Genscher injected a solemn note in what he characterized as 'a day of joy and jubilation'. 'In this hour, we remember the victims of war and totalitarian domination,' Genscher said. 'We are particularly thinking about the Jewish people. We would not want their agony to ever be repeated.'[15]

The Jewish claims, however, had attracted Germany's attention – at the behest of the US government. A week before the treaty was signed, Secretary of State James Baker sent the first of two letters to Genscher, seeking the German minister's 'clarification' of several bilateral issues. These would be 'of particular importance as the administration consults key Congressional leaders' on the unification treaty, Baker wrote. They concerned the property claims of US nationals against the GDR; Jewish claims; aviation rights; preserving the legal validity of actions taken during the Occupation, and Allied immunity; and property for the US military and diplomatic presence.

Baker asked Genscher for an 'appropriate commitment' to resolve US nationals' property claims against the GDR, which then were valued at $300 million. 'A related question involves Jewish claims. We have discussed this issue, and I know you fully appreciate the emotion and concern attached to the issue of claims against the GDR for victims of the Holocaust. The de Maiziere government has responded with sympathy and an acknowledgement of these claims. We support the negotiation of a fair settlement to these claims and feel an obligation to do everything necessary to ensure resolution of the Jewish claims,' Baker wrote.[16] Genscher 'did not want to put a specific provision in the unification agreement but did commit to take care of the issue, and he and Helmut Kohl were good to their word,' Baker said in an interview.[17]

The German commitment was contained in a letter from Genscher to Baker that accompanied the 2+4 agreement. In his letter of 18 September 1990 – which was addressed to '*Lieber* Jim' – Genscher said that united Germany accepted responsibility for the resolution of claims against the GDR, both those of American citizens and of Jewish Nazi victims. Genscher's letter committed his government to 'seek, shortly after unification, to provide expeditious and satisfactory resolution of claims of Jewish victims of the Nazi régime against the German Democratic Republic.'[18] Chancellor Helmut Kohl also made a pledge to Miller. 'I would like to assure you that there is no doubt that the federal government policy relating to indemnification will continue to apply after the German Democratic Republic's ascension to the Federal Republic of Germany on 3 October 1990,' Kohl said in his letter.[19]

When it became a sovereign state in 1949, the Federal Republic of Germany claimed to be the only free government authorized to act for all German people. However, in its negotiations with Israel and the Claims Conference, West Germany did not take responsibility for all of the former Germany's obligations. Instead, as the territory of West Germany covered only two-thirds of the former Third Reich, Bonn was liable for two-thirds of the debts, according to the unwritten understanding behind Protocol II of the Luxembourg Agreements. East Germany had an imputed obligation. It was clearly anticipated – but not part of the official record – that the remaining one-third would, at some unknown time, be assumed by the GDR.[20]

However, Goldmann had convinced Adenauer to makes payments to Nazi victims from East Germany for injuries and damages from persecution. This proved to be a double-edged sword. 'We have therefore lost our main ground for asking East Germany for individual reparations. Only [West Germany] could ask for its contribution to be repaid, but that is its own business,' Goldmann wrote. 'Of course, there is the question of communal assets nationalized by the GDR, but it must be admitted that the returns are paid to the Jewish community. This has 3,000 members and a satisfactory budget, which explains why I have never been very active about East Germany.'[21]

When the Conference initially undertook negotiations with the GDR, it sought $100 million. That amount was a rough estimate of the then-current value of the GDR's one-third 'share' of the collective payment under Protocol II.[22] However, the GDR rejected all claims that were based on Nazi crimes. 'The fact that the GDR had taken over part of the territory and assets of the former Reich, together with all Jewish property in the area, did not give rise, in their view, to either a legal or moral obligation,' said Ferencz. 'The GDR had chosen to consider itself the victim rather than a part of Germany, and felt that it could wash away the stain of the Nazi past by removing itself from German history.'[23] But, he said, 'The obligation cannot be discharged by simply taking off a brown shirt and putting on a red one.'[24]

The Iron Curtain and the absence of diplomatic relations with East Germany had made it impossible to pressure or persuade the GDR to provide compensation for Jewish Nazi victims who had left East Germany. However, the political circumstances changed in 1972. The two Germanies signed an agreement that, in effect, recognized the partition of Germany. That subsequently led to diplomatic recognition of East Germany by the West and to the admission of the two Germanies into the United Nations. And that, in turn, created the opportunity to press the GDR to pay its share of the amount due to the survivors of Nazi persecution.

Miller then was a delegate to the Conference representing the American Zionist Federation, a member organization. At the time, he also was the chairman of the Conference of Presidents of Major American Jewish Organizations, an umbrella organization representing American Jewish organizations in their collective dealings with the governments of Israel and the United States. In that capacity, Miller was recognized as the leader of American Jewry and was a familiar figure at the State Department.

Miller told Henry Kissinger, the German-born American secretary of state, that it was immoral for the United States to recognize East Germany and to grant it an ambassador to Washington before Nazi-era claims had been resolved. 'He of all people should recognize that they never accepted any kind of responsibility,' Miller said.[25] Supported by some members of Congress, the Conference urged the State Department to withhold recognition until East Germany acknowledged its responsibility for Jewish claims.[26] Those claims, however, were not a primary American concern. The United States was focused on European defence and other Cold War conditions. East Germany was the leading Soviet satellite, with large numbers of Soviet troops stationed on its territory. It also was closely aligned with Arab nations and was a supporter of the Palestine Liberation Organization.[27] The State Department contended that it could exert political and economic pressure on East Germany only if the two nations had diplomatic relations. And the Conference was not alone in pressing for compensation. The US Foreign Claims Settlement Commission, after years of adjudication on thousands of claims, ultimately issued some 2,000 awards, with a face value of $78 million, plus interest, to American individuals and corporations whose assets in the GDR had been nationalized.[28]

Nevertheless, Kissinger instructed the American negotiators to ensure that East Germany would agree to discuss compensation for Nazi victims.[29] Previously the GDR denied it was a successor to Nazi Germany, rejected any obligation to pay, and extolled its anti-fascist character and its special support for the small Jewish community in East Germany. The Americans made clear that normal relations with the US depended on East Germany's agreement to discuss compensation for Nazi victims. Diplomatic relations with the US could produce grants and non-discriminatory tariffs – compelling East Germany into a policy shift. For the new US ambassador to East Germany, John Sherman Cooper, 'an important part of his job will be to persuade the communist régime for the first time to indemnify Jewish victims of the Hitler era, as West Germany long has done,' the *New York Times* said in an editorial.[30] However, the GDR had balked at the notion of a government negotiating with the Conference, a nongovernmental organization. Instead, it agreed that 'talks' would be held between the Conference and East Germany's Committee of Antifascist Resistance Fighters, an organization with headquarters in Berlin.[31] But there was another hitch that had to be resolved. The Conference represented the interests of all Jewish victims of Nazi persecution, while the Antifascist Committee believed it was obliged to meet only with American citizens to discuss the war-era claims of American nationals.

In November 1976, Ferencz was in East Berlin for the fifth meeting with the Antifascist Committee. He was handed a formal 'declaration' announcing that $1 million was being given to the Conference as a one-time humanitarian gesture to help needy Nazi victims in the US. The committee insisted that the payment was unrelated to Jewish claims, which it said could not be discussed. The money was transmitted to the Conference in New York and, on Goldmann's instructions, it was promptly returned to East Germany. The payment was inadequate in amount and unacceptable in its restrictions. 'If receipt of the money was a surprise and an affront to Jewish organizations, its return was an even greater surprise and affront to the GDR,' Ferencz said.[32]

There was a breakthrough in June 1978, when Miller met in Washington with the GDR's foreign minister, Oskar Fischer, after the intervention of New York Congressman Jonathan Bingham.[33] At this first meeting with East German government officials, the Conference suggested that, as a token settlement of claims against the GDR, it would accept $100 million, payable in cash or goods over a number of years.

The proposal endured over the next decade, as the Conference held regular talks with the foreign minister. These took place at the East German Embassy in Washington, at lunches at the Harvard Club in New York and, on at least one occasion, Ferencz kibitzed with Fischer in the men's washroom at the United Nations. By the fall of 1983, the Conference had submitted to the GDR a proposal for a nonbinding agreement on compensation for Jewish victims of Nazi persecution.[34] It went unanswered. While the talks were friendly, they were unproductive. East Germany insisted on trade concessions before it would pay compensation to Jewish Nazi victims, while the Conference countered that moral claims should not be treated as a business deal, and that meeting the Jewish claims would be a gesture that would win favour among the Americans – implying that trade concessions would follow. The GDR believed that the Jewish community had great influence in the US, Miller said, adding, 'We keep holding out the carrot of most-favoured-nation status, which they do not have.'[35]

The Conference repeatedly passed resolutions in which it 'again solemnly [resolved] to urge the German Democratic Republic to enter into negotiations with representatives of the Claims Conference in order to seek agreement on a fair measure and means of humanitarian compensation for the surviving victims of Nazi persecution, taking into consideration, among other things, the extent and value of heirless and unclaimed Jewish property, including the property of communal organizations which still remains in the territory of the GDR; the costs of absorption and the rehabilitation of those who survived the Nazi persecution and adequate indemnity for the false imprisonment and slave labour performed by Jews within the territory of the GDR or for firms which have been nationalized by the GDR, and an appropriate global recompense as a successor to a proportion of the wealth and territory of the German Reich which inflicted incalculable losses upon the Jewish people.'[36]

Through four different American administrations, and vagaries in the American and international political climate, the Conference pursued its efforts to get payment from the GDR. There were setbacks after the Soviet Union invaded Afghanistan in 1979, and any prospect for 'most-favoured-nation' trade treatment by the US for the Soviet Union or its satellites evaporated. In 1986, the terrorist bombing of the La Belle discotheque in Berlin – which killed two American soldiers and a Turkish woman, and injured 200 others – was linked to the Libyan Embassy in East Berlin. The Conference's efforts, dependent on US government support, again were handicapped because relations between the US and East Germany were so strained that the GDR ambassador was no longer received by ranking State Department officials.

Miller cautioned at that time that it also was unlikely that the Jewish claims against East Germany would progress until the climate between the Soviet Union and the United States improved. 'We recognize that the green light is going to have to come from Moscow,' he said. When there were indications that the United States was hopeful about a meeting of US President Ronald Reagan and Soviet President Mikhail Gorbachev, Miller saw this as an opportunity for the Conference. 'I do not know whether it is good for the world, but for us this would be good,' he told the Conference's board.[37]

Throughout the 1980s, there also were a number of instances in which the State Department pursued a mechanism that would ease the trade relationship between East Germany and the US, to facilitate the settlement of American and Nazi-era claims. But the department was stymied by the objections of American commercial and security officials. When Miller met with Colin Powell, then the head of the National Security Council in the Reagan administration, he asked about most-favoured-nation status for the GDR. 'Nope, we're not going to make this kind of a deal with them,' Powell said. 'You're barking up the wrong tree, rabbi.'[38]

The GDR appeared to hold compensation for Jewish victims of Nazi persecution hostage to its demands for favourable trade relations with the US. The East German position was that any payment to the Conference would be similar to a 'broker's commission.'[39] East Germany had argued that the linkage was necessitated by its inability to raise cash. The Conference countered that the original compensation agreements with West Germany had taken into account the FRG's economic condition.[40] The West German payment schedule was adjusted accordingly – goods and services were accepted in lieu of cash, and payments were spread over a number of years. Moreover, after some 15 years of negotiations, the Conference was weary and wary of the GDR's pleas of poverty. In light of East Berlin's 'generosity' to Third World countries, the Conference thought it should be in a position to make humanitarian payments to Holocaust survivors.[41] Events were so sluggish that in 1989 when Lawrence Eagleburger returned to Washington as deputy secretary of state, five years after his stint as assistant secretary of state, he was startled at the stagnation in the compensation talks. 'Nothing seemed to him to have changed,' Miller said.[42]

In fact, there had been changes – cosmetic, substantive and atmospheric. The highlight had been the invitation to the Conference to visit Honecker, chairman of the Council of State of the German Democratic Republic. That visit placed negotiations on the highest level. 'I thought we had a breakthrough on the 750th anniversary of Berlin,' Miller said. 'They were making a big fuss about it in the West. The east decided they had to do something also, and so they invited me to be their guest on this occasion.'[43] Miller and Kagan agreed to go, on two conditions: that they be allowed to visit the Buchenwald concentration camp, and that they have a private meeting with Honecker. That meeting took place on 23 June 1987.

East Germans traditionally avoided specific references to the Nazi persecution of Jews. Instead, they stressed that Communists were among the first victims of the fascists. But in his welcome of Miller and Kagan, Honecker reminisced about his participation in the anti-fascist resistance and about his trial, after which he was sentenced to ten years in jail. Then he stressed that his co-defendant, a man named Baum, was sentenced to 13 years – because he was Jewish.[44]

As to the Conference's demand for $100 million, Honecker had two responses. 'One was that if we could get for them the most-favoured-nation status in terms of trade with the United States, they might be able to earn some foreign currency and maybe then they could talk to us. But basically they said, all of the fascists were on the other side. The next argument was that they had already paid reparations, because the Russians had picked up everything that was mobile and moved it to the East, which was undoubtedly true,' Miller said. 'Then they said to me, "We treat our Jews very well in East Germany."'

The Claims Conference visit got wide publicity in the GDR. 'My picture was on the front page every day,' Miller said. 'I was sort of an exhibit. They wanted to show that they were different than the other [Soviet] satellite countries. Here they were, entertaining Rabbi Miller.'[45] However, the purpose of Miller's visit was ignored by the East German media. He was not interviewed by the press and had no opportunity to publicly explain what the Conference sought from East Germany. The media coverage, extensive as it was, did not specifically mention restitution. A front-page story in the *Berliner Zeitung*, for instance, showed a picture of Honecker receiving Miller, but highlighted that the GDR 'stands for peace and friendship among nations.' The German side showed understanding of the 'wishes' of Miller's organization, and Miller emphasized the Conference's humanitarian concerns for the victims of Nazi and fascist persecution, according to the newspaper account. It also said the Conference was prepared to bring about a 'beneficial development' of relations between states – referring to economic ties between the US and East Germany.[46]

Miller returned to New York with oral and written assurances that the GDR was prepared to expand humanitarian aid for Jewish victims of Nazi persecution, but it had not accepted the Conference's demand for payment of $100 million.[47] That appeared to come a year later, when Heinz Galinski, the West German Jewish leader, said East Germany would pay $100 million.[48]

The Honecker invitation to the Conference was one of a number of conciliatory gestures by East Germany toward the Jews. These included the appointment of a Polish-born American rabbi, who survived the concentration camps, to serve the Jewish community of East Berlin,[49] and the commemoration of the fiftieth anniversary of *Kristallnacht*. The government also announced that East Berlin's Oranienburgerstrasse synagogue – pre-war Berlin's largest synagogue, which was burned by the Nazis in 1938 – would be rebuilt and turned into a Holocaust memorial centre.[50] Honecker also bestowed a state medal on Edgar Bronfman, who then was the Seagram chairman and president of the World Jewish Congress.[51] However, Miller warned that the Jewish claims would not be remedied by restoring a synagogue and a cemetery, as laudable as these acts might be.[52]

The conciliatory gestures increased. A month after the fall of the Berlin Wall, Modrow announced that East Germany wanted to establish diplomatic relations with Israel and was prepared to discuss reparations for Nazi victims.[53] Israel and East Germany held talks in Copenhagen, as the Conference held its negotiations with the newly democratic GDR in East Berlin. The Conference attempted to establish a formal coordinated approach with Israel, a move that quickly was rendered moot. Once the GDR introduced the Deutsche mark as its currency in July 1990, the government in East Berlin had no authority to enter new financial commitments.

German unification brought the 2+4 treaty. 'We were moving into an historic treaty that basically put to rest the issues that had been left open at the end of the Second World War; because of the divided nature of

Germany and the European continent, many of which had been left in limbo in the ensuing decades,' said Robert Kimmitt, who served from 1989 to 1991 as undersecretary of state for political affairs, and from 1991 to 1993 as US ambassador to Germany. 'What the 2+4 process was designed to do was to look into a collection of internal and external issues. The 2+4 meant you had the four historic Allied powers dealing with the external issues, working closely with the two Germanies that were looking at the internal issues. I would argue that the claims issues sat right atop the plus sign, because they affected both the external Allied interests and the internal German interests.'[54]

The Conference's agreements with unified Germany far exceeded the amount long sought from the GDR. Under Article II of the Agreement on the Enactment and Interpretation of the Unification Treaty, of 3 October 1990, tens of thousands of Jewish victims of Nazi persecution ultimately received additional compensation. In January 2001, Powell, the Army general who once had led the National Security Council, became the Secretary of State in the administration of President George W. Bush. When Miller sent a letter of congratulations, he reminded Powell of the Conference's futile efforts in favour of preferential trade status for the GDR. 'God was watching over us for you to say no,' Miller told Powell.[55]

NOTES

1 Miller interview, 31 January 2001.
2 See interview with Honecker, *Washington Post*, 11 June 1989, on conciliatory efforts aimed at the US and Western Europe.
3 Kagan interview, 6 February 2001.
4 *New York Times*, 9 February 1990.
5 English text provided by GDR Embassy, Washington, 12 April 1990; *Washington Post*, 13 April 1990.
6 Saul Kagan, 'Morality and Pragmatism: A Participant's Response.'
7 Interview, 29 April 2002.
8 Saul Kagan, 'Morality and Pragmatism: A Participant's Response.' Lothar de Maiziere of the CDU was the prime minister; Social Democrat Markus Meckel was the East German foreign minister.
9 Interview, 29 April 2002.
10 Miller letters to Kohl and de Maiziere, 28 August 1990.
11 Miller letter to Raymond Seitz, assistant secretary of state for European and Canadian affairs, 28 August 1990. This issue had arisen before – in January 1954. Goldmann asked US Secretary of State John Foster Dulles to preserve the external obligations of the FRG on a potentially re-united Germany. Dulles told Goldmann that a unified Germany should recognize the duty to redress the wrongs committed by the Nazis. However, in his letter of 1 February 1954, Dulles said that 'it is clear that unification would be impossible if there were a requirement in advance that existing international obligations of the Federal Republic ... should automatically be binding on a new all-German government.'
12 There were companion treaties dealing with German reunification. On 31 August 1990, the two Germanies signed the agreement that was the legal basis for political reunification. The 2+4 agreement dealt with the international aspects of German reunification, suspending the quadripartite rights and responsibilities, and thus resolving the 'external aspects' of German

reunification, including the withdrawal of the Occupation forces.

13 Miller memo to the Claims Conference Board, 13 September 1990.
14 Saul Kagan, 'Morality and Pragmatism: A Participant's Response.'
15 *Wall Street Journal*, 13 September 1990.
16 Baker letter to Genscher, 5 September 1990; Doc. No. 1990STATE297622; Declassification Case No. 200202683.
17 Baker interview, 9 July 2002.
18 President George H.W. Bush, statement accompanying submission of 2+4 agreement to US Senate, 25 September 1990. 'Treaty on Final Settlement with Respect to Germany and a Related Agreed Minute,' 101st Congress; 2nd Session, Treaty Doc. 101-20.
19 Kohl letter, September 1990 (n.d.).
20 Claims Conference Board meeting, 6 July 1990, Jerusalem.
21 Goldmann, *The Jewish Paradox*, p. 136.
22 After reunification, as it was preparing for negotiations with Germany, the Conference calculated that it was due DM 225 million as the former GDR's 'share,' which reflected the one-third outstanding obligation of the former GDR adjusted for inflation, or plus interest, since 1952.
23 Ferencz report to Claims Conference Board meeting, 8–9 July 1981, Geneva.
24 Claims Conference memo, 'Issues and problems regarding compensation claims against (East) German Democratic Republic,' 1973.
25 Miller interview, 31 January 2001, Jerusalem.
26 Ferencz report to Claims Conference Board meeting, 8–9 July 1981, Geneva.
27 West Germany and Austria each had faced pressure from the Arab world not to enter negotiations with Israel and the Claims Conference. Ferencz had speculated, in his 1981 report, that because the GDR was a 'vassal of the Soviet Union' and aligned with Arab nations, 'it is still unable to assess with precision the political and economic repercussions which might result from any claims settlement with the Conference.'
28 Kagan, memo to file, 26 April 1988.
29 Miller interview, 31 January 2001. See *New York Times*, 4 and 5 September 1974. The 'Agreed Minute' of 4 September 1974 between the US and the GDR states: 'Following the establishment of diplomatic relations and opening of embassies, upon the request of either side, the two governments will enter into negotiations for the settlement of claims and other financial and property questions which remain unresolved, each government being entitled to raise during these negotiations the questions it wishes to have dealt with. Included on the agenda will be property and other questions which arose prior to or since 1945 which have not otherwise been settled, including losses by victims of Nazism.'
30 6 September 1974.
31 At a media briefing on 4 September 1974, a US spokesman said the government had strongly urged the GDR to deal directly with the Claims Conference. 'This group is the group which has dealt with the Federal Republic of Germany. And we said, "Ideally, since these people have all the facts and know all the things, they are recognized as very reputable anywhere by anybody, deal with them, that's the simplest and best way to do it, work out something that would be mutually satisfactory." They did not agree to that. They said their government could not deal with a private organization ... These talks, which we would think would be the best, simplest, most efficient way to deal with the problem, of course, may not be successful. No one can predict that. We, therefore, made clear to the GDR that in the claims negotiations, which they agree shall be held after establishment of relations, that on the agenda either side is free to bring up whatever it may wish. That's a sort of standard thing for any claims talks. We made clear to them that in these negotiations the US side will be free to and will bring up, if warranted, the question of property and other losses incurred before 1945, including losses of victims of Nazi persecution.'
32 Ferencz report to Claims Conference Board meeting, 8–9 July 1981, Geneva. In his report, Ferencz said it was not clear what had prompted the payment. There was speculation that the US had prodded East Germany to make a symbolic gesture to the Jews. In addition, Ferencz said, shortly before the payment, East German ships had received permission to dock at US ports to load grain, which involved substantial savings for the GDR.
33 Claims Conference Board meeting, 1 July 1986, Herzliya, Israel.
34 Ferencz, memo to files, 3 October 1983.
35 Claims Conference Board meeting, 8–9 July 1981, Geneva.

36 Ibid.
37 Claims Conference Board meeting, 1 July 1986, Herzliya, Israel.
38 Miller interview, 31 January 2001.
39 Ferencz memo to Miller, 1 September 1989.
40 West Germany was impoverished at the time of the Luxembourg Agreements; Item 15 of Protocol I specifically stated that 'funds to be made available for any specific financial year shall be fixed in accordance with the Federal Republic's capacity to pay.' However, it should be noted that West Germany received aid via the Marshall Plan.
41 Ferencz, memo to file, 12 October 1988.
42 Miller interview, 31 January 2001.
43 Ibid.
44 Kagan, memo to files on meeting with Honecker, 23 June 1987.
45 Miller interview, 31 January 2001.
46 24 June 1987.
47 Claims Conference Board meeting, 14 July 1988, Tarrytown, NY.
48 *Los Angeles Times*, 9 June 1988.
49 *New York Times*, 15 August 1987.
50 Associated Press, 26 November 1987. Klaus Gysi, the GDR's secretary of state for religious affairs, said at a news conference: 'We want to get a monument [because] we feel we share responsibility for the past. The German Democratic Republic is not the legal successor of the Third Reich. But we are Germans, and therefore we are of course responsible for what has been done in our name, even if those who did it are our most bitter enemies.'
51 *Newsday*, 4 January 1989.
52 Ferencz memo, 25 September 1989.
53 *Los Angeles Times*, 26 January 1990.
54 Kimmitt interview, 7 August 2002.
55 Miller interview, 31 January 2001. See Chapter 5 on post-unification German compensation programmes.

Chapter 5

'Would Anne Frank Have Been Eligible?' Post-Unification Compensation

Forty years after the Luxembourg Agreements, more than 170,000 monthly pensions were being paid under the original West German indemnification legislation, and some 87,000 Nazi victims, primarily emigrants from the former Soviet Union, had received one-time payments of DM 5,000 from the 1980 Hardship Fund.[1] Yet there were still tens of thousands who had been barred from payments from West Germany for persecution during the Nazi era. The Cold War seemed to guarantee that new pensions were all but impossible.[2] Following German reunification, the Claims Conference successfully negotiated with Germany for two programmes that ultimately provided monthly payments to more than 76,000 Jewish victims – the first on-going Holocaust-related pension programmes since the 1950s.

The Conference had argued that it had long-unresolved claims against the former East Germany. These were addressed in conjunction with the 1990 German reunification agreement when German Foreign Minister Hans-Dietrich Genscher vowed, in letter to US Secretary of State James Baker, that Germany would deal with Nazi-era claims against the German Democratic Republic.[3] The specific commitment to negotiate with the Claims Conference on compensation was included in Article II of the Agreement on the Enactment and Interpretation of the Unification Treaty. 'The contracting parties express their intention to advocate, in accordance with the resolution adopted by the People's Chamber of the German Democratic Republic on 14 April 1990, fair compensation for all material losses suffered by the victims of the National Socialist régime. In line with the policy consistently pursued by the Federal Republic of Germany, the federal government is prepared, in continuation of the policy of the German Federal Republic, to enter into agreements with the Claims Conference for additional fund arrangements in order to provide hardship payments to persecutees who thus far received no or only minimal compensation according to the legislative provisions of the German Federal Republic,' it said.[4]

Despite the commitment to reach an agreement, from the outset, prospects were hobbled by ambiguities. The agreement simply called for 'additional fund arrangements.' The terms were vague, and no time frame was specified. Substantive negotiations on a compensation programme did not begin until July 1991, after Miller met with Chancellor Helmut Kohl.[5] They began with profound differences between Germany and the Conference over the nature of the compensation and its parameters. The Conference wanted to establish the principles of who would be eligible for compensation, while the German Finance Ministry wanted to know what the programme would cost. Germany originally sought to limit new compensation to a total of DM 300 million for Article II and hardship payments, while the Conference demanded on-going pensions.[6] 'At the first negotiation stage, we talked, we tried to talk, about criteria,' said Akiva Lewinsky, then the treasurer of the Jewish Agency and the head of the Conference's negotiating delegation. 'Our German partners tried to talk about finance.'[7]

For instance, Germany agreed to provide compensation for those who had received 'minimal' compensation – which went undefined. For the survivors, 'every amount you receive is the "minimum,"' said Lewinsky. 'There has to be some clear wording.' During the initial negotiations with the German delegation from the Finance Ministry, Lewinsky recalled, 'We had said, "Look, if somebody received DM 5,000, a one-time payment, this is undoubtedly negligible; it's not a serious amount."' The Germans agreed that DM 5,000 was a 'minimal' amount. That became one of the original benchmarks for the new compensation fund: Nazi victims were eligible if they had not received more than DM 5,000 in previous compensation. However, having established that the amount was minimal, the Conference argued it was too low to use as a cut-off for eligibility because it would exclude tens of thousands of *Freiheitsschaden* recipients. These were the survivors of concentration camps and labour camps who had received DM 5 for each day of confinement. The DM 5,000 limit had a perverse effect: Survivors who spent a relatively short time in concentration camps, and therefore received less than DM 5,000 in past compensation, would qualify for additional compensation, while those who endured the longest suffering in camps, and received DM 5 for each day, were excluded because their prior compensation exceeded DM 5,000.[8]

The negotiations dragged on through seven rounds, until October 1992, when Germany pledged to provide nearly DM 1 billion for continued financing of the Hardship Fund and for a new programme of 'continuing hardship payments,' which was called the Article II Fund.[9] As with the original West German indemnification programme, eligibility criteria for Article II fell into a matrix of interrelated categories. These were the nature of the persecution and its duration; the financial situation of the claimant, who was obliged to prove hardship (demonstrated by income limits) as well as limits on the amount of previous German compensation; and finally, geography. Nazi victims in Europe were excluded. The Western Europeans who were excluded were those Nazi victims who, before or during the Second World War, lived in countries that did not belong to the post-war Soviet bloc; Germany contended that these victims had been compensated through the bilateral agreements in the 1950s and 1960s. The Eastern Europeans historically were excluded from the West German compensation programmes for political reasons.

The 1992 agreement was expected to provide pensions to 25,000 of the 'severely persecuted', defined as those who had survived at least six months in a concentration camp or 18 months in ghettoes or in hiding, and who lived in Israel or the West (outside Europe). Monthly Article II payments were scheduled to begin in August 1995.[10] Unlike the Hardship Fund, which provided one-time payments of DM 5,000, the Article II Fund provided monthly payments of DM 500. Unlike the indemnification programme that was established by West German legislation, in which payments were the legal right of victims who met the criteria, there was no legal right to compensation under Article II. Instead, the Article II Fund was predicated on hardship, and seen by Germany as a humanitarian gesture to Holocaust survivors. And, like the Hardship Fund, the Claims Conference was obliged to administer it, according to rules and criteria negotiated with Germany.

Although the 1992 negotiations concluded with a plan to compensate some 25,000 survivors, it was impossible to determine how many survivors might benefit, and the Conference and the German Finance Ministry did not agree on the anticipated number of potentially eligible claimants.[11] Without a realistic estimate, it was impossible to determine whether Germany's DM 1 billion offer was sufficient to cover the claims. In theory, the Conference could have waited until all applications for compensation had been filed and reviewed, and then determined if DM 1 billion was adequate. 'That would be a very impractical matter,' Lewinsky told the Conference. While the negotiations proceeded, survivors were dying. 'We said to the Germans, "We are not going to permit any biological solution."'[12] After 16 months of negotiations, the Conference accepted what it believed to be the final German offer. 'At that time, we knew that at least 25,000 Holocaust survivors who suffered grievous persecution and who are in financial straits would be able to receive a modest pension for the rest of their lives, knowing at the same time there will be thousands of other survivors who will not meet the criteria,' Kagan said.[13]

In decades of dealings with the Germans, the Conference traditionally reserved the right to return to negotiations. When the talks ended in 1992, the Conference insisted on scheduling a meeting with the Finance Ministry, in two years, to review the programme as it developed. With German elections on the horizon, the Conference wanted to lock in government commitments to the programme.[14] In addition to discussing the number of applicants, Lewinsky wanted 'clarifications' from the Finance Ministry during the 1994 round regarding victims' eligibility. 'We are not negotiating something new,' he told the Germans. 'We are clarifying points.' At issue were the definition of a camp and the duration of persecution. For instance, the criteria said the victim must have spent six months in a concentration camp. The International Tracing Service had a list of 'officially recognized' camps, but it did not include some of the most brutal camps, such as labour camps run by the SS. 'We said, "Look, the idea was concentration camp." What happens if somebody spent five months in a concentration camp and 13 months in a ghetto? He would not be eligible. We came to the conclusion jointly that these times are interchangeable, meaning if somebody was 15 months in a ghetto and three months in hiding, he would still be eligible,' Lewinsky said. 'These are clarifications; these are not new criteria.'[15]

There also was the question of how to document that the victim was in hiding during the Nazi era, or lived under a false identity, which was known as 'living in a state of illegality.'[16] 'It's really a complicated matter, since if you lived in hiding or in illegality, what do you do? You try not to exist. If you try not to exist, it's very difficult to show that you were there.' Invoking the most famous symbol of life in hiding during the Second World War, Lewinsky asked if Anne Frank would have been eligible for compensation. 'Who can say she would not have been eligible?' he asked.[17]

When the talks resumed in 1994, the Conference achieved three significant improvements of the criteria: The upper limit of previous 'minimal compensation' was raised to DM 10,000, from DM 5,000; forced labour camps in Poland were recognized by the German government as concentration camps, which enabled former inmates to receive Article II pensions; and victims who were children during the war, separated from their families and living under false identities, became eligible because they were recognized as having lived 'in hiding.'[18] The Conference and the Finance Ministry estimated that the number of on-going payments would not exceed 31,500.[19]

The Article II Fund presented extraordinary administrative problems. The majority of the applicants were victims from the former Soviet Union, Romania, Hungary and Poland who left Eastern Europe in the first ten to fifteen years after the Second World War and who received some minimal compensation under the German indemnification laws. The records to document their individual previous compensation were four decades old, and had to be obtained from the archives of the decentralized West German indemnification agencies, as well as from the International Tracing Center in Arolson, Germany, Yad Vashem in Jerusalem, the Russian Red Cross and elsewhere.[20]

The October 1992 agreement provided funds that had been expected to pay pensions through 1999. However, it became clear that the Conference would run out of money to cover the payments to the Nazi victims who qualified. It approached the negotiations with the Finance Ministry in March 1996 with a dual agenda – to replenish the fund to cover the pensions that already had been approved, and to begin talks on 'open issues'.[21] Despite the 1994 changes in the fund's criteria, there were broad groups of Nazi victims who were not eligible. They fell into ten categories. Some had never received compensation from Germany, while others had received small amounts. These victims included Holocaust survivors living in Central and Eastern Europe; those who were in forced labour camps or other camps that had not been recognized by the German authorities; and those who had received more than DM 10,000 in previous compensation, or whose income was above the 'hardship' level. 'Article II, whether we like it or not, and we had to accept it, says it is "hardship" payments,' Kagan said. 'We don't like it, we fight it, but that is what it says.'[22]

The Conference told the Finance Ministry that it needed DM 546 million to pay pensions through 1999 for those who already qualified. 'Surprisingly, we immediately received an approval of this continuing money to conclude the programme,' said Rabbi Israel Singer, who in 1995 had replaced the ailing Lewinsky as the head of the negotiating team. 'This emboldened us. We immediately presented to them all 10 of our demands.'[23]

The head of the German delegation, Irmgard Karwatzki, the Parliamentary secretary of state of the Finance Ministry, said the government would advise the Bundestag that additional funds were necessary to meet the existing obligations. But she added, 'The mutual final point in this regard is that the on-going payments will benefit a peak number of 31,500.'[24] Nonetheless, she did not dismiss the prospect of additional beneficiaries; that decision rested with the chancellor. In the meantime, the Conference and the Finance Ministry agreed to create a joint 'working group' to estimate the number of victims potentially affected by the 'open issues'.[25]

More than 100,000 additional Jewish victims of Nazi persecution would be eligible for Article II if all the criteria were modified, according to estimates prepared by the joint working group, which met in Bonn on 6 and 7 May 1996. The estimates ranged between 106,500 and 119,500. The largest single category – 40,000 to 50,000 individuals – concerned victims who had been in open ghettos in the Nazi satellite states of Bulgaria, Romania and Hungary. Another 14,000 had received 'previous minimal compensation', referring to victims who received one-time payments of up to DM 34,000.[26] That new amount – DM 34,000 – represented the maximum lump-sum payments made under Article V of the Final (1965) BEG. 'If a survivor got an Article V payment, he shouldn't be excluded from the Article II Fund,' Brozik said.[27]

The Conference also estimated that there were 12,000 potential applicants in the former communist countries in Eastern Europe, who had been barred from compensation because West Germany had refused to make payments to victims behind the Iron Curtain. It anticipated a comparable number in Western Europe who had not been adequately compensated under the German bilateral programmes of the late 1950s and early 1960s.[28]

On 3 July, only days before negotiations were scheduled to resume in Bonn on 8 July, Karwatzki sent a letter to Singer that, in effect, cancelled the talks. Her letter declared that the German government had met its obligations under Article II. The Conference's proposal for new payments for tens of thousands of people would require another DM 700 million to DM 800 million a year. The Federal Republic's budget problems were causing 'marked reductions for the citizens of our country; it also means that the federal government has reached the limits of financial possibilities in all segments of policy-making,' she wrote. Further, the government contended it already had acknowledged the 'gravity of the problems' facing the Conference by agreeing to ask the Bundestag for DM 500 million to finance Article II through 1999. 'This must be recognized as a very important additional payment by the Federal Republic of Germany and can be viewed as a considerable negotiating success achieved by your delegation,' Karwatzki wrote. As far as the Finance Ministry was concerned, the additional Article II financing spelled the end of Germany's commitment. 'With this offer, the obligation of the Federal Republic of Germany as specified in the Annex Agreement to the Unification Treaty of September 18 [Article II] has been fulfilled completely.'[29]

The Conference was stunned by her letter – by its content, its tone and its timing. Some members of the negotiating team – the majority of whom were survivors – already had arrived in Germany when the letter was faxed to New York. It was, said Benjamin Meed, a member of the negotiating team and the president of the American Gathering of Jewish Holocaust Survivors, 'the greatest humiliation I received after the Holocaust'. He also assailed the German eligibility rules for imposing 'impossible, irrelevant and humiliating' conditions on the victims. 'We are sometimes presented like beggars, having nothing to do with the persecution which we suffered,' he said. 'Survivors are outraged because they're constantly told that Germany faces difficult economic circumstances, but they wonder, are the pensions or the other payments made to former Nazis and families of Nazis also negatively affected by the German economic conditions?' Noach Flug, Meed's counterpart from the Centre of Organizations of Holocaust Survivors in Israel, said the cost of expanding the eligibility criteria would amount to half a packet of cigarettes for every German. 'It's too much for the Holocaust?' he asked.[30]

In its negotiations, the Conference had two options: to present a list of compensation priorities or a complete set of demands. The committee resisted ranking, or otherwise choosing, which of its 'open issues' merited the greatest urgency; this would mean which group of survivors should be compensated first. The negotiating committee put forward the complete list of demands. It had expected, based on past experience, that the Finance Ministry would, in effect, begin negotiations by agreeing to discuss some, but not all, of the demands. 'None of us thought that all ten points were going to be given to us as a gift on a silver platter when we arrived on 8 July. We knew that those ten points would be the basis for a negotiation, protracted or otherwise,' Singer reported to the board.[31]

Singer, Miller and Ignatz Bubis, then the head of the *Zentralrat*, met with Kohl on 28 August 1996 to restart negotiations on Article II. The nature of the negotiations was elevated from the Finance Ministry to the political level when Kohl designated a senior member of his staff, Friedrich Bohl, to represent the chancellery on the German delegation.[32] By the end of the year, the Conference had reached an agreement with the German government that added 7,000 people to the Article II programmes by raising the ceiling on prior compensation. The talks were followed by letters both from Bohl and Karwatzki, saying that negotiations were closed until 1999, when the current financing for Article II would be exhausted.

'In my opinion, this modification solves all problems for a smooth completion of the Article II agreement until the year 1999,' Bohl said in a letter to Singer. 'I hope you understand that under the present circumstances, the federal government has shown a clear signal of its good will, to support the contemporary completion of assistance to the persons affected.'[33]

That attitude was echoed by Karwatzki. 'I welcome the fact that in our discussion of 19 December 1996, a definitive solution to an especially meaningful issue for your organization and the individuals whom you represent was able to be reached,' she wrote. 'It is expected that during 1999, further discussions will be held regarding the continuation of the implementation of the Article II agreement after the year 2000. Until the expiration of the agreement in 1999, you will make no further demands on the federal government of Germany.'[34]

Still without compensation were the Jewish victims of Nazi persecution in Eastern Europe. They were known as the 'double victims' – first of Nazi persecution and then of communist oppression – and they had not been eligible for the original West German compensation programmes, the 1980 Hardship Fund or Article II payments. The original German legislation limited payments to former Germans or Nazi victims who became stateless or who were refugees. Subsequently, the Germans used a variety of arguments to reject payments to Jewish Nazi victims in the East. 'Initially it was that there were no diplomatic relationships [with Eastern European nations], and in the later years that there was no guarantee that the money would reach the intended beneficiaries,' Kagan said. 'Whatever the argument was, the bottom line was that they were not ready to commit any more funds for any programme which would benefit Holocaust survivors resident in the former Soviet Union and the Eastern bloc.'[35]

The Claims Conference was not the only actor interested in these victims. Efforts on their behalf gained momentum in the 1990s due to a combination of independent factors. While Germany was steadily improving its relations with the Eastern nations, these states also were considering Nazi-era claims for their nationals. The Conference encouraged these endeavors. Before it reached the Article II agreement, the Conference was approached by Jewish communities and persecuted groups from Eastern Europe. Believing it was unlikely that Germany would revise its policy on compensation for victims in Eastern Europe, the Conference recommended that Jewish communities in the East urge their governments to seek bilateral agreements with Germany, akin to those with Western Europe decades earlier. In talks with the German Foreign Ministry, Brozik stressed that in these bilateral compensation agreements priority should be accorded to Nazi victims who were incarcerated in concentration camps and ghettos.[36]

Within Germany, the Greens – then a small, vocal opposition party that in 1983 had won representation in the Bundestag – had taken up the cause of the 'forgotten' Nazi victims (*vergessene Opfer*). The Greens hammered two points: that some perpetrators in Eastern Europe received government 'war victims' pensions, while their victims were barred from Article II payments. In 1995, the Greens filed a petition to halt pensions to former Waffen-SS members in the Baltic states. Volker Beck, a member of the Parliament from the Greens, subsequently released government data showing that West Germany paid war-disability pensions to thousands of Waffen-SS veterans abroad.[37] In 1997, a report on Germany's *Panorama* broadcast revealed that an estimated 50,000 Nazi war criminals around the world were among those receiving 'war victims' pensions from the German government. War criminals were eligible for the payments under the German 'Social Compensation and Assistance to War Victims' law if they could prove a war injury. In 1996 alone, the federal and *Länder* governments paid some DM 13 billion to more than 1.1 million 'victim' pensioners, according to the *Panorama* report.[38]

Soon after reunification, the German government had undertaken limited measures intended to compensate some Eastern European victims by financing so-called 'reconciliation foundations.' These foundations were the products of bilateral agreements between Germany and Russia, Poland, Ukraine and Belarus in which Germany made lump-sum payments for these states to use, as they saw fit, to compensate the Nazi victims in their populations.[39] The foundations suffered from many of the same problems as had the post-war compensation programmes in Western Europe. The Greens assailed them as inadequate, noting that Jewish victims were only a small minority of the recipients and that, because of currency depreciation, their compensation was worth significantly less than comparable one-time payments made decades earlier to victims in Western Europe. The foundations, the party said, 'have been endowed with such limited funds that, for instance, on average only a single payment of DM 550 could be made to each victim in Poland in compensation for all the suffering caused by persecution.'[40]

The foundations in the former Soviet Union came in for harsh criticism. 'They all devised structures of payments that used the lowest common denominator of "Nazi victims," so that well over 90 per cent of the recipients are not Jewish,' said Andrew Baker, the director of international affairs of the American Jewish Committee and a member of the Conference's Executive Committee. 'The effect is that the difference in a payment to a Jew who survived a concentration camp and a teenage Ukrainian farm worker who picked apples in Bavaria was a difference in a range of a few hundred marks.'[41]

When the German government made an informal offer to provide DM 300,000 for the private 'German-Baltic Parliamentary Friendship Fund' to assist survivors, it was rejected by Alexander Bergmann, chairman of the Federation of Holocaust Survivors of Latvia. He charged the German government with treating the impoverished victims in the Baltics like 'beggars to whom one has neither a moral nor a legal responsibility.'[42]

Jewish victims also were offended by Germany's bilateral agreements with the Baltic states to finance hospitals and old-age facilities as 'humanitarian gestures' for victims. The FRG reached an agreement in June 1995 with Estonia, in July 1996 with Lithuania, and in August 1998 with Latvia; Germany paid DM 6 million.[43] The Jewish victims recoiled at the prospect of sharing the facilities with local Nazi veterans. 'We would never live in an old-age home alongside former members of the SS, whose units killed our families and tormented us,' said Bergmann.[44]

In 1996, the Greens introduced legislation in the Bundestag calling for the government to reach an agreement with the Conference that would expand Article II compensation to survivors in Eastern Europe. It criticized the territorial boundaries that delineated German compensation programmes. 'It is not the severity of the injustice experienced in the Nazi period, but [the] present place of residence that determines whether a former ghetto or concentration camp prisoner receives restitution from the Federal Republic,' said Winfried Nachtwei, a member of the Greens who had forged special links with the Holocaust survivors in Latvia.[45]

Holocaust survivors had to emigrate to the West to receive an appreciable amount of indemnification from Germany. For the Greens, this was politically and morally unacceptable. 'This was unjust. It had a ridiculous effect – that they should leave the East because the only way to get compensation was in the West,' Beck said.[46] The German Parliament heard that sentiment echoed from the US Congress. In a letter to Burkhard Hirsch, the vice president of the Bundestag, US Representative Tom Lantos of California said the limited compensation available to survivors in the US and Israel appeared generous compared to the condition of Jewish victims in the East. 'For this group of largely elderly survivors, emigration to receive compensation is an impossible burden,' wrote Lantos, a Hungarian-born survivor.[47]

But it was the pensions to the veterans of the Waffen-SS that created a political and public relations nightmare that the German government could not ignore. While the Conference operated discreetly, its member organizations felt no such constraints. The American Jewish Committee, a founding Conference member organization that was expanding its activities in Europe, also was agitating in the US and Germany for assistance to survivors in Central and Eastern Europe. In 1997, the AJC launched a public campaign with newspaper advertisements on behalf of survivors in Central and Eastern Europe. The first appeared in May. It featured two photographs, one of a former Nazi officer and one of a Holocaust survivor. 'Guess which one receives a war victims pension from the German government. If you guessed the survivor, you're wrong,' the ad said. In August, the AJC published another ad, displaying an 'open letter' to Kohl signed by 82 American senators. The senators expressed their 'deep concern' about Germany's refusal to pay pensions to Holocaust survivors in Eastern Europe while it provided 'generous "war victims pensions"' to Waffen-SS veterans. [48]

The German government faced an internal political debate and an external image problem. 'We had argued for this over and over. Then came the political pressure – the ads with the AJC; we had a joint press conference at the Congress,' Beck said. 'It was cheaper to pay than to continue with the image problem. This was not about justice.'[49]

The German government's initial response to the AJC ad campaign was indignation at being pressured for additional compensation. Bohl said that Germany was committed to provide compensation to Nazi victims, but also noted that it had reached an agreement with the Conference only months earlier that no further claims would be made until 1999.[50] The Conference, however, had neither agreed nor disagreed. When the previous round of negotiations had concluded, the Conference ignored Bohl's and Karwatzki's statements of finality. 'We are confident that we will experience the goodwill of the federal government when we meet in the future to discuss our mutual challenges,' Miller and Singer wrote to Bohl.[51] Later, in a letter to Baker, Miller sought to clarify the 'confusion' on the Conference's position on the survivors in Central and Eastern Europe. 'We believe their urgent needs are just and long overdue, and we have pressed their cause in our own meetings with German government officials and Parliamentarians,' Miller said. 'The Claims Conference has never agreed to delay or defer their demands for redress.'[52]

After the public pressure for compensation for victims in Central and Eastern Europe, the German government agreed in July 1997 to resume negotiations. Weeks before talks were to resume, the AJC objected to the composition of the Conference's six-member negotiating committee. Although it was widely believed that Germany was prepared to deal exclusively with claims for survivors in Central and Eastern Europe, the negotiating committee did not include a representative from Eastern Europe, and its agenda included demands for compensation for survivors in the West.[53] 'We have serious doubts as to whether the

Claims Conference negotiating committee as it is presently constituted should undertake these discussions, unless it reconfigures its committee or clearly states that, while it may advise the German government, it will not "speak for" Eastern European victims or "negotiate" on their behalf,' AJC President Robert Rifkind and Baker wrote to Miller and Kagan.[54]

Miller then appointed Bergmann, the leader of the Latvian survivors, to its negotiating committee, which elevated the priority given to Eastern European victims.[55] A survivor of the Riga Ghetto and three concentration camps, Bergmann personally symbolized the geographical disparities in benefits for Nazi victims. Bergmann had never received compensation, while his brother, who shared his war-time fate, had moved to Germany in 1993 and became eligible for a pension. 'We were both in the same ghetto; we were both in the same concentration camps,' Bergmann said. 'What law can explain such an absurdity? Change the formula.'[56]

In talks in August, Germany and the Conference agreed to create two 'joint expert committees,' one to recommend compensation for the survivors in Central and Eastern Europe and the second to deal with other 'open questions'. In the 'Central and Eastern Europe' committee, the Conference called for the expansion of Article II for all Jewish Nazi victims in the former Eastern bloc, with monthly payments of DM 500, including pensions for Jewish victims who had not been covered by the foundations in Poland, Russia, Ukraine and Belarus. Using the Article II criteria, it estimated that there would be approximately 18,000 claimants, with the highest number – 6,000 – in Hungary. The Finance Ministry argued that it could not justify greater payments for Jewish victims than to other victims in Eastern Europe, saying, 'The consequence would be the danger of further demands in an incalculable financial dimension.' It also rejected the Conference's demand that the Jewish victims in the East get the same monthly pension – DM 500 – as those in the West. The Finance Ministry contended that because the cost of living was lower in the East, the payments also could be lower.[57]

The pressure did not abate. The AJC ads were followed by a Congressional resolution criticizing the inequities in Holocaust compensation. 'It is abhorrent that Holocaust survivors should live out their remaining years in conditions worse than those enjoyed by the surviving former Nazis who persecuted them,' said the resolution, which passed on 13 November 1997. It called on Germany to expand and simplify its compensation system so that all survivors would receive payments, regardless of their nationality, financial situation or duration or place of internment.[58] Soon after, some 90 members of the Israeli Parliament, representing parties on the left and the right, signed an 'open letter' to

Kohl and Rita Süssmuth, the chairperson of the Bundestag. 'We are aware that, under your current compensation legislation, the German treasury pays about DM 12 billion annually to some 1.3 million German 'victims of war', including many Nazi criminals. This sum is six times greater than that allotted to Holocaust victims,' the letter said. 'An absurd and terribly distorted situation has thus been created, in which post-war West Germany has favoured Nazi war criminals at the expense of their victims.'[59]

In January 1998, Germany and the Conference reached an agreement for compensation for Jewish victims in the East. Rather than expanding the Article II programme, the FRG said it would make a limited contribution to a new foundation, to be established and administered by the Conference, for needy Jewish Nazi victims in the East.[60] Germany would pay DM 200 million, over four years, with the understanding that the foundation would receive additional contributions from the Conference.[61] With the fund structured in this manner, Germany could avert the question of equity for non-Jewish victims.

Known as the Central and Eastern Europe Fund, the new programme used the same eligibility criteria as Article II. The 1998 agreement was based in the premise that initially up to 17,000 people might qualify, and that annual payments would not exceed DM 3,000 per year per person.[62] Kagan called the payments of DM 250 a month 'an austerity Article II'.[63] The amount seemed generous in the former Soviet Union, but was painful for the victims in Central Europe, where the cost of living neared that in Western Europe. 'I should not have agreed on the amount. It was too low, but we had to agree on something,' Singer said. 'We had to make a decision. What were we going to do? Take DM 250 a month, or were we going to hold out for the same DM 500 that Article II gave to people in the West? Were we going to accept the fact that they would be second-class citizens? Were we going to accept the fact that East European Jews in Hungary, Poland are going to be treated badly *again* as we treated them badly for 50 years, and now we'll treat them badly for the last 10 years of their lives? Are we going to stand on principle and give them nothing? ... I said, "Let's give them some-thing."'[64] As of 2002, 18,342 victims of Nazi persecution in two dozen countries had been approved for payments from the fund.[65]

At the same time, the Article II negotiations led to the liberalization of the criteria. The changes were incremental and very specific. As with the Central and Eastern Europe Fund, the German delegation resisted changes in eligibility that could have a ripple effect on demands from non-Jewish victims. The 1998 negotiations led to pensions for an additional 7,500 survivors, including 3,000 who had survived camps in Austria and forced labour battalions in Hungary. Article II, operating on the principle of hardship, took a claimant's income into account when determining eligibility. Another 4,500 people became eligible because of modifications in calculating individual income.[66]

'There were certain issues that were achievable at different times, depending on different factors,' said Gideon Taylor, who succeeded Kagan as the Conference's director. 'At the end of the day, it was a negotiation. We put all the issues on the table, and there were certain ones we could succeed on, and certain ones we couldn't. The Germans didn't say, "Here is compensation for 5,000 victims; which 5,000 do you want?"'[67]

Once the German government agreed to compensation principles, it continued to allocate the funds to meet its commitments. In March 2002, it reached an agreement with the Conference to continue financing the programmes, and again liberalized the criteria. Another 5,000 Holocaust survivors became eligible for compensation under the terms of the 2002 agreement, which recognized detainees from additional concentration-like camps as eligible for the Article II and Central and Eastern European Funds.[68]

For the first time, the German government also agreed to a Conference demand for 'cost of living' adjustments for these two funds. The cost of living had risen about 20 per cent since 1992, when the original agreement to create the Article II Fund was reached, but there had been no provisions to protect the real value of payments from erosion. The adjustment would be in the same proportion as that applied to BEG pensions, which were modified in line with those of German civil servants.[69]

A decade after German reunification, the Conference administered three parallel programmes, according to criteria negotiated with the German government: the 1980 Hardship Fund, as well as the Article II and the Central and Eastern Europe Funds. As the agency that determined who qualified, the Conference came in for harsh criticism from survivors over the requirements and limits of the compensation programmes. The Conference had recognized in the 1970s, when it was began negotiating for the Hardship Fund, that it was assuming a painful assignment – but it believed it had no choice. That judgment was confirmed by the Bundestag's tenacious victims' advocate, Beck. 'If the Claims Conference did not agree to administer the funds, it would not have gotten the agreements,' he said.[70]

Originally intended to benefit 80,000 people, the Hardship Fund made payments to four times that number. The original agreement for Article II called for pensions for 25,000 victims; through subsequent negotiations that expanded the criteria, the Conference was to double that number. By the end of 2002, the Conference made payments to individual victims through the three programmes totalling more than \$2 billion.[71]

NOTES

1 Kagan letter to Alan Rose, Canadian Jewish Congress, 13 August 1990, Kagan, memo to file, 20 August 1991. See Chapter 3 on the Claims Conference's Hardship Fund.
2 In the late 1980s, in the course of seeking money to replenish the Conference's Hardship Fund, Brozik lobbied the Bundestag for modest on-going 'emergency' payments for some 20,000 of the neediest Jewish Nazi victims. It appeared that he had succeeded in 1989; then the imminent collapse of communism and the subsequent reunification of Germany left the prospect suspended.
3 The Genscher letter was dated 18 September 1990. See President George H. W. Bush, statement accompanying submission of 2+4 agreement to US Senate, 25 September 1990. 'Treaty on Final Settlement with Respect to Germany and a Related Agreed Minute,' 101st Congress; 2nd Session, Treaty Doc. 101–20.
4 See Chapter 4 on the Conference's claims against East Germany.
5 The meeting was held in Bonn on 21 June 1991.
6 Kagan report to Claims Conference Board, 16 February 1996.
7 Claims Conference Board meeting, 17 July 1994, Stockholm.
8 Ibid.
9 Those funds were for the period 1993 to 1999. The new compensation fund was named 'Article II' after the clause in the unification implementation agreement under which Germany committed itself to make payments to Jewish Nazi victims.
10 Miller memo to Claims Conference Board, 29 October 1992.
11 Lewinsky originally had estimated that between 40,000 and 50,000 victims might be eligible, but the German government balked at this number and had proceeded with the negotiations only on the basis of a considerably lower estimate.
12 Claims Conference Board meeting, 17 July 1994, Stockholm.
13 Kagan interview, 4 January 2001.
14 The German delegation said a meeting should be held in 1998, when the programme funding was expected to be exhausted; the Conference prevailed in setting a meeting for 1994.
15 Claims Conference Board meeting, 17 July 1994, Stockholm.
16 The German delegation's view was that those who lived under false identities did not experience severe suffering. The Conference disagreed, arguing that these victims were daily in danger or betrayal and death.
17 Claims Conference Board meeting, 17 July 1994, Stockholm.
18 Jürgen Echternach, Parliamentary state secretary, German Finance Ministry, letter to Lewinsky, 14 June 1994.
19 Jürgen Quantz, director, German Finance Ministry, letter to Lewinsky, 20 April 1995.
20 Claims Conference Board meeting, 17 July 1994, Stockholm. The requirement that the Conference manage the new fund simply shifted an administrative burden that was widely recognized. In 1986, for instance, the German Greens Party sought to reopen the BEG. 'It was impossible; the BEG was complicated – the application process, documentation,' Volker Beck said. 'We changed our minds in the late 1980s and asked for a foundation for all neglected victims.' (Interview, 4 July 2002, Berlin.)
21 Kagan memo to Claims Conference Executive Committee, 28 February 1996.
22 Claims Conference Board meeting, 17 July 1994, Stockholm.
23 Claims Conference Board meeting, 10–11 July 1996, New York.
24 Statement of Karwatzki presented at the March 1996 discussions.
25 Minutes, meeting, Claims Conference and Finance Ministry, 12–13 March 1996.
26 Unsigned memo, 27 June 1996, 'Summary of the conclusions of the joint working party of the Claims Conference and the German Treasury with regard to the open questions'.
27 Correspondence with author, 11 June 2002.
28 Kagan memo to Executive Committee, 28 February 1996.
29 Karwatzki letter to Singer, 28 June 1996. Karwatzki did not refer only to Holocaust-

compensation issues. In her letter, she said, 'I would ask you to take into account, in this context, that the Federal Republic of Germany is contributing in a not insubstantial manner to the peace process in the Middle East and to enhancing the traditionally friendly relations with the State of Israel.'

30 Claims Conference Board meeting, 10–11 July 1996, New York.
31 Ibid.
32 Unsigned, undated summary in English of the problems in the 1996 negotiations.
33 Bohl letter to Singer, 23 January 1997.
34 Karwatzki letter to Singer, 10 January 1997.
35 Kagan interview, 4 January 2001. That attitude was not confined to the West Germans, but part of a long-standing resistance by the West to making funds available behind the Iron Curtain. After the end of the Second World War, when the US began restoring assets to nations that had been plundered by the Nazis, General Lucius D. Clay, the commander of the Office of Military Government for Germany (US), recommended against restituting to Hungary some $34.7 million in gold and silver that had been recovered in Germany by the American army. 'I was apprehensive that we were contributing to the communist treasure chest and strengthening its hand for heavier attacks against Western democracy' (Lucius D. Clay, *Decision in Germany*, Garden City, NY, Doubleday, 1950, p. 309).
36 Kagan letter to Brozik, 9 April 1993.
37 *Sunday Times* of London, 15 December 1996.
38 *Panorama* report by Volker Steinhoff and John Goetz, 30 January 1997, ARD television network. This was the second *Panorama* report on the subject; the first was broadcast on 29 March 1993.
39 Under these bilateral agreements, Poland received DM 500 million in October 1991; Belarus received DM 200 million in March 1993; Russia and Ukraine each received DM 400 million in March 1993.
40 Greens proposed legislation, 5 December 1996.
41 Interview, 22 May 2002, Washington.
42 *Jerusalem Post*, 25 February 1996. Survivors in the Baltics suffered other indignities as well; they were expected to apply to the foundations in Moscow and Minsk for compensation, which was an insult to populations that had been occupied by the Soviets in the Second World War and only regained sovereignty after the collapse of communism.
43 'German Compensation for National Socialist Crimes,' Background Papers series, Washington: German Embassy, Department for Press, Information and Public Affairs, and German Information Center. Under a Bundestag measure of 29 June 1994, Jewish victims in the Baltic states would get individual payments of perhaps DM 50 a month. The amount was assailed as too low. More important, the German government objected to the measure on grounds that the payments to Jewish victims might encourage additional demands from other victims in Eastern Europe. Institutional grants for old-age homes and hospitals were seen as an alternate that helped victims without creating a precedent that would prompt individual claims from members of other persecuted groups. Efforts to assist these Nazi victims also were complicated immensely by the twentieth-century history of the Baltic states. These nations focused almost exclusively on their national oppression and victimization by the Soviet Union and tended to resist efforts to distinguish Jews as uniquely endangered.
44 *Jerusalem Post*, 28 July 1996.
45 *Jerusalem Post*, 12 June 1997.
46 Beck interview, Berlin, 4 July 2002.
47 Lantos letter to Burkhard Hirsch, 9 September 1996.
48 The first ad was published in the *New York Times* on 7 May 1997. The second ad was published in the *Times* on 17 August 1997. The senators' letter was originally circulated by Kay Bailey Hutchison, a Republican from Texas, and Christopher J. Dodd, a Connecticut Democrat; see *Washington Post*, 26 June 1997.
49 Beck interview, 4 July 2002, Berlin.
50 *New York Times*, 10 May 1997.
51 Miller and Singer letter to Bohl, 29 January 1997.
52 Miller letter to Baker, 9 April 1997.
53 A Conference press release, dated 14 August 1997 did not distinguish claims for compensation for Central and Eastern European victims from broader Article II issues. It referred to negotiations to liberalize the eligibility criteria, including those for Holocaust victims who

were barred by income limits, those in former Soviet bloc countries, as well as people who were forced into military labour and labour camps.

54 Letter dated 4 August 1997.
55 The Conference's delegation was expanded again to include Tomas Kraus, director of the Czech Jewish community, after Czech Jews, while welcoming Bergmann, complained that the situation in the Baltics was not the same as that for the Czech Republic, and that Bergmann could not represent them. The delegation also included Joseph Bursuk from Ukraine and Tatyana Zhvanetskaya from Russia.
56 *Time* magazine, international edition, 25 August 1997.
57 Quantz letter to Kagan, 13 November 1997. The notion of a two-tier compensation programme also had been raised in the Greens' 1996 legislative proposal, which said that 'it should also be examined whether the monthly pension from Article II should be reduced in line with the standard of living in the country concerned.' The Greens accepted a differential in payments, so long as it was based on a standard measure that fairly reflected the cost of living.
58 Senate Concurrent Resolution 39, 105th Congress, 1st Session.
59 The letter was published as an ad, sponsored by the 'Israel Federation of Holocaust Survivors Organizations,' *Jerusalem Post*, 24 November 1997.
60 The fund was welcomed by the American government. 'We applaud this historic step forward,' State Department spokesman James P. Rubin said on 13 January 1998. 'For the first time, the German government will provide assistance to Holocaust victims in the East as it has in the West. "Double victims" – those who escaped the Holocaust only to be caught behind the Iron Curtain during the long decades of the Cold War and left out of earlier compensation programmes – can now seek justice.'
61 Bohl letter to Singer, 9 January 1998.
62 The payments would be retroactive to 1 July 1998. Kagan memo to Executive Committee, 2 June 1998. In March 2002, the German government agreed to continue financing this fund until at least 2005.
63 Kagan interview, 11 September 2002.
64 Singer interview, 6 June 2002.
65 Claims Conference, *Annual Report 2002*. Some 40 per cent of these recipients were in Hungary.
66 Miller and Singer letter to Bohl, 17 June 1998. The increase was based on Germany's agreement to exclude government old-age pensions from the computation of income for people who, in 1999, were 70 or older.
67 Interview, 30 July 2002.
68 The camps include labour camps and working battalions in Romania, Slovakia, the former Yugoslavia, Libya, Italy and Bulgaria. Claims Conference press release, 6 March 2002.
69 Kagan interview, 8 May 2002.
70 Beck interview, 4 July 2002. After the September 2002 Bundestag elections, Beck was the only legislator with significant experience in programmes to aid Nazi victims.
71 Claims Conference, *Annual Report 2002*.

Chapter 6

The Legacy of the Dead: Recovering Heirless Jewish Properties in the Former East Germany

Johanna Adler Markhoff sold her house at the corner of Raabestrasse and Winsstrasse in the Prenzlauer neighborhood of East Berlin on 11 December 1934. Markhoff, a widow, was deported to Theresienstadt on 1 September 1942 and died there seven weeks later. Her house, 50 years later, marked a watershed for the Claims Conference. It claimed the house as an heirless Jewish property. The house generated DM 941,500 – the first of thousands of payments the Conference received for heirless and unclaimed Jewish properties recovered in the former East Germany.

As significant as that claim was to the Conference, it was only one of 2.3 million claims for properties in the former East Germany.[1] The reunification of Germany entailed an extraordinary transfer of properties as part of a tumultuous effort to reverse the effects of more than four decades of partition, and to Westernize the economy and institutions in the former East Germany. Property restitution, in general, and Jewish property restitution, in particular, took place amid the overhaul of the German legal system, the integration of a new administration in the former German Democratic Republic, and the privatization of the formerly nationalized, state-supported East German economy through the *Treuhandanstalt*, the agency responsible for the sale of nationalized assets to private investors.

Within this massive property shuffle, the Conference was determined that no pre-war Jewish property in the former GDR would devolve to the 'Aryanizers' or to the German state. It fought to ensure that individual Jewish Nazi victims and their heirs had the right to recover properties that had been seized or sold under duress in the Nazi era.

These houses, farms, businesses and artworks had been out of reach for the four decades that East Germany had been in the Soviet sphere. And as the officially designated 'successor organization' (*Nachfolge-organisation*) the Conference sought all unclaimed and heirless Jewish properties in the former GDR, such as Markhoff's house, as well as the properties of dissolved Jewish communities and organizations.

The opportunity to recover properties radically changed the Conference's scope and its mission. A decade after the fall of the Berlin Wall, it had earned DM 1.6 billion from property sales – funds that suddenly were available to assist Jewish victims of Nazi persecution.[2] But the identification, recovery and disposal of unclaimed Jewish property was a formidable task that was conducted amid serious legal and logistical obstacles and that exposed the Conference to some of its harshest criticism within the Jewish community.

From the fall of the Berlin Wall on 9 November 1989 – the anniversary of *Kristallnacht* – the German reunification process hurtled forward. Between 1990 and 1992, the Bundestag passed more than 900 federal laws in an effort to reorganize and regulate the evolving conditions. The legal status of property was a major economic and social issue, one that preceded reunification.[3] There were hundreds of thousands of muddled property cases that had to be settled if economic development and investment in the Eastern part of the country were to proceed. The German law governing the 'open property issues' – the *Vermögensgesetz* – was, in essence, a partial reprivatization measure that recognized that 'a total revision of the socialist development of the society and the economy over more than 40 years would not have been possible'. The cases to be resolved were 'primarily those that were incompatible with the principles of the rule of law or represented particular examples of partition-related injustice'.[4]

The German property laws set off a frenzy of restitution claims. Privatization was intended to promote economic development and reduce the strain on the German treasury. Instead, it created economic uncertainty and impeded economic investment because competing claims put a cloud on property titles.[5] 'The moment the law provided for physical restitution, it created an obstacle,' Brozik said. 'If, theoretically, there was compensation in lieu of restitution, there would be no cloud.'[6] The property laws also bred social turmoil. Although the vast majority of the 2.3 million claims were submitted by Germans whose property had been nationalized after the Second World War, the restitution legislation was controversial and was considered by many, particularly in East Germany, to be one of the negative effects of reunification. Once the Berlin Wall fell, thousands of West Germans streamed into the GDR, looking for the properties they left behind when they fled from the communists after the Second World War. East Germans feared they would lose the homes in which they had lived for decades. When the freely elected Volkskammer convened in April 1990, protesters greeted the assembly in East Berlin with demands for housing guarantees and signs saying, 'German unity cannot allow us to be driven from our homes and gardens.'[7]

The East Germans feared they would lose their homes; the Conference feared Nazi victims would lose their rights. The restitution programmes that derived from reunification were concerned primarily with transfers that occurred once East Germany became a sovereign state. 'When the original legislation was drafted by the post-April [1990] government of the GDR, there was no reference to restitution of property resulting from takings and seizures in the period 1933–1945,' said Kagan. 'Everything was focused on what happened after 1949, once the GDR came into existence.'[8] Using the principles that had been established by the Allies after the war, the Conference successfully fought to ensure that the German reprivatization legislation included restitution to Jewish victims of Nazi persecution or their heirs who had property in the GDR, including East Berlin, that had been seized or sold under duress. The September 1990 law acknowledged that the GDR had failed to restore the Nazi-era confiscations. 'The former GDR, not having had sufficient regulations for compensation for wrongs perpetrated under National Socialism, the Property Act also applies to property losses due to persecution by reason of race, politics, religion or ideology in the years from 1933 to 1945,' according to the German Federal Office for the Settlement of Open Property Issues, or *Bundesamt zur Regelung offener Vermögensfragen* (BARoV).[9]

Although unified Germany made a commitment to address Jewish claims, it did not provide adequate redress for the losses. For instance, the 1990 restitution law included a provision (Paragraph 1.6) dealing with Nazi victims' claims for properties lost between 30 January 1933 and 8 May 1945 through forced sale, confiscation or similar measures. However, it restricted the possibility to restitution 'in natura' and provided only limited compensation to the original Jewish owners. And, while the measure recognized that heirless and unclaimed Jewish properties should be recovered by a successor organization, and designated the Conference for this role, it failed to incorporate the explicit provisions of the Allies' post-war restitution measures regarding the status and rights of the successor organization.[10]

In addition to legislative flaws, there were extraordinary administrative complications in property matters. By design, unified Germany was highly decentralized. Fearing abuses by an authoritarian state, the new system guaranteed that the federal government was deprived of absolute power. But the structural problems inherent in decentralization exacerbated the logistical burdens on the recovery of Jewish properties, because the system intended to implement the national restitution law was fragmented. It also was hampered by mechanical and procedural problems. There is no national restitution agency with the authority to issue directives binding on all restitution agencies in unified Germany. Instead, an assortment of new administrative networks was created in the Eastern *Länder*. There were 122 restitution agencies in the five new German states, which were overseen by state restitution agencies (*Landesämter*) acting as the higher authorities for the local agencies within their boundaries. And, although the restitution agencies had a common mission, they had neither uniform regulations nor computer software to register claims in each state.[11] Finally, the claims of Nazi victims did not occur in a vacuum. Properties were transferred and sold by current German owners before the original Jewish owners or the Conference had filed claims.[12] It was within this new, unwieldy and inconsistent restitution system that individual Nazi victims, heirs and the Conference pursued their property claims.

The Conference had secured the right to unclaimed and heirless property by invoking the principle that had been established in November 1947 under US Military Government Law Number 59 (*Rückerstattungsgesetz*). In the Occupation zones, the Jewish Restitution Successor Organization (JRSO), operating in the American Zone, and companion agencies in the British and French zones, were named as successor organizations with the right to claim the assets of Jews who perished without heirs and of dissolved Jewish organizations and communities.[13] However, there were massive logistical and legal differences between the post-war restitution in West Germany and that in the former GDR after reunification. These were due primarily to the passage of more than four decades and multiple layers of property ownership under different legal conditions.

In post-war West Germany, the Allies' restitution legislation essentially was a Jewish issue. It concerned property that had been taken through 'Aryanization' and forced sales. In contrast, in the former GDR, property had been 'Aryanized' during the Nazi era and subsequently nationalized by the communist régime. 'In West Germany and the western sectors of Berlin, [post-war] property restitution and Jewish claims for property were almost synonymous, while the Jewish component in the restitution claims for property in East Germany is small,' said Kagan.[14]

Jewish claims, in fact, were a 'side issue' in the practical work of the restitution agencies in unified Germany. Not only was the per centage of Jewish claims small, but the claims tended to be more complex and required much more time to complete, because of competing claims and the difficulties, after 60 years, of substantiating claims.[15] Further, the special character and origin of Jewish claims, arising from losses between 1933 and 1945, was alien to the German governmental and judicial apparatus of the 1990s. And the concept of the Claims Conference as the 'successor organization' was meaningless for restitution agencies. While a Nazi victim or his heir was a living claimant, the Conference was an 'abstraction'. This forced it to devote a considerable amount of time to educating restitution agencies on the historical circumstances under which Jewish property was subjected to forced sale or confiscation, and the rights of the Conference to submit claims, Brozik said.[16] The result was that the rate at which Jewish claims – both of individuals and of the Successor Organization – were settled was lower than that of other claims. 'The Jewish restitution cases are the most complicated ones, and the employees of the restitution agencies would gladly handle 10 simple GDR cases rather than one controversial Jewish case,' he said.[17]

The *Vermögensgesetz* established the Conference as the Successor Organization in the case of liquidated Jewish organizations and Jews who died without heirs.[18] The name 'Successor Organization' was deliberate. It embodied the legal notion that the Conference, as had been the JRSO a half-century earlier, was recognized by the authorities as the legitimate 'successor' that was entitled to inherit the heirless and unclaimed Jewish properties.

From·the Conference's base in Frankfurt am Main, Brozik quickly organized the Successor Organization to handle legislative issues, immense research projects on Jewish assets, claims for Jewish sites, and finally the management and sale of properties. Its initial handicap was that it had no money. Always a shoestring operation, the Conference had run out of money in the 1960s, when the funds that Germany made available under Protocol II were exhausted. In 1980, when it began to administer the Hardship Fund, the fund's administrative expenses were covered by West Germany. The Conference was in debt to the Memorial Foundation for Jewish Culture and had no additional funds for other Conference projects.

It had to borrow funds to hire researchers to scour archives to document Jewish properties that could otherwise be heirless and unclaimed in the former East Germany. '"Unclaimed" becomes the operative word, because all property restitution laws have filing deadlines,' said Kagan. 'We had to research it and claim it – the Germans didn't deliver it to us.'[19] The task was monumental, and the Conference was further handicapped by a series of severe limitations, even as it was racing against the early filing deadlines imposed by the German government. After Conference protests, Germany extended the claims deadline for real estate until 31 December 1992; the deadline for movable assets, such as furniture and art, was 30 June 1993.[20] 'These time limits, on the one hand, were to ensure legal certainty and, on the other hand, they gave former owners sufficient time to file their claims,' according to the German property office, BARoV.[21]

The Conference simultaneously began its research to identify Jewish properties in the former East Germany and established the administrative machinery to file claims. Unlike individual claimants who had the benefit of specific family knowledge or nostalgic reminiscences about properties – however limited those may have been some five decades after the war – the Conference had no first-hand information about the existence of properties, nor was it privy to the circumstances of their sale or confiscation. Its information had to be obtained from historical documents – a cumbersome task because many records had been destroyed during the war and, under the government of the former East Germany, public access to records had been denied. When the records existed, they were widely scattered among numerous institutions that had been involved in the process of 'Aryanization'.[22]

The Conference quickly created a massive research operation, digging in records and archives, including German archives located in Moscow and records at Yad Vashem in Jerusalem. 'We searched high and low, wherever there was anything that could lead to information on Jewish property in Germany,' said Kagan.[23] Brozik's researchers went so far as to read old issues of Julius Streicher's virulently anti-Semitic Nazi-era newspaper *Der Stürmer*, which had gloated about the pace of 'Aryanization'; the newspaper's 'progress reports' could identify Jewish confiscated properties.[24]

The Conference operated on the principle that, when in doubt, it was better to claim too many properties than too few. 'My arm ached from signing thousands of applications,' Brozik said.[25] As the deadline neared, in instances in which it did not have specific information, the Conference filed three sets of bulk – or 'global' – claims,[26] which referred to batches of possibly heirless Jewish properties cited in some German archives.[27] However, Brozik said it would be 'presumptuous' to believe the Successor Organization was able to file claims for all former Jewish properties. 'Some properties will remain forever undiscovered despite our efforts, and, considering the huge losses of records and the Nazi efforts to destroy all evidence, no other situation is imaginable,' he said. 'However, we assume that due to our efforts to follow all available and recognizable leads, a high rate of discovery will be achieved.'[28]

By the end of 2001, the Successor Organization had filed 98,417 claims, which represented if not all, at least the vast majority, of one-time Jewish property in the former East Germany.[29] However, the Conference consistently estimated that only some 5 per cent of its claims ultimately would result in restitution or compensation. The claims' initial validity was almost always uncertain and, from the outset, the Conference anticipated withdrawing a significant per centage of its claims. In its efforts to ensure that no one-time Jewish property would remain in German hands, it filed claims for everything it could identify, without knowing whether an heir existed, if the heir also had filed a claim, or if, in fact, the property was once owned by Jews.

There was a significant per centage of cases in which the Conference filed erroneous claims. These were for properties that, as it turned out, were not owned by Jews or represented multiple claims for the same property. German names and German-Jewish names were co-mingled on property lists. That led to the classic example of an erroneous claim, which had been filed under the post-war West German restitution programme. It was for a Berlin property sold by Alfred Rosenberg in 1937. 'Alfred Rosenberg is as good a Jewish name as it comes,' said Kagan. 'Alfred Rosenberg was the chief ideologue of the Nazi movement. You will find, I would say, thousands, certainly hundreds, of German family names that could be Jewish or German.'[30]

There were presumptions in the German property law that worked in favour of Jewish claims. Chief among them was that transactions after 1933 were presumed to have been involuntary. This is the concept of *Entziehungsvermutung*, or the presumption of confiscation, which meant that any sale between 1933 and 1945 was considered to be of dubious validity. Nonetheless, the pursuit of properties in the former East Germany was a field crowded with many competing claims. A claim filed by the Conference often competed against one filed by a rightful Jewish owner or his heir, as well as a claim from the 'Aryanizer' or his heirs, and a claim from an individual who purchased the property after 1945.

Individual claimants and the Conference were obliged to file claims by 31 December 1992 to the German restitution agencies in each of the five *Länder* of the former German Democratic Republic and in Berlin. The initial claim was primarily to 'protect the filing period' so that claimants were not shut out of the process because they missed the deadlines. Claimants were then bound to substantiate each claim, which typically required the collection and collation of documents about both the property and the claimant. The Conference – which had originally been ignorant about the ownership and history of individual properties – had to establish that the owner of the property was Jewish, that the property was confiscated or its sale was forced, and that the Jewish owner did not receive the proceeds.

For instance, if the Conference found a record saying that a certain Haim Schwartz sold a building at a certain address in Leipzig in 1935, it filed a claim for the restitution of the building. The Conference then had to document that Schwartz was a Jew and identify his fate (emigration, deportation, prohibition of exercising a profession, seizure and other persecution measures). If the Schwartz heirs also filed a claim by the 1992 deadline, the Conference withdrew its claim, once it was established that the applicants were the legitimate heirs. The settlement of the claim then depended on the heirs' ability to provide proof of inheritance to the restitution agency, which was a lengthy and complicated procedure. Once the Conference identified a property it thought might be 'Jewish', it was necessary to document the property's ownership, the type and date of the forced sale or confiscation, and the amount of the pre-war sales proceeds, if any. A claim also included material concerning the claims by the 'Aryanizer', and an examination of previous post-war restitution decisions about the site, including whether it had been purchased in good faith after 1945, was incorporated into a company, or designated for public use.

Pinpointing a specific property in the former GDR was particularly troublesome. 'The topographical classification of our restitution claims has been one of the most difficult problems for both the Claims Conference and the restitution agencies,' Brozik said. The archival material had its own limitations; much of the existing historical data was from the Weimar and Nazi periods, which was of limited value after the passage of more than 60 years. 'Items of real estate and plots of land have been separated, combined and divided anew,' Brozik reported. Where properties survived, their addresses often had shifted. 'Just the history of the naming of streets, which reflects the violent transformations of the German political system, is extremely complicated. In every town and village, the names and numbers of streets have been changed,' he said. There were thousands of duplicate claims because different teams of researchers, using different addresses from different periods, claimed the identical property. In many cases, street names were not unique. In Berlin, for instance, the street name 'Ackerstrasse' could be found multiple times in different districts of the city. In addition, the sequence of house numbers was changed for 400 streets.[31]

The Successor Organization had considered, then dismissed, the idea of a 'global' sale of its claims, either to private parties or the German states. Such a sale would have meant a quick infusion of cash for the Conference, but it also would have required that many claims be documented in advance, to ensure that the Conference did not undervalue properties. A private buyer likely would have been conservative in what it would offer for the claims. And it was not realistic to sell Jewish claims to the German government, which was saturated with properties it had acquired from the former GDR. 'They are having enough difficulty as it is selling the property they already own,' Brozik said.[32]

The Conference had never intended to become the landlord of the properties; it wanted to dispose of properties to raise cash to finance services for survivors. But it also was buffeted by the vagaries of the market. Only three years after unification, there was a general decline in sale prices – there was a surplus of properties in Berlin, Dresden and Leipzig, and banks became more cautious in extending credit. The quality of the Conference's properties varied widely. Land in the heart of Berlin was extremely valuable, but the Conference also had hundreds of rural agricultural properties of little value.[33]

As the Successor Organization, the Conference faced one of the most ticklish situations in its history, garnering wider publicity than its work in obtaining compensation or financing social welfare services for hundreds of thousands of Holocaust survivors. It was accused of competing with and cheating Holocaust survivors and heirs out of properties in the former East Germany.

One in 20 claims under the German restitution law was a Jewish claim, and one in 20 Jewish claims was a Successor Organization claim. This meant that the individual Jewish owners or heirs were the main beneficiaries of the Conference's efforts to improve the restitution measures, Brozik said.[34] However, among the thousands of properties claimed by the Conference, there were hundreds of cases in which the heirs of Nazi victims also had claims, but had not met the filing deadlines. The Conference had succeeded in obtaining two extensions of the filing period; 31 December 1992 was the final deadline for real estate claims, and it was merciless. 'It is irrelevant whether the potential claimant did not file a claim because he or she did not know of the inheritance, a lawyer filed a claim with improper information, or the potential claimant had difficulty in securing proof of inheritance,' Brozik said.[35] Under German law, a claimant who missed the deadline had no legal rights. The property would be forfeited. However, if the Conference had filed a timely claim, it recovered the property in its name. 'The German law establishes very clearly the legal rights and the legal position of the Claims Conference as the owner of any property that it claims under the law. That issue is not debatable,' said Kagan. 'The Claims Conference is not a legal trustee or a legal custodian for someone else.'[36]

There was a dilemma for the Conference when a 'defaulting' heir came forward. It could give up restituted assets in favour of the heir and, by doing so, diminish the collective funds available to aid Nazi victims. In 1994, the Conference established an 'equity fund,' saying it was a balanced compromise that met its moral obligation to the so-called 'late' heirs while also fulfilling its mission to assist survivors. There was a precedent for such a fund. A similar problem had been faced after the Second World War by the successor organizations in the western Occupied zones. They established 'equity funds' for individuals who did not meet the restitution filing deadlines. Using that model, the Conference decided to provide a share – on a sliding scale – of the proceeds to direct heirs who had missed the German deadline. The board originally set 31 December 1996 – four years beyond the German restitution deadline – for heirs to apply.

'We are a merciful people and so we said, "We will share the proceeds with you,"' Miller said of the fund, which was called the "Goodwill Fund".' 'We gave it that name because we thought we were doing a favour to the heirs.'[37] But the fund was controversial, and the reaction of the heirs was mixed. In many instances, they were relieved that the Conference had salvaged the property and that they would receive partial compensation. However, there were applicants who believed they should receive the full value of the property, discounting both the Conference's substantial efforts and its costs in recovering the property. 'It will be of little help to the Claims Conference if it points out the legal position and especially the legal fact that the heir himself is responsible for the non-observance of the time limit,' said Brozik. 'It will always be difficult to convey the insight that it was the Claims Conference who prevented the "Aryanizers" from keeping the dispossessed assets to themselves. The restitution of these assets to the Claims Conference will be viewed as a second expropriation, as long as the Claims Conference is not prepared to defer its rights almost completely.'[38]

There also were heirs who recovered properties, but who contended that the competing claim from the Conference had deprived them of the timely use or sale of the property and caused them to lose funds because, in the interim, the property deteriorated and lost value. In August 1998, Gabriele Hammerstein, a German Jewish refugee, filed a $25 million suit in New York State Supreme Court against the Conference. German authorities had awarded the property in Schwerin, Mecklenburg-West Pomerania, to her and her sister. However, she argued, the Conference had interfered in her attempts to recover her parents' estate, and had prevented her from renting, occupying or disposing of the property. She also contended that the Conference had attempted to obtain for itself the benefits of her families' businesses. The Conference rejected the contention. 'The Claims Conference, as the Successor Organization, has the responsibility to satisfy itself that the people to whom the property was awarded are the proper claimants,' Kagan said. 'As soon as the documentation was delivered, we withdrew the claim.'[39] Hammerstein's suit was dismissed in 1999.[40]

The general clamor over the Goodwill Fund began after scathing attacks in an Israeli magazine, the *Jerusalem Report*. The articles tarnished the Conference's reputation for integrity, embarrassed its board, and appeared to pit member organizations against each other, as some members publicly denigrated the Conference policy.[41] 'The problem is that now the Claims Conference has become the villain,' said Miller. 'Instead of the Germans, we have become villains.' It was under this cloud that the board revisited the Goodwill Fund at its annual meeting in July 1997, and again at a special meeting two months later. The meetings examined the principle, the character and the division of the proceeds under the fund. These were, in part, ideological questions – German law notwithstanding – about how the members viewed the Conference: whether it represented the interests of individual survivors and heirs or was the trustee of the collective interests of all survivors. The board voted to maintain the policy of the Goodwill Fund, but extended the deadline for applications until 31 December 1997, instead of 1996. The board, however, remained deeply divided. 'This is not a question of morality. You can find morality on both sides,' Miller said. 'It's not even a question of *halacha* [Jewish religious law]. You can find *halacha* on both sides ... It is a question of judgment. What is our judgment?'[42]

The discussions at Conference meetings were heated. At one end of the spectrum, there were Conference members who believed that late claimants should be given the proceeds, minus the Conference's expenses in recovering the property. This reflected discomfort with the publicity, a moral argument in favour of the heirs, and unease with the Conference's legalistic approach.[43] There were some who worried that assaults on its credibility and the apparent dissent within the Conference would undercut the organization's efforts to win concessions from Germany in negotiations for compensation programmes.[44]

Others, while favouring the rights of the former owner's immediate descendants, argued that the Conference had a more powerful moral claim than distant heirs. Moshe Sanbar, the president of the Centre of Organizations of Holocaust Survivors in Israel, supported the Goodwill Fund, but he wanted to limit the range of heirs with whom the Conference would share the proceeds. He argued that the Conference had an obligation to provide social welfare services to needy survivors – which required money. 'I never opposed returning the property to children and grandchildren. The problem is the wide definition of heirs,'

Sanbar said. 'Because of that, we have much less money for survivors.'[45]

The Conference's counsel, Manhattan attorney Julius Berman, cautioned that the argument was not between the organization and the heirs, but between the heirs and the Holocaust survivors who benefited from the services. 'The Goodwill Fund is a very, very substantial and adequate compromise between two conflicting substantial and meritorious claims.'[46] He also rejected the charges that the owners had been robbed by the Conference. 'The former owners were expropriated not by the Claims Conference,' Berman said. 'They were expropriated by the German government twice, twice – once way back when, and then with this statute. The German government said they have no right to [the property] anymore. They [the German government] could have kept it themselves from that point on. They could have left it to the immediate former owners. They didn't. They gave it to the Claims Conference.'[47]

The board subsequently revised its policy again, extending the deadline and the amount that the heirs would receive. Under the new guidelines, late heirs who applied to the Goodwill Fund by 31 December 1998 and who otherwise would have been eligible to recover the property in East Germany would receive some 80 per cent of the proceeds once the property was sold; the Conference retained the balance as an assessment for its services.[48] The Conference also established a review committee for applications that were submitted after the deadline. There were many. 'Although the deadline expired in 1998, as a gesture of generosity, the Claims Conference still accepts claims,' Brozik said. The number of claims against the Goodwill Fund rose from 231 in 1999 to 473 in 2001. By the end of 2001, the Goodwill Fund had paid some DM 224.1 million to the late heirs.[49]

The Conference faced another conflict with different kinds of heirs – German-Jewish communities and organizations. By 1933, the Jewish community in Germany – then some 600,000 strong – had built a well-developed communal and organizational network. Every town had *Gemeinden*, or congregations, that were legal entities. The members paid a 'church tax' to the state, which in turn gave funds to the *Gemeinden*. Under the Nazis, the *Gemeinden* had been dissolved and their properties seized. After unification – as had been the case after the war – there were communal claims for pre-war properties, although the post-war/post-GDR Jewish communities were only a remnant of their former selves, and many members were not the descendants of the communities' builders.[50] 'The Jewish communities of today are not the heirs of the community,' said Ignatz Bubis, then the president of the *Zentralrat*, the central organization of German Jews. 'It's a different community; the heirs are around the world, not in Germany.'[51]

The *Zentralrat* and the Conference struggled to reach an agreement over the division of property, compounded by domestic conflicts between the *Zentralrat* and local Jewish communities. The Conference, however, did not question the nationalities of the Jews in Germany. 'A reconstituted community has its needs and has to function,' Kagan said. The issue was not the origins of the members of the communities, but their numbers – what Kagan called 'numerical disproportion'. 'A community that today constitutes a fraction of the pre-Hitler community cannot assert a claim for all the assets of that community,' he said.[52]

In 1992, the Conference and *Zentralrat*, which was a founding member of the Conference, reached an agreement under which so-called 'indispensable' properties that were needed for the activities of the community – such as synagogues, cemeteries, social institutions and community centres – were returned to the community. Other communal properties within the locality, as well as communal properties in places in which there were no longer Jews, were to be sold. The Conference would retain 70 per cent of the proceeds. The *Zentralrat* would receive 30 per cent, which was intended to assist communities in the former GDR. The Berlin Jewish community, divided before 1990, was in an unusual position. After the Second World War, the Jewish community in the GDR had reached some property settlements with the East German government, while in the 1970s, the Jewish community in the West received 'equalization' funds from the West German government and waived claims for Jewish communal property in East Berlin. In addition, Adas Israel, an Orthodox community founded in the nineteenth century, was reorganized in 1986 in East Berlin. After reunification, it sought to restore the legal status it had attained a century earlier. In October 1994, the Berlin Administrative Court ruled that Adas Israel's corporate status remained in force, despite the organization's dissolution by the Nazi régime. 'The National Socialist legislation of 1938-39 was an arbitrary act that is now null and void and could not change that status,' the court said. 'Nor has it ceased due to the fact that Adas Israel revived its religious activities in Berlin after Nazi rule only since 1986.' That was affirmed by a German federal court in October 1997. The decisions meant there were two officially recognized Jewish communities in Berlin: Adas Israel and the *Jüdische Gemeinde*, the Jewish communal umbrella organization that operated in West Berlin after the war. The rulings gave Adas Israel the legal status to claim property it owned before the war, as well as access to public funds to support its activities. As of 2002, the Conference, which had the right under the federal law to claim properties of dissolved Jewish communities, had not fully resolved its relations with the Berlin community.[53]

The Conference encountered competing claims with another of its members, B'nai B'rith International. The fraternal organization, whose international headquarters are in Washington, had asserted claims for properties that had been owned before the Nazi era by B'nai B'rith's German affiliates, which were known as lodges. The Conference also had claimed the sites. It rejected B'nai B'rith's right to make a claim, saying the Conference was the only recognized authority for making collective Jewish claims, and noted that the statutes of the former East German lodges did not provide for the properties to be passed on to the international organization, as the 'supreme lodge', if the lodges were dissolved. B'nai B'rith and the Conference reached an agreement in 1998, under which all community properties to which B'nai B'rith International had a claim would be restituted to the Conference, and B'nai B'rith – like the *Zentralrat* – would receive 30 per cent of the proceeds.[54]

Among the multiple competitors confronting the Conference and Nazi victims' heirs were some who had no prior connection to the property – investors. Based on the experience of the JRSO in West Germany, the Conference originally had estimated that the recovery and disposition of property would take a decade. The German government, however, was impatient. It did not want property claims to hinder economic development in the East, but to contribute to it. And to the German government and its taxpayers, the restitution of Jewish property was but a minor aspect of a massive German plan whose primary purpose was to jumpstart and privatize the economy of East Germany. The government decided that priority in property claims would go to investors whose purchase of the sites would create jobs. As of the end of 2000, 949 properties claimed by the Conference had been taken under the German 'investment priority' plan.[55]

The Conference had two primary objections to the investment programme. In its efforts to entice investors to buy the properties, the government stripped the original owner of his rights. The former owner-claimant was given the chance to recover the property, instead of the investor, only if he could produce within 14 days an equivalent investment proposal. However, this time frame was impossible for claimants outside Europe, and it deprived the original owner of the right to use or dispose of the property as he wished.[56] Then there was the matter of compensation. Under the investment arrangement, the former owner would be compensated with the proceeds of the property sale. However, when the state agency sold the property, its purpose was to encourage investment, and it did not seek the optimal market price for the real estate. The former owner-claimant was in no position to influence the sale price. His only recourse, to realize the full value of the property, was to sue the German state authority, the *Treuhandanstalt*, to recoup the difference between the value of the property and the price paid by the investor.

In general, compensation in lieu of restitution was a sore issue for property owners. The German property law called for restitution, although there were many cases in which physical restitution was not possible. There were instances in which the buildings no longer existed, and cases in which, because of war-time destruction and post-war construction, plots of land had been combined and new structures erected on the sites. In addition, restitution was barred when the properties had been converted to public uses, such as schools, parks and roads. The number of cases for which physical restitution was deemed impossible was higher in urban areas than in the provinces because of the destruction of cities during the war and the construction of new buildings in the former GDR. Restitution also was complicated if the 'Aryanized' property subsequently changed hands in the German Democratic Republic and the new owner, unaware that the property had been confiscated from Jews, bought it in good faith. 'In the interest of a socially acceptable settlement, return is ruled out in cases where a third party acquired the property in good faith,' according to the German property guidelines.[57]

The Conference estimated that physical restitution would be impossible for up to 40 per cent of the properties it claimed in the cities.[58] When compensation was provided in lieu of restitution, a government agency calculated the amount to be paid to the claimant, which, as a rule, was lower than the market value of the property.[59] The Conference had numerous grievances as the property compensation policies evolved. The initial government proposal would have paid only 1.3 times the pre-war tax value of the property. In March 1993, Kohl's government approved a draft law that would place a tax on restituted properties; the tax revenue would be used to pay those who received compensation in lieu of restitution. Miller called the proposed levy 'immoral'.[60] The compensation provisions became increasingly complicated because the measures included both Nazi- and communist-era expropriations. The government liabilities potentially would be staggering if all properties earned a high compensation rate. At the same time, the authorities did not want a dual system that would make preferential payments for one type of confiscation at the expense of the other. It was only in late 1994 that the compensation law was enacted. The compensation for Nazi victims' property, in principle, was based on four times the assessed tax value of the property before its Nazi-era confiscation or forced sale, while compensation for nationalized property was to be paid on a reduced scale. In addition, the amounts awarded to Nazi victims would be paid immediately upon the approval of the award, while other awards were to be paid after 2004.[61]

Johanna Adler Markhoff's house in Berlin heralded a radical change in aid for Nazi victims. By the end of 2001, German restitution agencies had awarded 8,089 properties to the Successor Organization; more than 1,417 had been sold.[62] In 2001 alone, the Successor Organization generated revenue of about DM 245 million from property sales, rentals and compensation.[63] Collectively, these properties meant that, for the first time in four decades, the Conference had a significant, unrestricted source of funds to finance social welfare programmes for Nazi victims, and for Holocaust research, education and documentation.

NOTES

1 German Federal Office for the Settlement of Open Property Issues (*Bundesamt zur Regelung offener Vermögensfragen* [BARoV]), 'Information concerning "open property issues" in Germany after reunification', January 2000.

2 Claims Conference, *Annual Report 2001*.

3 The rapid changes regarding private property rights began in March 1990, when the Modrow government in the GDR announced that thousands of firms that had been nationalized in the 1970s could be reclaimed. In a joint declaration on 15 June 1990, West and East Germany announced their intent to restitute (or to provide compensation for) property that had been expropriated by the GDR. In one of its last formal acts, the GDR's Volkskammer passed a property law on 30 September 1990. The GDR initially set the deadline for filing claims at 31 January 1991, but subsequently advanced the deadline to 13 October 1990. (See State Department press release, 31 August 1990.) The deadline for registering claims preceded the development of standards and mechanisms for adjudicating claims. In the first five years of reunification, property laws were revised more than a half-dozen times.

4 BARoV statement, January 2000.

5 A German official estimated that there were five claims for every property in Berlin's Jewish district, the most disputed part of the city, according to a report by the Jewish Telegraphic Agency, 11 September 1995.

6 The principle of restitution had not come without a battle. The Conference had sought restitution, but the former East Germany and the FRG's Social Democratic Party favoured compensation in lieu of restitution. The conservative parties, led by the governing CDU, supported restitution. Brozik interview, 29 April 2002.

7 *Los Angeles Times*, 8 April 1990. A tragic protest was the 1992 suicide of Detlef Dalk, an East German politician, who feared he would lose his home in Zepernick. In a suicide note to Kohl, he called on the chancellor to stop the seizures of homes. 'Mr. Chancellor, there are many cleaning ladies, trash collectors, builders, workers and ordinary people in the former East Germany who own houses with gardens. And the overwhelming majority of these people were neither senior [communist] party functionaries nor Stasi spies. I am only one of many who have been threatened by ridiculous accusations that we unlawfully acquired our houses,' he wrote. 'Please listen to what I am saying – otherwise I will not be the last.' The letter was reprinted in *Harper's Magazine* in June 1992.

8 Kagan, 'Morality and Pragmatism: A Participant's Response.' Also excluded were claims for expropriations made on the basis of Occupation law or sovereign acts by the Occupying powers from 1945 to 1949, which were known in the GDR as 'land reform' properties. This exclusion was said to be a concession to the Soviet Union, in exchange for its support of German reunification. The former owners of properties lost during the four years of the Soviet Occupation were eligible for payment under the Equalization of (War) Burdens law. Some of these former owners have contended that their property rights have been violated by unified Germany. For an overview of property restitution in the former GDR as a form of 'corrective justice' in reunified Germany, see A. James McAdams, *Judging the Past in Unified Germany*, New York: Cambridge University Press, 2001.

9 BARoV statement, January 2000. The German restitution measures traditionally had built in some presumptions that favoured Jewish claimants, including the presumption that transfers after 1933 were under duress.

10 Claims Conference memorandum, 'Implementation of the German Restitution Legislation', 29 November 1991.

11 Brozik report, 'Problems of Increasing the Speed of the Restitution Procedure,' May 1995.

12 In addition to Jewish claims for nationalized properties, the US government also had claims that were made by American citizens for properties in the former GDR. The US and Germany did not reach an agreement on compensation for those claims until May 1992. Under that agreement, which was intended to settle some 1,900 claims, Germany pledged to pay up to $190 million to the US, which would be distributed by the Foreign Claims Settlement Commission, a division of the US Justice Department. The American claimants had the option of pursuing claims under the German property laws, or seeking compensation via the US–German property settlement.

13 The JRSO was based on a novel legal theory that a private international trust, in this case composed of voluntary organizations, could become the legal heir to property located in a sovereign state. German officials opposed the measure; they also insisted that the successor organization should be based in Germany and include primarily German victims. The Jewish Trust Corporation was the JRSO's British counterpart. A French branch of the JTC operated in the French Zone; the creation of the French branch was a means of bypassing problems in French law, which did not recognize the concept of a successor organization. After German reunification, the Conference was accepted as the logical successor organization because, by 1990, the JTC had been dissolved and the JRSO was dormant.

14 Kagan, 'Morality and Pragmatism: A Participant's Response'.

15 In addition, German claims were likely to be smoother because the claimants lived in Germany, often in the same town in which the claim was made, which was not the case for Jewish claimants.

16 Interview, 29 April 2002.

17 Brozik report, 'Problems of Increasing the Speed of the Restitution Procedure,' May 1995.

18 Brozik memo, 3 January 1996.

19 Kagan interview, 4 January 2001.

20 In 2002, the Conference reached an agreement with the German government for $69 million in compensation for the synagogues and contents destroyed during *Kristallnacht*.

21 BARoV statement.

22 Brozik report, 'Problems of Increasing the Speed of the Restitution Procedure', May 1995.

23 Kagan interview, 4 January 2001.

24 Brozik interview, 7 August 2001.

25 Claims Conference Board meeting, 23–24 July 2002, Luxembourg.

26 The global applications were submitted to more than 250 property offices in the former East Germany in December 1992. The global claims were differentiated according to how specific they were. See Brozik memo to Taylor and Kagan, 19 November 2002.

27 Because the bulk claims were later itemized, after the filing deadline had passed, the number of claims actually increased. In October 2002, a Berlin administrative court rejected a restitution agency's ruling in the Claims Conference's favour that was based on a claim from a global application a decade earlier. The court said the application was not specific and thus invalid. (*Wall Street Journal*, 14 November 2002.) However, Brozik expected to win an appeal because the global claims had been recognized by other restitution authorities and courts.

28 Brozik report, 'Problems of Increasing the Speed of the Restitution Procedure,' May 1995.

29 Claims Conference, *Annual Report 2001*. These claims were primarily for property and business assets, but also included works of art and the property of former Jewish communities in East Germany. The geographic distribution of the claims reflected the heavily urban distribution of the former Jewish population in East Germany. Nearly half were in Berlin; about 15 per cent (each) were in Sachsen and Brandenburg. The fewest claims – about 2 per cent – were in Mecklenburg-Vorpommern.

30 Kagan interview, 4 January 2001.

31 Brozik report, 'Problems of Increasing the Speed of the Restitution Procedure,' May 1995.

32 Ibid.

33 Kagan memo to Claims Conference Board, 11 October 1993.

34 Claims Conference Executive Committee, 3 July 1997, Jerusalem. Individual owners and heirs also had been the primary beneficiaries of the post-war restitution programme. In the US Occupation Zone alone, property worth some $250 million was restored to individual former Jewish owners; heirless assets valued at more than $25 million were recovered by the JRSO

35   Report on status of Successor Organization, 27 May 1994.

and used to aid Holocaust survivors, according to Ferencz, the founding director of the JRSO. (See his essay 'Restitution to Nazi Victims – A Milestone in International Morality,' in Harry Schneiderman, ed., *Two Generations in Perspective*, New York: Monde Publishers, 1957.)

36   Claims Conference Board meeting, 10 September 1997, New York. Under §2.1 of *Vermögensgesetz*, if the Jewish claimant or his heirs failed to file a claim within the time allowed by the law, the Conference is considered the legal successor.

37   Ibid.

38   Brozik memo, 'The Legal Position of the Claims Conference in its Function as the Successor Organization According to the Property Law,' 3 January 1996.

39   *Jerusalem Post*, 7 August 1998.

40   The ruling by Judge Barry A. Cozier did not deal with the factual allegations of the case. The dismissal was on grounds of *forum non conveniens*, meaning that the New York court was not the appropriate venue. The Conference argued that property, the documentation and the expertise on the restitution of German property were all in Germany. It also argued that 'the public policy underlying the determination of the parties' rights to the property and business assets at issue is uniquely German, relating to its objective of compensating victims of the Nazi era.'

41   Netty C. Gross, 'The Old Boys Club' (*Jerusalem Report*, 15 May 1997) and 'After Years of Stonewalling, the Claims Conference Changes Policy' (*Jerusalem Report*, 16 August 1997).

42   Claims Conference Board meeting, 10 September 1997, New York.

43   The publicity over the Goodwill Fund occurred amid demands for the recovery of dormant Jewish Holocaust-era accounts in Swiss banks, as well as the restitution of Jewish properties in Central and Eastern Europe. Some members of the Conference said that the Jewish community could not argue that it had a moral, if not legal, claim to bank accounts in Switzerland and properties in Central and Eastern Europe, and then use a legal argument to deprive a late heir of family property the Conference had acquired in Germany.

44   Claims Conference Board meeting, 10 September 1997, New York.

45   Sanbar interview, 26 August 2001.

46   Claims Conference Board meeting, 10 September 1997, New York.

47   Claims Conference Executive Committee, 3 July 1997, Jerusalem.

48   The revised Goodwill Fund guidelines were adopted by the Claims Conference Board on 19 July 2000.

49   Brozik interview, 10 October 2002. The most prominent Goodwill Fund case was the so-called 'Wertheim' claim for department store properties in the heart of Berlin that were owned, in part, by the KarstadtQuelle company after the Second World War. The potential claim came to the attention of the heirs of German businessmen Gunther and Fritz Wertheim in 2000, on the basis of research by a graduate student; the properties in former East Berlin also had been claimed by the Conference. The Wertheim case was extremely complicated, entailing proceedings under German property law for the Conference's claims; proceedings in US federal court, under American law, against the former 'Aryanizer' for actions taken after 1945; and a political dispute between the US and German governments about whether the case affected the law governing the German foundation Remembrance, Responsibility and the Future, which was established in 2000, on the basis of a bilateral German-American agreement, and which was intended to be the exclusive remedy for all remaining claims against the German government and industry. In December 2005, the Wertheim heirs' claim was validated by a German restitution court; the estimated value of the properties was about $350 million.

50   After the Second World War, many displaced persons and refugees were integrated into Germany, often because they were unable to emigrate elsewhere in the West. After reunification, the new immigrants were from the former Soviet Union. For instance, *The Week in Germany*, an official publication of the German Information Center in the US, reported on 12 April 1991 that the Jewish community of Brandenburg was to be re-established. At that time, there were 500 Jews in Brandenburg, of whom 486 were recent immigrants from the former Soviet Union.

51   Claims Conference Board meeting, 10 September 1997, New York.

52   Kagan interview, 24 June 2001. When the post-war successor organizations claimed the former Jewish communal and organizational properties, they divided the assets between the reconstituted Jewish communities in West Germany and programmes for Holocaust survivors outside of Germany. The communities received properties that were seen as essential to reconstruct Jewish social and cultural life; organizations that aided the resettlement and rehabilitation of victims abroad acquired the remaining proceeds of the properties.

53 For court decisions, see the *Forward*, 17 February 1995, and the Jewish Telegraphic Agency, 23 October 1997. The court did not specifically address the Claims Conference's role as the successor.

54 Conference memo to file, unsigned, 'Re: B'nai B'rith Property Claims,' 8 May 1994. Their agreement, dated 18 August 1998, included a provision under which B'nai B'rith would designate projects 'with a Holocaust component' that could be financed by the Conference from its 70 per cent share of the proceeds of the sales of B'nai B'rith properties.

55 'Status of Activities and Business Development as per 12/31/2000,' Successor Organization, 12 March 2001.

56 Claims Conference Board meeting, 28–29 May 1992, Madrid.

57 BARoV statement.

58 Brozik report, 'Problems of Increasing the Speed of the Restitution Procedure,' May 1995.

59 Brozik interview, 29 April 2002.

60 Miller memo to Claims Conference Board, 1 April 1993.

61 Brozik report, 8 November 1994.

62 Claims Conference, *Annual Report 2001*. However, it should be noted that the income was declining, in part, because the most valuable properties were sold earlier. In 2000, the income from the properties was DM 334.8 million.

63 Ibid. By that time, the German restitution agencies had ruled on 53,372 – about 54 per cent – of the Successor Organization's claims. As expected, the overwhelming majority did not devolve to the Conference. Of those claims, 22,315 were for properties that were not owned by Jews. Another 16,253 were duplicate claims for the same sites, and 6,715 were withdrawn in favour of Jewish heirs. Brozik estimated that the Conference will have disposed of its properties by 2010. (Brozik interview, 10 October 2002). The estimate considers the prospect of appeals and lawsuits. Under the German property law, there is an arduous appeals process in which either party has 30 days to appeal a decision by the restitution agency. There are four potential levels of appeal: Administrative Appeal Process; Court of First Instance; Court of Second Instance; and the Supreme Court.

Chapter 7

Surviving *Vernichtung durch Arbeit*: Compensation for Slave Labour

Norbert Wollheim, his wife and 3-year-old son arrived at Auschwitz on 5 March 1943, in one of the final Nazi transports from Berlin. Wollheim's wife and son were sent directly to the gas chamber. Tattooed with the number 107984, Wollheim was sent to work for I.G. Farben at the Buna sub-camp at Auschwitz. The commandants insisted that he run as he hauled sacks of cement. Later he worked, without protective gear, as a welder. Starved and terrified, his life depended on his labour. 'You were really a slave. You were rented out by the SS,' Wollheim recalled. 'I was a slave working for the benefit of the SS, and I was aware of the fact that I was allowed to live only as long as I was able to do this kind of work. The moment I became weak or the moment I would contract any illnesses – that was the end.'[1]

Farben, in consultation with the SS and with financial help from Deutsche Bank, had financed and built Buna, exploiting concentration camp slave labour in an attempt to produce synthetic rubber. Farben was only one of hundreds of companies that sought cheap concentration camp labour. This was part of a larger enterprise in which Jews were murdered through a scheme of *Vernichtung durch Arbeit* (destruction through work) that simultaneously produced commodities and matériel that would help the Nazi war effort and enrich German companies, said Benjamin B. Ferencz, a Nuremberg prosecutor who later represented the Claims Conference in Germany. 'If at any time along the road you were unable to work, you went to death immediately,' he said.[2]

'The Jewish concentration camp workers were less than slaves. Slave masters care for their human property and try to preserve it; it was the

Nazi plan and intention that the Jews would be used up and then burned,' Ferencz wrote in his book *Less Than Slaves: Jewish Forced Labour and the Quest for Compensation*. Ferencz used the term 'slave', he said, 'only because our vocabulary has no precise word to describe the lowly status of unpaid workers who are earmarked for destruction'.[3]

By 1944, the Nazis had pressed some 12 million people – Jews and non-Jews – into servitude; some conditions were far less coercive and brutal than others. Almost all German industrial companies sought cheap labour from the concentration camps. 'In company after company, the percentage of the labour force staffed with involuntary workers increased to over 50 per cent,' said Burt Neuborne, who represented Nazi victims in numerous class-action lawsuits filed in the 1990s in US federal courts, including a number filed against German companies, that were seeking compensation and disgorgement of profits made using slave labour.[4] The Nazi régime also profited handsomely from leasing slave labour to industry. It calculated that the 'profit per prisoner' from labour was at least 1,431 marks. That was based on a 'daily farming-out wage' of six marks (minus 0.70 marks for food and 'clothing depreciation'), multiplied by 270 days. That calculation of time was very telling; it was an official acknowledgement that conditions were so harsh that a slave labourer was expected to survive only nine months.[v]

The US war crimes tribunal known as the Subsequent Proceedings at Nuremberg brought indictments against three industrial companies that were accused of abusing concentration camp inmates: Farben, Krupp and corporations owned by the industrial baron Friedrich Flick. The tribunal already had determined that 'Auschwitz was financed and owned by Farben' and that its use of slave labour was 'a crime against humanity' when Wollheim saw a newspaper announcement in 1951. The Allied High Commission in West Germany was dismantling Farben and called on shareholders to register their claims.[6] 'All of a sudden I had a brainstorm. If they ask for claims to be registered, I also have a claim,' Wollheim said. 'They never paid me a penny for my slave work. I'm entitled to something.'[7]

He filed a suit against Farben for non-payment of wages and, on 10 June 1953 a court in Frankfurt ordered Farben to pay him DM 10,000, which was then the equivalent of about $2,500. When Farben appealed, Wollheim turned for assistance to the Claims Conference, which had been formed in 1951. 'My lawyer and I were not strong enough to fight this fight alone,' said Wollheim.[8] He was pursuing a principle, not the money. 'Twenty-five hundred dollars is nothing in America today,' Wollheim said in 1955, when he was living in New York. 'But the victory in court would open the way for thousands of suits totalling millions of dollars, and the money would mean something to many victims of the Nazis still in Europe.'[9]

Wollheim's initial success in his lawsuit against Farben established the obligation of German industry to pay compensation, at least in some limited form, to slave labourers. But the appellate court in Frankfurt left the determination of the company's legal liability in suspense. 'The appellate court was at a stage where it had to make a decision and, on an issue of such a delicate nature, it urged Farben to find a way for an amicable settlement to avoid litigation,' said Kagan.[10] That settlement was the first agreement between the Conference and German companies for compensation for Jewish slave labourers. However, Farben did not recognize a legal obligation to make payments. It paid DM 27 million to 'mitigate the suffering' of the victims.

One of every five inmates engaged in Nazi-era slave labour perished each month, according to Ferencz. At Buna, for instance, although no more than 10,000 persons worked at any one time, it was reported that during its three years of operation, more than 30,000 people perished there. Surviving slave labourers were in desperate condition after the war, while German companies began to regain their wealth. Immediately after Wollheim's case, the Conference, using records accumulated during the Nuremberg trials, demanded that German industrialists account for their brutal exploitation of the Jews.

From the outset, however, the obstacles to obtaining compensation were nearly insurmountable. There were no binding precedents in international or domestic German law that obliged companies to pay. No German company volunteered to aid survivors; rather, they intensely resisted compensation. 'The attitude was "What? We employed concentration camp inmates?" Next, they denied that they were in any way responsible or connected with it. "Ah, perhaps they were assigned to us by the SS. It could have been, but the conditions were really very good." So they denied the conditions,' Ferencz said. 'Then when you pointed out the conditions were really very terrible: "Ah, we were not responsible for that. We did the best we could under difficult circumstances." Then the ultimate payoff was, "Well, you know, if it hadn't been for us, they would have gone directly into the gas chamber. So, by our providing work, we saved their lives. Why are they complaining to us? They owe us."'[11]

Industry used other arguments to avoid compensation. Some companies contended that they already had paid via corporate taxes that the German government used to pay reparations, while Farben threatened that if it lost in court it would sue the West German government as the legal heir of the Nazi régime.[12] Some also argued that the slave labour claims were filed too late, invoking statutes of limitations under domestic German law. 'And if they did not come too late, they came too early,' before the signing of a final peace treaty with Germany, Ferencz said.[13]

The German 'economic miracle' was not anticipated after the war. Instead, the Allies initially planned to dismantle Germany to such an extent that it could not re-arm and threaten Europe in the future. However, the emergence of the Cold War radically altered the geopolitical landscape of Europe, and the West needed a vigorous and cooperative West Germany as a partner. While Bonn was negotiating with Israel and the Conference on compensation for Nazi victims, it was also talking to its creditors. In 1952, the London Debt Agreement – an arrangement between West Germany, the Allies and European nations to reschedule German debt – treated slave labour claims as reparations. These claims, however, were deferred until the conclusion of a peace treaty with Germany. Thus, slave labour compensation suits would be premature until there was a German peace treaty – which none at the time anticipated. The result, Ferencz said, was the companies that exploited them were legally immune from the slave labourers' claims.[14]

Without a legal determination of corporate liability, the Conference had no tools with which to compel West German companies to provide compensation for slave labour. Instead, it had to rely on economic pressure and political persuasion. The Farben agreement was the first of a handful, from among the hundreds, of German firms that exploited concentration camp inmates, that ultimately led to settlements totalling DM 51.9 million.[15] These few settlements were largely voluntary actions by industry, and none recognized the companies' legal obligation to the former slave labourers. In the case of Siemens, the company also rejected any suggestion of a moral debt.[16]

Those settlements reflected, in part, the extent and degree to which the German companies had been vulnerable to pressure. They were unequally so. Companies might be susceptible to mild forms of persuasion by their American business counterparts – such as the banker Eric Warburg or the industrialist Jacob Blaustein, who was the senior vice president of the Claims Conference – or to substantial threats to their business by the American government. Some of the companies might feel beholden to John J. McCloy, who, as the US High Commissioner, had granted clemency to the German industrialists convicted in the Nuremberg tribunals.[17]

Alfried Krupp was exposed to all these tactics. The Conference used 'what Germans might have regarded as a Blitzkrieg of pincer actions', according to Ferencz. 'There was a velvet-glove approach, in which several persons whom Alfried might regard as friends were recruited to try to persuade him to change his mind. There was also an iron-fist approach, which was designed to impress upon Krupp the risks he would run if he did not settle promptly. It was our hope that when Alfried weighed everything in the balance, he would recognize that it was clearly in his own interest to come to an early agreement.'

Krupp's family – which controlled the mammoth coal, iron and steel enterprise – had a long and early association with the Nazis. In 1933, his father, Gustav, had convened the Reich Association of German Industry, vowing to 'do everything in their powers to assist the government in its most difficult task'. For crimes against humanity and abuse of slave labour, Alfried had been convicted at Nuremberg. He was sentenced in 1948 to 12 years and loss of his property. He had been freed, and his property had been restored, when he was approached about compensation for slave labour. In approaching Krupp, Ferencz emphasized that the Conference regarded a settlement primarily as a humanitarian gesture, not a legal matter. Krupp resisted, in part, out of a sense of 'solidarity' with other German companies. Blaustein used his contacts with McCloy to approach Krupp, and also notified a Krupp advocate: 'We would regard it as unfortunate if you were to leave us no choice but to turn to the courts and to public opinion pursuant to our heavy obligation to assist these needy persons.' At the same time, the Conference tried to persuade the State Department to enforce the Allied law that required Krupp to sell his Rheinhausen steel operations. The linkage between the American government's interest in Rheinhausen and an inquiry about progress on the Jewish claims did not go unnoticed. The Conference and Krupp reached a settlement – of up to DM 10 million – in December 1959.

For the munitions company Rheinmetall, compensation for slave labourers was purely a business deal. It had been deaf to pleas for humanitarian aid. But compensation became enmeshed in military, political and economic considerations in 1965, when Rheinmetall expected a DM 300 million arms sale to the Pentagon. The arms deal was controversial, in part because Rheinmetall would displace an old American gun manufacturer. American Jews and some politicians also questioned the propriety of buying from a German company that had evaded its obligations to former slave labourers. The Conference did not want its moral argument inextricably linked with a military–commercial transaction, and rejected any suggestion that the American military's purchase of cannons from a German enterprise was conditioned on compensation for slave labourers.[18] Nonetheless, the Defense Department proceeded with the sale, and in 1966 the Conference received DM 2.5 million for former slave labourers.[19]

As part of the industrial agreements, the Conference was obliged to provide the companies with an indemnity against future claims by former Jewish slave labourers. For instance, in exchange for its arrangement with Krupp, 'the Claims Conference would have to guarantee that Krupp and its subsidiary companies, as well as persons acting on their behalf, would not be called upon to make any other payments arising out of forced labour claims by Jewish concentration camp inmates or their heirs'.[20] It also was obliged to administer the slave labour programmes, and created Compensation Treuhand, a special agency in West Germany, to screen and process the claims and distribute the funds.

The Farben agreement was reached in February 1957, after two years of negotiations.[21] It was 'the first time in the history of the Conference, since the Luxembourg Agreement, that we became a party to another special arrangement involving us directly, formally and officially, which will provide a sum from a source other than the German government for benefits to victims of Nazi persecution,' Kagan said.[22] The settlement was based on the Conference's participation as the intermediary because Farben declined to process the payments to the victims. It also was based on the Conference's guarantees and 'endorsement.'[23] 'They will never make an agreement with a committee of deportees,' Goldmann said. 'Every German knows the Claims Conference is a responsible body. We give a guarantee, it means something to them.'[24]

From the outset, the Farben agreement saddled the Conference with dilemmas. 'We don't want to have the same type of complaint coming against us as against the German government that we are too harsh,' Ferencz said. 'Everybody who is entitled to payment shall be paid. But how do you find out who is really entitled?'[25] And once the agreement was signed, survivors of slave labour for other companies approached the Conference. 'They reasoned that their claims were as justified as were those of the Auschwitz inmates who worked for the Farben company, and that they were entitled to the same measure of assistance as the Conference had given Mr Wollheim,' Ferencz said. 'They also noted that without such assistance they would be unable to obtain any compensation from the German firms involved.'[26]

There was not much time to act. The statute of limitations for such suits was due to expire at the end of 1957, and people who might have a claim would lose their rights by default if no means were found to assist them. However, the United Restitution Organization, the legal aid society for Nazi victims, was not prepared to help. Its mandate was to handle cases stemming from the German restitution and indemnification legislation, and it believed that the slave labour cases, which required a considerable amount of work, were 'of doubtful outcome'. Private lawyers shared that sentiment and declined to take the cases on a contingency basis. Conference officials in Germany recommended that it not get involved. They feared that a Conference connection to the slave labour cases might jeopardize the Farben deal, which was not yet final, and that the organization also would encounter opposition from West Germany, when the Conference needed support for legislative improvements in the existing German government compensation programmes for Nazi victims. However, Goldmann and Kagan 'felt that there was a moral obligation on the part of the Claims Conference do to something,' Ferencz said.[27]

Despite the unfavourable recommendation from its office in Germany, the Conference's New York headquarters office instructed the German office to submit test cases against nearly a dozen German companies in separate actions in courts in Berlin, Frankfurt and Munich.[28] The Conference remained in the background by establishing a 'Committee of Former Jewish Slave Labourers,' with an office for centralizing claims and a post office box to provide an address, although anonymous, to which claimants could turn.[29] None of the suits succeeded.[30] By the mid-1960s, 'there was nothing more that the Jewish organizations could do but to distribute whatever money had been obtained from a few companies to those particular classes of inmates for whom the payments were specifically earmarked,' Ferencz said. The former Nuremberg prosecutor was angered by the 'anomalous situation' in which German industrialists who had been prosecuted and convicted as war criminals for their abuse of slave labourers were not held civilly liable for the same deeds.[31]

Some 14,878 survivors in 42 countries got payments from those early agreements. However, there was no redress for labourers from enterprises that refused to pay, from those that were run by the Nazi government or SS – such as the Hermann Göring Werke and Organization Todt – or from private companies that were defunct, such as Messerschmitt and Junkers. Survivors whose labour was not covered under the agreements challenged the Claims Conference. 'What difference does it make if I worked for Krupp or Schmitt? It was the same kind of work in the same place in the same time and the same beatings and the same starvation. Why should he get it and not me?' Ferencz recalled the survivors saying. 'Morally, they were right, but we couldn't do anything about it.'[32]

Nor was the compensation consistent. These settlements established different conditions and terms. The payments themselves varied widely: The surviving Rheinmetall slave labourers received DM 1,700. By contrast, under the agreement with Siemens, claimants were to receive up to DM 5,000. Farben insisted on a two-tier payment schedule, with payments based on the duration of the victims' labour.[33]

Each agreement presented administrative problems. The relevant

Farben plants were all in one place and were named in the settlement. However, the Krupp, AEG and Siemens plants were scattered and were not specified in the agreements. It was difficult to ascertain the facts, especially because slave labourers often were ignorant of the identity of the firms for which they were compelled to work. AEG, for instance, demanded that the inmates specify the camp in which each person laboured. 'Complying with AEG's request was not as simple as it sounded. Over a hundred persons, for example, writing independently from different parts of the world, swore that they had worked for AEG at "Ankers," yet that name did not appear on any map of the region and AEG absolutely denied that it had ever had a plant at such location,' Ferencz recalled. In a poignant twist that showed the depths of the ignorance in which the victims laboured, it turned out that 'Ankers' was neither a town nor a factory. It was the German name for a part of a machine – a belt or *anker* – that was made by AEG in Riga. 'The workers only knew that they worked at 'Ankers,' without knowing that it was a thing, not a place,' Ferencz said.

By 1981, the slave labour programmes long had concluded. Compensation Treuhand had been dormant for a decade. In Germany, Katzenstein, as chairman of the Treuhand board, recommended that the Conference close it. There was no reason to keep it alive, he said, 'as an opportunity to call upon Compensation Treuhand to serve as an instrument of the Claims Conference will not present itself again, as the arena of [slave labour] compensation has been tightly walled off.'[34] Kagan and Ferencz, however, were 'reluctant to liquidate an entity which we have created in Germany as long as we are still actively in "business" there; one never knows when it may be useful to activate such a company,' Kagan said.[35]

The opportunity arose several years later when the Conference finally resolved the decades-old compensation claims for slave labour at Dynamit Nobel. The company was owned by Friedrich Flick, who had been indicted and convicted as a war criminal at Nuremberg for his abuse of slave labour. Flick, who served three years of a seven-year sentence, had insisted at Nuremberg, 'Nothing will convince us that we are war criminals.'[36]

'After intensive and many years of negotiation, we reached an agreement, at least we thought we had, in which [Flick] acknowledged some liability to pay DM 5 million, a totally inadequate sum, but the best that we could get, because the German courts in the last analysis refused to acknowledge the validity of such claims,' Ferencz said. 'The German Supreme Court said, no, these are in the nature of reparations claims, and they must be postponed until there is a final peace treaty with Germany, an event which will never take place. And so we were completely blocked despite the most strenuous efforts on all sides, and we had to take what we could get. And we did, in fact, adopt the principle of "Get as much as you can," and then accept that. But despite that, Mr. Flick, who was the richest man in Germany under Hitler, and who became the richest man in Germany after Hitler, when he was released from prison, absolutely refused to pay, and he died without having paid a cent.'[37]

'Am I right,' asked Katzenstein, 'in my assumption that the Dynamit Nobel case will be laid to rest with Flick's body?'[38] That was the Conference's sentiment until December 1985, when Karl Friedrich Flick, son of the founder and owner of the company then known as Feldmühle Nobel, decided to sell the private empire, which controlled some 300 companies, including Daimler-Benz.[39] Deutsche Bank bought it, for $2 billion, and planned to take the company public. Only days after the sale was reported, Miller wrote to Wilhelm Christians, the head of the bank's board. 'It has been reported that the Deutsche Bank is acquiring certain assets of the Flick Group, including the shares of Dynamit-Nobel. We wish to advise you that our organization – acting on behalf of surviving Jewish victims of Nazi persecution – has a claim against Dynamit Nobel that has not yet been satisfied', he wrote. 'The legal issue has never been resolved since German courts have deferred acting on such claims pending a final peace treaty with Germany. The claims remain, therefore, as an unsatisfied liability of the company and a continuing source of discontent. Since the survivors of Nazi persecution are now in advanced age, the problem calls for urgent solution.'[40]

The Conference's demand was echoed by Robert Kempner, a former Nuremberg prosecutor, who urged the bank to arrange the payment before it proceeded with a public stock offering, 'so that the new shares won't carry the smell of sweat and blood.'[41] The bank quickly instructed its former Flick subsidiary to pay, disregarding an attack by Hermann Fellner of Bavaria, the home affairs spokesman of the Christian Social Union. 'I see neither a legal nor a moral basis for this demand by the Jews,' Fellner said. 'It creates the impression that Jews are quick to show up when money tinkled in German cash registers.'[42]

However, in the decades between the agreement and the payment, the relative value of the original Flick settlement had eroded. 'This was not a point of negotiation any more,' Kagan said. 'This was an agreement that was reached 20-odd years ago, and the dead hand of Flick was lying there.' The result was that the 2,500 surviving Dynamit Nobel slave labourers received only DM 2,000 each. For Wollheim, who had successfully sued Farben 30 years earlier, the Flick payment was cause for soul-searching. 'I'm still fighting with a moral issue. Was it right to bring that suit, so that the Germans could say, "After all, we cleaned the slate, and now we have paid our dues"?' he told the Conference. 'When I hear that, for instance, Dynamit Nobel can only distribute DM 2,000 to my former slave labour colleagues, I must say, from a certain point of view, we rather do not accept this pittance of petty cash for the work we have done for them – because Dynamit Nobel, though there is now another management in charge, can say, "Well, we took care of the slave labourers" – for DM 2,000 per person. I think it's a shame.'[43]

It had been widely believed that the ability to secure compensation for slave labourers was all but exhausted in the late 1960s. The belated Flick payment encouraged Kagan to approach other German companies. Only a few responded. After goading by the Conference, Daimler-Benz in 1988 made a payment, but the nature of the compensation had changed. Citing 'humanitarian considerations', Daimler-Benz made DM 20 million available in 1988 to organizations that provide support for 'former forced workers in need.' But there was no plan to make payments to individual victims. 'After intensive discussions, we came to realize that individual compensation for the consequences of these terrible events would neither be practicable nor appropriate by the company,' Daimler chief Manfred Gentz said.[44]

The Conference's share of the Daimler payment was DM 10 million, which was used for grants to institutions, primarily in Israel, that assisted Holocaust survivors. 'At this point, we are past arrangements under which funds will be distributed to individuals,' Kagan told the board in 1990. 'The companies themselves are faced today with a different situation. When we come now and talk about Jewish Nazi victims, they are, of course, under pressure on behalf of non-Jewish forced labourers, who, although not in the same horrible circumstances as the Jews, nonetheless were forced to come to Germany, and in many cases were certainly not in very, let's say, comfortable circumstances.' Daimler-Benz, for instance, wanted to avoid individual payments to Jewish slave labourers because it feared setting a precedent that would prompt non-Jewish victims to demand compensation. The company had calculated that there were possibly 2,000 Jewish slave labourers, but there also were some 30,000 Nazi-era non-Jewish labourers, many from Poland.[45] The Conference also received DM 2.5 million from Volkswagen in 1992, but it came only after a struggle. Volkswagen argued that it had been a government firm and, since the German government had paid reparations, the company had no such debts. However, VW also was under pressure anew to make some gesture after a company-commissioned history of forced labour at VW, written by the German historian Hans Mommsen, was published in 1996.[46]

In West Germany, the issue of compensation for Nazi-era slave labourers began to surface in domestic politics amid new attention on the 'forgotten victims.' 'In 1986, there was an intense debate in the [Bundestag] Interior Committee about deficits in [Nazi-era] programmes in general; slave labour was one of those,' said Beck of the Greens.[47] The Conference called on the Bundestag to provide compensation to former slave labourers,[48] while the Greens – then a minor opposition party – with support of the Social Democratic Party in 1989 introduced a draft measure in the Bundestag calling for the creation of a German federal foundation, with the participation of private companies, to provide compensation for slave labour.[49] Experts told a Bundestag committee that the London Debt Settlement – long the reason for deferring slave labour payments – did not bar the German Parliament from enacting domestic legislation to compensate slave labourers.[50]

After German reunification, claims against German companies for Nazi-era use of slave labour were filed in German courts. In 1992, a Bremen court ruled that DM 15,000 in compensation should be paid to three Jews who had been slave labourers for the municipality for eight months during the war. However, the local court forwarded the case to the Federal Constitutional Court in Karlsruhe to decide whether the decision had to be deferred until there was a formal peace treaty under the terms of the 1952 London agreement.[51]

In a ground-breaking decision, Germany's highest court characterized the '2+4' reunification agreement as the equivalent of a peace treaty. This struck at the heart of the basis of the moratorium on compensation and opened the possibility for slave labour claims against German companies.[52] 'A combination of the 'postponements' imposed by the international community from 1946 to 1991, and the failure of the German reparations programmes to include compensation for forced labourers, left the involuntary labour population with no remedy for more than 50 years,' said Neuborne. 'To its credit, the German Federal Constitutional Court ruled in 1996 that claims against German corporations by slave labourers were no longer blocked by international law.'[53] In November 1997, a judge in Bonn ruled that Germany was liable for compensation to a Polish-born Jewish slave labourer who had worked at Weichsel Metall Union, a munitions plant near Auschwitz that subsequently was defunct.[54] In 1998, the Bremen *Landgericht* (District Court) ruled in favour of a Nazi-era Jewish slave labourer in Romania.[55]

In Frankfurt, Brozik wanted to take advantage of German court rulings – as well as the potential political changes after the September 1998 German federal elections – to press for slave labour payments. Although the Conference had reached slave labour agreements decades earlier with a few German companies, 'they were not appropriate and satisfying at all,' he said. 'Neither the amount of payments nor the number of companies willing to sign agreements was satisfactory because more than 90 per cent of the German companies employed slave labourers during the time of the Nazi régime.' Brozik recommended that the Conference enter into direct negotiations with industrial associations and individual companies. He also thought the Conference should press for negotiations with the German government, because the largest number of slave labourers had worked for state institutions and organizations as well as for local communities for whom the federal government was the legal successor. Finally, he suggested that the Conference support compensation lawsuits filed in Germany, as well as those in the US. 'Every one of these initiatives shows risks, advantages and disadvantages for the Claims Conference. An active support and involvement with individual lawsuits against German companies, for example, could cause ill feelings on the side of the German government. These ill feelings might effect the processing of the existing compensation funds,' Brozik said. 'Facing the unacceptable situation of the slave labour compensation, it is my opinion that we should not be afraid of this risk at all.'[56]

Lawsuits in American courts for compensation for Nazi victims had been more or less unknown until 1996, when class-action lawsuits were filed against Crédit Suisse and UBS – major Swiss commercial banks – for the recovery of dormant and unclaimed Nazi-era bank accounts. In August 1998, in US District Court in Brooklyn, a $1.25 billion settlement was announced.[57] In March 1998, the first slave labour suit was filed in the US, in US District Court in Newark. It was against an American corporation, the Ford Motor Company, and alleged that the company earned 'enormous profits' from slave labour during the Second World War at its Fordwerke German subsidiary in Cologne.[58] Soon after the Swiss banks' settlement, dozens of lawsuits on behalf of slave labourers were filed in US federal courts against Germany's industrial giants, including Daimler-Benz, Volkswagen, BMW, Degussa and Siemens. The claims were not limited to Jewish victims, but included non-Jewish forced labourers, primarily from Central and Eastern Europe.[59]

Nearly a half-century after the Nazi régime, the companies found themselves facing legal battles in both the US and Germany. In July 1998, Volkswagen reversed its earlier stance on compensation and announced that it would establish a fund for Nazi-era slave labourers.[60] The DM 20 million fund, which was portrayed as a voluntary humanitarian gesture based on the company's moral obligation, would pay all VW slave labourers DM 10,000 each.[61] Immediately after the announcement, the Claims Conference called on German companies that had used slave labour to enter talks on compensation.[62] Soon after, the electronics giant Siemens offered a DM 20 million fund for former slave labourers.[63] For Siemens, this also was a reversal of its previous attitude. When challenged by individual victims in 1997 – on the occasion of its hundred and fiftieth anniversary – Siemens said it had paid compensation via the Conference some 30 years before. 'Beyond that, I don't see any reason to reconsider this question any more,' Siemens chairman Heinrich von Pierer said at a news conference.[64]

The co-mingling of German political and economic interests also had a profound effect on compensation. VW, for instance, had announced its fund during the German electoral campaign. The SPD's candidate for chancellor, Gerhard Schröder, at the time was the minister-president of Lower Saxony. With 20 per cent of VW's stock, Lower Saxony was the company's largest shareholder.

When major German companies suggested a joint Holocaust fund to make payments to Nazi-era slave and forced labourers, Kohl, the Christian Democratic chancellor for the previous 16 years, dismissed the idea. 'What banks or insurance companies do is up to them,' Kohl said. 'But I say clearly "no" on behalf of the federal government, if you are asking whether it should open government coffers for reparations.'[65]

On 27 September 1998, Schröder defeated Kohl, and formed a coalition government with the Greens. The Red-Green coalition agreement called for a government foundation, together with German companies, to compensate Nazi-era slave labourers.[66] 'Our coalition agreement called for payments for slave labour,' Beck said. 'It was clear that the government would do something, even if there were no lawsuits.'[67] On the eve of taking power, the chancellor-elect met with executives of Germany's major enterprises to discuss how to deal with the American class-action lawsuits, saying, 'German companies have a right to be protected by the government.'[68]

The Conference was not a party to the lawsuits, but used them, as well as the change in the German government, as the opening to pursue its claims against German banks. The bank claims were not for compensation for slave labour, but linked to the banks' role in 'Aryanizing' Jewish property. 'Initially the idea was that we would try to reach a separate agreement with the banks on claims against banks,' Kagan said. 'They made the argument that there was no likely basis for claims. They were trying to minimize the size of the claims, the size of the demand.'[69] Those talks were interrupted in February 1999, when the chancellor and a consortium of twelve German banks and enterprises announced their plan for the 'Remembrance, Responsibility and the Future' fund. The fund was intended to provide 'humanitarian' compensation and meet the 'moral responsibility of German firms with regard to such issues as forced labourers, "Aryanization" and other injustice during the Nazi régime'.

The amount anticipated for the fund, financed by German industry, was DM 3 billion.[70] It also was suggested that a publicly funded German federal foundation would be created to handle claims – presumably for forced labour in agriculture and the public sector – that were not covered by the proposed industry foundation.

German companies referred to the fund as 'a gesture of reconciliation,' and rejected any legal basis for it. 'German enterprises recognize their moral responsibility, in particular where forced labour had to be performed under particularly harsh conditions and in cases where enterprises cooperated in discriminating against people who were persecuted on racial grounds during the Nazi régime.'[71] However, although the fund was cast in humanitarian terms, industry conditioned it on 'legal peace.' Schröder said it was 'to counter lawsuits, particularly class-action suits, and to remove the basis of the campaign being led against German industry and our country'.[72] Originally, it was envisioned that the fund would begin on 1 September 1999. The date had symbolic significance; it was the sixtieth anniversary of the invasion of Poland.

Previous efforts, decades earlier, by the Conference to craft an industry-wide settlement had come to naught. In March 1958, soon after the Farben settlement, Ferencz met with the *Bundesverband der Deutschen Industrie* (BDI, or the Federal Association of German Industries) to discuss a bulk settlement. 'My proposal was that German industrial firms contribute to a trust fund to be payable to former slave labourers along the lines of the Farben agreement,' he said. In addition to the moral arguments, Ferencz reasoned that an overall settlement would defuse any possible stigma against individual German companies and diminish the prospects of lawsuits against German firms.[73] The idea of a general settlement fizzled, in part, because the companies had different war-era histories, and because it had become clear that a global approach could backfire and solidly unite the companies against an industry-wide settlement because such a deal would imply industry-wide responsibility.[74]

In 1986, when the belated Flick payment revived attention on slave labour claims, Ferencz suggested another push for a bulk settlement. 'If German industry now feels political or other pressure to do something on behalf of uncompensated labourers, perhaps we can renew our earlier endeavors to have the [BDI] establish a general welfare fund to be divided among Jewish and non-Jewish organizations that represent Nazi victims,' Ferencz said in a letter to Kagan. 'If the heat on the German government gets too great, they might even welcome such a way out ... After our recent experience, who knows, anything may be possible!'[75] Although talks were held, again, a global approach failed.

The Conference, representing the interests of Jewish Holocaust survivors, traditionally had been the sole partner and vehicle for German companies' agreements on compensation for slave labour.[76] However, the February 1999 German proposal was intended to consolidate and resolve all remaining Nazi-era claims against the German government and industry, and it cast a net that went far beyond the Claims Conference.[77] The German government – which for decades had negotiated with the Conference – looked to the US government as the primary player, and it had other governments, public regulators and courts to satisfy. Before the final agreements were reached, there were twelve multilateral meetings to address forced and slave labour claims. They included major German multinational enterprises, who were linked in a consortium; German government officials; Stuart Eizenstat, who held positions in the US State and Treasury Departments and was the American government 'facilitator'; Central and Eastern European governments, representing their nationals – both Jewish and non-Jewish victims; the Claims Conference; and the class-action attorneys who filed the lawsuits. 'Everyone wanted to settle for different people,' said Taylor. 'It was a Rubik's cube. It was not fought on one plane.'[78]

The various parties had common interests and competing demands. However, these were not consistent, and the alliances shifted. Although, from a public relations point of view, Germany could not afford to win the lawsuits, German diplomats chafed at the American legal action as an intolerable attempt to interfere in German sovereignty and would never concede the right of an American court to have jurisdiction in German matters. German industry sought legal peace and shared the American government's interest in open markets. But the Germans and Americans disagreed about the role of the class-action lawyers. Unlike the US government, the German government thought that legal closure could be achieved without the consent of the lawyers.[79] The German government and industry were at times united, at other times not, over the obligation and strategy to address claims, the amount of the payment and the share to be borne by industry.[80] The five Eastern European countries sometimes acted in concert, sometimes not.[81] Although there were numerous actors representing victims, there was no natural 'victims side'. Jewish victims were lumped in with those from countries that had suffered under the German occupation, but whose national histories also included anti-Semitic violence against Jews and local collabouration with the Nazis.

The victims' advocates – the Conference and the class-action lawyers – also had different strategies, styles and tools in their negotiations. 'We negotiate with governments over moral and political issues and reach agreements on political grounds, regardless of the legal issues,' Taylor said. 'The legal side said law courts are the proper venue. We were coming from a completely different strategic position. There were arguments over strategy and tactics.' But the two were obliged, beginning with the 1996 class-action lawsuit against the Swiss banks, to reach a *modus operandi*. 'Everyone saw that the Swiss banks were not going to settle [the lawsuit] without the Jewish groups, and the Jewish groups were not going to settle without the lawyers. There had to be legal closure and political closure,' he said. 'It needed both sides; there was no solo deal that could be done with either.'[82]

All had to agree on the total amount of compensation, what Nazi-era damages the German payments would cover and how the fund would be divided among a staggering number of victims. Some one million surviving Nazi-era forced labourers ultimately could qualify for compensation, Eizenstat estimated in July 1999. The figures, which Eizenstat originally called 'ballpark estimates', included about 200,000 predominantly Jewish former slave labourers.[83] 'We must assume on principle that every concentration camp inmate was also a slave labourer, either in the camp or on building sites, in commands employed externally for industry or with the SS. A prisoner had to be able to work in order to survive,' Brozik said. 'The number of concentration camp prisoners is estimated at approximately two and a half million. The number of foreign workers is many times that amount, at least seven and a half million. Only a small number of concentration camp inmates survived, whereas most of the foreign workers and the forced labourers were not under threat of death.'[84]

The original German proposal was seriously flawed, Taylor said. From the outset, the Conference fought to establish definitive principles governing the Jewish claims. The first concerned German enterprises' moral responsibility for the exploitation of slave labour and industry's subsequent enrichment. Slave labour was 'primarily a moral issue and not just a political or legal issue', the Conference said in a position paper released as the slave labour negotiations got under way. German industry 'willingly participated and exploited a programme of the National Socialist régime that was morally unjustifiable. The acknowledgment of this fact and the public repudiation of the activities of the participating companies during the Second World War must form the underlying premise of all discussions,' the paper said.[85] For their part, the Germans repeatedly stressed the moral aspects at the same time they denied any legal obligations.[86]

Initially, the Germans, Eastern Europeans and Americans referred to the issue in general as 'slave labour'. The Conference insisted that a distinction be made between two categories of compulsory Nazi-era labour: slave and forced. The Nazis' forced labour policy was intended to provide a steady supply of workers, while slave labour 'was one of the three main methods used by the Nazis to murder Jews – the others being shooting and gassing. One of the purposes of slave labour was to work the individuals to death – *Vernichtung durch Arbeit*,' the Conference said.[87] The Germans quickly accepted the distinction. However, 'the Eastern Europeans' position was that everyone should be treated equally, that labourers were labourers, that they had been underpaid historically over the years, and we rigorously maintained, right from the beginning, again and again, there was a distinction between slave and forced labourers,' Taylor said.[88]

Under the definitions that evolved, slave labourers were those who had been inmates of a concentration camp, ghetto or similar facility; forced labourers were those who lived and worked under less harsh conditions.[89] The distinction was not based on religious or national origin, but on the severity of detention and labour. 'No racial, ethnic or religious group will get favourable treatment,' Eizenstat said. 'A slave or forced labourer is a victim of the Holocaust, whether he or she is a Czech, Pole, Jew, Romani or another nationality or religion.'[90] However, slave labourers were overwhelmingly Jewish, while forced labourers were overwhelmingly non-Jewish.[91]

The distinction between slave and forced labour also carried a financial impact, which reflected the differences in suffering. There were heated debates about what that differential should be. The Conference's original position was that slave labourers should receive five times the compensation of forced labourers. In the final agreement, former slave labourers received DM 15,000 – three times the compensation for forced labourers.

Industry argued that it was responsible only for slave or forced labourers who worked for private companies, not for those who worked for enterprises controlled by the SS or other Nazi entities. The Conference insisted that a private, industry-only fund was inadequate. 'The principle was that this was a fund for slave labour and *who* the labour was done for was not the main issue,' Taylor said.[92] The Conference demanded a single fund that would cover all labourers who worked for public and private companies, as well as for companies that were defunct a half-century after the Second World War. 'Jewish organizations cannot be expected to make selections and, for example, award a prisoner in Auschwitz who had to transport corpses from the gas chambers to the crematorium nothing or less than a forced labourer at Siemens,' Brozik said.[93] A general fund would benefit many more victims than those covered by the class-action lawsuits that had been filed in American courts, which targeted companies that conduct business in the US. 'For us, a company-specific solution would be completely inadequate because most of the survivors worked either for SS or other Nazi entities or for companies that are no longer in business,' Taylor said.[94]

The companies, contending that the fund was a goodwill gesture, said compensation should be based on the victim's need.[95] For the victims, this was irrelevant. 'The principle that was important to us was that compensation should be available regardless of need because it was not a humanitarian gesture for poor people,' Taylor said. 'This was compensation for people who had never gotten paid, and it was acknowledgment of their suffering.' The Conference also rejected a German proposal for a scale of payments linked to the standard of living in the victim's country of residence. 'We felt this was a moral gesture. If it is symbolic acknowledgement of suffering, there should be a uniform payment structure,' Taylor said.[96]

German enterprises also argued strongly that the German foundation would 'take into account' previous or ongoing payments by the German government to Nazi victims, including the pensions paid under the German indemnification legislation of the 1950s, the BEG. These offsets were a highly contentious issue in which the Germans insisted that slave labour was covered by the BEG, while the Claims Conference countered that the German indemnification laws covered incarceration, not slave labour. 'The German Government has paid – and this is to its great credit – something on the order of DM 100 billion since the early 1950s,' Eizenstat said. 'So if you had a dollar-for-dollar offset, then you'd basically be saying that very few people who received those payments would get anything [from the German fund].'[97]

The Germans argued that eligibility for labour should begin after six months of labour.[98] However, the Conference spurned any time 'threshold' before victims became eligible, primarily because these were symbolic payments. Further, it said, 'Since slave labourers were subject to immense suffering from the date they were forced to perform slave labour, there should be no minimum period before which slave labourers are eligible to receive compensation.'[99]

While the negotiations were under way, a US federal court issued the first ruling on German corporate liability for slave labour compensation. In September 1999, the court in Newark dismissed the class-action lawsuits against Degussa and Siemens. Compensation was a political question that was not subject to judicial proceedings, said US District Judge Dickinson R. Debevoise. 'Every human instinct yearns to remediate in some way the immeasurable wrongs inflicted upon so many millions of people by Nazi Germany so many years ago, wrongs in which corporate Germany unquestionably participated,' the judge wrote. However, he said he was bound to defer to the post-war treaties governing reparations claims, ruling that his court 'does not have the power to engage in such remediation.'[100]

The German companies welcomed the Newark court's dismissal of the lawsuits, but said they would still pursue their 'humanitarian' effort. German industry's fears were not limited to the battles in court; they also feared sanctions by American regulators. By this time, the German government negotiating team, headed by former Economics Minister Otto Graf Lambsdorff, had proposed a single national German foundation, to be established under German law and financed by the government and industry, that would make payments to victims of forced and slave labour for the German government, SS or private companies.[101]

The German offer was raised to DM 6 billion in October 1999, to DM 8 billion a month later, and to DM 10 billion in December.[102] The announcement came from the White House; President Bill Clinton said the German government and industry were prepared to commit DM 10 billion for what Clinton called 'the first important gesture made to those who were forced and slave labourers working for private industry.' The announcement conveyed a political settlement with legal and economic implications in the US. 'We believe this satisfies the requirements of those representing the victims,' Clinton said. 'We close the 20th century with an extraordinary achievement that will bring an added measure of material and moral justice to the victims of this century's most terrible crime ... They have been waiting a long, long time, and nothing can fully compensate [for] their searing loss. But we can accept our generation's responsibility to remember and to redress the injustices they suffered.' In return, Clinton pledged to 'do everything I can to provide legal finality for [Germany] and to remove the potential cloud hanging over German companies doing business here in the United States.'[103]

Days later, on 17 December 1999, there was a formal announcement that the German government and industry would pay DM 10 billion into the German 'Remembrance, Responsibility and Future' foundation. Although the negotiations were widely known as the 'slave labour' talks, and the primary issue concerned individual compensation for labour, the Conference had broader claims, including restitution claims for 'Aryanized' and heirless Jewish properties. The Conference demanded that the foundation include a humanitarian fund to cover those claims. 'The Germans wanted to deal with victims or heirs,' Miller recalled. 'We said, "You have a debt of honor to those who did not leave any heirs."'[104]

According to the December 1999 agreement, the foundation would 'cover all the Second World War injuries committed by German companies, including slave and forced labour to insurance, banking, "Aryanized" property and medical experiments.'[105] The language on property excluded those claims that were not based on racial persecution. 'To reopen a European reparation debate 55 years after the war could only have disastrous results for all nations involved,' Lambsdorff said.[106]

The agreement came with a powerful declaration from German President Johannes Rau that reiterated Germany's moral responsibility, acknowledged the role of German industry in the persecution, and made an appeal to the victims. 'We all know that no amount of money can truly compensate the victims of crime. We all know that the suffering inflicted upon millions of women and men cannot be undone. Nor is there any point in toting up past wrongs. Slave and forced labour did not merely mean that a just wage was withheld. Such labour meant being carried off, stripped of a homeland and rights, and having one's human dignity brutally violated. It often intentionally served the purpose of working people to death,' he said. 'This compensation comes too late for all of those who lost their lives back then, just as it is for all those who have died in the intervening years. I know that for many it is not really money that matters. What they want is for their suffering to be recognized as suffering and for the injustice done to them to be named injustice. I pay tribute to all those who were subjected to slave and forced labour under German rule and, in the name of the German people, beg forgiveness. We will not forget their suffering.'[107]

Three months following the agreement on the amount, an agreement was reached on the division of the fund. Of the DM 10 billion, DM 8.1 billion was for payments to individual slave and forced labourers. The Conference was to receive DM 2.072 billion to provide compensation to 129,000 Jewish slave labourers and 28,000 forced labourers in areas not served by the extant 'reconciliation foundations' in Central and Eastern Europe. The claims of another 9,000 Jewish former labourers in Eastern Europe would be served by those foundations.[108]

The German agreement earmarked DM 1 billion for property and insurance claims,[109] as well as DM 300 million as a humanitarian fund as redress for heirless assets.[110] The humanitarian fund, which was vigorously demanded by Singer, had been one of the most difficult elements for the Conference to achieve. 'The East Europeans were vehemently against any humanitarian funds at all; if there were to be any humanitarian funds, why only for Jews?' Taylor recalled. The humanitarian fund also was challenged by the plaintiffs' lawyers, who argued that all the money should be used for labour payments and other purposes. Another DM 700 million was set aside for the so-called 'Future Fund,' which was demanded by German industry and was intended for such projects as the promotion of tolerance. It did not have a specifically Jewish component.

Six months after the DM 10 billion agreement was announced, Eizenstat and Lambsdorff on 12 June 2000 finalized the mechanics of the provision for legal peace.[111] One month later, on 17 July 2000, the slave labour agreement was signed in Berlin. 'In the early 1980s when we at the Claims Conference commenced compensation and restitution negotiations with the leaders of the German Democratic Republic, the former East Germany, the reaction was so negative that I must admit I never imagined that one day I would be standing in the Foreign Ministry of the united Germany, located in the former Eastern sector of Berlin, to publicly welcome before the entire world and the international media the signing of an initiative that will provide a measure of justice to former slave labourers, those that Hitler had "marked for death," as well as former forced labourers. This is truly a historic day,' Miller said at the signing ceremony. However, he noted, 'A great challenge faces us now. We must reach potential beneficiaries as quickly as possible. Survivors are dying every day.' Roman Kent, vice-president and negotiator for the Claims Conference and chairman of the American Gathering for Jewish Holocaust Survivors, acknowledged the moral basis of the foundation. 'This foundation, approved by approximately 90 per cent of the Bundestag, is the conscience of the new generation,' he said. 'Yes, it was enacted 60 years late and is only a token gesture to financially compensate the slave and forced labourers. But it is the moral recognition for past wrongs, and we survivors take it as such.'

Payments ultimately would be sent to Jewish victims in 40 countries.[112] Although the slave labour compensation was considered a token payment, 'for individuals getting DM 500 a month [in pensions] under Article II, DM 15,000 is a significant amount,' Taylor said. And while the German government saw its foundation as the exclusive remedy for all remaining Nazi-era claims, the Conference preserved its separate demand that Germany maintain the financing and extend the eligibility requirements for the three funds it administers. 'When we came into this foundation, we were most concerned that the German government would say, "We're putting substantial funds into this foundation, and therefore this is closure for Article II, the Hardship Fund, the Central and Eastern Europe Fund – it's finished." We were most concerned about it, both for the financial implications and for the principle that there should not be closure with the German government. We cannot provide closure for the German government as long as there are survivors alive,' Taylor said. 'Ultimately, the German position was withdrawn. A letter from the German Finance Ministry acknowledged that the Claims Conference had open issues with Germany and confirmed that "the Foundation legislation will not impede such discussions in any way." Certainly, this letter was important for ongoing negotiations efforts with Germany on Holocaust compensation.'[113]

The day after the signing ceremony in Berlin, the Conference held its annual board meeting. Ben Helfgott, a survivor and a Conference negotiator, recounted an extraordinary turn of events. 'As late as the summer of 1998, the Conference received a letter from the [German] Chancellery saying they were not prepared to discuss the questions on slave labour – other matters they were prepared to discuss with us, but not slave labour,' he said. 'Today, two years later, there is an achievement that no one would have ever believed could have happened.'[114]

For Kagan, it was the end of decades-long struggle. In the midst of the slave labour negotiations, he had recalled a visit to Auschwitz, with its infamous sign: *Arbeit macht frei*. 'I could not help but say to myself that the slogan should have read "*Arbeit macht tot*," and not "*Arbeit macht frei*," because that was essentially the fate of the concentration camp inmates who were forced to do slave labour.'[115]

NOTES

1   Wollheim, Oral History interviews, 10 and 17 May 1991, US Holocaust Memorial Museum.

2   Claims Conference Board meeting, 6 July 1990, Jerusalem. Ferencz noted that Jews and non-Jews were compelled to labour for the Nazis and German companies. However, the intent in using Jewish slave labour was the destruction of the Jews through labour.

3   The German industrial use of concentration camp inmates as slave labourers, as well as the Claims Conference's early compensation agreements with German enterprises, are discussed in detail in *Less Than Slaves: Jewish Forced Labour and the Quest for Compensation*, Cambridge, MA: Harvard University Press (1979); reissued by Indiana University Press, 2002. All quotations from Ferencz are drawn from the book, unless otherwise cited.

4   Testimony, House Banking Committee, 13 September 1999. Neuborne also is the legal director of the Brennan Center for Justice at New York University School of Law.

5   Eugen Kogon, *The Theory and Practice of Hell: The German Concentration Camps and the System Behind Them*, New York: Berkley Publishing Group, 1980.

6   The announcement was published in a variety of newspapers, including the *New York Times*, 12 August 1951.

7   Wollheim, Oral History interviews. Former slave labourers might have been eligible for one-time payments or annuities for deprivation of liberty or damage to health under the West German indemnification programmes that resulted from the 1952 Luxembourg Agreements. However, the West German indemnification laws made no specific provisions for compensation for slave labour. In addition, some of the labour camps were not officially 'recognized' under the terms of the German legislation, thus depriving survivors of those camps of the possibility of receiving German government compensation.

8   Among those assisting Wollheim was Otto Küster, who had been co-chairman of the German delegation at The Hague negotiations. Küster had resigned from The Hague talks in protest when he believed that the German government was not acting in good faith; his resignation led to a reversal in the German position. He was hailed by the *New York Times* as a champion of slave labourers who 'sacrificed [his] public career in Germany to press their claims' (6 March 1955).

9   *New York Times*, 2 March 1955.

10 Claims Conference Board meeting, 19–20 January 1957. CAHJP 13625
11 Ferencz, Oral History Interview, US Holocaust Memorial Museum, 21 October 1994.
12 *New York Times*, 2 March 1955.
13 Claims Conference Board meeting, 2–3 March 1963. CAHJP 14164
14 Benjamin B. Ferencz, 'West Germany: Supreme Court Bars Claims of Forced Labourers,' *American Journal of Comparative Law*, Vol. 15, No. 3, 1967.
15 The other companies were Krupp, Siemens, AEG-Telefunken and Rheinmetall. An agreement in principle with Flick's Dynamit Nobel was not honored until after the company was sold, some 20 years later.
16 Katzenstein memo, 'The slave labour complex,' 1 March 1964. CAHJP 14855
17 By January 1951, none of the industrialists remained in jail. Shortly after McCloy read *Less Than Slaves*, he told Ferencz that the book had 'opened up a number of facts which were new to me'. In his 10 April 1980 letter, McCloy said, 'If I had all the facts I now have, I might have reached a more just result.'
18 Katzenstein also rejected the manner in which Rheinmetall intended to finance the slave labour compensation. Its DM 2.5 million payment would include funds from two other companies, both of which were involved in the Pentagon deal. Katzenstein, however, argued that the Conference could not take money from those firms, as there were no slave labour claims pending against them.
19 *New York Times*, 18 May 1966. The headline on the story made the linkage: 'Nazi Victims Win Pay With US Help. Arms maker to reimburse Jews used as slave labour.' A State Department source said he did not know whether Rheinmetall had explicitly been threatened with the loss of the contract. But, he told the newspaper, 'The threat was there anyway, and the company undoubtedly sensed it.'
20 Katzenstein memo, 'The slave labour complex', 1 March 1964. CAHJP 14855. See *Less Than Slaves* for details of the Claims Conference's indemnification. The indemnification provisions put the Conference in an awkward legal position some 40 years later, when the companies implied that the Conference bore liability for claims that arose from class-action lawsuits that had been filed in US federal courts. For instance, Siemens advised the Conference in a letter, dated 25 June 1999: 'Siemens AG continues to denounce the deplorable acts of the past, [but] Siemens AG does not believe the lawsuits have legal merit. We hope the American courts will decide that these issues are not appropriate for litigation. Until these cases are resolved, however, Siemens AG must continue to reserve all its rights, including those found in our 1962 agreement with the Claims Conference.' However, just as the companies sought 'legal peace,' so did the Conference. 'We accept and acknowledge the importance of the agreements reached [in 1962], even if done in a different era and in a different legal environment. The history of the Claims Conference is one, we believe, of integrity and propriety in all its activities,' Israel Miller and Israel Singer said in a letter to the German government negotiator, Otto Graf Lambsdorff, on 8 June 2000. 'However, we feel, with all due and appropriate respect for those agreements, that in the current environment in which all involved are reasonably seeking to find a way to have legal peace on these complex issues, it is appropriate that legal peace be equally applicable to the Claims Conference as well as to German industry.' Although the German companies never officially released the Conference from the indemnities, in the end, there was no public expectation that the Conference would abide by them.
21 *New York Times*, 7 February 1957.
22 Claims Conference Board meeting, 19–20 January 1957. CAHJP 13625
23 'I think it was wise to confirm the agreement with I.G. Farben,' said Ignacy Schwartzbart, a one-time World Jewish Congress representative on the Claims Conference Board. 'Usually in life, we have a choice between bad and worse, and not between bad and good. This is bad enough, but without the agreement, it would be worse,' he said in a letter to Kagan, dated 2 April 1958.
24 Claims Conference Board meeting, 19–20 January 1957. CAHJP 13625
25 Claims Conference Board meeting, 17–18 January 1959. CAHJP 13628
26 Ferencz memo to Claims Conference senior officers, 4 June 1958.
27 Ibid.
28 The targeted companies included AEG, Telefunken, Siemens, Rheinmetall, Brabag, Krupp, Holzmann and Heinkel.
29 Ferencz memo to Claims Conference senior officers, 4 June 1958.
30 There was a notable exception: after a German court ruling, in 1965 Büssing paid a single former slave labourer, Adolph Diamant, DM 178.80 [DM 178 and 80 pfennig]. Diamant was

awarded RM 1,788 for 1,778 hours of labour; the amount of the compensation was converted according to the *Währungsreform,* in which 10 Reichsmarks equaled 1 Deutschmark. In 1965, the award was worth approximately $60, which made Diamant's payment about 10 per cent of that paid to slave labourers from the Rheinmetall agreement.

31   Ferencz, 'West Germany: Supreme Court Bars Claims of Forced Labourers'. Farben's attorneys had argued, 'The issue here is not to develop a new Nuremburg trial.' (*New York Times,* 6 March 1955.)

32   Ferencz, Oral History interview.

33   Katzenstein memo, 'The slave labour complex.'

34   Katzenstein letter to Kagan, 31 January 1981.

35   Kagan letter to Avner Rom, 11 April 1983.

36   In *Less Than Slaves,* Ferencz noted that McCloy also intervened. In a 1969 letter to Friedrich Flick, McCloy recounted his role in reducing the sentences handed down by the Nuremberg tribunal, and said his clemency had been coupled with the hope that compensation would be provided by firms that had used slave labour. Flick's advocate told McCloy: 'Dr Flick is of the opinion that under no aspect, nor under a moral aspect either, it would be indicated or justifiable for Dynamit Nobel AG or the Flick group to fulfill the demand of the Claims Conference.'

37   Claims Conference Board meeting, 6 July 1990, Jerusalem.

38   Katzenstein letter to Ferencz, 24 July 1972; also cited in Ferencz, *Less Than Slaves.*

39   In late 1984, however, there had been a moment when Katzenstein thought that Flick might be amenable to making the slave labour payment. In light of the so-called 'Flick scandal,' in which the company was said to have made secret German political contributions valued at millions of dollars in exchange for preferential tax treatment, 'a re-approach to the Flick company through influential channels from abroad might make the Flick people think twice whether they do not want to make a tiny fraction of these huge bribery moneys at least available for their former Jewish slave labourers,' Katzenstein said in a letter dated 25 October 1984.

40   Miller letter to Wilhelm Christians, 18 December 1985.

41   *Wall Street Journal,* 9 January 1986.

42   *Los Angeles Times,* 7 and 8 January 1986. The opposition SPD and the Greens demanded that Fellner resign from the Bundestag, but he did not.

43   Claims Conference Board meeting, 6 July 1990, Jerusalem.

44   Manfred Gentz letter to New York City Comptroller Alan Hevesi, 21 October 1998. Several years before the Daimler payment, the company had commissioned research into its corporate history. In 1983, the Society for Entrepreneurial History (known by the German acronym GUG) began research on the history of the company during the Nazi years. In 1986, GUG was commissioned to look specifically at the issue of forced labour at Daimler-Benz.

45   Claims Conference Board meeting, 6 July 1990, Jerusalem. Survival rates were higher for non-Jewish labourers because the nature and purpose of the labour was different. Slave labour was a means of exterminating Jews, while forced labour of non-Jews was a means of supplementing the German war-time workforce.

46   Letter, Peter Frerk of Volkswagen to Kagan, 13 February 1992. In addition to the funds paid to the Conference for projects in Israel that would assist Jewish victims, Volkswagen made payments to Poland, Belarus and Ukraine, 'as representatives of the areas from which the majority of the forced labourers were deported,' Frerk said.

47   Beck interview, 4 July 2002.

48   Claims Conference press release, 24 June 1987.

49   Michael Geier, Symposium, 'Holocaust Restitution: Reconciling Moral Imperatives with Legal Initiatives and Diplomacy,' *Fordham International Law Journal,* Vol. 25, 2001.

50   Kagan letter to Brozik, 12 January 1990.

51   Jewish Telegraphic Agency, 25 September 1992.

52   *Jerusalem Post,* 4 July 1996. For an overview, see US District Judge Dickinson R. Debevoise's decision, *Burger-Fischer* v. *Degussa AG,* 65 F. Supp. 2d 248, 272–85 (D.N.J. 1999), and Libby Adler and Peer Zumbansen, 'The Forgetfulness Of Noblesse: A Critique of the German Foundation Law Compensating Slave and Forced Labourers of the Third Reich,' *Harvard Journal on Legislation,* Vol. 39, No. 1, Winter, 2002.

53   Testimony, House Banking Committee, 13 September 1999.

54   *New York Times,* 6 November 1997. Only one of the 22 slave labourers who brought the lawsuit was eligible for payment, because she had been behind the Iron Curtain and thus unable

to apply by the deadline for the original West German compensation programmes before she immigrated to Israel in the 1960s. 'The claims of the other women are not justified, because they all received compensation under the [West German] Federal Compensation Law and some are still receiving pensions,' Judge Heinz Sonnenberger said. 'No damage claims can be paid alongside this law – not even for slave labour.' He said the matter was 'a political issue for which lawmakers could find a new ruling.'

55 Bremen *Landgericht*, 1-0-2889/90 (1998). The Bonn decision was reversed on appeal; the German appellate court ruled that compensation programmes were issues for the legislative, not the judicial, branches. The ultimate German court decisions in the cases were sidelined by diplomatic agreements on slave and forced labour claims. Nonetheless, the initial rulings had created an environment that propelled German industry and the government to resolve the claims.

56 Brozik memo, 14 September 1998. Brozik was referring to three separate compensation programmes that were administered by the Conference, but financed by the German government: the Article II Fund, the Hardship Fund, and Central and Eastern Europe Fund.

57 *Wall Street Journal*, 14 August 1998.

58 *Wall Street Journal*, 5 March 1998. Few of the labourers in the Ford lawsuit were Jewish. They included French prisoners of war, some detainees from the concentration camp at Buchenwald, and Russian, Ukrainian, Italian and Belgian civilians.

59 *New York Times*, 1 September 1998. A separate lawsuit had been filed in June 1998 by Holocaust survivors in US court against Deutsche Bank and Dresdner Bank.

60 *Jerusalem Post*, 9 July 1998.

61 *Jerusalem Post*, 13 September 1998. The Volkswagen fund did not involve the Claims Conference, which, until that point, had administered claims for Jewish slave labourers. The fund was to be overseen by former Israeli Prime Minister Shimon Peres, former Austrian chancellor Franz Vranitzky, and former German president Richard von Weizsaecker.

62 Claims Conference press release, 10 July 1998.

63 *Los Angeles Times*, 24 September 1998.

64 *Newsday*, 13 October 1997.

65 Reuters, 21 August 1998. The Finance Ministry referred industry to German government-financed 'reconciliation foundations' for Nazi victims in Poland, Russia, Belarus and Ukraine. 'These are fed with government money, but are open for contributions from third parties,' a ministry spokesman said. 'The firms could pay into these, if they like.'

66 Associated Press, 20 October 1998. Schröder was re-elected in 2002; the second Red-Green coalition agreement made no reference to compensation for Nazi victims.

67 Beck interview, 4 July 2002. The SPD, many of whose members had been persecuted by the Nazis, also had a long-standing ideological commitment to compensation for victims. In the 1950s, the SPD – then in the opposition – had proposed that the financial burden of the West German government's indemnification programmes be eased by imposing part of the cost on the industrial employers of former slave labourers.

68 *Washington Times*, 22 October 1998.

69 Kagan interview, 12 December 2001. The *New York Times*, on 14 December 1998, reported on talks between Israel Singer and Rolf-Ernst Breuer, chairman of Deutsche Bank. The *Times* noted that Deutsche Bank was seeking to acquire Bankers Trust for $10.1 billion, and that the New York City comptroller, Alan Hevesi, 'vowed he would seek to block the huge takeover if the German bank does not resolve war-time claims.' Hevesi was a significant actor in the efforts to recover Holocaust-era assets from enterprises that conducted business in the US. As the New York City comptroller, Hevesi influenced business contracts awarded by the city as well as the investment of municipal pension funds. In 1997, he organized a national network of state and local government finance officers who had the power to regulate or influence multinational businesses operating in their jurisdictions. That group, whose members were not averse to imposing sanctions on industry, created an 'Executive Monitoring Committee' to monitor the negotiations on Holocaust-era assets.

70 *New York Times*, 17 February 1999. On 9 February, Schröder's emissary, Bodo Hombach, announced that the German government had agreed in principle to establish a government-industry fund for Nazi victims. At the time, DM 3 billion was roughly $1.7 billion, and there was speculation that the $1.25 billion settlement of the Swiss banks lawsuit was the 'starting point' for claims against German industry.

71 The language was important; the companies consistently avoided statements about legal

obligations that could boomerang and be used against them in the pending lawsuits. Hombach, the chancellor's adviser, noted that the idea of a voluntary settlement 'is not something that the head of the legal departments of German companies might subscribe to, but the CEOs understand the political importance.' (See *New York Times*, 10 February 1999.)

72 *New York Times*, 16 February 1999. For an account of these events from the US government's perspective, see the memoirs of Stuart E. Eizenstat, *Imperfect Justice: Looted Assets, Slave Labour and the Unfinished Business of World War II*, New York: PublicAffairs, 2003.

73 According to Ferencz, Krupp's general manager at that time had offered to intervene with the BDI. It was in Krupp's interest to pursue a 'global' settlement because, as more companies acknowledged their use of slave labour, the less offensive Krupp would appear.

74 Ferencz memo to Conference senior officers, 4 June 1958.

75 Ferencz letter to Kagan, 21 January 1986.

76 With the exception of Farben, in the early slave labour agreements, no German company had made provisions for non-Jewish labourers. In fact, Krupp had implied that the Jews were responsible for the omission of non-Jewish victims. 'With reference to your letter of January 7, 1960, we must inform you that in view of the considerable financial expenditures on behalf of the Jewish concentration camp prisoners, we unfortunately do not see ourselves in a position to make any further voluntary payments,' Krupp said in a letter to a group of non-Jewish victims, the Central Committee of Nazi Victims Refugees in the Free World. 'We ask that you have understanding for this.' In *Less Than Slaves*, Ferencz quotes an advocate for Alfried Krupp, who, when asked in a German television interview why Krupp did not pay non-Jewish labourers, said, 'Well, you know, the Jewish lobby was very active, and the non-Jews didn't have that kind of a lobby.'

77 Others wanted to ensure that their claims would not be excluded. Once it was reported that Germany was holding talks on Jewish claims, Poland insisted on inclusion of its claims (*Jerusalem Post*, 15 January 1999). Immediately after the German proposal officially was announced, Polish Prime Minister Jerzy Buzek's chief of staff, Wieslaw Walendziak, flew to Washington to discuss Poland's slave labour claim for its war-era nationals. Walendziak said that two million Poles had been deported to Germany to work under prison-like conditions for German companies or on farms, and that only one per cent of the funds Germany had paid to Nazi victims had been for former forced labourers in Central and Eastern Europe (*New York Times*, 15 February 1999). In the subsequent multinational negotiations, the Polish delegation insisted on receiving the same amounts as the Claims Conference. In his memoirs, *Imperfect Justice*, Eizenstat wrote that to placate the Poles he made a 'secret' arrangement in which Poland would receive $10 million of the $25 million that the US was to contribute to a new international relief fund for Nazi victims.

78 Taylor interview, 19 October 2001.

79 Lambsdorff letter to Eizenstat, 7 December 1999; interview, Michael Geier, German Ministry of Foreign Affairs, 2 July 2002.

80 Although Schröder's government had supported compensation for slave labourers, the chancellor originally rejected the prospect of government contributions to a fund (Bloomberg News Service, 12 February 1999).

81 For instance, Poland had festering claims against Germany, while the Czech Republic and Germany had signed a declaration of reconciliation in January 1997 that, among other thing, created a fund for special projects related to the Nazi era. 'The German side acknowledges its obligation and responsibility toward all those who fell victim to National Socialist violence,' the Czech-German declaration said. 'Therefore the projects in question are to especially benefit victims of National Socialist violence.' The declaration also included expressions of mutual regret about the Nazi occupation and the expulsions of the ethnic Sudeten Germans (*Sudetendeutsche*). However, it said, 'Both sides agree that injustice inflicted in the past belongs in the past, and will therefore orient their relations towards the future ... Both sides therefore declare that they will not burden their relations with political and legal issues which stem from the past.'

82 Taylor interview, 19 October 2001.

83 *Jerusalem Post*, 18 July 1999.

84 Brozik memo, 23 April 1999.

85 Claims Conference position paper on slave labour, 15 June 1999.

86 For instance, in an oft-repeated statement, Otto Graf Lambsdorff, the German chancellor's envoy, told the House Banking Committee on 9 February 2000: 'The German people and

German business and industry bear a special moral and historical obligation. I stress the word "moral," because I disagree with class action lawyers on the question of legal obligations.'

87 Conference position paper on slave labour.
88 Taylor interview, 19 October 2001.
89 These also were referred to as category A and category B.
90 Eizenstat testimony, House Banking Committee, 9 February 2000.
91 The forced labourers were primarily from Poland, Ukraine, Russia, Belarus and the Czech Republic – as reflected by these nations' participation in the negotiations. There also were intense debates about what constituted 'forced' labour. For the majority of Central and Eastern European victims, the German foundation would be the only mechanism for compensation for the suffering they endured during the Nazi era. Many of the Eastern European forced labourers had been agricultural workers. That category was 'a politically difficult step for the German government because many Germans feel that workers living mainly on family farms did not suffer greatly during the war', Eizenstat said in a statement to Hevesi's Executive Monitoring Committee on 16 September 1999.
92 Taylor interview, 19 October 2001.
93 Brozik, memo on 28 April 1999 meeting with German officials.
94 Taylor interview, 18 April 2002. The prospect that a single 'general' fund that would cover all slave and forced labourers could not be taken for granted. Lambsdorff warned, in a letter to Eizenstat on 7 December 1999 – only a week before an agreement was reached – of a 'growing tendency among German companies to look for individual solutions, given both the still unknown financial scope of the initiative and doubts about legal closure.'
95 The premise of 'need' was not a novel concept. It was the underlying basis of all German compensation programmes for Nazi victims since 1980, which were treated by Germany as 'humanitarian' programmes.
96 Taylor interview, 18 April 2002.
97 Eizenstat briefing, 15 July 1999. Previous payments for slave labour from all post-war company funds would be deducted.
98 The proposed six-month threshold, while unacceptable, was not arbitrary; it is the period used in the eligibility criteria for existing German compensation programmes, Eizenstat noted at a briefing in July 1999. The Farben settlement's payment scheme also took into account the duration of labour.
99 Claims Conference position paper on slave labour.
100 *Jerusalem Post*, 14 September 1999. Debevoise's decision is *Burger-Fischer* v. *Degussa AG*, 65 F. Supp. 2d 248, 272-85 (D.N.J. 1999). In a separate ruling in the same federal court on the same day, US District Judge Joseph A. Greenaway Jr. dismissed the class-action lawsuit against Ford.
101 US Treasury Department Fact Sheet, 'Chronology of Events in Slave and Forced Labour Talks,' 17 July 2000.
102 Once the negotiations reached DM 6 billion, the ruling SPD told its coalition partners, the Greens, it was time to halt. 'The SPD said, "It is good we are doing something, but now the amount is enough, so be quiet,"' Beck said in an interview (4 July 2002). 'My aim at the beginning was DM 10 billion, based on the number of people I thought would qualify. I never thought we would get it.'
103 Clinton statement on Nazi-era forced and slave labour agreement, White House Press Office, 15 December 1999.
104 Miller interview, 18 December 2001.
105 US Treasury Department Fact Sheet.
106 Testimony, House Committee on Banking and Financial Services, 9 February 2000.
107 The idea of an apology came from the Conference, Taylor said. 'We raised it informally with industry, with Lambsdorff, with Eizenstat. The formal request to Rau came at a meeting Singer and I had at the president's home in November 1999. He wasn't surprised when we came to make the formal request,' Taylor said in an interview on 18 April 2002. 'He prepared the text. There was not a negotiation over the text. This was not Adenauer, and this was not the first time there would be such a statement. We explained what we wanted, he understood what we wanted, and he did it. They didn't offer, and we didn't ask for, an advance text.'
108 Eizenstat letter to Miller and Singer, 28 April 2000. The countries with the foundations were Russia, Ukraine, Belarus, Poland and the Czech Republic. These had been formed earlier under bilateral agreements between reunified Germany and Eastern European states. The Conference

argued that it should handle all Jewish claims, but it did not prevail. Eizenstat told the Conference at its July 2000 board meeting that it was important that these national foundations administer Jewish and non-Jewish labour claims, in part because it increased the amounts they received from the German fund. He also suggested that this would reduce tensions between the Eastern Europeans and the Jewish community.

109 Although it set aside funds to cover insurance claims, the German foundation had come into existence at odds with the International Commission for Holocaust Era Insurance Claims [ICHEIC]. Chaired by former Secretary of State Lawrence Eagleburger, that commission was created in 1998 to resolve insurance claims after a class-action lawsuit against European insurers had been filed in federal court in New York. The commission's founding members included German, Swiss, French and Italian insurance companies. The German initiative covered all claims against German industry; within the insurance commission, there was wide discontent that the German companies had bypassed the commission by 'paying' insurance-related debts through the German foundation. The Eagleburger commission and the German foundation did not reach an agreement until 16 October 2002, under which the German foundation was to provide $275 million from German insurers for unpaid policies from the Nazi era. However, on 25 September 2002, US District Judge Michael B. Mukasey in Manhattan rejected the request of insurers Assicurazioni Generali and the Zurich Life Insurance Company to dismiss lawsuits that were filed in 1997; those suits sought compensation for the insurers' alleged failure to honour Nazi-era policies. Mukasey said the Eagleburger commission 'is manifestly inadequate because it lacks sufficient independence and permanence. ICHEIC is entirely a creature of the six founding insurance companies that formed the commission, two of which are defendants in this case; it is in a sense the company store. Virtually all of ICHEIC's funding – not only for claims payments, but also for all administrative expenses – comes from those insurance companies.'

110 The allocation was specified in the German law that created the foundation. It designated funds 'for social purposes to the benefit of Holocaust survivors through the Conference on Jewish Material Claims Against Germany.' See German *Federal Law Gazette* 2000 I 1263; and as amended, *Federal Law Gazette* 2001 I 2036.

111 US Treasury Department Fact Sheet. The mechanism for legal peace called for plaintiffs' attorneys to seek dismissals for all cases pending in US courts against German companies relating to Nazi-era wrongs. The US government agreed that it would file a 'Statement of Interest' in all pending and future cases stating that dismissals of the lawsuits are in the foreign policy interest of the US and recommending dismissal on any valid legal ground. This was challenged by a Miami federal judge, Ursula Ungaro-Benages, who filed a suit in 2001 against German banks for compensation for the loss of her family property, saying that the banks conspired with the Nazi régime to plunder the assets of German Jews. She also contended that the executive order signed by Clinton was unconstitutional. That lawsuit was pending at the end of 2002.

112 The German law entered into force on 12 August 2000 (*Federal Law Gazette* 2000 I 1263); it was amended on 4 August 2001 (Federal Law Gazette 2001 I 2036). There had been a delay because US District Judge Shirley Wohl Kram in Manhattan resisted dismissing the slave labour lawsuits, and the German Parliament would not implement the agreement until the legal peace was assured. The German foundation is governed by a Board of Trustees. The Bundestag legislation specified the composition of the 27-member board: the chairman, named by the German chancellor; four members named by German industry; five members named by the Bundestag and two by the Bundesrat; one representative each from the German Federal Finance and Foreign Ministries; one member named by the Claims Conference; one member named by the Central Council of German Sinti and Roma, the Alliance of German Sinti, and the International Romani Union; one member each named by the governments of Israel, the US, Poland, the Russian Federation, Ukraine, Belarus and the Czech Republic; one lawyer named by the US government; and one member each named by the United Nations High Commissioner for Refugees, the International Organization for Migration, and the Federal Information and Counseling Association for Victims of National Socialism.

113 Taylor interview, 18 April 2002; letter from German Federal Ministry of Finance to Brozik, 3 July 2000.

114 Claims Conference Board meeting, 18 July 2000, New York.

115 Seminar, Friedrich Ebert Foundation, Washington, 1 November 1999.

Chapter 8

Confronting the 'First Victim': Jewish Claims Against Austria

There was a Viennese mob in front of the German Tourist Bureau, where a flower-draped portrait of Adolf Hitler adorned the window. 'In the streetlights I noted faces of some of the individuals who made up this churning herd: a familiar sight it was to an old veteran of Nazi Germany. I had seen those faces at the party rallies in Nuremberg: the fanatical popping eyes, the gaping mouths, the contorted expressions of hysteria and paranoia. And now they were screaming: "Sieg Heil! Sieg Heil! Heil Hitler! Heil Hitler! Hang Schuschnigg! Hang Schuschnigg! Ein Volk, Ein Reich, Ein Fuhrer!" The Brownshirts at Nuremberg had never bellowed the Nazi slogans with such mania,' journalist William Shirer wrote of the *Anschluss*, the March 1938 German annexation of Austria. 'I had often seen the Vienna police break up Nazi demonstrations in this spot. But now they were standing with folded arms. And most of them were grinning.'[1]

That scene, and the passion it conveyed, haunted talks 14 years later when the Claims Conference met with the West German delegation in Wassenaar to negotiate for compensation for Nazi-era damages to Jewish victims. The Federal Republic of Germany refused to accept obligations for the Austrian Jewish victims, arguing that Austria, the birthplace of Hitler, also was guilty of Nazi crimes. Austria, in turn, contended that it was Nazism's 'first victim' and was not obliged to pay compensation. Indeed, it saw itself as the 'first claimant.'[2]

After six months of negotiations with the Conference, West Germany agreed in 1952 to the principles for compensation and restitution to Nazi victims. The FRG subsequently developed indemnification legislation, the *Bundesentschädigungsgesetze,* that provided monthly pensions to hundreds of thousands of Nazi victims.[3] By contrast, over five decades Austria grudgingly developed a labyrinth of measures for Nazi victims from Austria, always in response to the political exigencies of the moment. The measures were inequitable and fragmented, with gaps and deficiencies, some of which were not resolved before the end of the 20th century. Further, until 1995, the benefits were couched in terms that were politically palatable to Austria. Funds were given as charitable 'assistance,' not as an Austrian obligation to victims. The only ongoing benefit – one available to Nazi victims once they had reached a certain age – was the right to participate, on preferential terms, in the state 'social security' pension programme. 'Although the sums involved were tiny by comparison, it was much more difficult to negotiate with the Austrians than with the Germans,' said Goldmann. 'You never knew where you stood with them. Undertakings were always hedged with reservations; terms and promises were seldom honored.'[4]

There were 185,000 Jews living in Austria on the eve of the *Anschluss,* when more than 100,000 German troops marched in and annexed the country. Sixty-five thousand Austrian Jews perished in the Holocaust. In April 1938, a month after the *Anschluss,* Austrian Jews were required to register their personal assets – homes, businesses, bank accounts, jewellery, household goods and artworks. Walter Rafelsberger, the State Commissar in the Private Sector, in a report dated 1 February 1939, on registration of assets and on the 'de-Jewing' of Austria ('*Entjudung in der Ostmark*'), estimated the value of the Jews' registered assets at RM 2.042 billion. The Austrian Jews quickly saw their properties confiscated, looted, liquidated or drained by a series of special taxes for owning property (*Judenvermögensabgabe,* or JUVA) or for flight or 'emigration' – including forced deportation to concentration camps (*Reichsfluchtsteuer*).[5]

'The bitter fate of the Austrian Jews is a terrible one,' said Moshe Jahoda, director of the Claims Conference's Vienna office. 'They were in German concentration camps, they were slave labourers in German factories, and their Jewish brothers from Germany were getting compensation.'[6] When West Germany rejected the claims of Austrian Jewish Nazi victims, the Claims Conference established an affiliated committee to press Vienna. The committee's name reflected the awkward political sensitivities. It was called the Committee for Jewish Claims on Austria (CJCA), a name that avoided any implication of Austrian liability, as opposed to the assertive name of its German endeavor: the Conference on Jewish Material Claims Against Germany.[7]

In negotiations between 1953 and 1961, the CJCA was only one of many actors pressing the Austrian government. Austria simultaneously was developing domestic legislation to rehabilitate its economy and denazify its population; resolving its relations with West Germany; negotiating with the Allies on a treaty to restore its sovereignty; and acclimating itself to its role as a buffer state in the East–West divide of the Cold War.

In this environment, the claims of Jewish victims got short shrift. They were plagued by Austria's status as the 'first victim.' The 1943 Moscow Declaration called Austria 'the first free country to fall a victim to Hitlerite aggression.'[8] The declaration, issued by the then-foreign ministers of the US, Soviet Union and Britain – Cordell Hull, Vyacheslav Molotov and Anthony Eden – 'was allegedly a piece of some sort of convoluted psychological warfare where somebody thought that the courageous Austrians will rise up in 1943 in back of the Germans once this declaration was issued,' recalled Kagan.[9] With such a status, Austria felt no obligation to provide compensation. In fact, it was the reverse – the acknowledgment of any obligation would sabotage its own victim status. Austria used the declaration as a shield to thwart claims. 'The principle must be maintained that compensation has to be rendered by those who inflicted the damage,' said Chancellor Julius Raab. 'Therefore, compensation for the damage inflicted during the German occupation of Austria must be the obligation of the then occupier and his legal successor. Any payments by Austria can only serve to bridge, in the interest of those hardest hit, the period until such compensation can be made.'[10]

In its negotiations in Wassenaar with the Claims Conference, the West German delegation originally had agreed to provide compensation for claimants from Austria, but it quickly reversed its position. Bonn argued that Austria had been part of Greater Germany; that the majority of the Austrian population had greeted the *Anschluss* with joy; that Austrians participated in the illegal acts of the Nazi régime; and that Austria must be considered a successor state to Nazi Germany and responsible for the damages inflicted on Nazi victims in Austria.[11] 'While the Austrians are not so innocent as they pretend to be, the Germans are by no means so disconnected [from] events in Austria as they would have the world believe,' said Charles Kapralik of the Jewish Trust Corporation, which dealt with heirless Jewish property questions in the British Occupation Zone in West Germany.[12] The Conference argued that, whatever the sentiments of the Austrian population, the occupation of Austria had been a unilateral German act against the will of the Austrian government. Until the *Anschluss*, Austrian Jews had enjoyed all the rights of citizenship, and the anti-Jewish legislation was introduced by the German – not the Austrian – government. 'Even if it is agreed that Austria is a successor state to the Nazi Reich,' the Conference said, 'the obligations of the Federal Republic would by no means decrease.'[13] The Germans were unmoved. The Conference was caught betwixt and between. 'The Austrians say, "What do you want from us? The Germans took away everything to Berlin,"' Goldmann said. 'When you come to the Germans [for compensation for Austrian victims], they say, "What? Those bastards who gave us Hitler?"'[14]

And, unlike the negotiations with West Germany, when Israel conducted parallel talks alongside the Conference, Israel made no claims against Austria. 'Israel accepts the supposition that Germany is responsible for acts committed against Austrian Jews since they took place only after the *Anschluss*,' the Israeli foreign minister, Sharett, said in 1952.[15] That stance undermined the CJCA. 'Even Israel declared, for reasons that are still unclear to me, that it had no claim against Austria, and this seriously weakened the basis of our demands,' Goldmann recalled. Between the Allies' Moscow Declaration and the absence of an Israeli claim, Goldmann said, 'I had no leverage at all when I went to see Chancellor Raab.'[16]

The CJCA, however, had the support of the American government, one of the four Allied Occupation powers that also was engaged in negotiations with the Austrian government for a state treaty as well as for commercial claims by American businesses.[17] After intervention and pressure from various quarters, the Austrian Government invited CJCA representatives to negotiations in Vienna in June 1953. The talks began in 'an atmosphere of hopefulness' but degenerated into 'long and wearisome negotiations.'[18]

The Jewish claims fell into two categories: a global claim for heirless property in Austria, and amendments to the existing Austrian compensation and restitution laws dealing with Austrian Jews' material losses. The Committee argued on moral grounds that the Austrian economy could not be permitted to benefit from the assets it gained as a result of the Nazi persecution of the Jews. On political grounds, it contended that Austria was liable for Jewish claims because when states are unable to protect their people from injustice and illegal acts – especially annihilation and wanton spoliation – states must assume responsibility for the remedy when sovereignty is regained. It also noted that 'a regrettably important part of the Austrian populace participated with the Nazi terrorists in these acts, the illegality of which was proclaimed by the Austrian government after the war. Our claim is not based on war-loss compensation, nor are we seeking to establish any claims for reparation. We submit that the concept of *Rechtsstaat* – which Austria clearly is – carries with it the elemental duty to provide a measure of commensurate redress for illegal acts.'[19]

Talks between the Committee and the Austrian government began several years after domestic restitution initiatives had come into force under the supervision of the Allies. Akin to their actions in post-war West Germany, the Allies had installed an Allied Control Council with a prominent role in shaping Austrian policies.[20] At its first meeting, on 11 September 1945, the council issued a proclamation to the Austrian people declaring that one of its most urgent tasks would be to eliminate the effects of Nazi rule in Austria. 'Among these aftereffects was the unhappy condition of persons who had been despoiled of property or denied legal rights on grounds of racial or political discrimination,' according to the British representative, Sir Geoffrey Wallinger.[21]

There were repeated conflicts between the Austrian government and the council as Austria restored the rights of former Nazis before restoring those of their victims. 'Under pressure of its right wing, the Austrian government has been passing laws, one of which has already been vetoed by the Allied Control Council, diminishing the effect of previous restitution laws and permitting people who had been compelled to restore Nazi-seized property to its rightful owners to "re-acquire" it,' the *New York Times* noted in an editorial. 'These actions may find their inception in the growing bitterness of the Austrian people over the spoliation of their country by the Soviets, which [*sic*] seize Austrian property at will. But the Austrian government and people must realize that one wrong does not justify another, and that they cannot afford to impair Western goodwill, on which they must depend for their continued existence as an independent nation.'[22]

In 1954, the Allied Control Council unanimously rejected two Austrian laws – one that would have restored property that had been confiscated from former Nazis and one restoring pension payments to Nazi-era civil servants. 'It is under these circumstances – before certain victims of Nazi oppression have had their wrongs set right – that we are requested to give approval to the two laws before us which are designed to relieve former Nazis who participated in that oppression from the legal penalties imposed,' Wallinger said, also signaling that Austria's restitution efforts for victims were insufficient.[23]

The Allied Occupation ended with the State Treaty. The Allied–Austrian pact was signed on 15 May 1955 – some 17 years after the *Anschluss*. The treaty included a provision, Article 26, that addressed Nazi-era claims. The Republic of Austria, 'in all cases where property, legal rights or interests in Austria have since 13 March 1938 been subject of forced transfer or measures of sequestration, confis-cation or control on account of the racial origin or religion of the owner,' foresaw returns of the properties, legal rights and interests 'together with their accessories.' Where restoration was impossible, Article 26 called for compensation to be paid to the same extent that Austrian nationals were compensated for war losses.

The CJCA used Article 26 to press victims' claims, many of which had yet to be satisfied. The Committee contended that the existing Austrian legislation had failed to offer redress for more than three-quarters of the Jewish assets that had been registered upon Nazi orders – and lost. The Committee's assessment was disputed by Raab. 'Their demands called for legislative actions involving an expenditure of AS 1.2 billion and cash payments of AS 1 billion. It might therefore be assumed that this programme was drafted without any regard for Austrian realities and possibilities. We therefore had to reject these unbearable demands,' the chancellor said in a 1955 radio address. 'They were based on exaggerated evaluations of the Jewish assets in 1938, and various foreign publications mentioned sums which amounted to more than a quarter, almost one-half of Austria's national wealth.'[24]

The scope of Article 26 was hobbled by the conflicting interpretations by the Americans and Austrians.[25] During negotiations on the treaty – and continuing for several years afterward as the two struggled with its implementation – there was no agreement on what constituted 'property, legal rights or interests'. This vague concept was treated differently by the American and Austrian legal systems. 'This particular article has been a source of controversy because of the difficulty in interpreting the language "property, legal rights or interest" in terms of specific claims,' said Assistant Secretary of State C. Burke Elbrick. The US State Department considered tenancy rights, mortgages, insurance policies, pensions, bank accounts, discriminatory taxes, securities and money subject to restoration under Article 26, according to an October 1958 department memorandum. Austria was prepared to negotiate a lump-sum settlement for the losses, but it disputed which properties were covered. Austria specifically rejected claims for bank accounts, mortgages and securities, maintaining that the German authorities had required Austrian banks to liquidate and deliver the assets to the Nazis. Under those circumstances, even if the assets were treated as 'property, legal rights or interests', they were not in Austria and thus not subject to 'return or restoration', Austria argued.[26]

The post-treaty talks moved sluggishly, and the Americans, like the CJCA, were frustrated.[27] The State Department's Austrian Desk officer, Frederic Chapin, in late 1957, noted that the Austrian Foreign Office's legal department 'appears very adept at finding the legal difficulties and exceptional cases, which is of course consistent with the Austrian position that the government has no legal liability under the treaty, a point of view with which we most emphatically disagree'. In a letter to a colleague at the US Embassy in Vienna, Chapin advised: 'You can emphasize that we are always working within a financial range which is, if anything, so modest that it seems hardly appropriate to engage in interminable, legalistic arguments.'[28] The US had proposed a formula under which Austria would pay $5 million to settle Jewish claims. That would average less than $200 each for an estimated 30,000 claimants around the world, and represented only a fraction of the Jewish property that had been seized. The State Department told Raab in 1958 that if the negotiations between the two governments resulted in satisfactory settlements, the US was prepared to deliver a formal note stating that Washington would no longer intervene diplomatically on behalf of claimants under Article 26. However, it also said the US government could not prevent private persons from advancing claims.[29]

Several months later, after Raab had agreed to a $5 million settlement, CJCA negotiator Seymour Rubin told the State Department that the CJCA sought more than $5 million.[30] An official from the US Embassy in Vienna broached the topic, which apparently was not well received by Austrian authorities. He reported back to Washington: 'I also do not see why six or seven million [dollars] would be any more reasonable than five million, as no accurate estimate can be made of the amount necessary to satisfy the categories of claims, as that depends on the type of claims to be included, the number of claimants who will assert a claim and many other factors.'[31] Further, the State Department advised Rubin, 'The $5 million lump sum offer is a political offer to settle a problem which has resulted in protracted negotiations between Austria and the United States, the United Kingdom and France.'[32] When the CJCA persisted, the department dispatched a special delegation to Vienna in November 1958 to negotiate. Raab raised to $6 million the Austrian offer to settle Article 26 claims, which the Allies accepted in May 1959.[33]

The new Austrian offer – and the Allies' acceptance – put the CJCA in a bind. The State Department was determined to conclude the issue, in view of the time that had elapsed since the treaty was signed. The CJCA considered the increased amount insufficient, but it could not influence the outcome. 'The power of the organizations to negotiate a settlement of Article 26 is extremely limited due to the fact that the treaty is only subject to negotiations by governments,' Kagan advised the Committee. 'And the Austrian government made it very clear that it cannot deal with the Jewish organizations on the implementation of the treaty.'[34]

The State Treaty led to two new 'property' compensation funds: the 'Claims Fund' (*Abgeltungsfond*) and the 'Collection Agency Fund' (*Sammelstellen*). The 'Claims Fund' was created in 1961, with the $6 million Raab had pledged. It paid limited compensation for loss of cash, securities, bank accounts and mortgages and for the discriminatory taxes (JUVA and *Reichsfluchtsteuer*) that had been levied on the

Jews.[35] Two special collection points – *Sammelstellen* – were created to handle additional restitution claims and to recover unclaimed and heirless property, both Jewish and non-Jewish.[36] *Sammelstelle* 'A' recovered Jewish property and 'B' was responsible for non-Jewish property that had been subject to Nazi confiscations. The collection points recovered more than AS 320 million, which was used to compensate individuals for property losses and to make grants to institutions that aided Nazi victims.[37]

While property compensation negotiations were under way, the CJCA also pressed for improvements in the Austrian social welfare legislation known as the Victims Assistance Law, or *Opferfürsorgegesetz* (OFG). The American and British envoys in Vienna also wanted extensions in the OFG legislation, but were cautious about conditioning a settlement of the obligations in the State Treaty on the enactment of Austrian law. Austria chafed at what it saw as external meddling in its civil matters. 'I consider all the other attempts at interference in our domestic legislation through the Allied Powers as extremely unhappy,' Raab said in a radio address only weeks before the treaty was signed. 'The internal pacification of the Austrians is a purely Austrian affair. I hope that the hotheads who suggested these ill-conceived steps now understand this. We will do what we regard as just in the field of care for our fellow citizens and for our former fellow citizens who were political persecutees, as well as in the field of the liquidation of the Nazi problem, and we will not deviate from this path under pressure.'[38]

When the OFG was expanded, the improvements derived from Austria's bilateral agreement with West Germany. Until 1957, West Germany had resisted treating Austria as a 'liberated' country, arguing that Austria was responsible for claims from Austrian Nazi victims.[39] In November 1961, after four years of talks that overlapped with those on the implementation of Article 26, Vienna and Bonn signed the Bad Kreuznach Treaty. The pact was intended to settle the the Second World War-era financial claims between them, including indemnification for displaced persons and victims of persecution. Once again, as with the State Treaty, Jewish claims were a component of treaty negotiations between governments, but Jewish representatives were not direct participants.

By century's end, the OFG had been amended 62 times, mostly as a result of Allied intervention or pressure from Nazi victims' associations.[40] It was emblematic of the incremental manner in which Austria created a complicated patchwork of compensation and restitution measures in which some laws were repeatedly modified, and in which different groups became eligible for benefits under different conditions and at different times.[41] Payments were treated as humanitarian gestures, not the government's obligation or the victims' legal right. 'The Austrians are allergic to the business of having proper indemnification legislation as explicit as it is in Germany, which starts with the premise that the predecessor government was the cause of, and was responsible for, the persecution,' Kagan said.[42] Raab himself had laid out the terms in a 1955 radio address. 'I regard it as our duty to do something for these poor devils.' However, he said, 'All that we plan to do is nothing but a social measure for the benefit of those with whom we feel ourselves connected through a common past, and we are ready to make grants to them in accordance with our abilities in order to relieve their distress. This, however, should in no way be regarded as the payment of a claim.'[43]

Complications were threaded through all Austrian programmes. For instance, through dozens of amendments, the OFG had evolved into a mélange of social welfare benefits for victims who were Austrian citizens. The OFG, as initially enacted on 17 July 1945, aided only 'resistance fighters'. It was devised to compensate those who were involved in the 'struggle for a free and democratic Austria', not victims. Two years later, it was replaced. The 'second' OFG included a clause covering 'political' and 'religious' persecutees.[44] But the definition of 'victim' favoured political resisters over victims of Nazi persecution, and there was a severe distinction in benefits; Jewish victims were entitled to less than the 'resistance fighters,' meaning 'those who fought with a weapon in hand ... for an independent, democratic and ... conscious Austria, especially against ideas and aims of National Socialism.'[45] After intensive lobbying by the CJCA and the Austrian victims' organization KZ-Verband, the twelfth amendment of the OFG was approved in March 1961.[46] This was a key amendment for Austrian Jewish victims, because it added benefits for those who had been confined in ghettos or other concentration-like camps, who were compelled to wear the Jewish star, and who suffered loss of income and education. However, these benefits were limited to Jewish victims who retained Austrian citizenship.[47]

The Austrian government passed the amendment expecting that West Germany would contribute to its costs under the terms of the Bad Kreuznach agreement, and that the amendment spelled the conclusion of CJCA claims. To that end, Goldmann pledged in a letter on 19 December 1961 that, after the twelfth amendment went into effect, the Committee would 'not undertake any steps against the Austrian government to demand further legal measures for the benefit of those Jewish victims who were persecuted by the Nazis in Austria'. However, Goldmann's letter was not a blanket renunciation of claims. It imposed several conditions, including that the rights of the persecutees would not deteriorate.[48]

In 1956 Austria agreed to create the *Hilfsfonds* for which AS 550 million would be allocated for one-time payments to Austrians who were persecuted for political reasons, including race, religion and nationality. It operated on the principle of a hardship fund, with payments based on such factors as physical suffering, previous imprisonment and current need, rather than on the victims' damages or losses. The fund made payments to 33,223 victims in amounts ranging between AS 7,000 and 30,000. When the funding proved insufficient to cover the claims, the CJCA negotiated for supplemental appropriations. The *Hilfsfonds* was augmented in 1962 (the so-called *Neuer Hilfsfond*) and again in 1976. In the aggregate, the Austrian government appropriated AS 1.590 billion for these *Hilfsfonds*.[49]

In addition, Austria agreed in 1961 to the restitution of pension rights, allowing Austrian-born Jewish victims of Nazi persecution to participate in the Austrian national social insurance system (the General Social Insurance Law, or ASVG). Because they had been banned from employment and later deported, Nazi victims received 'credit' for years of foreign residence between the *Anschluss* and 31 March 1959. Further, victims who were at least 16 years old at the time of the *Anschluss* were given the option of participating in the pension system by retroactively purchasing pension rights at a preferential rate.[50]

Years before it had agreed to these compensation measures, Austria had enacted a series of laws for the restitution of property. The result was 'a confusing and partly contradictory web,' according to the official Austrian Historical Commission, known as the Jabloner Commission. 'It is made up of numerous laws and regulations, of the conflicting interests of political parties, economic associations, victims' organizations and the Allies.'[51]

The restitution measures were initiated immediately after the Second World War. In 1945, the government declared as null and void 'all legal transactions during the German Occupation if undertaken in connection with persecution and racial discrimination'. This was followed by restitution measures whose fragmentation foreshadowed Austria's subsequent disjointed approach to compensation. Between 1946 and 1949 – when Austria was still under Allied control – the Austrian Parliament passed seven restitution laws, the *Rückstellungsgesetze*, covering property losses between 1938 and 1945.[52] The laws varied according to the nature of the property and in whose hands it fell after the war. Some assets were excluded.

The First Restitution Act concerned property seized by Germany – not by private individuals or companies – that was administered after the war by the Republic of Austria or one of its federal states. The Second Restitution Act dealt with property seized during the Nazi era that had become the property of the Republic on the basis of forfeiture (for instance, if the holder was a war criminal). The Third Restitution Act was the general restitution law for the return of property wrongfully taken from its owners – including through forced sales or 'Aryanizations' – that was in private hands after the war. The third law, which was passed in February 1947, was the key measure for Nazi victims – and the most politically controversial, according to the Jabloner Commission. 'Even the draft of the Third Restitution Act was contested by interest groups representing business,' the commission reported. 'The main argument was that restitutions introduced uncertainty into economic life, and should therefore be kept as low as possible! This line was pursued in the further legislation until the 1960s and to a large extent ensured the delays in the legislative process. It was the Western Allies, in particular the US, who continually pushed for the restitution of expropriated property.'[53]

'The fact that Austrian restitution legislation was divided into seven separate laws covering different types of property, based on the current owner or caretaker, complicated the restitution process for Jewish owners right from the start,' said Laurie Cohen, a historian who served as deputy director of the Claims Conference office in Vienna. 'Despite the seemingly broad scope of property covered, Laws One, Two and Three were deceptively restrictive. It is clear that only a small amount of property assets were recovered by former Austrian Jews. Some historians estimate that only 10 per cent of the value of Jewish property was restituted.' The restitution laws were plagued by flaws in design and administration, Cohen said. 'The intent of the legislation was to restore properties that still existed, to relieve the government of paying compensation for destroyed or liquidated properties. This contrasted with West Germany, which provided compensation or restitution for all real estate, based on the 1938 land registries.'[54] A majority of the Austrian Jewish properties were not recovered or compensated. For instance, of 33,326 Jewish-owned businesses in Vienna, former owners could make claims only for the 4,286 that were 'Aryanized'.[55]

Claimants often were discouraged from seeking their properties for a variety of reasons built into the laws: Although impoverished after the Second World War, the victims often had to pay the current owners' 'purchase' price, for any improvements on the property, and for discriminatory taxes. In addition, the claims periods were limited, and notice often was inadequate for Austrian Jews living abroad. In addition, Cohen said, a disproportionate number of former members of the National Socialist régime were employed by the restitution agencies, which may have led to numerous decisions favouring the 'Aryanizer' over the previous owner. For instance, a Jewish businessman who, in 1961, filed a claim for the loss of office equipment was told by Austrian restitution authorities: 'By opening an office on January 11, 1937, it should surely have been clear that there was a threatening régime on the horizon; thus it is unbelievable, without documented proof, that you really did outfit your office within a year.'[56]

The restitution statistics are illuminating: by the end of 1957, there were 39,766 applications under the Third Restitution Law. Of these, 12,544 claims were settled out of court, 8,113 claims were accepted, and the rest were rejected, withdrawn or 'transferred' to another authority.[57] 'In other words, twelve years after the end of the Holocaust, a mere 20 per cent of Austrian claims against private – not state – "Aryanization" had been accepted, 33 per cent were faced with rejection of their claim or striking some sort of last-resort deal, most often with the "Aryanizer,"' Cohen said.[58]

In Austria, the post-war restitution processes were cumbersome, and claimants faced onerous requirements that militated against successful claims. 'Penetrating this labyrinth required an act of both financial and mental strength,' the Jabloner Commission said. 'For the victims of Nazism who had escaped with their lives and who wanted their plundered possessions back in order to be able to ensure some form of survival, it was extremely difficult to orient themselves. In Federal Germany, where in principle two laws regulated restitution and compensation, access to the law was easier.'[59] In many cases – not unique to Austria – victims simply were not in a position to pursue claims. They were scattered around the world and often unaware of the post-war restitution policies in their native countries, including deadlines for filing property claims. After the original restitution laws lapsed, restitution in Austria was moribund until Nazi-hunter Simon Wiesenthal intervened and Austria passed a law in 1969 under which claims for artworks, which had been seized between 1938 and 1945, would be accepted until the end of 1972.[60]

Then, in 1984, an article in *ARTnews* magazine exposed the existence of Nazi-looted and confiscated art that was in Austrian government possession and stored in the Mauerbach monastery near Vienna. The report, entitled 'A Legacy of Shame: Nazi Art Loot in Austria,' raised serious questions about the extent to which Austria and its institutions had benefited from looted art.[61] The Mauerbach revelation was the first of a series of events – some political, some related to war-era anniversaries and commemorations – that created an environment in which, after two decades, the CJCA renewed its efforts for Austrian Jewish Nazi victims.

Alerted by the magazine article to the existence of the art, Miller and Kagan met with the Austrian chancellor, Fred Sinowatz, and other officials, insisting that individuals be given the right to claim their family objects in the Mauerbach collection. The Austrian Parliament unanimously passed a law requiring the state to return to the Jews the Nazi-confiscated works, including some 600 paintings, as well as books, medals and coins.[62] Between 1984 and 1996, some 400 Mauerbach items were restituted to individuals. The process was slow, impeded by Austrian evidentiary requirements, heirs' dim memories, and the nature of the objects themselves, which were subject to conflicting claims. 'These were not the Rembrandts and Picassos. They were good, 19th-century bourgeois paintings,' said Kagan. 'Many of the claimants were teenagers at the time [of the plunder]. Their recollection is that in the salon, there was a painting of a farmer with a horse at the brook, and such were more than one in good Austrian bourgeois homes.'[63]

The Austrian measure also had included an important principle: that none of the Mauerbach objects would remain in custody of the Austrian government. The legislation provided that whatever went unclaimed would be sold, and the proceeds would be used to aid Nazi victims in and from Austria.[64] The auction of the residual Mauerbach objects was held on 29 and 30 October 1996 at the Austrian Museum of Applied Art (MAK). Christie's, which conducted the auction, originally had estimated that it would generate about $3.5 million. Instead, it raised $14.5 million.[65] 'Nobody expected $14 million from this sale,' Miller said. 'Part of it was due to the fact that these items – objects of art, armor, books, coins – were things that people could see and feel and touch. It hit a responsive chord.'[66]

It also was bittersweet. It had been more than a decade since Miller and Kagan had learned of the Mauerbach art. 'It took much too long a time, but it is that legislation enacted subsequently by the Austrian Parliament that made it possible to return thousands of objects to their former owners or heirs and to create the basis for the auction. I would have been more pleased had every object been returned to the original owners or their heirs,' Miller said in Vienna on the eve of the sale. 'I hope that the sale will be successful, and will raise a significant sum of money. The survivors for whom the proceeds will be used are aged and many of them are infirm, and many are in need,' he said. 'But this sale is not just about money. It is primarily about justice and morality and Jewish dignity. It reminds the present generation of the sins of the past. It has excited the imagination of people the world over because it is the right thing to do. The art will be purchased by caring individuals, aesthetically and morally, but we – all of us – must never forget why we are here, the events which led up to our presence here.'[67]

Mauerbach was the first in a revival of efforts on behalf of Nazi victims. Miller viewed political and commemorative events as opportunities to advance Jewish claims. When Kurt Waldheim was seeking the Austrian presidency, the World Jewish Congress revealed that the former U.N. secretary-general had concealed much of his record as an officer in the German army in the Balkans during the Second World War.[68] The storm over Waldheim created an environment in which Austria's links to its Nazi past were discussed and one in which the claims of Nazi victims could be pursued. Soon after Waldheim was elected, the Austrian Cabinet decided to mark the fiftieth anniversary of the *Anschluss*, 13 March 1988. Miller used the occasion to remind Chancellor Franz Vranitzky that there were deficiencies in the Austrian compensation measures for Jewish victims. In view of the 'historic and humanitarian importance' of these issues, he called on the chancellor to 'discuss specific steps that should be taken to ensure that the fiftieth anniversary of the *Anschluss* will mark the enactment of a series of measures for the benefit of the most tragic victims of the *Anschluss*.'[69] After talks with the Conference, in March 1988 the Austrian Parliament passed the Honorary Grants and Assistance Fund Act (*Ehrengaben und Hilfsfondsgesetz*), which provided one-time grants to Austrian resistance fighters and victims who had been persecuted on political grounds or on the basis of origin, religion or nationality, and to those who emigrated to escape persecution. Individuals got token compensation ranging from AS 2,500 to AS 5,000.[70] Freda Meissner-Blau, of the Austria Green Party, voted for the legislation, but she said, 'This paltry sum makes my face red with shame.'[71]

The CJCA sought additional compensation. 'Fifty years after the *Anschluss*, we were greatly concerned about the need to provide former Austrian Jews who were reaching retirement age with the possibility to claim pensions. And thus at our initiative, we turned to the Austrian government. It's not a gesture that they made of their own goodwill,' Miller said.[72] In fact, there were serious doubts whether anything tangible would be achieved, because of the Austrian government's traditionally negative attitude about Jewish claims. The Austrian government also confronted the CJCA with Goldmann's 1961 letter, which said that the Committee would not advance any further demands. 'I just ignored it,' Miller recalled.[73]

The Committee successfully negotiated for changes in the Austrian social insurance law (ASVG), a measure that had assumed great significance to Austrian-born Nazi victims. Because Austria had never enacted annuities akin to those created by the West German indemnification legislation, the ASVG pensions became the primary means through which Austria compensated Jewish Nazi victims. The government acknowledged that the pensions were not restitution in the strict sense. However, it said, 'in many respects [the pension programme] nevertheless contains important elements of restitution and compensation (preferential treatment) for victims of National Socialism with respect to pension rights'.[74]

There were incremental changes that expanded the number of victims who participated in the pension system on the basis of their birth years. By gradually adjusting the age limits, Austria agreed to make eligible those who were forced to leave the country long before they were old enough to join the work force. In 1989, Parliament approved an amendment that enabled Jewish Nazi victims from Austria who were born in 1930 (who would have been 8 years old at the time of the *Anschluss*), or earlier, to apply for social insurance pensions.[75] In 1993, the CJCA was the catalyst for legislation under which Austrian Jews who were born as late as 31 December 1932 – who were 6 at the time of the *Anschluss* – became eligible for social insurance pensions. Under traditional social insurance pensions, individuals make regular contributions to the system during their years of employment and draw pensions on retirement. For the Nazi victims to qualify, many were obliged to make payments into the system, to 'buy back work months'. 'One of the most difficult negotiations was to make sure that these payments are relatively tolerable,' Kagan said. In most cases, the payment required of the Nazi victims was less than two years of the value of what the pension eventually pays.[76] By century's end, more than 30,000 victims had been approved for such pensions.[77] In addition, there was a 'collective' payment in 1989, when Austria agreed to provide some AS 300 million (about $25 million) to the CJCA for projects that provide shelter or social care to aged and infirm Austrian Jewish Nazi victims.[78]

Despite these improvements, there were issues that remained unresolved. These included the failure of the Austrian government to compensate for certain material losses, as well as some discriminatory measures in social welfare laws, including provisions that excluded non-residents from benefits. This was especially troubling because the majority of the surviving former Austrian Jews lived abroad.[79] Domestic Austrian politics provided an opening to raise these claims in June 1991, when Jörg Haider, of the right-wing Freedom Party and governor of Carinthia, praised the Nazis during a debate in Parliament. 'An orderly employment policy was carried out in the Third Reich, which the government in Vienna cannot manage,' Haider said.[80] In his powerful reaction to Haider, Vranitzky broke a long-standing taboo and all but reversed Austria's customary portrayal of itself as a victim of Nazi aggression. In a speech to Parliament, he issued an apology. 'We must not forget that there were not a few Austrians who, in the name of this

[Nazi] régime, brought great suffering to others, who took part in the persecutions and crimes,' the chancellor said. 'We own up to all facts of our history and to the deeds of all parts of our people. As we take credit for the good, we must apologize for the evil.'[81]

Those remarks 'laid the foundation for a new approach by Austria to reach out to those who were forced to leave the country in 1938. At the same time, it was made clear that many Austrians shared the responsibility for the Holocaust and that Austria missed many opportunities where just and moral action would have been required,' Vranitzky told Miller.[82] The chancellor again raised the topic in June 1993, in a speech in Jerusalem. 'We clearly have to face the catastrophe which the Nazi dictatorship brought upon my country,' he said in an address at Hebrew University. 'There were those who were courageous enough to offer active resistance against the madness or tried to help the victims, risking their lives by doing so; but many more joined the Nazi machinery, and some rose through its ranks to be among the most brutal, hideous perpetrators. We have to live up to this side of our history, our shame of the responsibility for the suffering which not Austria – for the state no longer existed – but which some of her citizens inflicted upon other people, inflicted upon humanity.'[83]

A year later, Waldheim's successor as president, Thomas Klestil, became the first Austrian head of state to appear before the Israeli Knesset. His speech mirrored those of Vranitzky. 'We know full well that all too often we have only spoken of Austria as the first state to have lost its freedom and independence to National Socialism, and far too seldom of the fact that many of the worst henchmen in the Nazi dictatorship were Austrians. And no word of apology can ever expunge the agony of the Holocaust,' he said in his address on 15 November 1994. 'On behalf of the Republic of Austria, I bow my head with deep respect and profound emotion in front of the victims. We know full well that for far too long we have not done enough, and not always the right thing, to alleviate the plight of the survivors of the Jewish tragedy and the victims' descendants. And we know that for far too long we have neglected those Jewish Austrians who were forced to leave their native land, humiliated and embittered.'[84]

The speeches were welcomed, but they were insufficient. 'There was continuous pressure for Austria to do something tangible to show that the speeches were not just pious declarations,' Kagan said.[85] The CJCA, the Austrian Jewish community and sympathetic members of Parliament pressed for compensation. In conjunction with the 50th anniversary of the Second Austrian Republic, in 1995, Austria established the National Fund for Victims of National Socialism. 'On the occasion of its 50th birthday, the Republic of Austria wanted to give a manifestation of its goodwill and is now in the process of setting up a fund for the victims of National Socialism,' Vranitzky told Miller. 'The idea underlying this endeavor has been to include also victims who hitherto – be it intentionally or unintentionally – have been disregarded.'[86] The fund was expected to make payments to estimated 30,000 victims.[87] The government's $50 million fund, however, did not have universal support. The Green Party, which had demanded $150 million, opposed the measure, saying it was too little, too late. Green Party deputy Johannes Voggenhuber said it would 'turn the compensation fund into little more than a poor box.'[88]

Unlike earlier measures, the fund was historic because it was not linked to financial need. Instead, it made lump-sum payments to Nazi victims who had been Austrian citizens or long-term residents before the *Anschluss*. 'For the first time, with this new law of the National Fund, there is an inkling of restitution – not only restitution, but of recognition and justice,' said Paul Grosz, then-president of the IKG. 'It was an uphill struggle to make the Austrians agree finally to the fact that the moneys are not given because the victims are poor or destitute, but because justice asked that every victim, every survivor of the Holocaust, should by this token be recognized for the first time as victims.'[89] As of October 2001, more than 27,800 victims had received a payment from the National Fund, according to Hannah Lessing, the fund's secretary-general. Some 95 per cent were Jewish. 'This is a gesture, not compensation,' she said. 'The word "compensation" is not a word I use; there is no way of compensating.'[90]

While domestic Austrian events created opportunities to pursue compensation for Nazi victims, there also were international forums at which the anticipation of compensation was raised. The first was in December 1997, when the British government hosted an international 'Nazi gold' conference in London. During the war, the Nazis had confiscated tons of gold, primarily from the national treasuries of occupied European countries. A substantial portion had been recovered by the Allies after the Second World War and was restituted to European nations by the Tripartite Gold Commission (TCG), a post-war agency created by Britain, the US and France. The claimant nations received, on average, about 60 per cent of their claims. By 1997, the commission was due to close. At the London meeting, dozens of nations discussed their outstanding gold claims and how to use the residual looted gold that still was held by the commission. In light of the attention on Nazi victims' losses, there was international pressure for nations to commit their share of the residuals to aid the victims.[91] The London conference became the venue at which nations formally pledged to use the estimated $70 million in residual gold to assist victims.[92]

Austria was the first to make the pledge. In August 1997, Austria officially was notified of its share of the residual gold, and four weeks later, the Austrian government decided to use the funds – AS 102 million (about $8.5 million) – for victims. 'We have from the beginning shared the view that, taken as a global amount, the sum to be distributed seems a pittance, but it could nevertheless significantly help in particular those aging survivors of the Nazi atrocities who have not received anything so far close to the justice they deserve,' Hans Winkler, the legal adviser of the Austrian Foreign Affairs Ministry, said at the London conference. 'The irrefutable proof that at least a portion of the gold restituted to the claimant countries since the end of the war as well as of the gold still in the vaults of the Federal Reserve and other banks was non-monetary, belonging to individual victims of the Nazi persecution, confirmed our conviction that a moral obligation exists to making available the amount still held by the TGC to the benefit of needy survivors of the Holocaust. We regard this as a humanitarian gesture, as expression of shared international solidarity with the victims of the Holocaust.'[93]

The second international forum was in December 1998, when more than 40 nations convened at the State Department for the Washington Conference on Holocaust-Era Assets. Second World War-era plundered art was among the items on the agenda. By that time, Austria was grappling anew with the question of Nazi-looted art that was in its federal institutions' possession. Attention had sharply focused on Austria after the January 1998 detention in New York of two Egon Schiele paintings that had been on loan from the Austrian Leopold Foundation to an exhibition at the Museum of Modern Art. While in New York, two of the paintings were claimed by heirs of Nazi victims. Once the Schieles were seized, the Austrian minister for education and cultural affairs, Elisabeth Gehrer, established a 'Commission for Provenance Research,' whose work served as basis for a federal law on the restitution of war-era art in federal museums.[94]

Nonetheless, in light of the fragmented nature of Austrian compensation and restitution, the Conference still had 'open issues.' The First Austrian Republic failed to protect its Jewish citizens' lives and properties, and the Second Republic had been remiss in remedying the past, it contended. One of the issues was compensation for the loss of movable properties. Austria had traditionally argued that it was not liable for the loss of these assets because properties had been liquidated and moved to Berlin. The Conference disputed that assertion. In the State Archives in Vienna, there were tens of thousands of property declarations that Austrian Jewish households had been obliged to file after the *Anschluss*. 'These declarations contained a record of everything that every Jewish family in Austria possessed, starting with silverware and furniture and household goods and anything else that had any kind of value,' Kagan said.[95] The declarations also included securities and business inventories. 'Austria reaped disproportionately large benefits from its incorporation into Germany and a large part of the Jewish assets which were confiscated in Austria remained there,' Kagan said. 'We have found, for instance, that all securities confiscated from Austrian Jews were sold in Austria. Only non-salable securities were shipped to Berlin.'[96] In addition, Jews had had valuable tenancy rights to apartments. Among those who were evicted after the *Anschluss* was Jahoda's family. 'They threw us out with five days' warning. Did they send 75,000 rented flats to Berlin or did they remain in Vienna?' said Jahoda, who as a child fled to Palestine and returned to Vienna decades later as the Conference's representative.[97]

However, the Conference had 'not devoted enough time or effort to [Austria], one of the reasons being that it was very difficult to get the United States to move in this area,' said Miller, underscoring the Conference's reliance on American government.[98] This was due, in part, to the traditional view of Austria as a Nazi-occupied country, as well as Austria's importance as a Cold War buffer state. While the US had political reasons to ignore claims, Israel and Jewish organizations deferred them for humanitarian reasons. From the days immediately following the Second World War until the collapse of communism decades later, Austria's geography made it an important transit point for Jews fleeing the Soviet Union and Eastern Europe. Israel and most Jewish organizations feared jeopardizing the transit routes if they antagonized Austrian authorities. By 1999, the climate had changed. The Cold War was over and there was an international focus on Nazi victims' losses. The Conference opened its first office in Austria and formed a negotiating committee that included the *Israelitische Kultusgemeinde* (IKG), organizations of former Austrian Jews living in Israel and the US, the World Jewish Congress and the Ronald S. Lauder Foundation, which had substantial philanthropic interests in Central and Eastern Europe.[99] Its prospects were uncertain. The public mood in Austria was embodied in a quip that made the rounds, said Ariel Muzicant, who in 1998 succeeded Grosz as president of the Austrian Jewish community: the Austrians who were alive in the Nazi era were the first victims and should not pay; those who were not alive in those days cannot be bothered.[100]

By this time, however, there was another venue in which Nazi victims pressed claims against Austria – the US federal courts. Lawsuits involving Austrian enterprises followed those against Swiss banks, which were sued for failing to restore dormant and unclaimed Holocaust-era accounts, and against American and German companies for the war-time use of slave labour. Austrian companies – Anker and Wiener Allianz, a subsidiary of German's Allianz – were among the European insurers sued in 1997 for allegedly failing to honour Nazi-era policies. And Creditanstalt, a wartime subsidiary of Deutsche Bank, was included in the class-action lawsuit filed in June 1998 against Germany's Deutsche Bank and Dresdner Bank.[101] In March 1999, Bank Austria and Creditanstalt agreed to a $40 million settlement for Holocaust-era Austrian bank accounts; the Conference negotiated a companion agreement of $5 million to be used for the benefit of Holocaust survivors of Austrian origin.[102]

In the interim, the October 1999 national elections ended the long history of coalition governments formed by the Socialists and the People's Party. Haider's Freedom Party won some 27 per cent of the vote and joined the coalition of Chancellor Wolfgang Schüssel of the People's Party on 1 February 2000. This caused an uproar in Israel and Europe, where the European Union (EU) nations imposed diplomatic sanctions to protest the inclusion of Haider's party in the government.[103]

The new government, anxious to shed its pariah status and to prove that it was committed to democratic values, immediately contacted the Conference. 'I would like to reiterate the commitment of Austria to continue to cooperate with all international institutions and bodies that were formed in the last few years to look into all questions relating to Holocaust assets,' Schüssel, on his third day as chancellor, wrote to Taylor. He was willing to act quickly on an 'interim' humanitarian gesture to surviving victims, 'especially those who live in difficult personal financial circumstances', he wrote, although he did not provide details.[104]

The US had not imposed sanctions on Austria, which was delighted to show the EU that it had a friend – Washington. On the ninth day of the Schüssel government, Eizenstat reported to Congress that the Austrians had vowed to resolve the 'outstanding questions' relating to Nazi-era slave and forced labour, to continue to restore Nazi-looted art, and to proceed with a review of its the Second World War record. For Austria, slave labour was primarily an issue for Central and Eastern Europe. The Jewish interests in Austria concerned property losses.[105] The chancellor appointed Maria Schaumayer, the former head of Austria's National Bank, as the government envoy to lead the negotiations on slave and forced labour compensation.[106] Months later, the government appointed Ernst Sucharipa as the 'special negotiating partner for victims' organizations' to deal with restitution claims.[107]

The overtures created a quandary for the Conference. Israel had recalled its ambassador from Vienna. A Conference member organization, the Jewish Agency, whose raison d'etre was immigration to Israel, imagined a mass exodus of Austrian Jews and rejected Austria's offer to negotiate, calling it a 'cynical attempt' to breach the international boycott.[108] Oscar Deutsch, a member of the IKG board, did not want to defer the claims, but wanted some indirect approach to Austria, saying, 'If we should start now direct negotiations with this government, we would *kasher* [give approval to] this government.' However, Kurt Ladner, representing Austrian Jews living in the US, thought it was 'silly' not to speak to an Austrian government. 'You've got to speak to the Austrian government, whoever is in the government ... We spoke to all of them,' said Ladner, who was 11 in 1938 when the Nazis marched into Vienna. 'I'm 73 years old. If you're going to wait for another government, I'll be 93.'[109]

'We were torn,' Taylor said. 'We didn't want to enhance the legitimacy of a government that had the Freedom Party in it. On the other hand, we felt that we didn't have the right to not pursue issues on behalf of victims from Austria because of Haider. The claim was every bit as valid, if not more so, and not less so, because Haider's people were in the government.'[110] A middle ground was found when Eizenstat became the 'facilitator' of the talks with Sucharipa. 'If it had not been for Eizenstat, we would not have reached an agreement,' Miller said. 'The United States never broke relations with Austria. Eizenstat served as the coalescing force to bring the various parties together, and kept their feet to the fire.'[111]

By the close of the century, there were some 21,000 surviving Austrian Nazi victims scattered around the world. They were seeking compensation for confiscated and looted properties, including apartments, businesses, household contents, bank accounts and securities, as well as compensation for discriminatory taxes, and improvements in social welfare pensions.[112] The Austrian Jewish community, the IKG, also had claims for the restitution of Jewish communal property that remained in public hands.[113] While they had common interests, the Conference and the IKG also were at odds with each other. The Conference primarily was seeking compensation and social welfare benefits for individual Austrian Nazi victims, while the IKG, with 6,500 members and buckling under debt, wanted to recover property that would generate income to relieve its financial burdens and fund its communal activities. Each apparently feared that the other could prevail at their expense.

Together they faced an Austrian government that resisted assertions that its previous laws were as deficient as the victims' groups maintained. Further, Austria also contended that it had satisfied its post-war treaty obligations to the Allies. 'The Austrian restitution and compensation legislation between 1945 and 1955 was adopted with the explicit knowledge and approval of the four Allied Powers, including the United States of America,' according to Sucharipa. 'Thus, at the time, the Allied Powers must be held to have considered the Austrian measures suitable remedies for claims of restitution or compensation.'[114]

In neighbouring Germany, the government was negotiating to establish a foundation that would pay compensation for slave labour and all other Nazi-era claims against Germany and German industry. Austria, however, originally limited its focus to slave labour, and in late 2000 Austria established an AS 6 billion fund for slave labour, which was known as the 'Austrian Fund for Reconciliation, Peace and Cooperation.'[115] At the time, it was estimated that some 150,000 victims would be eligible for compensation, of whom roughly 10,000 were Jewish – primarily from Hungary.[116] In exchange for the fund, Austria sought 'legal peace' from lawsuits in the US courts. That fund, however, did not address the losses of Jewish property, and victims' groups would not agree to forgo the labour lawsuits – some of which also dealt with property restitution – without a commitment by Austria to deal with property claims.[117] The US also linked the two. While commending Austria for compensating slave labourers, it also reminded Vienna of other outstanding claims. 'The establishment of the Austrian Reconciliation Fund, which will provide many aged survivors with a measure of justice in their lifetimes, will be a historic achievement,' President Bill Clinton told Klestil days before the labour agreement was signed. 'We look forward to working with you and Chancellor Schüssel's government to find a similar resolution to the remaining property and "Aryanization" issues arising out of the Nazi era and the World War II.'[118] At the 24 October 2000 signing of the labour agreement in Vienna, Eizenstat announced that immediately after the ceremony, Austria, victims' groups and lawyers would begin to discuss property restitution and compensation issues. 'It is critically important that these talks succeed,' he said.[119]

Negotiations on Jewish claims subsequently proceeded at an accelerated pace.[120] Austria quickly agreed to provide $150 million that, similar to the National Fund years earlier, would distribute one-time payments of $7,000 to all Nazi victims originating from or living in Austria.[121] The payments were not dependent on legal peace from the pending lawsuits. 'Getting this $7,000 without legal closure, and getting it as a guaranteed amount for everyone, with little bureaucracy, was critical,' said Taylor. However, there was a dispute over what the payment covered. The Austrians insisted that it was compensation for three categories of losses: apartment and business leases, household contents and personal effects, for all victims.[122] For the Conference, however, this was simply the first round, a 'down payment' on outstanding claims. 'The Austrians were trying to minimize what was left to discuss and treated the $150 million payment as having dealt with the majority, if not all, of the issues,' Taylor said. 'We wanted to make clear that there were still many issues to be discussed.'[123]

Social welfare benefits were a priority. 'The survivors on our delegation were saying over and over again that this was the most important and effective way to aid survivors,' Taylor said. The Conference demanded an amendment to the social insurance law (ASVG) to enable people born in Austria between 1932 and 1938 to receive the minimum Austrian social insurance pensions. It also insisted that Austria remove the limitations on a special 'nursing allowance' that severely discriminated against disabled Austrian Nazi victims living abroad. These benefits were the major sticking points in the negotiations, and the Conference entered the eleventh hour of negotiations certain that it would be rebuffed. The costs were difficult to quantify; the benefits were open-ended and would have significant financial implications for the Austrian social welfare system for years. Nonetheless, Taylor said, 'for us, this was the red line.'[124]

An agreement was concluded on 17 January 2001 in the final days of the Clinton presidency. It was a combination of funds, social welfare benefits and property restitution valued at $480 million, and financed by the Austrian government and industry. An estimated two-thirds of the benefits would go to individuals, either in direct payments through the National Fund or in the form of social welfare benefits. The Austrian legislation to implement that agreement was passed weeks later, on 31 January 2001. Through a General Settlement Law and amendments to existing laws, the agreement would improve social welfare benefits for Jewish victims of Nazi persecution from Austria by expanding eligibility for pensions and the nursing allowance.[125] It also pledged direct restitution of Jewish properties in public hands, as well as a limited compensation package for some property claims.[126]

On the one-year anniversary of the agreement, Jahoda convened a seminar in Vienna with representatives of the Austrian government and Parliament, the National Fund, Austrian industry and US State Department. The 2001 agreement was hailed as a 'historic breakthrough,' but the social welfare package had yet to be realized because there was not yet legal peace.[127] 'I was naïve last January. I thought we'd achieved something, and had no idea that the legal peace issue would prevent suffering people from receiving their just, humanitarian payments,' Jahoda said on the anniversary of the agreement. 'How can I convince Parliament to accept the split, and allow the social benefits without legal peace? We're talking about a few hundred shillings more per month for a few hundred people.'[128]

Sucharipa also said he believed that Austria needed to begin enforcing the measures to demonstrate that it took the agreement seriously. That sentiment was echoed by Terezija Stoisits, a member of Parliament from the Green Party. 'I wasn't part of the negotiations, but I voted for passage of the laws,' she told the seminar. 'But it doesn't look like anything was done. Here I hear the spirit was warm, strong, unified – well, what about the social welfare benefits that haven't been paid? That seems totally against the spirit.'[129]

Two weeks later, Stoisits recounted to a parliamentary session that Jahoda had spoken of being 'naïve'. 'I would say that this victims' representative wasn't speaking about being naive, but that in a certain way they have been a little taken for a ride – in spirit, not directly – as far as their hopes for the compensatory payments,' she said. 'What we are doing is not an act of mercy or an act of any special generosity, but ... rather the only possibility to fulfill the legislation we agreed to last year.'[130] On 30 January 2002, the Parliament passed a measure authorizing the payments of the additional social welfare benefits and permitting Nazi victims from Austria who were born was early as 1 January 1933 to purchase pension rights.[131]

The Conference has rued its limited success in securing compensation for victims from Austria. Its efforts to get benefits for Jews who survived the *Anschluss* 'did not reach the proportionate order of magnitude of the results of our efforts in Germany,' Kagan said. 'Nonetheless, it provided some limited compensation and restitution and continues to provide, particularly through the social insurance legislation, ongoing payments to thousands of Jewish Nazi victims in and from Austria.'[132]

Nor did Austria fully acknowledge its history in the manner of Adenauer and Rau, and the January 2001 agreement did not resolve the question of the adequacy of Austria's post-war compensation and restitution measures. In the joint statement, it simply acknowledged 'that there were certain gaps and deficiencies in such measures.' 'In my eyes,' said Jahoda, 'the difference between Austria and Germany and other countries is that the Austrians don't feel any remorse, and this is our main problem.'[133]

NOTES

1 This account of the crowd's rejection of Austrian Chancellor Kurt von Schuschnigg and of its enthusiastic embrace of the Nazis appears in William L. Shirer, *The Nightmare Years, 1930–1940*, Boston: Little, Brown and Company, 1984, p. 296.
2 For instance, in 1946, Austrian Parliamentarian Ernst Kolb said that 'the first entitled claimant' to the proposed Austrian restitution laws was 'the Republic of Austria itself,' and that 'Austria had nothing to compensate for, as it had not broken any laws.' The Allies' post-war Tripartite Gold Commission also treated Austria as a legitimate claimant nation with the

right to recover gold that had been looted by the Nazis.
3 For details on the *Bundesentschädigungsgesetze*, see Chapter 2.
4 Goldmann, *Autobiography*, p. 282.
5 The Germans initiated the JUVA after *Kristallnacht* – the November 1938 anti-Jewish rampage known as the 'Night of Broken Glass' – on the grounds that the Jews 'had provoked' the outrage of the German people and had to make good for the damages. According to the Austrian Historical Commission, which was established in October 1998, the JUVA initially amounted to 20 per cent and in October 1939 was increased to 25 per cent of the assets that Jews had been required to register. Other taxes included the *Passumlage* ('passport fee') and the *Auswanderungsabgabe* ('emigration levy'). The Austrian Historical Commission, which submitted its final report to the government in January 2003, attempted to determine the value of the Jewish assets based on surviving 1938 property registration documents. The commission said that the estimates ranged between RM 1.842 billion and RM 2.9 billion, depending on methods and assumptions used in the calculations. Historian Helen B. Junz, in her 1999 'Report on the Pre-War Wealth Position of the Jewish Population in Nazi-Occupied Countries, Germany and Austria' (Annex to Report on Dormant Accounts of Victims of Nazi Persecution in Swiss Banks, Independent Committee of Eminent Persons), said a conservative valuation of Jewish assets in 1938 was RM 1.4 billion. That figure, based on property declarations of more than 45,000 Jews in Austria in 1938, did not include items such as pensions, salaries, household contents and rental properties.
6 Claims Conference Board meeting, 14 July 1999, New York.
7 At the end of 1952, some Conference members had argued against a distinct committee for Austria, fearing both the expense and the unwieldy nature of a new structure. However, the proponents contended that there was a need for some 'international' vehicle to deal with compensation for Austrian Jews, as well as concern that, in the absence of such a vehicle, independent Jewish groups would try to broker separate deals. The Committee's members were the same as those of the Claims Conference, minus German Jewish organizations, plus the World Council of Jews from Austria.
8 *A Decade of American Foreign Policy: Basic Documents, 1941–49*, Washington: Government Printing Office, 1950. The second paragraph of the declaration, which was traditionally overlooked, stated: 'Austria is reminded, however, that she has a responsibility, which she cannot evade, for participation in the war at the side of Hitlerite Germany, and that in the final settlement account will inevitably be taken of her own contribution to her liberation.' According to the Austrian Foreign Ministry, the second paragraph was unrelated to Nazi victims, but was inserted at the insistence of the Soviet Union; it permitted Moscow to seek reparations from Austria and to seize assets and dismantle industry in the post-war Soviet Occupation Zone.
9 Claims Conference Board meeting, 6 July 1990, Jerusalem.
10 Raab letter to Goldmann, 13 November 1953.
11 The Austrian victims were included in the Joint Recommendations of April 1952 that were issued in Wassenaar, but were excluded in the final agreement between West Germany and the Claims Conference. See Claims Conference, 'Memorandum concerning the liability of the Federal Republic for damage inflicted upon Jewish victims of Nazi action in Austria,' 6 August 1952. In excluding Austria, West Germany also said that if it were not accepting liability for Eastern Germany, it could not accept liability for an independent state such as Austria, according to Moses Leavitt's personal diary of negotiations.
12 Kapralik letter to Kagan, 14 October 1952. In his letter, Kapralik also said that West Germany would be able to afford compensation because it would have a healthy economy supported by a population of some 50 million workers, while the Austrian economy rested on a population of seven million, which would limit its ability to pay.
13 Claims Conference, 'Memorandum concerning the liability of the Federal Republic for damage inflicted upon Jewish victims of Nazi action in Austria.'
14 Claims Conference Board meeting, 30–31 January 1960, Amsterdam, CAHJP 13630.
15 There was speculation that one of the reasons for Sharett's declaration was that the National Bank of Austria had just credited AS 100 million ($2.5 million) to Bank Leumi in Israel. *Jerusalem Post*, 18 August 1952.
16 Goldmann comments on the negotiations both in *Autobiography*, p. 281 and in *The Jewish Paradox*, p. 137. In *Paradox*, Goldmann was somewhat forgiving of Raab, saying that the chancellor 'in any case had nothing to reproach himself for, because he himself had been in a

concentration camp'. Not only was there no direct Israeli claim against Austria to bolster the Jewish claims, but there was powerful Arab opposition to Austrian negotiations on Jewish claims. Arab nations threatened to oppose a United Nations resolution on the restoration of Austrian sovereignty if Austria opened negotiations on claims (*New York Times*, 24 November 1952). Israel said it would support the UN resolution, but also said it believed that Austria had the 'serious intention' of fulfilling its obligation to Nazi victims.

17 Austria was occupied by the Four Powers from 1945 to 1955. Because Austria was treated as a liberated – not a defeated – country, in January 1947 negotiations began for a 'state treaty', not a peace treaty.

18 CJCA memorandum to Senators Alexander Wiley and Walter F. George, 19 November 1954, CAHJP 14105.

19 Claims Conference, 'Final Document Submitted by the Jewish Negotiating Team to the Austrian Negotiating Team', 1 July 1953, CAHJP 14107.

20 This was less-complicated than in Germany because, unlike Germany, Austria was not a divided nation. In Germany, various measures for indemnification and restitution were developed at different times in the Western Occupation Zones; these subsequently were harmonized by West German federal law. See Chapter 2.

21 The comment was recounted at the Allied Control Council meeting; summary by British Embassy, Vienna, 13 August 1954, CAHJP 14105.

22 *New York Times*, 31 August 1952. The newspaper revisited the issue the next year, when there was a deadlock in talks on Jewish claims. 'There is one point that would seem to take precedence over all others, and this is that the issue is not primarily a legal once, and in view of the sum involved not even one of economics, but first and foremost a moral one,' it said an editorial on 21 December 1953. 'Since the anti-Jewish atrocities were perpetrated not only by German but also by Austrian Nazis, it would seem that the Austrian Government would act in its own best interest if it did its utmost to settle the issue in conformity with the conscience of the Western world, to which it belongs'.

23 Allied Control Council meeting; summary by British Embassy, Vienna, 13 August 1954, CAHJP 14105. The Allies' veto was denounced by Herbert A. Kraus, the parliamentary leader of the League of Independents. Kraus called the veto 'an unheard-of interference in Austrian legislation', in a statement published in the right-wing party's weekly newspaper, *Neue Front* (*New York Times*, 20 August 1954).

24 Kagan memo to CJCA, 9 September 1957, CAHJP 14106.

25 The treaty was subject to negotiations by governments; the CJCA consulted regularly with State Department and Austrian officials, but had no direct role in the talks. The American interest in the matter was based on its role as one of the Allied powers, plus the fact that about half the Austrian claimants were thought to be residents of the US. Internal State Department memo, 20 October 1958, NARA, NND959204.

26 C. Burke Elbrick, Assistant Secretary of State, letter to Congressman Emanuel Cellar, 24 July 1957, NARA, NND959204.

27 The Jewish claims were not the only source of aggravation. Austria was to have settled the claims of American and British oil companies by April 1957, but 'protracted negotiations since 1955 are having an increasingly adverse effect on Austrian–American relations', according to a May 1958 memorandum by Mr. Jandray to the Secretary of State, 'Briefing Memorandum for the Meeting with Chancellor Raab', NARA, NND959204.

28 Frederic Chapin, the Austrian Desk officer in the State Department, letter to Walter Löhr, US Embassy, Vienna, 30 December 1957, NARA, NND959204.

29 Memorandum of conversation, State Department, unsigned, 19 May 1958, NARA, NND959204.

30 Rubin was an ideal candidate to press the issue with the US government because he previously had served as a State Department negotiator handling several post-war American-European treaties. According to a letter dated 8 September 1958 from Chapin to Löhr, the State Department believed that the US government should not approach the Austrians for an increase.

31 Löhr, US Embassy, Vienna, letter to Chapin, 19 September 1958, NARA, NND959204.

32 Richard Kearney, assistant legal adviser, State Department, letter to Rubin, 3 October 1958, NARA, NND959204.

33 State Department press release on Austrian agreement and claims, 18 April 1961, CAHJP 14104.

34 Kagan memo to CJCA officers, 3 February 1959, CAHJP 14106.
35 There was a one-year deadline to apply, which later was extended by six months. The fund received 11,098 claims; approximately 8,330 were accepted, of which roughly half were from Jewish Nazi victims (or heirs) who lived in the US. The successful applicants received, on average, $700, according to the Claims Conference's Vienna office (position paper, November 2000).
36 Much of that property was situated in the zone that had been occupied by Soviet forces before the State Treaty was signed. The Soviet Occupation authorities in Austria – like their counterparts in Occupied Germany – had not respected the local restitution laws. By the time the Soviet forces withdrew, the filing deadlines under the 1947 Austrian restitution laws had expired; property owners were directed to make restitution claims via the *Sammelstellen*. There was a one-year filing deadline for claims. George Weis, who had been a member of the staff of the Jewish Restitution Successor Organization in Berlin, headed both funds.
37 Eighty per cent of the proceeds from *Sammelstelle* A went to 7,458 individuals, in amounts ranging from AS 2,000 to 22,800 per claim. In addition, the Collection Agency Fund provided AS 23 million to the Jewish Community of Vienna for the construction of an old-age home; AS 19 million toward the construction of an old-age home near Tel Aviv for Austrian Nazi victims; and additional funds for projects in New York, Linz, Salzburg and Innsbruck. The remaining proceeds (*Sammelstelle* B) were used to benefit non-Jewish victims. They concluded their activities in 1972.
38 Text of radio address by Raab; 6 March 1955, CAHJP 14109.
39 Nazi victims were not the only population at issue between West Germany and Austria. West Germany also had rejected financial responsibility for the *Volksdeutsche,* more than 400,000 ethnic Germans who were expelled after the Second World War from the Sudetenland, Romania and Hungary and who subsequently settled in Austria. An estimated 12 million so-called expellees had settled in West Germany, where they were entitled to significant benefits under the Equalization of Burdens law. By 1961, the expellees who had settled in Austria had acquired citizenship and represented a large bloc of voters who sought the war-related compensation for which they would have been eligible had they continued on to Germany. West Germany had argued that Austria should meet the demands of the ethnic groups, contending that the state had benefited from the *Volksdeutsche*, who contributed to the growth of the Austrian economy and the expansion of its industry.
40 Austrian Historical Commission, English summary of final report, February 2003.
41 Compensation and restitution programmes for Nazi victims occurred at the same time that Austria passed laws governing denazification, which included benefits for former Nazis that often pitted the victim against the perpetrator. For instance, according to Claims Conference research, in March 1957, there was a general amnesty for 'severely incriminated' Nazis who were eligible to recover land and flats. Victims who were renting the flats, which had been arranged by the state, were obliged to turn them over to former Nazis or to pay for them.
42 Claims Conference Board meeting, 17 July 1994, Stockholm.
43 Text of radio address by Raab; 6 March 1955, CAHJP 14109.
44 OFG, 1947, Article 1: 'According to this federal law, victims of political persecution are defined as having suffered between 6 March 1933 and 9 May 1945, based on political or family background, religious or national grounds.'
45 For instance, Jewish victims generally received a 'victims' identification document' (*Opferausweis*) that allowed little more than minor tax relief. However, 'resistance fighters' were entitled to an 'official certificate' (*Amtsbescheinigung*) that foresaw a pension supplement.
46 KZ-Verband, in a 14 July 1955 letter to Raab, demanded improvements in the Victims Assistance Law, as well as compensation for property losses, special taxes, emigration costs, loss of employment and interruption of education. The association also lobbied Parliament and demonstrated in front of the Finance Ministry. The Federation of Austrian Jewish Communities, which was established in 1953, also pressured officials.
47 The requirement of Austrian citizenship would be resolved decades later, after the Austrian–US agreement of January 2001 came into force.
48 Goldmann letter to Finance Minister Josef Klaus, 19 December 1961.
49 Kagan letter to Lewinsky, 22 January 1993. The fund was supervised by a board that included a total of four representatives from the CJCA and the Jewish community of Austria. Under the original measure, payments were to be distributed over ten years. However, to expedite the

payments, Austria took out loans – from Austrian banks and from the European Recovery Plan/Marshall Plan – and most of the money was distributed within three years. The 1962 *Hilfsfond* used funds from West Germany. The 1976 moneys were the result of Kagan's negotiations with Chancellor Bruno Kreisky, despite Goldmann's 1961 agreement that there would be no additional claims.

50　The significance of the age is that these victims would have been too young to join the labour force and acquire pension rights in the traditional manner. Kagan letter to Lewinsky, 22 January 1993; Office of the Special Envoy for Restitution Issues Ernst Sucharipa, 'Survey of Past Austrian Measures of Restitution, Compensation and Social Welfare for Victims of National Socialism', October 2000.

51　The Austrian Historical Commission, which was chaired by Dr Clemens Jabloner, the president of Austria's Administrative Court, was established 'to investigate and report on the whole complex of expropriations in Austria during the Nazi régime and on restitution and/or compensation (including other financial or social benefits) after 1945 by the Republic of Austria.' According to the commission, there were different partisan political considerations propelling the dominant Socialist and Peoples parties. The Socialist Party 'made its agreement to the restitution acts, which it saw as a main Peoples Party (ÖVP) issue, conditional on measures in favour of its organizations. The ÖVP, however, was not pursuing the restitution acts as its own aim at all, but regarded their enactment as something imposed by the Allies and a necessary measure with regard to the rapid conclusion of the Vienna State Treaty.' See interim reports issued 6 June 2002.

52　The initial restitution efforts were stormy and ran into a 'vicious circle', according to a 14 February 1946 dispatch by the Jewish Telegraphic Agency. 'The Allied Control Council has ordered that administrators of 'Aryanized' property be placed under their supervision. This was done in a move to insure [*sic*] justice to the Jews, but as a result, the [Austrian] government is claiming that it is impossible to restore property to anyone until the country has regained its full sovereignty', JTA reported. 'Government spokesmen also say that any decision on property cannot be made until the Allies decide what is Austrian property and what is German property, because enterprises falling into the latter category as subject to seizure as reparations.'

53　Austrian Historical Commission; interim reports.

54　Cohen interview, 17 January 2002.

55　Claims Conference Vienna office, position paper on prior Austrian restitution efforts, November 2000.

56　Cohen interview, 17 January 2002.

57　Claims Conference Vienna office, position paper on prior Austrian restitution efforts.

58　Cohen interview, 17 January 2002.

59　Austrian Historical Commission, English summary of final report.

60　Paul Grosz, president of IKG, Mauerbach catalog, Christies, New York, 1996. One of the complaints about the earlier art-restitution programme was its limited notice. In 1969, the Austrian government had published notices of the artworks in the Austrian government newspaper *Wiener Zeitung*, but not in the general circulation media. Austrian historian Oliver Rathkolb referred to the newspaper as one that 'is barely read outside Austrian government circles'. For all practical purposes, this amounted to a failure to publicize the assets and the restitution procedures.

61　The article by Andrew Decker was published in December 1984. After the Second World War, the Allies had recovered tens of thousands of works of art, artifacts and books that had been plundered by the Nazis. The Allies repatriated the objects to the country of origin, intending that the country would locate the original owners or heirs. Austria was not the only European nation to face questions about its post-war art-restitution policies. By the end of the twentieth century, virtually all Western European nations were compelled to examine the extent to which their public museums and institutions had benefited from the Allies' repatriation of Nazi-looted art, often at the expense of Nazi victims. In the US, the Presidential Advisory Commission on Holocaust Assets, which examined how the Second World War-era American military and civilian authorities handled the identification, collection and restoration of Nazi-looted assets, found no evidence that the US had monitored the recipient countries' compliance with their expected restitution responsibilities. See *Plunder and Restitution: Findings and Recommendations of the Presidential Advisory Commission on Holocaust Assets in the United States*, Washington: US Government Printing Office, December 2000.

62 'Mauerbach items seized by the Nazis to be sold for the benefit of victims of the Holocaust,' Christie's press release, Vienna, 1996.

63 Claims Conference Board meeting, 6 July 1990, Jerusalem.

64 The 1995 law transferred residual objects to the Austrian Jewish community – *Israelitische Kultusgemeinde* (IKG) – which was to dispose of them. Unlike the case in Germany, where the Conference is recognized as the successor organization, the CJCA was not recognized as the successor organization of unclaimed and heirless Jewish property in Austria.

65 Not all of the proceeds were used for Jewish victims. Twelve per cent was given to agencies that aided non-Jewish victims of Nazi persecution. For the Jewish victims, the allocations from the 'Mauerbach Hardship Fund' were determined by the Claims Conference, the Austrian survivors' organization in Israel, the IKG, and the Ronald S. Lauder Foundation. The fund provided for a one-time payment of AS 12,000 ($1,000) to Jewish Nazi victims who resided in Austria in March 1938 and whose current gross annual income did not exceed $16,000. As of 31 August 2001, the fund had approved 6,828 applications. The eligibility criteria were comparable to those used by the Conference in its Article II programme.

66 Miller interview, 16 December 2001. The auction was a prestigious event, in part because it was led by luminaries of the art and the Jewish worlds, including Ronald Lauder, who had served from April 1986 to October 1987 as the US ambassador to Austria.

67 'Address on the occasion of the Mauerbach auction,' 28 October 1996, Vienna.

68 Waldheim was subsequently elected in 1986 with 54 per cent of the vote. He later was placed on a US 'watch list' and barred from travelling to the US. The Justice Department said that the 'evidence collected establishes a prima facie case that Kurt Waldheim assisted or otherwise participated in the persecution of persons because of race, religion, national origin or political opinion'.' Waldheim did not seek a second term in 1991.

69 Miller letter to Vranitzky, 13 August 1987.

70 Individual payments were dependent on the victim's income and were offset by prior compensation. It was not known how many beneficiaries were Austrian nationals or former Austrian Jews. There is anecdotal evidence that many victims rejected the offer. The fund drew the contempt of the *New York Times* in a 2 April 1988 editorial entitled, 'What Austria can't buy for $416', a reference to the then-dollar equivalent of the highest individual payment. 'If Austrians truly believe they were only victims, no reparations are required,' the *Times* said. 'If they are finally coming to terms with a painful past, then reparations payments of $416 are macabre.'

71 *Washington Post*, 24 March 1988.

72 Claims Conference Board meeting, 6 July 1990, Jerusalem

73 Miller interview, 16 December 2001. The Austrian government routinely referred to the pledge in Goldmann's 1961 letter. 'Of course we raised it. When the question of new demands came up, Goldmann's letter was our bible,' Hans Winkler, the head of the Legal Office of the Austrian Federal Ministry of Foreign Affairs, said in an interview on 28 June 2002.

74 Office of the Special Envoy for Restitution Issues Ernst Sucharipa, 'Survey of Past Austrian Measures of Restitution, Compensation and Social Welfare for Victims of National Socialism.'

75 Miller memo to Claims Conference Board, 12 December 1989.

76 Claims Conference Board meeting, 17 July 1994, Stockholm. According to the Austrian Information Service, Nazi victims have 'advantageous stipulations and their contributions were minimal – only approximately 10 per cent of the usual requirements.'

77 See Claims Conference motion to intervene, In Re: Austrian and German Banks Holocaust Litigation, Master File No. 98-CIV-3938 (SWK), US District Court for the Southern District of New York.

78 Of that amount, $18.5 million was used for projects in Israel and $1 million in the United Kingdom.

79 For instance, the Austrian coverage of medical expenses was not equitable; those who lived outside of Austria received a lower level of reimbursement for their medical expenditures. The requirement of Austrian citizenship was resolved once the Austrian–US agreement of January 2001 came into force.

80 *Washington Post*, 19 June 1991. The government condemned Haider's statement, saying that 'defames the millions of people who endured unending suffering under the Third Reich ... Forced labour, concentration camps and military buildup were the central elements of this labour policy.'

81 *New York Times*, 19 July 1991.

82 Vranitzky letter to Miller, 14 August 1995.
83 The chancellor's speech was quoted by Sucharipa, then Austria's ambassador to the United Nations, in a speech in New York to the American Jewish Committee, 8 October 1998. Vranitzky's speech – delivered after he received an honorary doctorate from Hebrew University – was important, but it did not fully distinguish the persecution and suffering of Jews from the war damages sustained by the Austrian population. He also said that 'hundreds of thousands of Austrians, many of them Jewish, were thrown into prisons and concentration camps, perished in the Nazi slaughterhouses or were forced to flee and leave everything behind – victims of a degenerate ideology and the totalitarian quest for power. And many other Austrians died on the battlefield and in the bomb shelters.'
84 Text from Office of President.
85 Kagan interview, 16 December 2001.
86 Vranitzky letter to Miller, 14 August 1995.
87 All Austrians persecuted by the Nazis received payments of AS 70,000. There also were a limited number of 'hardship' cases who received up to AS 210,000.
88 Reuters, 1 June 1995. In April, the Green Party threatened to boycott national celebrations marking the end of the Second World War, saying the government had failed to honor its 1994 pledge to establish the fund. The government then committed itself to submit a measure.
89 CJCA Board meeting, 10–11 July 1996, New York.
90 Lessing interview, 17 January 2002.
91 In addition to the national gold reserves of the occupied states, it was clear that during the Second World War the Nazis also trafficked in 'victim gold,' according to a May 1997 US government historical report (*Preliminary Study on US and Allied Efforts To Recover and Restore Gold and Other Assets Stolen or Hidden by Germany During the World War II*), conducted under Stuart Eizenstat's leadership. This gold – which included jewelry as well as dental fillings of concentration camp victims – was widely believed to have been mingled with the gold supply.
92 The residual gold was less than 2 per cent of the total recovered by the Allies after the war. Months before the London conference, the three member states of the Tripartite Gold Commission proposed setting up a new fund, using the residual gold to aid Nazi victims. *Jerusalem Post*, 14 September 1997.
93 Winkler interview, Vienna, 28 June 2002; Winkler's statement on behalf of the Austrian delegation to the London Conference on Nazi Gold, Lancaster House, 2–4 December 1997.
94 More than eight years after the Schiele paintings first were detained by Manhattan District Attorney Robert Morgenthau, one painting – *Portrait of Wally* – remained in New York, the subject of a lawsuit in federal court over whether it was, in fact, stolen property. However, there had been significant restitution of art in Austria after the Schiele detention. In 1999 Bettina Looram-Rothschild, the daughter of Alphonse and Clarice Rothschild, recovered more than 200 paintings from four museums in Vienna, as well as illuminated manuscripts, under the new Austrian art-restitution law. When the objects were auctioned in London in July 1999, they fetched a record-setting $88 million.
95 Claims Conference Board meeting, 9–10 July 1998, Jerusalem.
96 Kagan letter to Charles Kapralik, 23 October 1952.
97 Jahoda interview, 16 January 2002.
98 Claims Conference Board meeting, 14 July 1999, New York.
99 The Claims Conference opened the Vienna office on 15 March 1999. 'It is being established to ensure smooth cooperation and coordination with the Austrian Parliament and government, as well as the recently created [Austrian] committee of historians that will look into restitution issues,' the Conference said in a 9 March 1999 press release. These organizations, with the exception of Lauder's foundation, were represented by the original CJCA. For most of its existence, however, the CJCA was not as well-organized as the Conference was in dealing with West Germany, and did not have a negotiating committee. By the time the Claims Conference opened an office in Vienna, its activities were in the name of the Claims Conference, not the CJCA.
100 Claims Conference Board meeting, 14 July 1999, New York.
101 This was a source of consternation to the Claims Conference, which originally was not a party to the lawsuits and believed that its customary role as the representative of heirless Jewish victims had been diminished, if not usurped, by the lawsuits. It also was alarmed because the Austrian banks simultaneously negotiated both with the Claims Conference and with the

class-action lawyers who filed the suits to resolve the disposition of the Nazi-era assets that had been in Austrian banks. See Claims Conference motion to intervene, In Re: Austrian and German Banks Holocaust Litigation, Master File No. 98-CIV-3938 (SWK), US District Court for the Southern District of New York.

102 *Los Angeles Times*, 9 March 1999. In 1999, Creditanstalt was a subsidiary of Bank Austria. The US District Court in Manhattan gave final approval to the settlement on 6 January 2000.

103 The EU sanctions – which were symbolic, not substantive – were lifted after eight months. *Wall Street Journal*, 13 September 2000.

104 Schüssel letter to Taylor, 4 February 2000. Schüssel's government was so new that his office had not yet received its official stationery at the time he wrote to Taylor. As Taylor recalled: 'They didn't have printed paper; his office had to type at the top of a blank sheet of paper, "Office of the Federal Chancellor Wolfgang Schüssel."'

105 Eizenstat testimony, House Banking and Financial Services Committee. *Jerusalem Post*, 10 February 2000.

106 According to Peter Moser, Austria's ambassador to the US, 'At the time of the Austrian State Treaty, the question of slave and forced labour was not discussed, as most of the victims had returned behind the Iron Curtain and could not be reached. The Soviet Union did not show interest in pursuing their claims due to obvious reasons.' See remarks in the proceedings 'Fifty Years in the Making: the Second World War Reparation and Restitution Claims,' *Berkeley Journal of International Law*, Vol. 20, No. 1, 2002.

107 Reuters, 18 May 2000.

108 *Jerusalem Post*, 16 February 2000.

109 Claims Conference Executive Committee meeting, 15 March 2000, New York. Avraham Hirschson, a member of the Israeli Knesset from the Likud Party and the chair of a parliamentary panel on restitution, ruled out any discussions with any Austrian government that included Haider's party. 'I am caught between two justices. Survivors need money now. But there also is justice for the dead, and their blood is shouting that we should have no business with this [Austrian] government,' he said. 'I am listening to the dead.' *Jerusalem Post*, 10 February 2000.

110 Taylor interview, 18 April 2002.

111 Miller interview, 16 December 2001. Although Eizenstat played a central role, Austrian negotiators repeatedly reminded the US of the 1959 'Exchange of Notes' concerning Article 26 and the State Treaty, in which Washington assured Vienna that it would 'neither advance nor support through diplomatic channels' certain claims against Austria by Nazi victims.

112 The issue with apartments referred to long-term tenancy rights that, in Austria, were a valuable and traditional type of property right that could transferred. According to reports of the Austrian Historians Commission, released in September 2000, about 59,000 leased apartments were 'Aryanized' between 1938 and 1945; very few victims regained their flats.

113 The Austrian government had transferred to the IKG the heirless and unclaimed Mauerbach art, as noted above. However, representatives of former Austrian Jews living abroad disputed the IKG's exclusive right to the heirless and communal properties, arguing that the properties belonged to the pre-war Jewish community, whose survivors were now dispersed.

114 Office of the Special Envoy for Restitution Issues Ernst Sucharipa, 'Survey of Past Austrian Measures of Restitution, Compensation and Social Welfare for Victims of National Socialism.' However, 'as a legal matter, the [Allied–Austrian] treaty provisions had no impact on the property negotiations. Although the 1959 Exchange of Notes does constitute a waiver by the United States of its rights under Article 26 to support certain categories of private claims by diplomatic means, it does not affect the ability of victims to pursue their claims directly against the Austrians, for example, in US courts,' according to Eric Rosand of the State Department, who served as a legal adviser to Eizenstat. 'Moreover, it does not affect the ability of the United States to facilitate discussions between victims' representatives and the Austrians concerning the establishment of a humanitarian fund, particularly where the Austrians themselves requested the United States to assume this role.' See remarks in the proceedings 'Fifty Years in the Making: the Second World War Reparation and Restitution Claims.'

115 There were 'territorial' disputes over which labourers – such as former inmates of Mauthausen and its sub-camps, and Dachau sub-camps in Austria – would be covered by the Austrian or the German foundations.

116 Compensation for non-Jewish labourers served not only a humanitarian purpose, but also a political one. Most of these beneficiaries were from Central and Eastern European nations that

were in the process of joining the European Union; it was in Austria's national interests to strengthen relations with them. As Moser noted: Austria 'was looking at the question of slave and forced labour not with cold legal logic, but rather with an acceptance of a moral obligation to people who in many cases had been victimized a second time through communist rule. Some of the former communist countries, where most slave labourers presently live, will join the European Union sooner or later, and thus come even closer to Austria.' See remarks in the proceedings 'Fifty Years in the Making: the Second World War Reparation and Restitution Claims.'

117 According to Rosand: 'For different reasons, both the class action attorneys and the Jewish organizations insisted that Austria make certain commitments on the property side of the equation before they would agree to support the labour deal. The class action lawyers had filed a number of cases, which included both labour and property claims. The Austrians wanted the plaintiffs' attorneys to bifurcate their claims, and dismiss those related to labour, before any payments would be made by the labour fund. The plaintiffs' attorneys, however, would only agree to take such steps if Austria agreed to address property issues on an expedited, albeit separate track. They knew they could use their labour claims as leverage against an Austrian side that was most anxious to dispose of those claims.' See remarks in the proceedings 'Fifty Years in the Making: the Second World War Reparation and Restitution Claims'.

118 Clinton letter to Klestil, 19 October 2000.

119 Eizenstat remarks, 24 October 2000, Vienna.

120 The pace was determined by a variety of factors. Most important was the impending change in the American government. Clinton's term concluded in January 2001, and there was a full-court press to reach agreements with European governments and enterprises on all Nazi-era claims before Clinton left the White House.

121 The payment in dollars, a strong currency, was used in the second round of the National Fund to try to avert exchange-rate depreciations that had undercut the value of some payments in the original allocations from the fund.

122 The 1958 Law on Material Damage Resulting from War and Persecution had been designed to compensate for damage or loss of household belongings and business equipment. However, it was a hardship-like fund in which claimants were required to demonstrate financial need, and compensation risked being offset by any payments from the 1956 *Hilfsfond*. The maximum allowances under the 1958 law were AS 15,000 for belongings and AS 25,000 for equipment.

123 Taylor interview, 18 April 2002.

124 Ibid.

125 Claims Conference Board meeting, 17 July 2001, Washington. Under the settlement, the allowance for the nursing service (*Pflegegeld*) will pay up to $1,400 a month for victims living abroad who reach a certain level of disability.

126 Ultimately, the CJCA and the IKG reached a settlement under which the local community received 95 per cent of the first $50 million of the recovered communal properties. The additional proceeds would be divided along the lines of the agreement between the Claims Conference and the German Jewish community: 70 per cent for the Conference and 30 per cent for the community. Although this was primarily a restitution matter, it had an important sociopolitical element that dealt with the future as well as with the past: 'It is very, very important for all of those involved in Austria and in the United States to recognize that one of the key components of this is to assure the continued viability of the Austrian Jewish community which is in difficult straits. And this is a process which is in part designed to help them,' Eizenstat said when the agreement was concluded. On the one-year anniversary of the Austrian–US agreement, Kagan and Kurt Scholz, of the Vienna Municipality's restitution office, also stressed the need to ensure an active Jewish community in Austria, saying this was as important for the country as it was for the Jewish community. Austria agreed to provide compensation to the local Jewish community for the loss of Hakoah, a powerful and internationally acclaimed Jewish sports association; in addition to a lease for a property, it would contribute $8 million for the construction of an appropriate facility. The municipalities of Vienna and Graz also agreed to maintain the Jewish cemeteries.

127 At the time, there were lawsuits pending in federal courts in New York and Los Angeles, in which the IKG was an *amicus curiae*. It was not until November 2005 that an American federal appellate court dismissed the last lawsuit against the Republic of Austria for

Holocaust-era claims, which permitted the allocation of the Austrian funds that had been negotiated in the final days of the Clinton administration.
128 Seminar, Literatur Haus, Vienna, 17 January 2002.
129 Ibid.
130 Austrian Parliament (Nationalrat), 30 January 2002.
131 'Additional Social Benefits for Victims of National Socialism,' press release, Austrian Press and Information Service, Washington DC, 11 February 2002.
132 Kagan interview, 10 January 2002.
133 Claims Conference Board meeting, 14 July 1999, New York.

Chapter 9

Sacred Spending: The Claims Conference's Institutional Allocations

Het Apeldoornsche Bosch in Holland was the only modern Jewish mental hospital in Western Europe in 1943 when the Nazis deported its 1,150 doctors, nurses and patients, many of whom were foreign-born Jews. More than a decade after the deportations, there was no Jewish psychiatric hospital in Europe to care for traumatized Holocaust survivors. More than 100 Jewish patients were institutionalized in the Netherlands, scattered among 23 mental hospitals, some of them under Christian auspices. These Jewish patients were a minority everywhere. Half were schizophrenic, which made the need for specifically Jewish medical care urgent. 'Many psychotic patients have lost contact with their fellow man, and they are in a permanent struggle to regain and in permanent terror of losing their relations,' the Central Association for Jewish Mental Health in the Netherlands reported in 1954. 'Their living in unfamiliar surroundings increases their apprehension.' The association appealed to the Claims Conference for funds for a Jewish facility, saying that treating patients in a familiar milieu would enhance their chances of recovery.[1] The Claims Conference assisted with the financing; the Joint Distribution Committee also contributed. The Dutch government pledged to pay a portion of the costs and to permit the entry of Jewish mental patients from abroad. A foundation stone was laid in June 1958 for a Jewish mental facility in Amersfoort, with 76 beds – for 49 women and 27 men. On 18 October 1960, Queen Juliana came to Amersfoort, lit a candle to commemorate the murdered staff and patients of Het Apeldoornsche

Bosch, and officially opened the first Jewish psychiatric hospital in Western Europe after the Holocaust.[2]

Since its establishment, the Claims Conference's objectives have been to secure compensation for individual Jewish victims of Nazi persecution, as well as to obtain collective funds to finance services to victims and to help reconstruct the Jewish communities, institutions and cultural life that were destroyed by the Nazis. In its first 50 years, the Conference received $353.5 million and DM 515.8 million.[3] The funds came in three different periods, from different sources and with different conditions. Although the Conference's objectives did not change, its ability to meet them changed dramatically over time.

The Conference's programme of institutional allocations began with funds generated by the 1952 Luxembourg Agreements. Under Protocol II, West Germany pledged to provide the Conference, via Israel, with DM 450 million over a dozen years. Those funds, which arrived in increments of about $10 million a year, were distributed primarily to agencies and institutions for the relief and resettlement of Jewish Nazi victims, and to rebuild Jewish communities and cultural life outside of Israel.[4] In the second allocations period, between 1981 and 1993, there were smaller funds available from the German and Austrian governments, as well as modest payments from two German companies. All came with restrictions on their use.[5] The third period of institutional allocations began in 1995, once the Conference began recovering and selling one-time Jewish properties in the former East Germany. These funds differed markedly from the previous periods. They were discretionary funds from Jewish properties that were recovered in the name of the Jewish people. No restrictions were imposed by governments or enterprises, which enabled the Conference to finance social welfare projects and programmes for Nazi victims and cultural projects that would otherwise have been barred. With these funds, the Conference for the first time made direct allocations to Jewish communities in Eastern Europe and the former Soviet Union, and undertook long-term commitments to projects on research, education and documentation about the Holocaust.

In the 1950s and 1960s, the Jewish organizations' funds were spent primarily in Europe, and financed a wide gamut of services for Jews of all ages. There were allocations for kindergartens as well as old-age homes. At the end of the twentieth century, the overwhelming majority of the funds were used in Israel and the former Soviet Union for social welfare programmes and capital projects to aid elderly Nazi victims.

With the exception of modest relief programmes for former European Jewish communal leaders and support for *Hassidei Umot*

Haolam, righteous non-Jews who had saved Jews during the Nazi era, the Protocol II funds were not intended for payments to individual victims of Nazi persecution. Those victims were expected to be compensated through the West German indemnification and restitution legislation that evolved from Protocol I.[6] Nonetheless, there were appeals to the Conference for individual payments from the Protocol II funds. 'We received countless letters from individuals to the effect that "There are so many survivors and so much money; when the money is divided up, my share is $1,400. Please send me a check,"' according to Kagan.[7]

The West Germans also suggested that the function of Protocol II was to serve as a 'hardship fund', particularly for Jewish victims whose claims for indemnification had failed. 'We said under no circumstances would we accept this concept,' Leavitt said. 'Relief and rehabilitation would have to be based on need, and not on whether a Nazi victim was a successful or unsuccessful claimant. It was obvious that they wanted to be able to refer unsuccessful claimants to us and thereby save themselves money and annoyance.' The language of Protocol II said the funds would be used according to 'the urgency of the need' as determined by the Conference. This was the so-called 'purpose clause'. West Germany wanted the clause to be as specific as possible, and insisted during the Wassenaar negotiations on inserting language that would demonstrate to the Bundestag that the money was being used for the purpose intended. 'Every day they came with new ideas on this purpose clause,' Leavitt said. 'One of the big fights we had centered on their proposal that the purpose clause contain the phrase *nach billigen Ermessen*. Translated it meant that we must use the funds with equity and justice or fairness.' This was insulting, as it implied that the $1 billion that Jewish agencies had already spent on post-war relief and rehabilitation had been used unfairly.[8]

The Conference made a specific decision to give the Western European countries that had been occupied by the Nazis the first priority for Protocol II funds, even though thousands of victims had left Europe and settled elsewhere. Not only had individual members of the European communities suffered grievously, but the entire framework of their institutions and services had been decimated. 'The German funds were not given exclusively for individual victims of Nazi persecution. More than that, the funds are to rebuild Jewish life, particularly on the destroyed continent of Europe. It would be easy for the Conference to give each individual $20 to $25, and to fritter away the funds in this manner. There is always a conflict between the claims of individuals and the needs of the community,' Goldmann said. 'This is a unique opportunity for the rebuilding of Jewish life, which the Conference must take.'[9]

The Conference saw the Protocol II funds as a 'Jewish Marshall Plan' that could address the multiple needs for relief, rehabilitation and reconstruction – benefiting individuals, institutions, communities and cultural activities. The funds were 'the vital infusion' that helped European communities rebuild, expand and improve the network of communal facilities and services, and were 'decisive in launching the communities on the road of independence,' said Kagan.[10]

Each year, requests from Jewish communities and agencies far exceeded the funds available. The Dutch appeal for funds for a psychiatric facility in Amersfoort was one of 300 applications from 26 countries seeking a total of more than $35 million from the Claims Conference's earliest allocations. Jewish organizations in France, for instance, sought about 700 million francs. 'In some instances, [French] organizations have presented what amounts to a bill for losses incurred during the [Nazi] occupation; in other instances, funds have been requested as reimbursement for expenditures made since the liberation,' said Auren Kahn, the JDC director in France. 'And in many instances, their requests were pure fantasy.'[11]

Protocol II funds financed medical care, housing, education, transit and vocational training in Europe that were organized or provided primarily by the Joint Distribution Committee. The Conference also undertook more than 470 capital projects in 29 countries – a building programme so extensive that virtually every community in Western Europe that had been under Nazi occupation had at least one capital project that had been built, renovated, repaired or equipped with Conference funds.

When the Protocol II funds became available, nearly a decade after the end of the Second World War, the issue facing European Jewry was no longer the survival of the individual, but the survival of Jewish life and its traditional institutions, said Leavitt. 'Capital investment is an investment in Jewish survival,' he said. 'Here in Europe today we are no longer faced with the problem of survival as human beings, but we do wish to survive as Jews, maintaining cultural and social patterns within the general community that will preserve and carry on our most glorious traditions... We don't want to erect monuments. We want to erect or help maintain institutions that will make Jewish community life richer, fuller and, we hope, more Jewish.'[12]

In its first decade, the Conference's capital projects included 150 schools – from primary schools through rabbinical seminaries; 107 community and youth centres; 65 religious institutions; 56 homes for the aged; 41 children's homes and kindergartens; 17 summer camps; and 12 medical institutions. They served a function that far surpassed the value of the physical structures themselves. 'The reconstruction of

Jewish communal institutions attracts the interests not only of the Jewish population, but the population of the country,' said Charles Jordan, then the director of European operations of the Joint. 'The effects of these accomplishments in the development of Jewish life, the prestige of the Jewish community and the inspiration to other Jewish communities in Europe are immense ... [They] provide a spirit of hope that attracts people back to the community.'[13]

The projects were tailored to meet the specific needs of the communities. With the exception of Denmark, whose Jews had been dramatically saved by their countrymen, all European Jewish communities were remnants of their former selves. Their demographics, communal conditions and financial resources varied considerably. In Italy, a decade after the war, the Jewish population was impoverished, in part because of the local economic conditions and the undeveloped public welfare system. The Italian Jewish community, expanded by refugees and migrants from Central and Eastern Europe, was somewhat youthful; Jewish schools were the major beneficiary of Conference funds in the country. In Austria and Germany, by contrast, the average age of the Jewish population was above 45. One-third of all Conference capital projects were in France, primarily for community and youth centres and Jewish schools, because France was a magnet for Jewish refugees from Eastern Europe and North Africa, and was the largest Jewish community in Europe West of the Soviet Union.

Holocaust survivors in Central and Eastern Europe were beyond the direct and immediate reach of the Conference. With the Cold War's division of East and West, the FRG refused to finance programmes in the Soviet sphere. In addition, the rigid policies initiated by Stalin's régime, which were intended to isolate and diminish the Jewish communities, made it difficult to penetrate the Iron Curtain to reach the victims. However, in 1954 Conference began financing a secret welfare programme for those victims. Known by the ambiguous name of 'relief in transit,' the programme – operated by the Joint Distribution Committee – ultimately used some $48 million from the Conference to provide cash and material goods to Jews in Central and Eastern Europe. In its first ten years of operations, 'relief in transit' helped more than 200,000 people. Families would receive a parcel of dungarees, stockings, coats or some other valuable barter commodity, from an unknown 'uncle' or 'cousin' abroad, usually in Ireland or Switzerland.[14] In 1955, for instance, some 55,000 packages found their way to Jews in Eastern Europe. In 1957, 100,000 packages went into Hungary, Romania and Poland, and tens of thousands into the Soviet Union.[15]

The balance of the Protocol II funds – about 20 per cent – was used for cultural and educational reconstruction, as well as for documentation of the Shoah. The Nazis had destroyed centuries of vibrant Jewish cultural, religious and intellectual life in Europe. They had plundered and razed synagogues, schools and libraries, and murdered Jewish cultural and spiritual leaders. The shortage of communal leadership posed as serious a threat to the reconstruction of European Jewish life as did the shortages of funds and facilities. The Conference's cultural and educational programmes focused on training a new generation of rabbis, teachers, social workers and administrators to lead the communities. Each year of the Conference's first decade, 13,000 people studied at Conference-supported Jewish primary and secondary schools, yeshivot and seminaries, teachers' colleges and adult education programmes.

In its cultural programme, the Conference's principle was diversity – that is, the right of groups of every shade of opinion to their particular cultural, spiritual, ideological and religious beliefs. 'To this end, we try to ensure that every facet of Jewish cultural and religious life should be aided in its struggle for survival,' Kagan said.[16] The cultural programme was seen as the guarantee of Jewish continuity. 'We can provide the bricks and mortar, the old-age homes, orphanages and sanatoria, which are essential for the survival and health of our people,' he said. 'But they will become archeological exhibits if there is no conscious and determined effort to ensure that these buildings and institutions become meaningful to the life and members of the next generation.'[17]

With aid from the Conference in its first dozen years, Nazi victims produced more than 400 books in a dozen languages, including literature and poetry, religious texts, children's stories and Jewish social studies. 'But mere numbers alone are not the criterion. The programme has been a great stimulus to Jewish cultural creativeness and to Jewish scholarship,' said the American Jewish Committee's Blaustein.[18]

The Conference took special pride in its fellowship programmes for Jewish scholars, artists and writers. About 1,800 Nazi victims were Conference fellows, studying at Jewish teachers' colleges and graduate schools, and conducting independent work in Jewish studies, arts and literature. Among the fellows was Nathan Rappaport, whose 'Wall of Remembrance', a bronze sculpture commemorating the Warsaw Ghetto uprising, is a centrepiece at Yad Vashem. In 1959, Rappaport won a prize in fine arts, the Alfred Steele Memorial Prize in sculpture.

Another Conference fellow, André Schwarz-Bart, at 31 'earned his livelihood as a porter in Les Halles, the food marketing centre of Paris, up to the day that fame caught up with him,' said Leavitt.[19] Schwarz-Bart's novel, *Le Dernier des Justes* (*The Last of the Just*), won the French literary Prix Goncourt in 1959. Yet another fellow, Anna Langfus, a refugee from Poland, three years later also won the Prix

Goncourt for her novel *Les Bagages de sable* (*The Lost Shore*). Louis Copelman was a refugee from Romania in 1961. The next year, he became a Conference fellow. In November 1963, he won one of the highest awards in the medical world, when the French Academy of Medicine named him a laureate in recognition of outstanding research in the field of psychological and physical trauma among concentration camp survivors. 'In no other Conference programme have pleasant surprises cropped up at more frequent intervals than in the fellowship programme. The surprises were surprises in the true meaning of the word since they were never anticipated when the programme was launched,' Leavitt said. 'We share a foster parent's joy in the *simcha*.'[20]

The Conference also was a founding partner of Yad Vashem in 1953. 'The Claims Conference was created for one purpose – to be the organized instrument, the organized spokesman for the rights and interests of survivors. You cannot restrict dealing with the consequences of the Shoah by strictly dealing with the physical needs of the survivors or the physical needs of the reconstruction of the communities. The Holocaust destroyed a millennium-old culture, and lessons of the Shoah had to be learned. Yad Vashem was an instrument that Israel created to be the centre,' Kagan said. 'What was, for me, almost symbolic was that this institution that was created by the Knesset to be the institution in the field of research and commemoration saw its first building funded 50 per cent by the Claims Conference.' The rest of the financing for the construction of Yad Vashem on Har Hazikaron in Jerusalem was paid by the Jewish Agency and the State of Israel.[21] During Yad Vashem's first eleven years, the Conference also provided funding for its research and documentation projects, such as the bibliographical series *The Sources and Literature of the Catastrophe*, the first annals of the Jewish communities (*Pinkasey Hakehilot*) and the publication of archival documents.[22] In the first decade, the other primary beneficiaries of Conference aid for commemoration and documentation of the Shoah were the YIVO Institute in New York, the Centre de Documentation Juive and the Tombeau in Paris, and the Wiener Library in London. In addition to preserving the records of lost communities and witness testimony about the Holocaust, documentation also helped validate individual claims and assisted with the prosecution of war criminals.

Several years before the Protocol II funds were exhausted, members of the Conference began to debate how to meet the Conference's few ongoing financial obligations and how to handle what the members thought were the final allocations. This was the 'post-1964' dilemma. The final year's funds could be spent in the traditional manner, with most used for relief and rehabilitation. An alternative was for the greater part of the 'residual' funds to be used 'to preserve the spiritual and cultural values of the six million who perished.' There were heated battles between these two very different points of view. The lines were drawn primarily between the Joint, which believed that funds should be used for relief and rescue, and Goldmann, who insisted that the money be used for Jewish culture. He argued that the Nazis had not only killed Jews, but Jewish culture in Europe. Jordan, speaking for the Joint, countered that one cannot make a good student out of a child with an empty belly.[23]

Simon Segal of the American Jewish Committee sided with Goldmann. 'I'm not underestimating the importance of the need for relief, but funds spent this way will not have the same lasting results as they might if they were used judiciously for cultural, educational, social and religious programmes. Funds are more readily available for physical relief and rehabilitation than for cultural and spiritual purposes,' he said. 'Thus we might save the individual and risk losing the community. If, in addition to having saved the individual victims of Nazism, the Conference can do more toward saving a generation and substantially contribute to the preservation of the Jewish group, then indeed the Conference would become a vital, unique phenomenon of our times.'[24]

Goldmann was more emphatic. He opposed more funds for relief. 'The moment you open the door to relief, I am afraid of the good heart of all Jews. *Tzedaka* [charity] is a very dangerous thing with Jews; billions have been wasted on that. But what maintains the people is cultural life, and not the hospitals,' he said. 'I know that it sounds brutal ... What I want is that out of this activity at the Claims Conference should come at least one foundation which is earmarked for the rebuilding of the cultural life of the Jewish people. What Hitler has done away with is much more serious – he has destroyed Jewish culture, not only six million Jews. This also sounds brutal. But the fact is that he destroyed six million bearers of Jewish culture – so many thousands of intellectuals, so many thousands historians and so on. This ruins the Jewish people. The six million also represent a great tragedy, do not misunderstand me. But, if I had all the hundred thousand intellectuals buried in Auschwitz, I would rebuild the Jewish people. But if you go on and spend for relief, then everything will become meaningless.'[25]

Ultimately, at the final allocations meeting in May 1965, the Conference focused on the preservation of culture: Some $10 million was used to establish the Memorial Foundation for Jewish Culture; another $5 million was earmarked for special relief projects. The Conference then linked its future with that of the Memorial Foundation. Its constituent members became half the membership of the new foundation's board. At its board meeting in Copenhagen, in March

1962, the Conference decided that two-thirds of the funds accruing after 1964 would be allocated to the foundation; the remainder would be used by the Conference for relief, rehabilitation and resettlement.[26] Once its institutional allocations were concluded, the Conference became a skeletal operation. It had limited, residual responsibilities for two small 'relief' funds. These were exceptions to the Conference's policy on providing compensation to individuals from Protocol II, which it struggled to finance once the funds were exhausted. The first, the Community Leader Fund, provided monthly support to the needy former leaders of Jewish communities that were destroyed in the Holocaust. From the programme's inception, the Conference provided more than $2.2 million to aid more than 60 community leaders.[27] The second programme helped *Hassidei Umot Haolam*, the Righteous Among the Nations who, at considerable personal risk, had saved Jews and who later needed financial assistance. The Conference was the first organization to establish a special programme recognizing the Jewish community's moral obligation to the rescuers. From the programme's initiation in 1963, the Conference provided more than $2.4 million to assist 784 non-Jews who were recognized as Righteous Gentiles by Yad Vashem.[28]

For more than a dozen years, the Claims Conference functioned as an appendage to the Memorial Foundation.[29] So indebted was the Conference to the Memorial Foundation that the Conference board, meeting in Israel in 1986, approved a measure under which the Memorial Foundation would forgive the Conference's $137,080 debt on condition that the Conference agree that, 'upon its dissolution, the net assets of the Conference for Jewish Material Claims Against Germany will be transferred to the Memorial Foundation for Jewish Culture.'[30]

The Conference, however, was not dissolved. It continued to monitor the implementation of the West German indemnification programmes and to press Bonn for additional compensation for Jewish victims. That led, some 15 years after the Conference had exhausted the Protocol II payment, to the Conference's second phase, with a new source of funds for institutions that aided Nazi victims. These came from the 1980 agreement between the Conference and West Germany for the establishment of the Hardship Fund, which provided modest payments to individual Nazi victims who arrived in the West after 1965. The fund set aside 5 per cent of the total provided by West Germany for grants to institutions for shelter and social services for needy survivors. However, these were restricted to projects and programmes in the West. The first institutional grants were made in 1981: DM 2.5 million to 34 organizations in 13 countries.[31] All told, some DM 63 million was made available for institutional allocations via the Hardship Fund, which was used for 166 programmes in 16 countries, primarily in Israel. In addition to the German government funds, another DM 12.75 million came from separate agreements with Volkswagen and Daimler-Benz, which had been pressed to help victims because of their use of slave labour during the Second World War.

The third financing phase began after German reunification in 1990. For some 17 years, the Conference had negotiated with East Germany to reach an agreement in which the GDR would recognize its obligations as a successor state to the Nazi régime and assist Nazi victims, parallel to what West Germany had provided under Protocol II. No such agreement was reached. However, Nazi-seized Jewish properties were included in the post-unification German property law that 'reprivatized' properties in the former East Germany. Under the German law, the Conference was named the 'successor organization' for unclaimed and heirless Jewish properties and the properties of dissolved Jewish communities and organizations. By the end of 2001, the properties recovered by the Conference's Successor Organization had generated more than DM 1.6 billion.[32]

Unlike the moneys the Conference received in its previous four decades, there were no external restrictions on the use of the Successor Organization funds. This permitted the Conference, for the first time, to make overt allocations in Eastern Europe and the former Soviet Union (FSU) for programmes benefiting Nazi victims. And for the first time since 1965, it generated funds for research, documentation and education about the Shoah.[33]

From 1995 through 2000, the Conference distributed more than $400 million to more than 700 programmes and projects from the funds generated by sales of properties in the former GDR. In 2000 alone, the Conference allocated $81.86 million to projects in 26 countries.[34] In addition to funds from the Successor Organization, the Conference received 'humanitarian funds' from the German Foundation, 'Remembrance, Responsibility and the Future', which raised its institutional allocations in 2001 to $91.6 million.[35]

These sums made the Conference one of the largest Jewish charitable agencies in the world. The funds also prompted extraordinary demands on and participation in the Conference. While the organization could barely maintain a quorum at its meetings in the 1970s, by the mid-1990s, board meetings were packed, with more than 50 delegates from member organizations and numerous observers.

With Protocol II funds in its early years, the Conference's objective had been to help displaced surviving Jews rebuild their lives, communities and cultural institutions. More than a half-century after the liberation of the concentration camps, the Conference remained preoccupied with social welfare. But the geographical focus had shifted and the population had dramatically changed. Nazi victims were now elderly; the priority was to provide shelter and basic social services to help them live out their lives in dignity. Reminiscent of the clash decades earlier about how the Conference should use the 'post-1964' funds, the income from the German properties created momentous practical and philosophical problems. 'I used to think collecting money was difficult,' Miller said. 'I learned a *Gemara*, where giving away money is much more difficult than collecting money.'[36] And however massive the amounts seemed, as in the days of Protocol II, the requests far outpaced the resources. There were competing pressures to spend funds as they became available as well as to retain funds in anticipation of future needs as the 'younger' survivors aged. Unlike the finite amount of Protocol II, the total amount, the duration and the flow of the funds via the Successor Organization were unknown. They depended on the quantity, disposition and the market value of the Jewish properties in the former East Germany.[37]

The Conference had acquired properties as the 'successor organization'. 'Successor to what?' Miller asked. 'Successor to people who are no longer alive, who left properties in East Germany – in Dresden, in Leipzig, in East Berlin – who have no heirs who will claim these properties.' The Conference's post-1990 incorporation certificate stated that all funds would go for Holocaust survivors. 'What does that mean? Does it mean directly? Does it mean indirectly?' Miller asked. 'What is the heritage of the Holocaust? Is the heritage of the Holocaust just that it shall never happen again, or is it that Jewish life must flourish, be reconstituted in the fashion in which we would like it to be reconstituted, that it would flourish and bring its values to the generations that are to come?'[38]

Within the Conference, there were recurring debates about whether the funds were for the Jewish people or for Holocaust survivors. If the funds were for survivors, which survivors? A related issue concerned who was a 'survivor'. The German indemnification laws referred to 'victims of National Socialist persecution,' and it was customary for the Conference to demand that Germany provide funds for 'Jewish Nazi victims'. 'I think we should be very careful in not creating some kind of categories of Jews who suffered the consequences of Nazi persecution,' said Kagan. 'We've fought long and hard with the Germans to recognize that all individuals, all Jews who were exposed to all forms of Nazi persecution have to be considered and recognized both for compensation and also for their social needs and social care.'[39]

There was a practical effect to the broader definition, because it encompassed a far greater number of Jews competing for the funds.

'Survivors' traditionally referred to the victims who had been detained in concentration camps, labour camps and ghettos. Under the wide definition, a Nazi victim was any Jew who lived in a country when it was under a Nazi régime, Nazi occupation or Nazi collabourators, or who fled to escape the Nazis.[40] At the end of the century, there were an estimated 820,000 Nazi victims scattered around the world. They represented about 6 per cent of world Jewry, but about 30 per cent of all Jews over the age of 60.[41]

Planning also was hampered by other delicate questions about the demographics of the Nazi victim population – how long the survivors were expected to live and what kinds of aid would be available to them from other sources. There also were ideological and pragmatic debates about what form the Conference aid should take, how much the Conference should invest in capital projects or use to underwrite social services, and in which countries the funds should be used. The largest number of survivors was in Israel; with an estimated 300,000 Nazi victims, Israel was home to 37 per cent of the survivor population.[42] The Nazi victims in Israel had come in two waves: immediately after the Holocaust and after 1990, with the immigration to Israel of more than 100,000 elderly Soviet Jews – among them, thousands of victims.[43] Twenty-four per cent of the Nazi victims, or 200,000, lived in the former Soviet Union. In Eastern and Western Europe, there were about 143,000 Nazi victims, compared to 137,000 in the US. The remaining 5 per cent – some 40,000 victims – were in other countries.[44]

The allocations of funds generated by the Successor Organization's recovery of properties in the former East Germany began in 1995. The Conference's guidelines called for a substantial majority of funds to be allocated for projects in Israel, where most Nazi victims lived. At the same time, there was a priority for social care programmes for elderly Holocaust survivors, with 'special consideration' for the needs of Nazi victims in Eastern Europe and the former Soviet Union, because they had not benefited from German compensation programmes. The Conference's Executive Committee also called for funds for research and documentation of the Holocaust 'and to ensure the broad dissemination of its lessons for the Jewish people, giving priority to projects from established institutions which have a significant record and wide impact in these fields'.[45]

The general principles were that 80 per cent of the funds would be used for social services; the rest would be for research, education and documentation of the Holocaust. About 60 per cent of the funds were to be used in Israel. Although the Conference board members professed an emotional attachment and commitment to Israel, that policy aroused a debate that did not subside.

In the first five years of Successor Organization distributions, the single largest category of allocations – more than 40 per cent – was for social welfare programmes and projects for Nazi victims in Israel.[46] It was the Conference's policy to assist survivors with social services that would permit them to live as independently as possible, and to provide institutional care for those who could not function otherwise. Because of the compact size of the state, Israel was the one place in which the Conference could provide a continuum of services from the time a survivor begins to fail through death – including home care, day-care centres, sheltered housing, geriatric programmes on kibbutzim, nursing homes and psycho-geriatric facilities. Much of these funds – $81.4 million between 1995 and 2000 – were used for capital projects and infrastructure, all of which met a gaping need.[47]

Beginning with its allocations in the 1980s of moneys from the Hardship Fund and from Daimler-Benz, the Conference developed an allocations policy in which it leveraged its funds with Israeli government ministries and non-profit agencies, both to defray the costs and to ensure there would be an ongoing commitment to the projects once the Conference funds were exhausted. 'I found it very exciting – how you can leverage even $25 million into $100 million,' Miller said.[48]

With the new allocations beginning in 1995, the Conference continued its emphasis on alleviating the shortage in Israel of nursing and psycho-geriatric beds, and made funds available to establish geriatric day centres to delay or prevent institutionalization as long as possible.[49] These allocations were under way in 1998 when the primitive conditions in Israeli psychiatric facilities were publicly exposed.[50] In 1999, a commission led by retired Judge Ya'acov Bazak denounced the Health and Justice ministries for the crude, often barbaric, institutional conditions that amounted to incarceration, not protection, of psychiatric patients, including hundreds of victims of the Nazis. In some instances, patients had been warehoused in wards without indoor plumbing. 'From the beginning, government mental hospitals have been at the bottom of state priorities, run on a poverty budget,' the commission said.[51]

Conference funds had served as a catalyst for Israeli government and non-profit agencies to undertake long-term commitments to the care of the elderly. The construction of three hostels accommodated most of the mentally ill Holocaust survivors who previously had been living in the harshest conditions.[52] Among the projects was Lev Hasharon, a residential facility serving dozens of Holocaust survivors with chronic psychological problems. Until they were moved to Lev Hasharon in the mid-1990s, they were among the saddest group of victims to emerge after the Shoah. While the majority of victims were able to build new and successful lives, many were so traumatized that they were incapable of fending for themselves. 'These survivors had never really set foot in Israel. They arrived in the state from the DP camps in Europe, and went right from the boat to a mental hospital here. For almost 50 years after their liberation, they were living in big, barn-like wards that had been British army barracks during the Mandatory period,' recalled Miller. 'There was one barracks for the men and one for the women. We built hostels and a hospital for them, together with the Ministry of Health, in which there were two people in a room; there were private bathrooms. We are helping them to live out their years in dignity.'[53]

With Conference participation, more than 3,800 new nursing beds, which gave priority to Holocaust survivors, were established in Israel between 1995 and 2001.[54] 'Claims Conference support invariably serves as a decisive factor in the decision to undertake these projects, and leverages funding from the other partner agencies and sometimes from private American foundations,' said Avraham Pressler, the Conference's representative in Israel. The funds transformed the nature of care and dramatically improved these facilities. 'The increased level of privacy, higher standard of hygiene and expanded space all contribute to a greatly improved quality of life,' Pressler said.[55] The Conference's share of the construction cost was modest. 'In general, we're giving somewhere around 25 per cent of the cost of a bed, and we're looking at the cost of our contribution being somewhere in the region of $10,000 or $12,000,' said Taylor.[56]

However, there were increasing demands from Israeli survivors for funds for social services and, in its crudest form, the debate came down to whether the funds would be spent for buildings or for services for people, and what those services would be. Capital projects were of special interest to the Conference, because such investments aided victims while they also expanded the geriatric infrastructure of Israel. For instance, subsidizing the construction of a kosher kitchen in a day-care centre served a larger purpose than simply providing low-cost meals to impoverished survivors, said Miller. 'I feel that when we make a contribution to help the poor, the sick, the needy people in Israel, what we are doing to help these people as we help build this kitchen is also a great *mitzvah* in Israel, because it will remain there. After our money runs out, it will remain the *rechush* [property] of the Jewish people,' Miller said. He illustrated his point by drawing on his decades of experience as a pulpit rabbi in New York before moving to Israel in 1999. 'I had a synagogue in the Bronx. We sold it to a public school. The Jews are not there any more,' Miller said. 'What the Conference is doing in Israel for Israel is not ephemeral. It is for the future.'[57]

After several years of allocations, however, the Conference began a transition from primarily capital projects in Israel and also began financing home-care services and emergency assistance grants. Part of the shift reflected the fact that much construction already had been undertaken in Israel, and many of the institutional building projects had been completed. Nearly 4,000 nursing beds, 100 day-care centres, and 80 geriatric centres on kibbutzim had changed the landscape of geriatric care in Israel. 'We already had done a great deal, and it is a small country,' said Greg Schneider, the Conference's chief operating officer.[58]

Social services in Israel were provided, in part, through the Foundation for the Benefit of Holocaust Victims (known as the 'Keren'), which was administered by survivors and financed by the Claims Conference. In 2001, the Conference allocated more than $17 million to the Keren to finance supplemental home care to more than 3,600 of the most disabled Nazi victims, and one-time emergency grants for items not provided under the Israeli national health service. In its first seven years, the Keren provided individual emergency aid to more than 50,000 victims.[59] The projects and services supported by the Conference and its partner organizations over the last ten years 'have changed the face of geriatric treatment in Israel, which can now be favourably compared with the best in public services for the elderly in the Western world,' said Pressler.[60]

The Conference also financed projects that changed the character of social welfare services for victims in theNazis in the former Soviet Union – a region that had been beyond its direct reach before 1990. It was not until funds became available via the Successor Organization that the Conference was able to openly aid survivors in the Nazi-occupied countries that, after the Second World War, were behind the Iron Curtain. However, 'it was difficult to convince many of our own people that people in the former Soviet Union were Nazi victims of the Holocaust. Since many of them fled and saved their own lives, and went, let's say, to Siberia, they were not considered victims,' Miller said. 'It became a problem to convince our people that our resources should go to the former Soviet Union.'[61] Ultimately, social services in the FSU accounted for some 30 per cent of the allocations from the Successor Organization's funds between 1995 and 1999 – second only to allocations for social services in Israel.[62]

In Israel, the Conference had support from and a partnership with government and non-profit agencies that enabled them to expand and enhance the existing social welfare services. In the FSU, by contrast, there was no functioning public welfare system. And decades after the Stalinist policy of eviscerating the Jewish community – which had preceded the Nazi régime – there was no Jewish communal structure to aid survivors. The vast majority of Nazi victims in the former communist bloc were among the neediest in the world. They never had been eligible for the German compensation programmes. About three in 10 survivors world-wide were thought to live in poverty; nearly half of the poor survivors lived in the FSU.[63]

In the major cities of the former Soviet Union, working with the Joint Distribution Committee, the Conference financed regional welfare centres, known as 'Hesed' centres. The centres provide an extensive array of social services for the elderly, including meals, medication, medical equipment and consultations, and limited social activities. 'The core of this programme is really a hunger relief programme,' said Greg Schneider. In 2000 alone, the Conference financed more than 1.48 million food packages, 4.2 million hot meals and 3.3 million 'meals on wheels' for victims in the former Soviet Union.[64] 'These are the forgotten survivors of the entire Shoah,' Miller said at the 1996 dedication of the Hesed centre in Kiev. 'We have a holy responsibility to use the money from people who did not survive for the benefit of those who did.'[65] For the Jews in the FSU, cut off from the Jewish world for three or four generations, the Hesed centres were also another step in the effort to reclaim them for the Jewish people, said Asher Ostrin, the Joint's director for the FSU. 'It's not just a physical rescue. It's not simply bringing a food package or a book. All people engaged in this enterprise are reclaiming the Jewish people,' said Ostrin. 'That's the majesty of what's going on.'[66]

The early allocations of Successor Organization funds had been used for projects that met clearly identifiable needs. As allocations continued and many projects neared completion, adjusting the priorities became increasingly urgent. 'We must have knowledge of who the needy survivors are, who is actually needy, and try to establish some criteria for who is needy and who is not needy. And we also have to take into account comparative standards between different countries,' said Michael Schneider, then the executive director of the Joint. 'Is an American survivor who doesn't have Social Security and doesn't have a health service and a safety net in a better or worse position than a needy survivor in Israel who has a national health service, who has a local municipality and social services, who gets a monthly Social Security check? Likewise, is an impoverished Nazi victim in the former Soviet Union, who does not have enough to eat, lives in a nonexistent health system and survives in the most appalling housing conditions, better or worse off than his or her counterparts in Israel and the United States?'[67]

In 1999, Miller convened a broad 'planning committee' of board members, survivors and Jewish professionals, both American and Israeli, to grapple with these issues. 'This is a subject that cannot be discussed only within the Claims Conference,' he said. 'It has to be discussed by people who are serious about the future of the Jewish people.'[68] Researchers commissioned by the Conference attempted to identify the number, location and socioeconomic conditions of Jewish victims around the world, including the relative degree of economic and social deprivation in different geographical areas and the existence of alternative sources of economic and social support. The research organization Ukeles Associates in New York found that, while the number of Nazi victims was declining each year, life expectancy for the group as a whole tended to exceed projections, in part because there were many more relatively younger Nazi victims than previously believed. 'The most striking finding from this projection is that the population of Nazi victims is declining more slowly than many had believed, and that as a consequence there are likely to be substantial numbers of surviving victims for at least another 20 years,' the Planning Committee reported.[69]

The geographic distribution and demographics of the Nazi victims varied dramatically. In the FSU, Nazi victims constituted a significant proportion of the total Jewish community, especially of older Jews. Nazi victims represented more than one in four of the Jews in the FSU, two of five in Eastern Europe, one in 16 in Israel, and one in 33 in the US. In Israel, which has the youngest Jewish population of any Jewish community in the world, Nazi victims were a significant proportion of the older population, but not a significant proportion of the total population, according to Ukeles Associates.[70]

There was little specific data available on the economic situation of Nazi victims. Much of the information was inferential and anecdotal, but it showed that the victims' conditions varied significantly. In the FSU, there were very large numbers of poor Nazi victims, and poverty trailed them; in both the US and Israel, the immigrants from the FSU were among the poor. Ukeles Associates estimated there were some 120,000 indigent Jewish victims in the FSU, compared to about 65,000 poor Nazi victims in Israel, about 17,000 in the US, 40,000 in Europe, and about 9,000 in the rest of the world.[71] Poverty was also relative. The needs in the FSU tended to be the desperate lack of essentials, including food, medical care and heat. In Israel, there was a safety net of social services, although there were significant gaps. In the US, an affluent society, the social safety net was not as systematic as in Israel; the needy survivors tended to live in states where the safety net was weakest.

Over ten months, the Planning Committee struggled to identify Nazi victims and their needs, and to recommend Solomonic principles and criteria for allocating the Conference's funds among competing needs. 'The Claims Conference faces agonizing choices among valid claims for the use of these resources,' the committee said. 'The pain associated with the Shoah and the sense of individual and collective abandonment expressed by surviving victims of Nazi persecution weighs heavily on the allocation process.'[72]

There were also philosophical disputes within the Claims Conference about whether its funds were for survivors or for the Jewish people. 'Let's not forget history, and let's remember what the prime purpose of the Claims Conference was,' Miller admonished. 'It is not the "Conference on Material Claims for Survivors." It is a conference on "Jewish material claims." This is for the Jewish people, and we decided – it was our decision – the money should go first to the survivors.'[73] As the Planning Committee noted: 'Whether one believes that Successor Organization funds belong to the Jewish people or to victims of Nazi persecution or both, the highest priority should go to social welfare needs of the most vulnerable surviving Nazi victims.' It essentially confirmed the Conference's existing allocations criteria, recommending that priority should go to meet the welfare needs of the neediest Nazi victims based on their economic circumstances, and on the availability of health and other social services.[74]

The recommendations also called for 'special priority' for programmes benefiting needy Nazi victims 'that enhance and strengthen the State of Israel as in the past'. That geographical division of funds was one of the most contentious topics in the Planning Committee and within the Conference itself. The tradition of using about 60 per cent of the Conference's funds for Israeli projects had been based not solely on a commitment to Israel; it was established with the allocations of institutional moneys from the Hardship Fund, which developed before the collapse of communism provided direct access to the Jews in Eastern Europe and the FSU. The division became known informally as the 60–40 split, and it aroused strong emotions.

'I'm not saying I'm against the 60–40,' said Schneider of the JDC, which was a major beneficiary; it used Conference funds to open and operate welfare centres in the FSU. 'I'm saying that 60–40 has to be backed up by proper data, not sentiment and not politics.'[75] There also was consternation among American survivors. 'This body cannot allocate 60 per cent of the money to the survivors in Israel and then 25 per cent to the survivors in Eastern Europe, and have almost no money left for the survivors everywhere else. We have to consider survivors everywhere,' said Kent, of the American Gathering of Jewish Holocaust Survivors and a member of the Conference's Executive Committee. 'In the past, we spent 60 per cent of the money in Israel. There was another reason for it too – because we did for Israel what we did not do basically for any other country – namely, we have spent a lot of money for building, for building hospitals and old-age homes. Because it was for Israel and a lot of survivors, we did not mind. But we cannot continue like this as long as there are living survivors who need help in other countries.'[76]

Among Conference members, it was not clear whether the allocations criteria were considered guidelines or quotas. Nor was it clear how the Conference would navigate conflicts between funding projects outside Israel that were based on need, or those for Israeli agencies and institutions that met the so-called geographical criteria, but were less urgent. When the 60–40 ratio first was adopted, the funds went primarily for capital projects in Israel. 'Miller often argued that, when we support these facilities in Israel, we know they will always benefit the Jewish people, even after survivors die. But it is not necessarily the case if we are supporting the development of facilities in Romania or Slovakia, for example,' said the American Jewish Committee's Baker. 'I think he had an important – and persuasive – point when we were devoting so much money to actual buildings. But now that we are putting emphasis on home care and other services, it seems to me it no longer has much merit.'[77]

However, the Israeli contingent on the board had argued vehemently in favour of the traditional allocations, viewing them as sacrosanct. The Conference accepted the Planning Committee's recommendations with modifications that appeared to specify the Israeli share. 'The Board of Directors notes that the recommendation regarding the per centage of Successor Organization funds that should be spent in Israel is reflected in the wording "as in the past" – namely that approximately 60 per cent of the allocations of the Successor Organization should be spent in Israel,' it said in a resolution at its 2000 meeting.[78] The Jewish Agency touted its chairman, Sallai Meridor, and claimed 'victory.' The Planning Committee 'recommended giving priority to projects in Israel without defining a precise exact budget framework,' the agency said. 'Meridor scored a victory, when his demand to preserve the principle whereby 60 per cent of the money is allocated to projects in Israel and 40 per cent to projects abroad is preserved.'[79]

The money raised by the Successor Organization also offered the single largest source of funds for research, education and documentation of the Shoah. This 'cultural' category included building projects as well as programmes. In the first five years of Successor Organization allocations, funds were distributed to 131 institutions in 26 countries for research, education and documentation. The funds were targeted toward established, influential institutions; 20 institutions received about 90 per cent of the funds. The capital projects in Israel for documentation and research were major beneficiaries and originally skewed the use of Successor Organization funds; from 1995 to 1999, these allocations amounted to more than those for social welfare projects in the US and Europe.[80] Yad Vashem was the primary recipient; the Conference Allocations Committee's first recommendations, in 1995, for distributing DM 42.4 million worldwide set aside DM 9 million for Yad Vashem – 21 per cent of all funds and 36 per cent of the funds designated for Israel.[81] Yad Vashem's archives and library building, which officially opened in 2000, consumed a significant portion of the Conference's research and documentation funds, but Miller considered it of prime importance. 'If archives are not saved now, in many cases they will never be saved,' Miller said. 'The archives at Yad Vashem were going to waste. The paper upon which they were written was just disintegrating, and we are living in the year 2000, where there is technology that can preserve all of these things.'[82] As it had been in the 1950s, Yad Vashem was especially significant to the Conference. A half-century after the Holocaust, museums and memorials were not uncommon, Miller noted at a ceremony at Yad Vashem marking the fiftieth anniversary of the Conference. 'There is a beautiful museum in Washington. There is a meaningful museum in Paris. They are building a beautiful memorial in Berlin, of all places,' he said. 'But unless we have the institutions of remembrance here in the State of Israel, we would have failed in our mission. And therefore, for the Claims Conference it is so important for us to support these institutions and to say this is holy ... What we are talking about is the remembrance of righteousness and goodness and of what we stand for as Jews. And we can only find its essence here in the State of Israel.'[83]

The other major institutions that benefited were Beit Lohamei Haghetaot (Ghetto Fighters' House–Holocaust and Jewish Resistance Heritage Museum), Massua (Institute for the Study of the Holocaust), Moreshet (Mordechai Anilevich Memorial Study Centre for Teaching the Holocaust) and Beit Hatefutsoth[84] in Israel, and the US Holocaust Memorial Museum and YIVO in the US.[85]

As was the case with social welfare, there were serious disagreements about the use of the funds. Within the Conference and among survivors, there was no consensus about the extent of financing research, education and documentation, or, indeed, what it entailed. There also were serious philosophical debates about the nature, scope and audience for Holocaust education, including whether the Conference should aim at non-Jewish audiences or finance education programmes exclusively for Jews.[86] There were disputes as well about where the Shoah fits into Jewish education and history. 'The greatest danger seems to me that education about the Holocaust becomes a category of its own in Jewish education,' said Jean-Jacques Wahl, director-general of the Alliance

Israélite Universelle in Paris. 'Judaism should not be perceived as what existed before and after the Shoah, at the risk of making a new religion out of the Shoah.'[87] And there were questions about what time frame should be covered by 'Holocaust' research. Some argued that it should be limited to the Nazi period, between 1933 and 1945. Others, such as Anita Shapira, a historian at Tel Aviv University and president of the Memorial Foundation, said Holocaust studies should entail a broad conception of modern Jewish history. 'We cannot keep out of Shoah studies the area of Jewish society in the wake of the Holocaust – how the Holocaust impacted Jewish society and culture everywhere, even to this day,' she said. 'We cannot limit ourselves only to the 15 years from the rise of Nazism until the establishment of the State of Israel ... You cannot isolate the history of the Holocaust from Jewish history, European Jewish history.'[88]

There also were voices insisting that the lingering question of Jewish survival was among the legacies of the Holocaust, and that assimilation further threatened the Jewish future. There was strong pressure from Israel – primarily from the Jewish Agency, which ran educational programmes – to expand the focus from the Holocaust to a broader and more-general Jewish education. These advocates believed it was imperative to ensure a community of 'literate Jews' to keep alive the lessons of the Shoah in future generations. Without such a focus on Jewish education, these advocates said, the number of Jews for whom the Holocaust is important would shrink in the future.[89] Kagan suggested that there also was a 'collateral' benefit to Holocaust education that extended beyond its intrinsic value. This would instill a commitment to Holocaust survivors so that the Jewish community would feel a moral responsibility to care for needy victims once the Conference's funds were exhausted.[90]

Again, there was no consensus among the survivors. Adi Steg of Paris, a survivor who was chairman of the Alliance Israélite Universelle, backed Conference support of education. 'The survivors have needs. The survivors have rights. But I think that the survivors also have duties,' he said. As those who endured persecution and witnessed the endangerment of the Jewish people, survivors should make education a priority, he said.[91] Others, however, contended that agencies, museums and institutes should raise funds for research and education from alternate sources. 'Everything is important. We never said that Jewish education is not important,' said Sanbar. He offered to help other agencies raise funds, but said the Conference money was 'earmarked' for survivors. Kent was more emphatic. He rejected the notion that the organization bore responsibility for the community at large, saying that the Conference exists solely for the benefit of the survivors. 'The Claims

Conference is not another Jewish organization that is supposed to support all Jewish causes,' he said. 'For this we have Hadassah and B'nai B'rith and all other organizations.'[92]

Despite the contention among its members, the Conference developed a broad policy on how to spend its funds – for whom, for which projects and in which locations. The next issue was when to spend: how to balance the immediate needs of survivors against what they might need in the future. With so much income, and so many survivors in need, there was enormous pressure on the Conference to spend funds as they became available, rather than its practice of limiting annual allocations. Some members thought that the Conference was too cautious and that limiting its allocations would harm the survivors of concentration camps and ghettos who were the most vulnerable population and who needed immediate aid. These advocates said that the 'child survivors', those victims who were very young during the Nazi era, had had greater post-war opportunities for educations and careers. Thus, they were unlikely to feel any material impact of the Holocaust and would be less dependent on Conference aid in the future.

'We have a problem, a sort of political problem,' said Sanbar, chairman of the Centre of Organizations of Holocaust Survivors in Israel. 'My own survivors are saying, "You are sitting on money and you don't spend it."' However, with an unknown future income, the Conference would not take on unlimited liabilities. At the same time, once it began to provide services for individuals, it could not stop, but it also was expected to be able to provide for additional survivors who would require aid in the future. Sanbar advocated the creation of a reserve fund that would allow the Conference to meet ongoing obligations and also would ensure that funds were available to aid survivors who became needy at a later date. 'If we start assisting some-one who is unable to carry out basic functions such as eating, washing, we must carry on doing so until his last day,' Sanbar said. 'For this we need sufficient long-term reserves.'[93]

According to Ukeles's estimates, in 2000, the largest group of Nazi victims – 41 per cent – was between 65 and 74 years old; 17 per cent were under 65.[94] At its board meeting in July 2000, the Conference, acting on the recommendations of its Planning Committee, set aside $100 million for the 'reserve' fund.[95] By then, the Conference was dispersing some $80 million a year. The allocations were primarily for on-going programmes, including the Keren in Israel, which received about $20 million a year, and the Hesed centres in the FSU, which received about $25 million.[96] In the US, the network of Jewish Family Service agencies received about $10 million to aid survivors.

'Restitution income will come in over the next few years, but it is clear that the needs will extend for many years beyond that,' Taylor said. 'We should seek to help the neediest Nazi victims over the duration of their lifetimes rather than spend the funds as they come in. There are many Nazi victims who thankfully do not need help today but as they get older and sicker will be in desperate need in a few years time. We need to be there to help them. That was the philosophy that lay behind the creation of the Fund for Long Term Needs.'[97] It was a sentiment that Greg Schneider shared. 'We have a tradition of being responsible,' he said. 'The absolute number of survivors will decrease, but the per centage in the 75-and-older range who need services will remain constant in the next 10 years. I think we have a moral obligation to be prepared.'[98]

The total amounts that may ultimately become available to the Claims Conference are unknown. In addition to the discretionary funds generated by the Successor Organization's sales of properties in the former East Germany, there were 'humanitarian funds' of some DM 276 million in 2001-02 from the German 'slave labour' foundation, known as the Foundation for Remembrance, Responsibility and the Future. Another $132 million in humanitarian funds for victims' social needs were anticipated from the International Commission of Holocaust-Era Insurance Claims, a consortium of European insurers, American state insurance regulators and Jewish organizations that was formed in 1998 to resolve the claims for Holocaust-era policies. There also were expected to be humanitarian funds associated with settlements of Nazi-era claims against European governments and enterprises.[99] While the amounts are unknown, it is certain they are finite.

Although the Conference devoted its substantial funds overwhelmingly to the social welfare of needy survivors, it insisted that it not be the exclusive financial source for programmes for Nazi victims. It traditionally leveraged its funds not only to provide more services and facilities than it could finance on its own, but also to engage existing institutions in providing care to needy survivors. 'It is important for us to bring in partners with the understanding that as time goes on and there will be a need to care for Holocaust survivors, we may not be able to contribute at all,' Kagan said. 'They have as great and as equal a responsibility as we have to make sure that the social care needs of Holocaust survivors are met.'[100]

The Conference's allocations always have come with an emotional edge. In the 1950s, there were violent demonstrations against negotiating with West Germany, on the grounds that German funds were tainted as 'blood money'. When West Germany paid DM 450 million under Protocol II, Leavitt said the money could be viewed in two ways: 'Either it is dirty, filthy money, or it is sacred money,' he said. 'I believe it has to be used as holy money.'[101] It helped transform Western European Jewish life between 1954 and 1964. The European communities had been destroyed; their members had been murdered; the few survivors were destitute and traumatized; their institutions were reduced to ruin. But some communities endured. 'The reconstruction of the Jewish communities has been an expression of the spirit more than of the purse strings,' Kagan said. 'Their will to build and to grow, to make sacrifices for it when necessary, have been essential ingredients in that reconstruction. The indomitable spirit to live on, to refuse to be subdued and conquered, was even alive in the darkest hour of the concentration camps and ghettos.'[102]

The sacred nature of the funds was apparent again at the turn of the century when the Successor Organization commenced its work in Eastern Germany. 'It is property, the homes of people who were killed in the Shoah, the victims, the people who didn't survive, the people who were gassed, who were shot – it's their property, their houses, their homes,' said Greg Schneider. 'And that leaves us with a special responsibility, with a sacred task, I think, unparalleled in Jewish life.'[103]

NOTES

1   Centraal Israelietisch Krankzinnigengesticht in Nederland (Central Association for Jewish Mental Health in the Netherlands), allocation application, July 1954. See also Centrale Vereniging Voor de Joodse letter to Claims Conference, 24 April 1956, CAHJP 690.

2   Renate G. Fuks-Mansfeld and Armand Sunier, editors, *Wie in tranen zaait ... : geschiedenis van de Joodse Geestelijke Gezondheidszorg in Nederland*, Van Gorcum Publishers, 1997. The pre-war Jewish psychiatric hospital was never again used for its original purpose; the building subsequently became a non-Jewish children's hospital.

3   The funds were received in different currencies over different periods of time, and cannot be combined into a single amount without distorting the value of the collective sums. Further, the sums are nominal and are not adjusted to reflect current values. Data on allocations, unless otherwise noted, is drawn from two Claims Conference publications: *Twenty Years Later* and *An Overview of Allocations 1952–1999*.

4   For a detailed review of the Conference's use of German funds until 1965, see Zweig, *German Reparations and the Jewish World*.

5   For instance, in 1992, Volkswagen provided DM 2.75 million to the Claims Conference, which came with a geographical restriction. There funds were to be used exclusively in Israel for survivors' shelter and social care.

6   The Conference's position was validated by American courts. In *Wolf v. Federal Republic of Germany and the Conference on Jewish Material Claims Against Germany*, the US federal court ruled that the protocols did not 'expressly create any right to recover for particular individuals or classes of individuals.' (No. 93-C-7499, 1995 WL 263471 [N.D. Ill. May 1, 1995], aff'd, 95 F.3d 536 [7th Cir. 1996].) See Chapter 2 on the West German indemnification and restitution legislation.

7   Kagan, *Exchange*. In addition to the individual appeals, there was a collective claim for Protocol II funds from the committee representing the remaining 1,400 Jews at Camp Föhrenwald, the last displaced persons camp in Germany. Moses Beckelman of the Joint Distribution Committee complained that Jewish organizations had encouraged, or had failed to quash, the Föhrenwalders' high expectations of aid. Since the Wassenaar negotiations had

began, the Föhrenwalders had received letters and oral assurances that they would get 'adequate funds,' which they had interpreted as $5 million, Beckelman wrote in a letter dated 1 March 1954. [Letter in JDC Archives, New York, 45/64 Collection, File 397]

8 Claims Conference Policy Committee meeting, 24 September 1952, CAHJP 16723. German historian Constantin Goschler observed that, for instance, West Germany was displeased that the Claims Conference used Protocol II funds to found Yad Vashem, the Holocaust memorial authority in Israel, because Yad Vashem was a constant reminder of German crimes, while Bonn viewed the funds as a means to improve Germany's image (Goschler interview, 3 July 2002, Berlin).

9 Claims Conference Board meeting, 14–15 January 1956, CAHJP 14150. The Luxembourg Agreements had caused some commotion about the charitable responsibilities of American Jewish communities, which saw the funds as an opportunity to recoup some of their post-war aid to Nazi victims. Leavitt rejected the prospect of spending Protocol II funds in the US. 'I would have very great doubts and I certainly would feel that it is not the proper thing to do, to utilize money of the Conference in American communities, thereby relieving American Jews of their obligations to take care of new immigrants,' Leavitt wrote in a 6 July 1953 letter.

10 Kagan, 16th Annual JDC Overseas Conference and Second Assembly on European Jewish Community Services, 25 October 1961, CAHJP 15058.

11 Excerpt from 1954 country director's report, American Joint Distribution Committee, JDC Archives, New York, 45/64 Collection, File 309. The Conference distributed some 30 million francs for those French requests, less than 5 per cent of the requests.

12 Claims Conference press release, 4 May 1956, CAHJP 15018.

13 Claims Conference Board meeting, 30–31 January 1960, Amsterdam, CAHJP 13630.

14 Zweig, formerly a professor at Tel Aviv University, has spoken of 'relief in transit' in his classes and, on occasion, a startled student from the former Soviet Union would say, 'We received such a package; we never knew we had relatives in Switzerland.'

15 Claims Conference Board meeting, 22 July 2002, Luxembourg. Conference officials privately had advised German authorities of how the money was used. The West Germans did not object, as Kagan recalled, in part because they had similar operations to help their compatriots in the East.

16 Kagan, *Exchange*.

17 Kagan statement to JDC meeting, 1954.

18 Claims Conference Board meeting, 7 March 1964, Brussels, CAHJP 14166.

19 Claims Conference Board meeting, 30–31 January 1960, Amsterdam, CAHJP 13630.

20 Claims Conference Board meeting, 7 March 1964, Brussels, CAHJP 14166.

21 Kagan interview, 18 November 2001.

22 Kagan letter to Yitzhak Arad, 28 May 1993.

23 Claims Conference 'Post-1964 Committee' meeting, 6 February 1961, New York, CAHJP 14909.

24 Segal, undated position paper to the Claims Conference 'Post-1964 Committee.'

25 Claims Conference 'Post-1964 Committee' meeting, 6 February 1961, New York, CAHJP 14909.

26 Claims Conference document 63/29-D, 'Utilization of Conference funds after 1964.'

27 Claims Conference, *Annual Report 2001*. By the end of the century, there were only two recipients of Community Leader grants, in the US and Israel, and the annual cost of the programme in 2000 was about $1,500.

28 Claims Conference Board meeting, 17–18 July 2001, Washington. The Conference was unable to maintain the programme without assistance. It had virtually no income in the 1970s and 1980s, even as the number of non-Jews designated as Righteous Gentiles climbed, leaving the Conference to rely on the Jewish Agency and the Joint Distribution Committee to maintain the programme. In 1989, the Jewish Foundation for the Righteous assumed the responsibility for assisting the newly recognized *Hassidei Umot*, while the Conference retained responsibility for aiding those recognized before 1989. At the end of 2000, there were 165 grant recipients in 10 countries – all but 15 in Poland. In 2001, the Conference also transferred the administration of the programme to the Jewish Foundation for the Righteous.

29 The Conference was so impoverished that its 1981 budget was less than $300,000. It had board members on five continents, but lacked the funds to pay the expenses of delegates who attended its meetings. It was able to hold board meetings by convening them for a few hours at the conclusion of the Memorial Foundation board meetings.

30 Claims Conference Board meeting, 1 July 1986, Herzliya, Israel.

31 Kagan, memo to Claims Conference Board, 23 November 1981.

32 Claims Conference, *Annual Report 2001*. All of the proceeds of the property sales were not available to the Conference for institutional allocations. See Chapter 6 on the Claims Conference Successor Organization for a discussion of the Goodwill Fund, under which the Conference shares the proceeds of recovered properties with Jewish property owners and heirs who missed the German deadline for filing property claims. Income generated by property sales is reported in Deutschmarks; Conference allocations are reported in US dollars.

33 Claims Conference Planning Committee meeting, 23 November 1999, New York.

34 Claims Conference, *Annual Report 2000*.

35 Claims Conference, *Annual Report 2001*. The German foundation was established in 2001 primarily to compensate former slave and forced labourers. The Conference was among the parties negotiating with the German government and industry to resolve remaining Nazi-era claims, which also included German banks' obligations for 'Aryanized' Jewish properties. In addition to payments for individual Nazi-era labourers, the joint German government–industry fund included a 'humanitarian' portion of DM 276 million (some $127 million) for Claims Conference allocations to social service agencies and institutions. The Conference allocated these funds in 2001 and 2002.

36 Claims Conference Board meeting, 9–10 July 1998, Jerusalem.

37 In its *Annual Report 2001*, the Conference noted that, through 2001, the Successor Organization sold 1,417 properties, but advised that many of the properties still to be recovered in the former East Germany were smaller and of lesser value than those already recovered.

38 Claims Conference Planning Committee meeting, 23 November 1999, New York.

39 Claims Conference Planning Committee meeting, 31 May 2000.

40 Under the definition traditionally used by the Claims Conference, a Nazi victim is any Jew who was in (or subsequently was deported or fled from) Germany as of January 1933; Austria in March 1938; Czechoslovakia in October 1938; Poland after September 1939; Denmark, Norway, Belgium, Netherlands, Luxembourg and France, after April/May 1940; Yugoslavia and Greece after April 1941; Bulgaria, Romania and Hungary, as of April 1941 when these governments enacted anti-Jewish measures on the demand of the Nazi government; and the Soviet Union after June 1941. See Kagan memo to Joint Distribution Committee – Israel, 19 August 1991.

41 Ukeles Associates, 'An Estimate of the Current Distribution of Victims of Nazi Persecution,' appendix in Claims Conference Planning Committee, 'A Plan for Allocating Successor Organization Resources,' 28 June 2000. Ukeles reported that there were no reliable statistics on the number of Nazi victims alive in 2000. His methods for estimating the number and social conditions of Nazi victims varied by location; the best information was available for those in Israel; there also was some hard data concerning victims in the former Soviet Union. Estimates on Nazi victims in the West were based on extrapolations from the Israeli data; in Central and Eastern Europe, Nazi victims' conditions were assumed to be similar to those in the former Soviet Union. In 2003, Ukeles and Israeli demographer Sergio Della Pergola each were commissioned by the International Commission on Holocaust Era Insurance Claims to determine the number and location of survivors. Ukeles's adjusted figure was 688,000. Della Pergola reported 1,092,000. The major difference in their count is based on Della Pergola's inclusion of Jews who had lived in Arab countries that passed had anti-Jewish laws. I rely on the data assembled by Ukeles Associates, in part, because it is the basis of Claims Conference planning.

42 Ukeles Associates, 'An Estimate of the Current Distribution of Victims of Nazi Persecution.'

43 Claims Conference Tel Aviv office, 'Report for the Last Decade of the Millennium in Israel (1990-1999),' 4 July 1999. Fifty years earlier, the proportion of people over the age of 65 was less than 4 per cent of Israel's population; by the century's end, it was close to 10 per cent, and growing more than twice as fast as the general population. This was due both to immigration from the former Soviet Union and a general increase in life expectancy.

44 Ukeles Associates, 'An Estimate of the Current Distribution of Victims of Nazi Persecution.'

45 Israel Miller memo to Claims Conference Board, 19 July 1995.

46 Claims Conference Planning Committee, 'A Plan for Allocating Successor Organization Resources,' p. 55.

47 Figures provided by Caroline Lerner, Claims Conference Allocations Department, 21 October

2002. Correspondence on file with author.

48 Claims Conference Board meeting, 6 July 1990, Jerusalem. The DM 10 million from Daimler-Benz was allocated to 56 institutions in 15 countries; more than half went to 23 institutions in Israel, which pledged to give special preference in admissions to Holocaust survivors.

49 Israel Miller memo to Claims Conference Board, 19 July 1995.

50 After reports in the Israeli newspaper *Ma'ariv*, there was an outcry about the living conditions of institutionalized survivors who were wards of the state, and over revelations that government trustees had withheld Holocaust-compensation payments that had been made over four decades to individual survivors. Israeli doctors complained that the government trustees refused to allow the accumulated funds to be used for items to improve survivors' living conditions, such as televisions and air conditioners. According to news accounts, trustees approved requests only for purchases that would assist individual survivors. Other requests were refused on the grounds that other patients would benefit from the use of the individual survivor's funds. 'Unfortunately, there are still eight patients in a room,' said Avner Elitsur, director of the psychiatric ward at the Abarbanel Hospital near Tel Aviv. 'We pointed out that the other patients are also Holocaust survivors, but it didn't help.' Associated Press, 5, 6 August 1998.

51 *Jerusalem Post*, 30 March 1999.

52 Claims Conference Office of the Controller-General, Audit Report Number 27, 'Implementation of the recommendations of the public commission [Bazak Commission] to examine the condition of mentally ill Holocaust survivors who are incarcerated in mental hospitals in Israel', April 2003.

53 Miller interview, 31 January 2001.

54 Claims Conference, *Annual Report 2001*.

55 Claims Conference, Report on Activities of the Tel Aviv office 2000/1, May 2001.

56 Claims Conference Board meeting, 17–18 July 2001, Washington.

57 Claims Conference Board meeting, 18–19 July 2000, New York.

58 Greg Schneider interview, 2 January 2002.

59 Claims Conference Board meeting, 17–18 July 2001, Washington. The Keren was intended to provide basic needs that were not met elsewhere. For instance, between its inception and 1997, it distributed more than $7 million in 8,700 grants; more than 90 per cent of the grants were for dental care. Demands on the Keren grew with the immigration of Nazi victims to Israel from the FSU.

60 Claims Conference, Report on Activities of the Tel Aviv office 2000/1, May 2001.

61 Miller interview, 23 December 2001.

62 Claims Conference Planning Committee, 'A Plan for Allocating Successor Organization Resources,' p. 55.

63 Ukeles Associates, 'An Estimate of the Current Distribution of Victims of Nazi Persecution.'

64 Claims Conference Board meeting, 17–18 July 2001, Washington.

65 *Jerusalem Post*, 7 November 1996. In 2002, the Kiev centre was renamed Hesed Avot-Azriel in honour of Miller.

66 Ostrin interview, 5 November 1996. There were similar linkages in other Conference-financed programmes. For instance, the Yiddish Theatre in Israel received a grant from the Conference that was conditioned on the theater staging performances for Nazi victims in Israeli geriatric institutions.

67 Claims Conference Planning Committee meeting, 15 March 2000, Jerusalem.

68 Claims Conference Planning Committee meeting, 23 November 1999, New York.

69 Claims Conference Planning Committee, 'A Plan for Allocating Successor Organization Resources.'

70 Ibid.

71 Ukeles Associates, 'An Estimate of the Current Distribution of Victims of Nazi Persecution.' The Planning Committee report also noted that with the exception of recent immigrants from the FSU, the economic situation of Nazi victims in Israel was probably significantly better than that of immigrants in Israel from Moslem countries.

72 Claims Conference Planning Committee, 'A Plan for Allocating Successor Organization Resources.'

73 Claims Conference Planning Committee meeting, 23 November 1999, New York.

74 Claims Conference Planning Committee, 'A Plan for Allocating Successor Organization Resources.'

75 Claims Conference Planning Committee meeting, 15 March 2000, Jerusalem.
76 Claims Conference Board meeting, 18–19 July 2000, New York.
77 Interview, 9 September 2002.
78 Claims Conference Board meeting, 18–19 July 2000, New York.
79 Jewish Agency press release, 'Success for the Chairman of the Jewish Agency: No Cut in Claims Conference Allocation For Jewish Education and Projects in Israel,' 1 June 2000.
80 Claims Conference Planning Committee, 'A Plan for Allocating Successor Organization Resources,' p. 55.
81 Israel Miller memo to Claims Conference Board, 19 July 1995. Of the first allocations to Yad Vashem, DM 7.5 million was for construction of an archives building and DM 1.5 million was for the computerization of archival materials. In numerous ways, the Conference was instrumental in helping to rescue Yad Vashem. The institution was 'about to close down in 1988 because of debts', Avner Shalev, the director, told the Knesset's Finance Committee at a meeting on 2 May 2001. 'All of the [Israeli] organizations that have to do with ensuring the memory of the Holocaust received significant aid [from the Claims Conference], Yad Vashem among them. And we would have disappeared off the map if it wasn't for this organization's help to us in raising a lot of private money.'
82 Claims Conference Planning Committee meeting, 15 March 2000, Jerusalem.
83 Miller speech, 27 November 2001, Yad Vashem, Jerusalem.
84 The Conference has a special affinity with Beit Hatefutsoth because of its links with Goldmann, the Conference founder. It was on Goldmann's initiative that the museum was established in the 1960s. Beit Hatefutsoth also is known as The Nahum Goldmann Museum of the Jewish Diaspora. When it was established, the museum was 'jointly owned' by Tel Aviv University, the Jewish Agency, the World Jewish Congress, the Israeli government and the Tel Aviv Municipality. The museum was hobbled by debt in 2001. Under a recovery plan, the Tel Aviv Municipality would help reduce the museum's debt, but relinquished its ownership, while the university and the Jewish Agency became the key forces.
85 Claims Conference symposium on Holocaust research, education and documentation, 16 May 2001, Jerusalem.
86 Interviews undertaken on behalf of the Conference by Ukeles Associates appeared to indicate that there was greater interest in Holocaust education in the general community than in the Jewish community.
87 Claims Conference symposium on Holocaust/Jewish education, 16 May 2001, Jerusalem.
88 Claims Conference symposium on Holocaust research, 15 May 2001, Jerusalem.
89 Claims Conference Board meeting, 9–10 July 1998, Jerusalem.
90 Claims Conference Planning Committee meeting, 15 March 2000, Jerusalem.
91 Ibid.
92 Ibid.
93 Correspondence with author, 22 October 2002.
94 Ukeles Associates, 'An Estimate of the Current Distribution of Victims of Nazi Persecution.'
95 Claims Conference Board meeting, 18–19 July 2000, New York.
96 Greg Schneider interview, 2 January 2002.
97 Taylor interview, 19 October 2001.
98 Greg Schneider interview, 2 January 2002.
99 The insurance commission was chaired by former US Secretary of State Lawrence S. Eagleburger; the funding was reported by the Jewish Telegraphic Agency, 26 February 2003. In addition, the Conference was one of the channels for distributing funds through the Nazi Persecutee Relief Fund. This fund was created at the 1997 'Nazi Gold Conference' in London, in which nations relinquished their claims to the residual resources of the Tripartite Gold Commission, and pledged additional contributions to aid needy Nazi victims. These were not discretionary funds. Nations identified which projects they would support and channeled grants through non-governmental organizations. The Conference was the vehicle for funding from the US, French, Austrian and Spanish governments for projects in 15 countries, as mandated by the donor nation. For details, see Claims Conference, *Annual Report 2001*.
100 Claims Conference Planning Committee meeting, 15 March 2000, Jerusalem. Kagan also sought to wean the Keren from its total dependence on Conference funds. The Keren 'should not depend 100 per cent on the funds of the Claims Conference alone,' he said. He called on philanthropists within the Holocaust survivor community to assist the needy among them.
101 Minutes, Claims Conference Policy Committee meeting, 24 September 1952, CAHJP 16723.

102 Kagan, 16th Annual JDC Overseas Conference and Second Assembly on European Jewish Community Services, 25 October 1961, CAHJP 15058.
103 Claims Conference symposium on Holocaust research, education and documentation, 16 May 2001, Jerusalem.

Chapter 10

The Claims Conference: Fifty Years of the Luxembourg Agreements

'We are ready to negotiate on certain claims of a material nature.'[1] With that opening statement in 1952 in Wassenaar, the Claims Conference began a historic mission for compensation and restitution for Jewish victims of Nazi persecution. It was guided by the premise that, however repugnant the task and irreparable the loss, it was immoral to permit Germany to profit from the murder of six million Jews. 'Nobody is saying to the Germans: "You pay us; we forgive you,"' Goldmann said. 'We are promising nothing; we are offering nothing. We are simply claiming what is ours, morally and legally.'[2]

The Conference's negotiations with West Germany culminated in the Luxembourg Agreements, which became a model for individual redress for abuses of human rights. For the first time in modern international law, a non-governmental organization representing individuals had successfully defended individual human rights on the international level.[3] The Conference continued to defend them for more than 70 years after Hitler's rise to power.

The Claims Conference, however, never intended to exist in perpetuity. In 1965, it had finished distributing the funds West Germany paid under Protocol II and it was thought that it had 'lived out its ordained lifespan'.[4] Under Protocol I, Germany agreed that it would 'endeavor to carry out the whole compensation programme as soon as possible but not later than within 10 years'.[5] The Conference had successfully negotiated for three indemnification laws between 1953 and 1965, but the indemnification programme moved at a slow pace. The Conference would not defer to the Germans to ensure it was fulfilled. Nor was it willing to abandon the claims of Jews who had not been eligible for compensation under existing measures, or to abandon the pursuit of East Germany to acknowledge its share of the German obligations to Nazi victims.

And because it was so dogged in its determination, the Conference – understaffed and operating with virtually no resources – remained prepared to exploit every opportunity to press claims in Bonn, East Berlin, Vienna and Washington. Many of the Conference's material successes were monumental. Others were painfully incremental.

When a New York magazine published an article in 1984 about Nazi-looted art that remained in the hands of the Austrian government, Miller and Kagan demanded that the Austrian chancellor grant individuals the right to claim their properties. That effort ultimately reopened the art claims as well as questions regarding Austria's responsibility for compensation for Nazi-era damages. In 1985, when Deutsche Bank acquired Feldmuehle Nobel, the company built by Friedrich Flick, Miller told the bank of a decades-old slave labour claim that Flick had refused to honour. Deutsche Bank paid the Flick claim, which was distributed to individual former slave labourers. That, in turn, encouraged Kagan to approach other German companies to reopen discussions about compensation for slave labour. When the US recognized East Germany, Miller reminded the State Department of unsatisfied claims against the GDR and obtained US support for what amounted to some 17 years of prodding East Germany. After the fall of the Berlin Wall, the Claims Conference was ready to press its claims; its efforts subsequently led to new compensation programmes for tens of thousands of Nazi victims. Its insistence on the protection of victims' property rights led to the recovery of thousands of Jewish properties in the former East Germany. For individual victims and their heirs, it had been unimaginable that properties in the GDR would be restored after five decades. For the Jewish world, the Conference's claims for heirless properties generated the single largest source of discretionary funds to aid Holocaust survivors around the world.

And after years of unrecognized labours by its few active members, its success also brought criticism about how well it did its task. 'I don't like people to criticize us at all, but I am realistic,' said Miller. 'If we didn't have any money, nobody would criticize us. Nobody would even want to join us. I remember when the Claims Conference couldn't get a quorum or couldn't get a *minyan* together. We have a few *Shkalim*, and so we are subject to all kinds of criticisms.'[6]

Because of its tenacity, more than a half-million Nazi victims ultimately received more than DM 100 billion in compensation, and the Conference was able to allocate more than $500 million to organizations providing social welfare services to survivors. How it secured those amounts is little understood, in part because the Conference shunned publicity and because it insisted that its members keep information confidential. It persisted in pushing West Germany into seemingly continuous negotiations and feared that publicity could jeopardize pending or potential agreements. Some of its fears were well-founded; West Germany did not want 'forgotten victims' to demand comparable compensation.

Over 50 years, the Conference's negotiations with Germany have been labourious and have entailed a heart-wrenching balance between morality and pragmatism. 'We came to The Hague demanding $500 million; we accepted DM 450 million. We had no choice,' Kagan said. 'The overarching reality of our entire existence is the fact that at every stage of our activities, we were confronted with the question: After serious negotiations, after using all the means at our disposal, are we going to achieve what we set out to achieve? Do we ultimately settle because a significant number of Holocaust survivors will benefit, or not? Whatever we have achieved was always some kind of a compromise. Our overriding consideration, from Day One, is to secure optimum compensation for the survivors within the framework of the attainable.'[7]

The 'attainable' was always dictated by Germany's focus on its finances. In Wassenaar, the Conference presented a series of demands for improvements in the scope and amount of compensation to individual survivors. It argued that the extant German indemnification and restitution measures were improperly implemented and did not cover sufficient categories of people who suffered. The preamble to Protocol I of the Luxembourg Agreements stated that West Germany and the Conference have 'agreed on a number of principles for the improvement of the existing legislation as well as on other measures,' but these were linked to the Federal Republic's 'capacity to pay'.

West Germany's paramount attention on the costs was evident in its choice of negotiators. The government vested that authority in its Finance Ministry. 'The initial fatal deficiency in the statutory structure, the competence accorded to the Treasury and not invoking the ministries of justice or of the interior, always displayed its paralyzing impact,' Katzenstein said. Regardless of the nature or gravity of the claims presented, the Germans invoked 'the plea of a precarious budgetary situation implying the tendency to overshadow and brush aside moral considerations'.[8]

It was in this environment that the Conference also faced an early decision about how to present its demands to the Germans, and whether these demands should be ranked. There were members who argued that the organization should present the totality of its demands and should not renounce any, because the notion of favouring one group of victims over another was abhorrent. Goldmann, however, insisted that the Conference was 'duty-bound' to conduct negotiations, not simply to submit a list of demands. 'If we presented a long list of demands, but without indicating priorities at any stage, the German authorities would gain *carte blanche* to distribute as they saw fit the funds they were prepared to grant. Distribution in the manner the German authorities may choose is not necessarily the manner we would choose,' he said. 'If compelled to do so, the Conference must make choices, must establish priorities, must accept responsibilities, and must be prepared to negotiate on them, even at the risk of strong criticism.'[9] In fact, vehement criticism, hostility and the occasional threats of violence stalked the Claims Conference. In the early days, Goldmann was accompanied by a bodyguard, and some New York hotels, fearing confrontations, refused to allow the Conference to rent space for meetings. 'We had sit-in strikes by amputee victims of Nazi persecution, one of whom one day unscrewed part of his wooden leg and was about ready to crack my head open,' Kagan recalled.[10]

Despite the enmity, the Conference persisted. 'Those who were involved in the negotiations used as many different means as possible, and as great an effort as possible, to secure as much funding as possible, to help as many survivors as possible, as soon as possible,' Taylor said.[11]

First among those on whom Jewish organizations have relied is the US government, which devoted significant attention to restitution and indemnification at key moments. When it was impossible to reach a consensus for a quadripartite restitution law in Occupied Germany, the US acted unilaterally. It established the principles governing restitution in 1947 in the US Occupation Zone of Germany under Military Government Law Number 59 (*Rückerstattungsgesetz*). The law provided for individuals to recover property that had been seized or stolen between 1933 and 1945, and introduced the presumption of duress in property transfers, which relieved the victims of the need to prove that their properties had been confiscated. The US also recognized a 'successor organization' – the Jewish Restitution Successor Organization – with the right to claim and recover heirless Jewish properties. That concept overturned the tradition of escheat, under which heirless properties reverted to the state, because the US would not permit Germany to benefit materially from the *Endlösung*.[12] The basic principles governing individual indemnification also were established in the US Occupation Zone. In 1949, American military authorities oversaw *Länder* legislation for the General Claims Law, which included compensation of DM 150 to victims for each month of incarceration in concentration camps and ghettoes, as well as redress for injuries and losses that were not covered by restitution laws.[13] Those laws were the blocks on which all subsequent indemnification and restitution measures were built.

Jewish organizations, fearing that that the creation of the West German state would adversely affect Holocaust-related compensation measures, believed that Allied supervision was essential to ensure that sovereign West Germany would fulfill its obligations.[14] When the Allies loosened their control on the FRG, the rights of Nazi victims were protected in the German–Allied contractual agreement; in the 1952 Treaty on the Settlement of Problems Resulting from War and Occupation, the FRG committed itself to enact indemnification and restitution legislation that would be no less favourable than the existing laws in the American Occupation zone. And in every subsequent treaty dealing with German sovereignty, the US insisted that Germany retain its commitment to victims. During the negotiations on German reunification, the Conference reminded the US government of its historic commitment and, in turn, the US again protected the rights of victims.[15] Shortly before the 2+4 Agreement was signed, Baker, the secretary of state, told his German counterpart that the US felt obliged 'to do everything necessary to ensure resolution of the Jewish claims. There is also close interest in this issue in Congress,' Baker wrote to Genscher, the German foreign minister. 'A commitment from your government now to resolve these claims expeditiously and equitably following unification will help ensure the continued support of the American people and Congress for the German-American partnership we have so effectively consolidated over the past year.'[16]

Baker had deliberately reminded Genscher of the need to ensure support for that partnership. 'German unification would not have happened without America. The Soviets were dead set against it, at least initially, and the British and the French were extraordinarily lukewarm – they didn't want to do it. They were worried that history would repeat itself,' Baker said. 'So when we went to the Germans and said, "Hey, there is another issue here that is of concern to us," we got their ear. We had been there for the Germans on the fulcrum issue on unification. They needed us. They could not have unified Germany without us. That is why when we raised this issue of compensation, it was received positively, because it came from us.'[17]

The US again exercised its political muscle in 2000, this time in Austria. While most of the West shunned the new Austrian coalition government that included Jörg Haider's right-wing Freedom Party, US Treasury Deputy Secretary Stuart Eizenstat acted as the 'facilitator' of negotiations on claims for Nazi-era damages. When Austria and the advocates reached an agreement on compensation for war-time slave labourers, Eizenstat issued a statement that combined congratulations with warnings about diplomatic relations. 'I am confident that Austria's actions on the range of Holocaust issues will be important in how we judge the way Austria has lived up to the commitments embodied in the coalition government's own programme, and thus will play a crucial role in any decision we might make about future engagement between the US and Austrian governments,' he said.[18]

Immediately after the Second World War, the Americans' interest in Jewish claims was far more sympathetic than that of the British and French. But it was not altruistic. The recovery of Jewish assets was a means of making funds available for the resettlement and rehabilitation of refugees, which relieved the burden on Western governments. The US government was also responding to pleas of German-born Jews who had immigrated to the US and who appealed to Washington for assistance; they were the primary beneficiaries of the early restitution laws.[19] And, as individuals appealed to the American government to represent their interests, so too did the Conference, which was seen as an American Jewish organization. Although the Conference advocates for survivors around the world, its leadership and gravitas were American. Goldmann was considered a 'genius' for incorporating the Claims Conference in the US, rather than in Israel, 'because he knew that we would need the clout of a major, major player in the international community in bringing justice to the Jewish people,' said Miller. 'I know where the power is in this world. It is important to have Israel on my side. But it is more important in this relationship to have the US ambassador, the US secretary of state.'[20]

However, the Conference's demands and US government's interests did not always converge.[21] For instance, less than a decade after reunification, they were often at loggerheads over German compensation for Nazi-era slave and forced labourers. The Conference, accustomed to being the sole victims' advocate, found itself in multi-party negotiations, facing competing demands from attorneys who had filed class-action lawsuits in US federal courts on behalf of Nazi victims, and from Eastern European governments acting on behalf of their nationals. The US government acted as a mediator. Whatever its sentiments about the justice of Jewish demands, its foreign policy interests in Europe transcended them, and the US government called on the Conference to subvert its claims to those of Eastern Europeans. Nonetheless, the US remained the most stalwart and potent ally of the Conference, which had no independent means by which to compel any agreement.

The Conference's relations to Israel have been both intimate and complex. The Conference originally was convened in 1951 to support Israel's claim against Germany for funds to resettle tens of thousands of European Jews in Israel. When the Conference insisted that there was also a collective Jewish claim against West Germany, the Israeli ambassador initially warned that the diaspora claim could sabotage that of the Jewish state. The Conference subsequently negotiated alongside Israel in Wassenaar in 1952, subverted its collective demands in favour of the Israeli claim, and received its payments from West Germany, under Protocol II, via Israel. However, Israel did not join the Conference in making post-war claims against Austria. And after the fall of the Berlin Wall, Israel distinguished between its bilateral agenda and the Jewish agenda. The Conference and Israel did not hold joint talks for compensation from East Germany. Instead, the Conference met with GDR officials in East Berlin, while Israel conducted separate negotiations with East German officials in Copenhagen. Following reunification, Israel's German agenda did not include Holocaust claims; it negotiated with Germany on trade and security issues, such as submarines.[22]

As the Conference began to recover Jewish properties in the former East Germany, it confronted varying sentiments from Israeli officials about how funds should be used. At times it appeared as if the government viewed the Conference as an instrument to raise funds for Israel, not for survivors. 'The Israeli government feels that this property, and compensation received for it, should be used mainly for financing the absorption of newly arrived Jews and other important social goals,' Finance Minister Avraham Shochat said in 1993. 'Absorbing these newcomers is the central goal of the Jewish people and the State of Israel in our generation.'[23] At century's end, the State of Israel and its envoys floundered on the government's role in Holocaust compensation claims, especially as the prospect of funds from additional sources began to materialize. Successive Israeli governments or members of the Knesset periodically asserted Israel's role, but they pursued the issue on the basis of individual initiative and with inconsistent vigor.[24] Israel was not automatically seen as the representative of the Jewish people by either its government, Jewish organizations, Holocaust survivors or other nations. And although the Holocaust inevitably remains an ineffable characteristic of Israeli life, it was not an explicit aspect of Israeli foreign affairs; there was no organized set of instructions for Israeli diplomats on the Holocaust *vis-à-vis* foreign policy.[25] 'There are no position papers [on the issue] in Israeli diplomacy, not today and not in the past,' Danny Scheck, director of the European Division of the Israeli Foreign Ministry, told diplomats from more than two dozen nations at a meeting in Jerusalem in 2001.[26]

The tensions over Israel's role were illuminated in a debate in 2001 in the Knesset Finance Committee, which was considering a law to establish a 'Fund for the Jewish People' that, according to its sponsors, would be financed with the proceeds of Holocaust-era claims. When Knesset member Avraham Hirschson said the State of Israel was the legal heir of all Jewish assets for which there are no heirs, he was challenged by Moshe Bejski, a survivor who had retired as an Israeli Supreme Court judge. Bejski contended there was no legal basis for such a claim.[27]

The Knesset committee hearing turned into something of a free-for-all for Nazi victims' grievances, including those against the State of Israel. Holocaust survivors, many of whom had had prominent careers in the Israeli public sector, vehemently expressed a lack of confidence in Israel's treatment of Holocaust survivors. They assailed the Israeli government for failing to aggressively pursue victims' claims in Europe. They also criticized the relatively low levels of compensation it provided to Holocaust survivors; 'unfair and even degrading,' said Dov Shilansky, a Nazi victim and former speaker of the Knesset. 'What has the State of Israel done in order to secure the money?' Bejski asked. 'The only people who did anything were the survivors themselves, and once it seems likely that there will be more money, then suddenly the government says that it will be in charge of it.' Nor was Israel itself immune from claims for dormant Nazi-era accounts in its own banks. There were revelations in 1997 that Bank Leumi, the successor institution to the Anglo-Palestine Bank, had more than 10,000 such accounts. Another Israeli institution, the Jewish National Fund, controlled parcels of land that may have belonged to Nazi victims. The dormant and unclaimed assets in Israel – primarily land and bank accounts – were valued at as much as 25 billion shekels, according to Colette Avital, the head of the Knesset committee that examined war-era assets in Israel.[28] 'Ladies and gentlemen,' Bejski said at the Knesset hearing, 'the State of Israel has left a bitter taste in my mouth.'[29]

Survivors also have had serious grievances with the Claims Conference, over the amount of compensation, the use of the Conference's income, and the role of survivors in the organization. Although the Conference's agenda was to secure compensation for Nazi victims, survivors' groups were not members when the organization was established. 'A good part of the criticism of this nature may be theoretically meritorious – and not practical,' said Kagan.[30] For many years, survivors were not organized to advocate for redress for material losses. Instead, when survivors emigrated from Europe and formed organizations, they tended to be concerned with commemorative activities and with the relentless search for kin.[31]

Although the Claims Conference had dramatically succeeded in negotiating for German legislation to provide compensation to scores of thousands of Jewish victims, the Conference itself long remained invisible to individual survivors. They received indemnification payments directly from West Germany, and most were unaware of the Conference as their advocate. Yet, throughout its history, the Conference's primary focus was on obtaining aid for individual victims. In the Wassenaar negotiations, the Conference's delegation gave priority to individual compensation over the collective claim. A half-century later, when the Conference insisted on the right to recover Jewish properties in the former East Germany, individual Nazi victims and their heirs were the primary beneficiaries. The Conference sought for itself the heirless and unclaimed properties that otherwise would have remained in German hands.

Survivors' organizations – the American Gathering/Federation of Jewish Holocaust Survivors and the Centre of Organizations of Holocaust Survivors in Israel – were admitted to the Conference in 1989. That move was initiated by Israeli survivors who in 1988 had organized the Centre, intent on obtaining additional compensation from Germany. When the Centre asked the Israeli Finance Ministry for advice on how best to approach the Germans, the Ministry directed it to the Conference.[32] Once the Israeli survivors applied for membership in the Conference, the American group followed.[33] Their applications placed the Conference in a quandary. At the time, it had an uncertain future and few funds at its disposal for institutional allocations. It persisted in appealing to East Germany for compensation, but the prospect seemed remote. 'We are in a moral dilemma,' Miller said when the Conference convened to consider the applications of the survivors' organizations. 'When the Claims Conference was organized, the survivors were then a beaten group that had no organization of its own and there was no way in which they could be represented. But we are dealing with a different survivor group. It is 40 years, 45 years thereafter. And we are all faced with the dilemma – how does one say "no" to a survivors' group, if indeed we are acting on their behalf?'[34]

Within the Conference, some members objected to expanding the organization, fearing that there would be additional applications from other survivors' groups. That was immaterial to the chairman of the American Gathering, Roman Kent. 'We, the American Gathering, represent maybe 65,000 to 70,000 survivors. I realize that when the commission was created we were not in existence; we were children out of the camps. But there is a time that we are grown up and we should be part of it,' said Kent. 'This particular commission did a wonderful job for many, many years. But there is nothing wrong with recognizing, right now, new members. It would enhance the value of the commission rather than [be a] hindrance to it ... We should not be asking you people to join the organization. You people should ask us to join the organization by acclamation.'[35]

Ferencz, the long-time negotiator, opposed admitting the survivors' organizations as members. 'Will it help you to be a member?' he asked. 'My personal feeling is it will not help you. It will not help the Claims

Conference; it will not help you.' By then, West Germany had paid some DM 80 billion to survivors. 'This is a continuing effort being made by very competent people, skilled people ... I am not pointing to it with pride because we never have done enough. The only question is, can we do it better if you are in the organization or if you are outside the organization?' Ferencz argued that the survivors could be a force outside the Conference that would not be bound by its earlier agreements with West Germany. 'What can you really do to persuade the German government to pay more than what we are now trying?'[36]

The Conference also discouraged the survivors by noting that the Conference expected 'discipline' from its members. 'You can't go by yourself to Chancellor Kohl or to Honecker and say, "I am part of this group but I don't agree with them." Once a decision has been made, we will live by that decision,' Miller said.[37] Nonetheless, the survivors organizations were adamant about joining and agreed to abide by the Conference's rules. Soon after their organizations were officially admitted, survivors became the majority on the Claims Conference's negotiating committee.[38] A decade later, however, Holocaust survivors formed a 'victims-only' international organization, the World Confederation of Holocaust Survivors Organizations, seeking a specific role in Holocaust commissions and class-action lawsuits on Nazi-era claims. 'Survivors must raise their voices on all kinds of international issues,' said Sanbar, a founding member of the confederation, as well as the leader of the Israeli survivors and, by then, a Conference official. 'We will do our utmost to cooperate with the Claims Conference and the World Jewish Restitution Organization, but we will be independent.'[39] Some survivors complained that their positions have been compromised by or outvoted in the Conference, and Israeli survivors resented their limited representation. 'It can't be democratic when 60 per cent of the people [survivors] are represented by only five per cent,' Noach Flug, an official of the Israeli survivors organization, said at the Knesset Finance Committee hearing. 'It might be undemocratic, but that doesn't damage the essence of the matter,' said the Romanian-born committee chairman, Avraham Poraz. 'It could be that they act fairly with everyone.'[40]

Except for the addition of the Israeli and American survivors' organizations, for decades the Conference membership remained a reflection of the post-war Western Jewish world. The member organizations – overwhelmingly from the US, Britain and France – were those that had been invited to the Waldorf meeting because of their relations and influence with the Occupation governments in Germany. By the century's end, the logic of that criterion had disintegrated. Most organizations had undergone upheavals in their roles, relevance and prestige; some were weakened versions of their former selves. As the

Conference evolved and the political climate changed, the exclusions also were jarring. When it was founded, the Conference was a diaspora entity that was expected to support Israel, not represent its interests. Decades later, and in light of survivors' grievances with the Israeli government, that meant a severe under-representation of Israelis' interests.[41] Nor were Eastern European Jewish communities directly represented. 'This is an organization that addresses the needs worldwide of Holocaust survivors, but we know it does not represent world Jewry, and in particular what is absent is representation at the table from Central and Eastern Europe, the former Soviet Union,' said Andrew Baker of the AJC. 'I think ten years after the fall of communism, there is something wrong that we do not have at our table representation from these communities.'[42] However, the Conference executives were unwilling to expel any veteran members or to substantially expand to accommodate new ones. In lieu of a major structural change, the Conference in 2000 provided a seat for 'pan-European representation,' as well as membership for 'four eminent Israeli personalities.'

Jewish organizations – some of whom were relentless antagonists – had coalesced in 1951 for a particular mission, putting aside their intense differences to present a united front against the German delegation in Wassenaar. 'The Conference would have found itself in a very difficult position if it could not have reached unanimity, because it was not a conference which could have reached decisions by majority votes,' Goldmann said at the conclusion of the Waldorf meeting. 'It was no parliament. It was not an elected body. There is no possibility to force Jewish organizations who disagree to accept a certain line. There was no binding power to the decisions of this conference, and therefore we had to work in order to reach unanimous agreements.'[43] Unanimity often is elusive, and the Conference has had to tread carefully when members' interests clashed. For instance, in 2000, Israel was among the states that broke diplomatic relations with Vienna after Haider joined the government. When Austria offered to negotiate on Nazi-era claims, the Jewish Agency, a Conference member, rejected the offer; it was determined not to confer legitimacy on the new Austrian government. Austrian survivors, however, wanted the talks to proceed. Caught in the middle, the Conference turned to the US government to mediate.

The Conference is an umbrella organization that cannot – and will not – control its members, who had their individual agendas, roles and strategies quite apart from their cooperation with the Conference. In 1952, when the Conference was forging its distinctive identity and negotiating for its collective claim, it confronted German suspicions about some of its members. These were indirectly addressed in Protocol

II's so-called 'purpose clause.' Protocol II did not simply commit West Germany to provide the Conference with funds; it stated a broad principle about how the funds would be used. The Germans 'know there are agencies in the Conference that attack Germany,' Leavitt reported after the Luxembourg Agreements had been signed. 'They do not want to be placed in a position of subsidizing such organizations for attacks on Germany, which is understandable. They certainly could not ask Parliament for an appropriation to an organization attacking them.'[44]

By the end of the century the German government had decades of experience with the Conference. It also had honed some of its attitudes about individual Conference members – sentiments that could ricochet in favour of or against the Conference's interests. For instance, Chancellor Helmut Kohl was wary of the World Jewish Congress, which he said had 'polemicized in an outrageous manner against German reunification, and thereby against Germany's right to self-determination.'[45] While the WJC disputed the accusation, Kohl's grudge cast a shadow. By contrast, the FRG enjoyed a warm relationship with the American Jewish Committee, which in 1998 became the first American Jewish organization to open a branch office in Germany.[46] However, the government was vexed when the AJC launched a public campaign in 1997 for compensation for Holocaust survivors in Eastern Europe. The campaign was antithetical to the conservative negotiating manner of the Conference and, the German government snapped, the Conference had agreed not to press additional demands until 1999.

The Conference is also a member of another umbrella organization: the World Jewish Restitution Organization, which it helped found in 1992 to recover Jewish properties confiscated during the Nazi and communist eras in Eastern Europe.[47] The WJRO, in turn, includes organizations that themselves also are members of the Conference. The styles and interests of these overlapping organizations are as likely to intersect as to collide; at times they appear to operate at cross purposes.

Although the Conference is apolitical, some of its member organizations and board members are highly politicized. And while it was not shy about exploiting board members' political muscle or moral authority when it suited, the Conference could not ensure they would reliably toe the official line.

For instance, Roman Kent, chairman of the American Gathering of Jewish Holocaust Survivors, was an unimpeachable moral voice in castigating Germany for failing to provide Holocaust survivors with the same level of health care as that given to German military veterans. 'I have heard German politicians and people from all walks of life express regret and shame for the brutal and inhuman acts committed by their forefathers,' Kent wrote in an opinion piece in a New York Jewish weekly newspaper. 'It seems to be a bit paradoxical to acknowledge guilt and shame, yet at the same time provide medical care for the perpetrators but not for the victims.'[48]

Kent's presence also lent symbolic heft to the signing ceremony in Berlin in 2000 of the hard-won agreement to provide compensation to former slave labourers. But a year later, Kent was agitated by some of the agreement's terms. At a public event to announce the distribution of these funds, he said, 'I am ashamed that I was participating in these negotiations.'[49]

The most visible member of the Claims Conference in recent years has been Israel Singer, who wore multiple hats that tended to blur the roles of the different organizations he served. He was an official of the World Jewish Congress and the World Jewish Restitution Organization, and became president of the Conference after Miller's death. Where Miller was modest, Singer was flamboyant. 'He was brilliant, fast-talking, a gifted speaker, magnetic. He could be witty and charming one moment and truculent the next, his engaging smile turning to a scowl,' Eizenstat wrote in his memoirs. 'He was an extraordinary negotiator, tough in pursuing his goals, possessing a sixth sense for when it was time to cut a deal.'[50]

Singer's independent streak, which irritated Eizenstat,[51] occasionally embarrassed the Conference. For instance, in an essay called 'Transparency, Truth, and Restitution,' Singer wrote, 'Survivors should not decide all questions about funds restored to the Jewish people from the Holocaust.'[52] There were, of course, many who agreed with him. But Singer's essay was a public relations nightmare for the Conference at a time of heightened awareness of survivors' poverty, anger and belief that they were still victims – not of persecution, but of condescension.[53]

In the essay, published in the second month of Singer's presidency, the new leader of the Conference proposed that decisions on the use of Holocaust funds 'should be entrusted to a new body that would include the Conference on Jewish Material Claims Against Germany, the World Jewish Restitution Organization, and the government of Israel, along with Holocaust survivors, Jewish educators, and innovative thinkers.' The proposal ignored many realities, most notably Holocaust survivors' stormy relationship with Israel, and the fact that the State of Israel had not formally participated in any restitution matter with the Conference after the Luxembourg Agreements.[54] The proposed plan also would undercut the legal authority and recognition the Claims Conference had attained over 50 years.

Although the Conference generally resisted lawsuits as a means to resolve claims and, although its focus was on claims against Germany and Austria, by 1997, it found itself actively involved in broader activities – in court settlements or commissions targeting European enterprises for Nazi-era damages either because of its membership in the WJRO or because it was the only Jewish agency experienced in handling claims. For instance, it figured prominently in the 2005 settlement in US federal court of the so-called 'Hungarian Gold Train' case, in which the US government agreed to pay up to $25.5 million. Of that, some $21 million was designated for social service projects for which the court asked the Conference to propose an allocations plan.[55]

More than a half-century after the Holocaust, the Conference's task had not finished. Its pursuit of property in Germany was dependent, in part, on the BARoV, the German agency handling property claims. Fifteen years after the enactment of a German law governing property restitution in the former East Germany, the BARoV reported that it still was processing more than 130,000 applications seeking properties seized during the Nazi era.[56] In its negotiations with Germany, the Conference broke extraordinary ground in May 2005, when it succeeded in obtaining compensation for survivors of labour camps in Tunisia, Morocco and Algeria. These North African nations had been Nazi battlegrounds, yet the victims had traditionally been overlooked, in part because the Holocaust was seen as a European phenomenon and because post-war Arab and Moslem governments did not advocate for Jewish victims. 'As long as there is one survivor alive, our work will continue,' Taylor said.[57]

In 1951, the Claims Conference assumed the daunting task of attempting to deal with the cultural and physical consequences of the greatest tragedy to befall the Jewish people. There were no precedents to guide it – neither in its negotiations with West Germany or in its decisions about how best to aid Nazi victims with the limited funds it received from Protocol II. Those who survived the atrocities of the Holocaust are not a monolithic group. They originated in various European nations, endured different fates during the Second World War, settled in numerous countries at different times after the war, and had varying needs, aspirations and degrees of success in rebuilding their lives.

Nor were they treated equitably in the German compensation and restitution measures. Compensation was not determined solely by the damage and duration of persecution the victims had suffered, but on their citizenship, legal status and residence before and after the Second World War. Some victims had the legal right to compensation, while others received 'humanitarian' payments; many others received nothing. Some survivors of similar fates received pensions, while others received one-time 'hardship' payments. For more than five decades, the Conference steadfastly pursued negotiations to improve the amount and scope of payments and to remedy deficiencies in the German programmes. Seen in the broad perspective, its efforts have been nothing short of remarkable. At the close of the twentieth century, there was a whirlwind of negotiations, lawsuits and conferences involving dozens of governments, lawyers, victims' advocates and organizations, historians and enterprises – all focused on Nazi-era claims. Collectively, their efforts generated about $7 billion. This is a considerable sum, and these payments are important to the victims. But they amount to only a small fraction of the funds generated by the Conference from the Luxembourg Agreements.

Protocol I of the agreements was a set of principles about West Germany's commitment to redress for victims. The principles were essential, but their true significance is found in the legislation that gave them meaning. This is where the endeavours of the Conference are especially notable. Some of its greatest achievements came long after American pressure, international attention and West Germany's need for integration into the West all bolstered the Jewish moral claims. The Conference recognized its disadvantages; in 1964, it was in the eighth year of a struggle to amend and expand the German compensation legislation. 'The weight of our weapons has weakened, and their firepower was considerably greater in 1952, when indemnification payments had not yet begun, than it is today,' Goldmann said.[58] The Conference did not surrender. It achieved the amendments the following year, in the 'final' German indemnification law. 'A good deal of the Conference's successes came in the years following the Luxembourg Agreements, without the help of Israel or any other government. The Conference's successes did not come at a time when the world was feeling guilty, but rather as a slow process, over the next 20 years,' Dean Silvers wrote in a 1980 legal analysis. 'Without the constant work, negotiation, collective bargaining and post-treaty work of the Claims Conference the successes would not have come even close to the standards now in existence.'[59] The Conference remained a thorn in Germany's side. 'The Germans had a problem in dealing with Goldmann – no "final" deal was ever final,' said German historian Constantin Goschler.[60]

The Conference also has undertaken distasteful tasks that have benefited victims, often at the expense of its relationship with those victims. Despite the finality of the 1965 German law, the Conference relentlessly demanded that West Germany provide compensation to additional victims. In 1980, West Germany agreed to the Hardship Fund – on condition that the Conference administer it. The Conference faced the quandary of rejecting the FRG's offer or of operating the fund and rejecting some victims' claims. 'I could not bear that on the stationery of the Conference on Jewish Material Claims Against Germany, we would have to tell thousands of survivors, the answer is no,' Kagan said.[61] Indeed, some would have applauded the Conference if it dismissed the

German plan as morally unacceptable and closed its doors. Nonetheless, the Conference agreed to operate the fund, which transformed it into an uncomfortable German partner. However unpleasant, it was the right choice. The fund ultimately made payments to more than a quarter of a million victims and kept the Conference alive to pursue claims against East Germany, with stunning results after the collapse of communism. 'We have succeeded – with obstacles, difficulties and crises along the way – to achieve something tangible,' said Kagan, the surviving member of the Jewish delegation in Wassenaar. But he noted, 'Any time a survivor complains that compensation is inadequate, they will never have an argument from me.'[62]

The agreement signed in Luxembourg was the first of some two dozen agreements the Conference reached that provided material aid to Jewish victims of Nazi persecution. By century's end, individual victims had received some DM 100 billion in payments from the German indemnification laws – a startling sum that was more than ten times the original estimates. Nonetheless, one could not look at this compensation 'as an abstract and absolute figure freed from the events that led to it and from all the misery it reflected,' Katzenstein said as his decades of service to survivors was ending. 'I did not say that it should not be quoted, as it was impressive indeed. But the quotation should not be made without at least trying to ascertain how much, or rather little, of it was held out as compensation to the individual persecutee and how adequate, or rather inadequate, this was when it came to the yardstick by which all the annihilation, extermination, destruction, humiliation and suffering had to be measured.'[63]

It was, in fact, the yardstick. The Conference delegation went to The Hague determined that 'whatever will come out of these negotiations is not going to be German philanthropy or charity or goodwill, but it will be in payment of legally established and legally anchored claims and demands,' Kagan recalled.[64] It succeeded. The Luxembourg Agreements represent a milestone both in Jewish history and in international law. They established the precedent by which individual victims of human rights abuses and atrocities are entitled to redress. 'This was the moment at which the modern notion of restitution for historical injustices was born. In the public's memory of gross historical injustices, the Holocaust is unique in the very debate about its uniqueness,' said Elazar Barkan, a professor of history. 'It has become a yardstick for the ultimate genocide against which victims of other historical crimes measure their own suffering. The German reparation that followed the war became the gauge for future restitution claims.'[65]

These agreements 'are not some historical relic, but – in ways we could never have imagined – are a living, breathing instrument,' Kagan said.[66] Many of the principles embodied in the Luxembourg Agreements have had influence far beyond Germany and German history. For instance, the legacy of the Luxembourg Agreements is enshrined in the Rome Statute of the International Criminal Court, which includes provisions for victims of human rights abuses.[67]

'The Luxembourg Agreements represent our efforts to achieve a measure of justice for Holocaust survivors. The principles embodied in them have aided hundreds of thousands of victims of Nazi persecution and have radiated far beyond Germany. What began as a revolutionary idea between a voluntary Jewish organization and the new state of West Germany has attained a transcendent and enduring significance.'[68]

NOTES

1   Claims Conference Delegation Statement, *Documents Relating to the Agreement Between the Government of Israel and the Government of the Federal Republic of Germany.*
2   Quoted in Balabkins, *West German Reparations to Israel,* p. 94.
3   Dean Silvers, 'The Future of International Law as Seen Through the Jewish Material Claims Conference Against Germany,' *Jewish Social Studies,* Vol. XLII, Nos. 3–4, Summer–Fall 1980, pp. 215–28.
4   Kagan, *Exchange.*
5   Protocol I, Item 15.
6   Claims Conference Planning Committee meeting, 15 March 2000.
7   Kagan interview, 4 January 2001.
8   Katzenstein letter to Ferencz, 6 June 1983.
9   Claims Conference Board meeting, 2–3 March 1963, New York.
10 Kagan interview, 10 December 1971, American Jewish Committee (William E. Wiener) Oral History Library, New York Public Library, Dorot Jewish Division.
11 1 November 2001, Symposium, 'Holocaust Restitution: Reconciling Moral Imperatives with Legal Initiatives and Diplomacy,' proceedings at *Fordham International Law Journal,* Vol. 25, 2001.
12 The US adopted the principle demanded by Jewish organizations. In his letter to the Allies of 20 September 1945, the Jewish Agency's Weizmann wrote: 'Property by crime rendered masterless should not be treated as *bona vacantia,* and fall to the governments which committed the crimes, or to any other governments or to strangers having no title to it. It is submitted that the provisions for heirless property falling to the state were not designed to cover the case of mass murder of a people. Such properties belong to the victim, and that victim is the Jewish people as a whole.'
13 The advisers on Jewish affairs to the US Military Government were instrumental in these efforts, especially in ensuring that the laws did not exclude victims in displaced persons camps, as well as in protecting the laws from corrosive amendments. Advisers William Haber and his successor, Harry Greenstein, were ardent advocates for Jewish claims and the role of the US. 'Every effort should be made to persuade the German authorities to pass a law that will adequately indemnify all who are not likely to be reimbursed from such reparations as Germany may eventually be required to pay, and will in other respects conform to American standards of equity,' Haber wrote to Acting Secretary of the Army William H. Draper in his final report, which was released 7 February 1949. 'In the event that such efforts do not meet with success, it would be far more prudent to veto the [General Claims] Law rather than to permit the Germans to cleanse their conscience with a law that is fundamentally unjust.' For more on the advisers, see Louis L. Kaplan and Theodor Schuchat, *Justice – Not Charity: A Biography of Harry Greenstein,* New York: Crown Publishers, 1967, and Abraham S. Hyman, *The Undefeated,* Jerusalem: Gefen Publishing House, 1993.
14 Anxiety about German intentions – though subsequently unfounded – had merit. Germany had a history of reneging on its reparations commitments. In addition, a post-war incident in

Westphalia had been unnerving: According to Elazar Barkan, the *Land* government, which had budgeted funds to compensate surviving relatives of the SS, tried to retroactively collect property taxes from the Jewish community for the years 1938 to 1945 for a synagogue that had been destroyed during *Kristallnacht*. Although Westphalia rescinded its demand for back taxes, 'there was nothing to indicate that state governments in Germany were going to recognize claims for Jewish compensation.' (*The Guilt of Nations: Restitution and Negotiating Historical Injustices*, New York: WW Norton & Company, 2000, pp. 3–4.)

15 Throughout its history, the Conference recalled the significance of the US government's original efforts on behalf of victims and the urgency of retaining that commitment. For instance, Blaustein, an industrialist with exceptional access in Washington, appealed to Secretary of State Dean Rusk on 2 June 1964, writing: 'It was in great measure due to the interest and help of our government, through President Truman and US High Commissioner John J. McCloy, that the original indemnification and restitution legislation was effected. And just as it is clear that the original programmes would not have been accomplished without the top level representations by our government, just so do we feel that now only top level representation by our government to [West German] Chancellor [Ludwig] Erhard will avoid a crisis and ensure a successful conclusion of a humanitarian effort which has brought so much goodwill to the German Federal Republic and some material compensation to the survivors of tragedy.'

16 Baker letter to Genscher, 5 September 1990; Doc. No. 1990STATE297622; Declassification No. 200202683.

17 Baker interview, 9 July 2002.

18 Treasury Department Office of Public Affairs, Press Release LS–634, 17 May 2000.

19 Of the individuals who recovered property in the US Occupation Zone and West Berlin, under the early restitution measures, 42 per cent were residents of the US, 18 per cent lived in Germany, 11 per cent in Britain, and 5.4 per cent in Israel. See In re Holocaust Victim Assets Litigation (Swiss banks settlement), CV 96-4849(ERK)(MDG), Special Master's Proposed Plan of Allocation and Distribution of Settlement Proceeds, 11 September 2000, Annex E (Holocaust Compensation), p. E-64.

20 Claims Conference Board meeting, 13 July 1999, New York; Miller interview, 24 July 2001.

21 An early clash had occurred shortly after the Second World War, when the Jewish Restitution Successor Organization, the antecedent of the Claims Conference, contended that some $6 million in unclaimed accounts in American banks may have belonged to Jews killed in the Holocaust. The US government paid $500,000 in 1963 to settle the JRSO's claims for the accounts; under that settlement, the funds were to be used for the rehabilitation of Nazi victims in the US (*Jerusalem Post*, 2 April 1997).

22 Israel Miller, Claims Conference Executive Committee meeting, 22 November 1999, New York. Israel received three Dolphin-class submarines from Germany; two of the submarines, which cost about $150 million each, were financed by the Germans (*Jerusalem Post*, 25 October 2000).

23 Letter from Finance Minister Avraham Shochat to Israel Miller, 8 June 1993.

24 The tumult over Israel's role was illustrated by the failure of a 1997 agreement between the Italian insurer Assicurazioni Generali and Knesset members to resolve claims of Holocaust survivors and victims' heirs. MKs Rabbi Avraham Ravitz, Avraham Hirschson and Michael Kleiner signed the agreement, which created a $12 million fund based in Israel. The so-called Generali Fund, although brokered by Israeli officials, did not impede the American class-action lawsuits against the insurer. Kleiner subsequently emerged as one of the Conference's most vociferous critics.

25 At the height of the international commotion over dormant Jewish Holocaust-era accounts in Swiss banks, the Israeli ambassador to Switzerland, Gabriel Padon, had urged the government to become involved in the dispute. When he asked Foreign Minister Shimon Peres what position to adopt, he was told not to intervene. 'I was just to observe and report,' Padon said in an interview when he retired (*Jerusalem Post*, 14 August 1998, 22 September 1999).

26 25 January 2001. However, in August 1998, weeks after the $1.25 billion settlement in US federal court of claims against Swiss banks, Israeli Prime Minister Binyamin Netanyahu announced the creation of an interministerial committee to deal with the restitution of Jewish property. Although Israel was not a party in the litigation against the Swiss banks, the Prime Minister gave his support to Israeli legislation that presumed to oversee allocations from the settlement. However, the Israeli Foreign Ministry had declined in 1997 to act as a 'guarantor' of any agreement when the Swiss banks raised the prospect, saying: 'This is absolutely not a

bilateral issue. It is an issue for the entire Jewish people' (*Jerusalem Post*, 15 December 1997).

27 15th Knesset, Third Session, Finance Committee Meeting 276, 2 May 2001.

28 *Jerusalem Post*, 9 November 2001. The bank accounts were first brought to light by Israeli historian Yossi Katz in his book *Forgotten Assets* (1997, Hebrew); the restitution of those accounts had not been concluded by 2005.

29 15th Knesset, Third Session, Finance Committee Meeting 276, 2 May 2001.

30 Kagan interview, Hebrew University Institute of Contemporary Jewry, Oral History Division, 24 March 1971. Holocaust survivors were among the members of the organizations represented on the Claims Conference, and among those at the founding meeting in 1951 were organizations from communities that had been victimized by the Nazis, including German and French Jews.

31 Immediately after the war, many survivors organized in the displaced persons camps; those organizations generally represented victims' interests as DPs seeking relief and resettlement assistance. The most prominent group was at Bergen-Belsen, under the leadership of Josef Rosensaft. For later developments, see *New York Times*, 15–16 June 1981 about the first 'World Gathering of Holocaust Survivors' in Jerusalem.

32 Sanbar interview, 26 March 2001.

33 The two organizations declined to join forces and insisted on separate memberships.

34 Claims Conference Board meeting, 14 July 1988, Tarrytown, NY.

35 Ibid.

36 Ibid.

37 Ibid.

38 Sanbar interview, 26 March 2001. Two member organizations voted against the admission of the survivors' organizations: Agudath Yisrael and the Central British Fund for World Jewish Relief.

39 *Jerusalem Post*, 17 October 1999.

40 15th Knesset, Third Session, Finance Committee Meeting 276, 2 May 2001.

41 The question of Israeli interests was especially ticklish. The Conference, which allocated substantial funds to Israeli social service and educational institutions, sought Israel's support but also resisted Israeli government interference. The Israeli organization on the Conference's board was the Jewish Agency. Before 1948, the Jewish Agency, representing the Jews in Mandatory Palestine, had a quasi-governmental structure and its leaders subsequently became Israeli government officials. While the agency continued to exist after the establishment of Israel, most of its traditional functions were assumed by the state. And although the agency had had an important role in the rescue and resettlement of European Jews in Palestine, it had no specific mission on behalf of Holocaust survivors after the establishment of the state.

42 Claims Conference Board meeting, 14 July 1999, New York.

43 Claims Conference founding meeting, 25–26 October 1951, CAHJP 16600.

44 Minutes, Claims Conference Policy Committee meeting, 24 September 1952, CAHJP 16723.

45 Wall Street Journal, 31 March 1992.

46 The German government considered the event significant enough for German Foreign Minister Klaus Kinkel to speak at the opening.

47 The WIRO had no significant restitution successes to its credit in its first decade.

48 *Forward*, 6 May 2005.

49 *New York Times*, 20 June 2001.

50 Stuart E. Eizenstat, *Imperfect Justice: Looted Assets, Slave Labour and the Unfinished Business of World War II*, New York: PublicAffairs, 2003, pp. 53–44.

51 Eizenstat, page 131.

52 The article in the June 2002 issue of *Sh'ma: A Journal of Jewish Responsibility* identified Singer as 'chairman of the World Jewish Congress, and chairman of several restitution organizations, including the World Jewish Restitution Organization and Conference on Jewish Material Claims Against Germany'.

53 Survivors complained that they were not adequately represented in the Conference or commissions and international forums on Nazi-era assets, and that the restitution campaigns oen robbed them of their dignity by presenting an image of survivors as helpless and incapacitated a half-century afier the Holocaust (*Jerusalem Post*, 20 September 1998).

54 Although the Conference's Protocol II funds from West Germany were paid via Israel, that was an accounting procedure and did not reflect a partnership between the Conference and the state.

55 The class-action lawsuit, *Rosner* v. *United States*, was filed in May 2001 in US District Court for the Southern District of Florida. Hungarian Jewish Nazi victims sued the US government, alleging that the US military mishandled plundered Jewish properties when the 'Hungarian Gold Train' came into US custody in Austria at the end of the Second World War. The train was said to have included some 24 freight cars of properties that had been confiscated by the Nazis and their Hungarian collabourators from Hungarian Jews. The US has denied legal liability in its handling of the contents of the train.

56 Deutsche Presse-Agentur (DPA), 14 March 2005.

57 Taylor interview, 19 October 2001.

58 Goldmann to Claims Conference Board, 7 March 1964, Brussels.

59 Silvers, 'The Future of International Law as Seen Through the Jewish Material Claims Conference Against Germany.'

60 Interview, 3 July 2002, Berlin.

61 Interview, 26 December 2000.

62 Interview, 15 October 2001.

63 Katzenstein letter to Ferencz, 6 June 1983.

64 Kagan interview, 10 December 1971, American Jewish Committee (William E. Wiener) Oral History Library, New York Public Library, Dorot Jewish Division.

65 Elazar Barkan, 'Restitution and Amending Historical Injustices in International Morality,' Claremont: European Union Center of California, November 2000. See also Barkan's essay, 'Between Restitution and International Morality,' *Fordham International Law Journal*, Vol. 25, 2001.

66 Speech, November 21, 2002, German Historical Institute, 'Commissioning History in the United States, Germany and Austria: Historical Commissions, Victims, and the Second World War Restitution,' New Orleans.

67 Article 75 states that the court 'shall establish principles relating to reparations to, or in respect of, victims, including restitution, compensation and rehabilitation.'

68 Speech, November 21, 2002, German Historical Institute.

Appendix I

Protocol No. I
Drawn Up by the Representatives of the Government of the Federal Republic of Germany and of The Conference on Jewish Material Claims Against Germany

Representatives of the Government of the Federal Republic of Germany and of the Conference on Jewish Material Claims Against Germany have met in The Hague to discuss the extension of the legislation existing in the Federal Republic of Germany for the redress of National-Socialist wrongs and have agreed on a number of principles for the improvement of the existing legislation as well as on other measures.

The Government of the Federal Republic declare that they will take as soon as possible all steps within their constitutional competence to ensure the carrying out of the following programme:

I. Compensation

1. The Government of the Federal Republic of Germany is resolved to supplement and amend the existing compensation legislation by a Federal Supplementing and Coordinating Law (*Bundesgänzungs-und Rahmengesetz*) so as to ensure that the legal position of the persecutes throughout the Federal territory be no less favourable than under the General Claims Law now in force in the US Zone. Insofar as legislation now in force in the *Länder* contains more favourable regulations these will be maintained.

The provisions contained hereinafter shall apply throughout the whole territory of the Federal Republic.

2. Jurisdictional gaps resulting from the residence and date-line requirements of the compensation laws of the various *Länder* will be

eliminated. A change of residence from one *Land* to another shall not deprive anyone of compensation.

3. Where residence and date-line requirements are applicable under compensation legislation, compensation payments for deprivation of liberty shall be granted to persons who emigrated before the date-line and had their last German domicile or residence within the Federal territory.

4. Persecutees who were subjected to compulsory labour and lived under conditions similar to incarceration shall be treated as if they had been deprived of liberty by reason of persecution.

5. A persecutee who within the boundaries of the German Reich as of December 31, 1937, lived "underground" under conditions similar to incarceration or unworthy of human beings shall be treated as if he had been deprived of liberty by reason of persecution, in the meaning of that term under compensation legislation.

6. Where a persecutee died after May 8, 1945, his near heirs (children, spouse or parents) shall be entitled to assert his claim for compensation for deprivation of liberty, if this appears equitable by reason of the connection between the persecutee's death and persecution or of the indigence of the claimant. This provision shall not apply if the deceased was at fault in failing to file his claim in time.

7. Where the computation of annuities payable to persecutees is or will be based on the amounts of pensions payable to comparable categories of officials, all past and future changes in the pensions payable to comparable categories of officials will also be applied, as from the effective date of the future Federal Supplementing and Co-ordinating Law, to the annuities payable to persecutees. If at that time the persecutee has received no such annuities, such changes shall be effective as of April 1, 1952.

8. The Future Federal Supplementing and Co-ordinating Law in supplementing the present legislation will grant to members of the free professions, including self-employed persons in trade and industry, agriculture, and forestry, the choice between a capital payment and annuities as compensation for loss of opportunities to earn a livelihood (*Existenzschäden*). The capital payment shall be granted up to a ceiling of DM 25,000 in each case as compensation for the damage suffered before the former vocation was fully resumed. Instead of the capital payment the persecutee may elect an appropriate annuity corresponding to his former living standards. The annuity shall, however, not exceed DM 500 per month. The persecutee shall be entitled to such choice only if at the time the choice is made, he is unable to or cannot be reasonably expected to

fully resume his former vocation. The choice shall be final. If the beneficiary elects annuities, payments will be computed as from the day one year prior to the date of election.

9. The Government of the Federal Republic of Germany will provide compensation to persons who suffered losses as officials or employees of Jewish communities or public institutions within the boundaries of the German Reich as of December 31, 1937.

Insofar as these persons have a claim against public authorities for compensation under existing or future compensation legislation, they will receive temporary relief pending the beginning of these compensation payments. If the persons involved do not have such claims, their maintenance will be secured by monthly payments based on their former salaries.

10. The future Federal Supplementing and Co-ordinating Law shall, in providing compensation for damage to economic prospects, include in an appropriate manner provisions for compensation for damage to vocational and professional training.

11. Persecutees who have their domicile or permanent residence abroad shall be compensated for deprivation of benefits accruing to victims of the First World War if they were deprived of such benefits by the National-Socialist régime of terror because of their political convictions, race, faith or ideology.

12. Persons who were persecuted because of their political convictions, race, faith or ideology and who settled in the Federal Republic or emigrated abroad from expulsion areas within the meaning of that term in the Equalization of Burdens Law shall receive compensation for deprivation of liberty and damage to health and limb, in accordance with the provisions of the General Claims Law of the US Zone. This applies only if they settled in the Federal Republic or emigrated abroad before the general expulsion measure taken against German nationals and ethnic Germans in connection with the events of the Second World War. Survivors of such persecutees shall receive annuities if all other conditions prescribed in the General Claims Law of the US Zone for the grant of survivors' annuities are fulfilled.

Such persecutees shall receive compensation for special levies, including the Reich Flight Tax, which were imposed upon them as a result of acts of terror of the National-Socialist régime, either by law or arbitrarily. Such special levies shall be taken into account up to a ceiling of RM 150,000 in each individual case. The claim shall be converted at the rate of DM 6.5 for RM 100, in the same way as savings accounts of expellees from the East are being converted.

For damage to economic prospects compensation shall be paid

insofar as such damage made it impossible for the persecutee to provide for old age maintenance, wholly or in part, out of his own resources. In such case the damage will be determined, taken into account also up to a ceiling of RM 150,000 in each case converted at the rate of DM 6.5 for RM 100.

If the claimant is aged or permanently incapable of earning a livelihood because of illness or physical disability and the compensation paid to him for personal damages and for special levies, together with his own property and his other income, is insufficient to provide for his livelihood he may elect, instead of a capital payment for damage to his economic prospects, a requisite annuity.

Compensation in accordance with paragraph 1 shall also be paid to persecutees who emigrated abroad or settled in the Federal Republic during or after the time the general expulsions took place.

13. The residence and date-line requirements of the General Claims Law of the US Zone shall not be applied to persecutees who suffered damage under the National-Socialist régime of terror and who, as political refugees from the Soviet Zone of occupation, moved into the Federal Republic and legally established their permanent residence there (so-called "double persecutees").

14. Persons who were persecuted for their political convictions, race, faith or ideology during the National-Socialist régime of terror and who are at present stateless or political refugees and who were deprived of liberty by National-Socialist terror acts shall receive appropriate compensation for deprivation of liberty and damage to health and limb, in accordance with the basic principles of the General Claims Law of the US Zone and in line with (*in Anlehnung an*) the compensation payments established therein, i.e., as a rule, not less than 3/4 of those rates. This does not apply, however, if the persecutee's needs are or were provided for by a State or an international organization on a permanent basis or by way of a capital payment because of the damage suffered from persecution. Persecutees who acquired a new nationality after the end of persecution shall be assimilated to stateless persons and political refugees.

Survivors of such persecutees shall receive corresponding annuities if all other conditions established in the General Claims Law of the US Zone for the grant of survivors' annuities are fulfilled.

If the compensation granted to the claimant, together with his own property and other income, is insufficient to provide for his livelihood he shall, in recognition of the persecution, be granted a corresponding equalization payment out of the Hardship Fund referred to elsewhere which is to be established by the Government of the Federal Republic of Germany.

The provisions contained herein shall not be applicable insofar as a persecutee is covered by the provisions of 12 above.

15. The Government of the Federal Republic of Germany will endeavour to carry out the whole compensation programme as soon as possible but not later than within ten years. They will see to it that the necessary funds shall be made available, as from the financial year 1953–54. The funds to be made available for any specific financial year shall be fixed in accordance with the Federal Republic's capacity to pay.

16. The Federal Supplementing and Co-ordinating Law shall, in recognition of general social principles, provide that claims of persons entitled to compensation who are over 60 years of age, or who are needy, or whose earning ability has been considerably impaired because of illness or physical disability shall be accorded priority over all other claims, both in adjudication and payment. Full compensation for deprivation of liberty and for damage to life and limb shall in these cases be payable at once. Property damage and loss of opportunities to earn a livelihood insofar as they are compensated by capital payment shall be payable at once up to an amount of DM 5,000 in each case. Insofar as payments are granted to such beneficiaries by way of annuities full payment shall begin at once.

17. The Government of the Federal Republic of Germany will see to it that, taking into account the principles contained in 15 above, funds shall be provided in such amounts, during the first financial years, that not only the claims referred to in 16 above can be satisfied, but, in addition, claims of other beneficiaries can also be appropriately dealt with.

18. No distinction shall be made concerning the treatment of claimants living outside of the territory of the Federal Republic, insofar as compensation is concerned.

19. Where evidence is required equitable consideration shall be given to the probative difficulties resulting from persecution. This shall apply particularly to the loss or destruction of files and documents, and to the death or disappearance of witnesses. The compensation authorities shall *ex officio* make the investigations necessary to establish the relevant facts and seek appropriate evidence. The special conditions affecting the persecutees shall be taken into due consideration in interpreting the terms "domicile" (*'rechtmässiger Wohnsitz'*) or "residence" (*'gewöhnlicher Aufenthalt'*).

20. A principle corresponding to the legal presumption of death contained in the restitution laws of the US and British Zones shall be inserted in the Federal Supplementing and Co-ordinating Law. This

presumption of death shall also be applied in the procedure before the Probate Courts dealing with the issuance of a certificate of inheritance (*Erbschein*), provided that the validity of the certificate of inheritance be restricted to the compensation procedure.

II. <u>Restitution</u>

1. The legislation now in force n the territory of the Federal Republic of Germany concerning restitution of identifiable property to victims of National-Socialist persecution shall remain in force without any restrictions, unless otherwise provided in Chapter Three of the "Convention on the Settlement of Matters Arising out of the War and the Occupation".

2. The Federal Government will see to it that the Federal Republic of Germany accepts liability also for the confiscation of household effects in transit (*Umzugsgut*) which were seized by the German Reich in European ports outside of the Federal Republic, insofar as the household effects belonged to persecutees who emigrated from the territory of the Federal Republic.

3. The Government of the Federal Republic of Germany will see to it that payments shall be ensured to restitutees – private persons and successor organizations appointed pursuant to law – of all judgments or awards which have been or hereafter shall be given or made against the former German Reich under restitution legislation. The same shall apply to amicable settlements. Judgments or awards based on indebtedness in the *Reich Marks* of the former Reich for a sum of money (*Geldsummenansprüche*) shall be converted into *Deutsche Marks* at the rate of ten *Reich Marks* for one *Deutsche Mark*. Judgments or awards for compensation for damage (*Schadenersatz*) shall be made in DM and assessed in accordance with the general principles of German law applicable to the assessment of compensation for damage.

In accordance with Article 4, paragraph 3 of Chapter Three of the "Convention on the Settlement of Matters Arising out of the War and the Occupation", the obligation of the Federal Republic of Germany shall be considered to have been satisfied when the judgments and awards shall have been paid or when the Federal Republic of Germany shall have paid a total of DM 1,500 million. Payments on the basis of amicable settlements shall be included in this sum. The time and method of payment of such judgments and awards shall be determined in accordance with the Federal Republic's capacity to pay. The Government of the Federal Republic of Germany will, however, endeavour to complete these payments within a period of ten years. In settling the liabilities of the German Reich the claimants in the French Zone shall not be treated less favourably than those in other parts of the Federal territory.

4. Monetary restitution claims against the German Reich up to an amount of DM 5,000 in each case, as well as claims of beneficiaries who are over 60 years of age, or are needy or whose earning ability has been considerably impaired because of illness or physical disability shall be accorded priority over all other monetary restitution claims against the German Reich, both in adjudication and payment.

5. The Government of the Federal Republic of Germany shall continue to grant exemption from taxation to charitable successor organizations and trust corporations appointed pursuant to restitution legislation.

6. In equalizing the burdens arising from the war ('*Lastenausgleich*') the position of persons entitled to restitution is given special consideration as concerns the tax on property. Reference is made to the particulars contained in the provisions of the Law on the Equalization of Burdens of August 14, 1952 (BGB1. I. S. 446).

7. It is the intention of the Government of the Federal Republic of Germany in implementing the principle of law contained in Article 359, paragraph 2 of the Law on the Equalization of Burdens to bring about the following:

a) Compensation in accordance with the principles of the Equalization of Burdens Law shall be provided for damage to and losses of such material assets as are described in Section 12, paragraph 1, sub-paragraphs 1 and 2 thereof, if the persecutee suffered these losses as a result of confiscation as defined in the restitution legislation, and in the expulsion areas within the meaning of that term in the Equalization of Burdens Law. This applies, however, only if the losses occurred before the general expulsions took place and if it may be assumed that the persecutee would have been subjected to the expulsion measures taken against German nationals and ethnic Germans in connection with the events of the Second World War.

b) In implementing the principle of law referred to above, the provision of the Equalization of Burdens Law requiring that the persecutee had his permanent residence in the Federal Republic or in West Berlin on December 31, 1950, shall not apply.

c) The indemnification of persecutees from expulsion areas whose permanent residence is outside the boundaries of the former German Reich will be taken over only in part. This part shall be determined by taking into account the distribution of expellees between the Federal Republic and the Soviet Zone of occupation.

d) In cases where household effects in transit belonging to such persecutees were confiscated in European ports outside of the Federal Republic these confiscations shall be treated as confiscations within the meaning of paragraph a) above.

IN WITNESS WHEREOF the Chancellor and Minister for Foreign Affairs of the Federal Republic of Germany, of the one part, and the representative of the Conference on Jewish Material Claims Against Germany, duly authorized thereto, of the other part, have signed this Protocol.

Done at Luxembourg this tenth day of September 1952, in the English and German languages, each in two copies, the texts in both languages being equally authentic.

For the Government of the
Federal Republic of Germany

For the Conference on Jewish
Material Claims Against Germany

(Konrad Adenauer's signature)

(Nahum Goldmann's signature)

Appendix II

Protocol No. II
Drawn Up By Representatives of the Government of the Federal Republic of Germany and of The Conference on Jewish Material Claims Against Germany Consisting of the Following Organizations:

Agudath Israel World Organization
Alliance Israélite Universelle
American Jewish Committee
American Jewish Congress
American Jewish Joint Distribution Committee
American Zionist Council
Anglo-Jewish Association
B'nai B'rith
Board of Deputies of British Jews
British Section, World Jewish Congress
Canadian Jewish Congress
Central British Fund
Conseil Représentatif des Juifs de France
Council for the Protection of the Rights and Interests of Jews from Germany
Delegacion de Asociaciones Israelitas Argentinas (DAIA)
Executive Council of Australian Jewry
Jewish Agency for Palestine
Jewish Labour Committee
Jewish War Veterans of the US
South African Jewish Board of Deputies

Synagogue Council of America
World Jewish Congress
Zentralrat der Juden in Deutschland

The Government of the Federal Republic of Germany, of the one part, and the Conference on Jewish Material Claims Against Germany, of the other part,
WHEREAS
The National-Socialist régime of terror confiscated vast amounts of property and other assets from Jews in Germany and in the territories formerly under German rule;
AND WHEREAS
Part of the material losses suffered by the persecutees of National-Socialism is being made good by means of internal German legislation in the fields of restitution and indemnification and whereas an extension of this internal German legislation, in particular in the field of indemnification, is intended;
AND WHEREAS
Considerable values, such as those spoliated in the occupied territories, cannot be returned, and that indemnification for many economic losses which have been suffered cannot be made because, as a result of the policy of extermination pursued by National-Socialism, claimants are no longer in existence;
AND WHEREAS
A considerable number of Jewish persecutees of National-Socialism are needy as a result of their persecution;
AND HAVING REGARD
To the statement made by the Federal Chancellor, Dr Konrad Adenauer in the Bundestag on September 27, 1951, and unanimously approved by that body;
AND HAVING REGARD
To the Agreement this day concluded between the State of Israel and the Federal Republic of Germany;
AND HAVING REGARD
To the fact that duly authorized representatives of the Government of the Federal Republic of Germany and of the Conference on Jewish Material Claims Against Germany have met at The Hague;
Have therefore this day concluded the following Agreement:

ARTICLE 1
In view of the considerations hereinbefore recited the Government of the Federal Republic of Germany hereby undertakes the obligation towards the Conference on Jewish Material Claims Against Germany to

enter, in the Agreement with the State of Israel, into a contractual undertaking to pay the sum of DM450 million to the State of Israel for the benefit of the Conference on Jewish Material Claims Against Germany.

ARTICLE 2

The Federal Republic of Germany will discharge their obligation undertaken for the benefit of the Conference on Jewish Material Claims Against Germany, in the Agreement between the Federal Republic of Germany and the State of Israel, by payment made to the State of Israel in accordance with Article 3, paragraph (c) of the said Agreement. The amounts so paid and transmitted by the State of Israel to the Conference on Jewish Material Claims Against Germany will be used for the relief, rehabilitation and resettlement of Jewish victim of National-Socialist persecution, according to the urgency of their needs as determined by the Conference on Jewish Material Claims Against Germany. Such amounts will, in principle, be used for the benefit of victims who at the time of conclusion of the present Agreement were living outside of Israel.

Once a year the Conference on Jewish Material Claims Against Germany will inform the Government of the Federal Republic of Germany of the amounts transmitted by Israel, of the amounts expended as well as of the manner in which such expenditure has been incurred. If, for any adequate reasons, the Conference on Jewish Material Claims Against Germany has not spent the moneys it has received, it shall inform the Government of the Federal Republic of Germany of the said reason or reasons.

The information herein referred to shall be supplied within one year from the end of the calendar year in which the relevant amount had to be transmitted to the Conference in pursuance of Article 3, paragraph (c) of the Agreement between the State of Israel and the Federal Republic of Germany.

The Conference on Jewish Material Claims Against Germany undertakes to spend, not later than three months before the penultimate installment payable to Israel falls due, all moneys referred to in Article 3, paragraph (c) of the Agreement between the State of Israel and the Federal Republic of Germany and which have been received seven months prior to the date on which the said penultimate installment becomes due as aforesaid, and to inform the Government of the Federal Republic of Germany accordingly.

ARTICLE 3

The Conference on Jewish Material Claims Against Germany shall be entitled, after prior notification to the Government of the Federal

Republic of Germany, to assign its rights and obligations derived from the provisions of this Protocol and of the Agreement between the Federal Republic of Germany and the State of Israel to one or several Jewish organizations which are qualified to assume such rights and obligations.

ARTICLE 4

Disputes arising out of the interpretation and the application of Articles 2 and 3 of this Protocol shall be decided, in accordance with the provisions of Article 15 of the Agreement between the State of Israel and the Federal Republic of Germany, by the Arbitral Commission established by virtue of Article 14 of said Agreement.

IN WITNESS WHEREOF the Chancellor and Minister for Foreign Affairs of the Federal Republic of Germany, of the one part, and the representative of the Conference on Jewish Material Claims Against Germany, duly authorized thereto, of the other part, have signed this Protocol.

Done at Luxembourg this tenth day of September 1952, in the English and German languages, each in two copies in both language being equally authentic.

For the Government of the   For the Conference on Jewish Material
Federal Republic of Germany   Claims Against Germany

(Konrad Adenauer's signature) (Nahum Goldmann's signature)

References

Adler, Libby and Peer Zumbansen, 'The Forgetfulness of Noblesse: A Critique of the German Foundation Law Compensating Slave and Forced Labourers of the Third Reich,' *Harvard Journal on Legislation*, Vol. 39, No. 1, Winter, 2002.

Balabkins, Nicholas, *West German Reparations to Israel*, New Brunswick, New Jersey: Rutgers University Press, 1971.

Elazar, Barkan, 'Between Restitution and International Morality,' *Fordham International Law Journal*, Vol. 25, 2001.

— *The Guilt of Nations: Restitution and Negotiating Historical Injustices*, New York: WW Norton & Company, 2000.

— 'Restitution and Amending Historical Injustices in International Morality,' Claremont, California: European Union Center of California, November 2000.

Claims Conference, *Activities of the Claims Conference 1952–1957*.

— *Annual Reports*.

— *Report for the period October 1, 1975 to September 30, 1978*.

— *Twenty Years Later: Activities of the Conference on Jewish Material Claims Against Germany, 1952–1972*.

Claims Conference Planning Committee, *A Plan for Allocating Successor Organization Resources*, 28 June 2000.

Clay, Lucius D., *Decision in Germany*, Garden City, New York: Doubleday, 1950.

Deutschkron, Inge, *Bonn and Jerusalem: The Strange Coalition*, Philadelphia, Pennsylvania: Chilton Book Company, 1970.

Eizenstat, Stuart E., *Imperfect Justice: Looted Assets, Slave Labour and the Unfinished Business of World War II*, New York: PublicAffairs, 2003.

Ferencz, Benjamin B., *Less Than Slaves: Jewish Forced Labour and the Quest for Compensation*, Cambridge, MA: Harvard University Press, 1979; reissued by Indiana University Press, 2002.

— 'Restitution to Nazi Victims – A Milestone in International Morality,' in Harry Schneiderman, ed., *Two Generations in Perspective*, New York: Monde Publishers, 1957.

— 'West Germany: Supreme Court Bars Claims of Forced Labourers', *American Journal of Comparative Law*, Vol. 15, No. 3, 1967.

'Fifty Years in the Making: the Second World War Reparation and Restitution Claims,' *Berkeley Journal of International Law*, Vol. 20, No. 1, 2002.

'Focus On ... German Restitution for National Socialist Crimes,' New York: German Information Center, January 1997.

Geller, Jay Howard, *Jews in Post–Holocaust Germany, 1945–1953*, New York: Cambridge University Press, 2004.

Goldmann, Nahum, *The Autobiography of Nahum Goldmann: Sixty Years of Jewish Life*, New York: Holt, Rinehart and Winston, 1969.

— *The Jewish Paradox*, New York: Fred Jordan Books/Grosset & Dunlap, 1978.

Goschler, Constantin, 'German Compensation to Jewish Nazi Victims after 1945,' in Jeffry M. Diefendorf (ed.), *Lessons and Legacies VI: New Currents in Holocaust Research*, Evanston, Illinois: Northwestern University Press, 2004.

Henry, Marilyn, 'Fifty Years of Holocaust Compensation,' *American Jewish Year Book*, 2002.

Herf, Jeffrey, *Divided Memory: The Nazi Past in the Two Germanys*, Cambridge, MA: Harvard University Press, 1999.

Kagan, Saul, 'The Claims Conference and the Communities,' *Exchange*, Vol. 22, 1965.

— 'Morality and Pragmatism: A Participant's Response,' Symposium on Shilumim in the 1950s, 15 March 1991, Deutsches Haus of Columbia University, New York.

Kapralik, Charles I., *Reclaiming the Nazi Loot: The History of the Work of the Jewish Trust Corporation for Germany*, London: The Corporation, 1962–1971.

Kogon, Eugen, *The Theory and Practice of Hell: The German Concentration Camps and the System Behind Them*, New York: Berkley Publishing Group, 1980.

McAdams, A. James, *Judging the Past in Unified Germany*, New York: Cambridge University Press, 2001.

Miller, Rabbi Israel, 'The Conference on Jewish Material Claims

Against Germany,' *Cardozo Law Review*, Vol. 20, No. 2, December 1998.

Moeller, Robert G., *War Stories: The Search for a Usable Past in the Federal Republic of Germany*, Berkeley, California: University of California Press, 1999.

Presidential Advisory Commission on Holocaust Assets, *Plunder and Restitution: Findings and Recommendations of the Presidential Advisory Commission on Holocaust Assets in the United States*, Washington: US Government Printing Office, December 2000.

Pross, Christian, *Paying for the Past: The Struggle Over Reparations for Surviving Victims of the Nazi Terror*, Baltimore, MD: Johns Hopkins University Press, 1998.

Robinson, Nehemiah, *Indemnification and Reparations: Jewish Aspects*, New York: Institute of Jewish Affairs, 1944.

— 'Ten Years of German Indemnification,' New York: Conference on Jewish Material Claims Against Germany, 1964.

Rosensaft, Menachem Z., and Joana D. Rosensaft, 'The Early History of German–Jewish Reparations,' *Fordham International Law Journal*, Vol. 25, 2001.

Sagi, Nana, *German Reparations: A History of the Negotiations*, Jerusalem: Hebrew University, 1980.

Schwartz, Thomas Alan, *America's Germany: John J. McCloy and the Federal Republic of Germany*, Cambridge, MA: Harvard University Press, 1991.

Silvers, Dean, 'The Future of International Law as Seen Through the Jewish Material Claims Conference Against Germany,' *Jewish Social Studies*, Vol. XLII, Nos. 3–4, Summer–Fall 1980, pp. 215–28.

Simpson, Christopher, *The Splendid Blonde Beast: Money, Law, and Genocide in the Twentieth Century*, New York: Grove Press, 1993.

State of Israel, Ministry for Foreign Affairs, *Documents Relating to the Agreement Between the Government of Israel and the Government of the Federal Republic of Germany*.

Shirer, William L., *The Nightmare Years, 1930–1940*, Boston, MA: Little Brown and Company, 1984.

Ukeles Associates, 'An Estimate of the Current Distribution of Victims of Nazi Persecution,' in Claims Conference Planning Committee, *A Plan for Allocating Successor Organization Resources*, 28 June 2000.

Zweig, Ronald W., *German Reparations and the Jewish World: A History of the Claims Conference*, 2nd edn, London: Frank Cass, 2001.

— 'Restitution and the Problem of Jewish Displaced Persons in Anglo-American Relations, 1944–1948,' *American Jewish History*, Vol. LXXVIII, No. 1, 1988, pp. 54–78.

Index

Meed, Vladka, xv
Meissner-Blau, Freda, 165
membership of Claims Conference, 7, 9, *24n31*, 222–4
Memorial Foundation for Jewish Culture, 14–15, 109, 192–3
Mendor, Sallai, 203
Messerschmitt, 130
Miller, Rabbi Israel, 20, 215, 219, 222, 223; Article II Fund, 19, 89, 94; Austria, 164, 165, 170, 172; Central and European Fund, 98, 99; GDR, 74, 79–80, 81, 82, 83–4, 85; heirless assets, 142; institutional allocations, 195, 197, 198, 199, 200, 202, 203, 204; property in former GDR, 114, 115, 119; reunification, 76–7, 78; slave labour, 132, 144
Modrow, Hans, 75, 84
Moldova, 70
Mommsen, Hans, 133
Moreshet, 204
Moses, Siegfried, 6
Muzicant, Ariel, 170

Nachmann, Werner, 67–8
Nachtwei, Winfried, 97
National Fund (1995) (Austria), 15, 167–8
'Nazi gold' conference, 168–9
needs analysis, 200–2
negotiating, principle of, 10, 217
Netherlands, 31, *54n18*, 185–6
Neuborne, Burt, 125, 134
New York Times, 11, 80, 156
Nuremberg trials, 125, 126, 127, 128, 131

objectives of Claims Conference, 17, 20–1, 63–4
Occupation-era laws, 4, 8, 10; indemnification laws, 32–3, 38, 42, *55n27*, *55n28*, 217–18; restitution laws, 50–1, 108, 217
Organization Todt, 130
Ostrin, Asher, 200

pensions (Article II Fund), 90, 100, 101
pensions (BEG), 29, 49; cost of living

adjustment, 33; Israel, 32, 40; paid, 30, 50, 53, 88
pensions (Central and Eastern Europe Fund), 100, 101
pensions (social insurance): Austria, 153, 161, 165–6, 174, 175; FRG, 49
pensions to Waffen-SS veterans, 96, 97–8
Pierer, Heinrich von, 136
Poland, 42, 49, 60, 75, 99, 100; Article II Fund, 91, 92; bilateral agreements (FRG), 32, 96; 'flight cases', 69–70; forced labourers, 133, *149n77*; funds spent in, 189; indemnification laws, 35, 40, 42
Poraz, Avraham, 223
Powell, Colin, 82
Pressler, Avraham, 198, 199

Raab, Chancellor Julius, 154, 157, 158, 159, 160
Rafelsberger, Walter, 153
Rappaport, Nathan, 190
Rau, President Johannes, 143
Reagan, President Ronald, 22n5
'reconciliation foundations', 96–7, 143
Reconciliation Fund (2000) (Austria), 173
Remembrance, Responsibility and the Future fund *see* slave labour agreement
restitution laws: Allies in FRG, 50–1, 108, 217; Austria, 155–9, 161–4, 169, 174; Equalization of Burdens law, 51; Federal Restitution Law (1957) (BRüG), 51-2, 53; 'hardship fund', 52; on reunification, 106–7, 109, 111 *see also* heirless properties in former GDR
reunification of Germany, Jewish claims on, 18, 76–8, 84–5, 88–9, 105–6
Rheinmetall, 128, 130
Rifkind, Robert, 99
Righteous Gentiles (*Hassidei Umot Haolam*), 14, 186–7, 193
Robinson, Jacob, 6
Robinson, Nehemiah, 3–4, 6, 14, 51; indemnification laws, 33, 34, 35,